CIMA

GW01425273

STUDY TEXT

MANAGEMENT

PAPER E2

ENTERPRISE MANAGEMENT

Our Text has a brand new look for CIMA's new 2010 syllabus.

In this edition we:

- **Highlight** the **most important elements** in the syllabus and the **key skills** you will need

- **Signpost** how each chapter links to the syllabus and the learning outcomes

- **Provide** lots of **exam alerts** explaining how what you're learning may be tested

- **Emphasise key points** in **section summaries**

- **Test your knowledge** of what you've studied in **quick quizzes**

- **Examine your understanding** in our **exam question bank**

- **Reference all the important topics** in the **full index**

FOR EXAMS IN MAY 2010

BPP LEARNING MEDIA

First edition May 2009

ISBN 9780 7517 7501 3

British Library Cataloguing-in-Publication Data
A catalogue record for this book
is available from the British Library

Published by

BPP Learning Media Ltd
BPP House, Aldine Place
London W12 8AA

www.bpp.com/learningmedia

Printed in the United Kingdom

Your learning materials, published by BPP
Learning Media Ltd, are printed on paper sourced
from sustainable, managed forests.

We are grateful to the Chartered Institute of
Management Accountants for permission to
reproduce past examination questions. The
suggested solutions in the exam answer bank have
been prepared by BPP Learning Media Ltd.

Contents

How the BPP Learning Media Study Text can help you pass

Streamlined studying	• We show you the best ways to study efficiently
	• Our Text has been designed to ensure you can easily and quickly navigate through it
	• The different features in our Text emphasise important knowledge and techniques
Exam expertise	• **Studying E2** on page (xii) introduces the key themes of the syllabus and summarises how to pass
	• We highlight throughout our Text how topics may be tested and what you'll have to do in the exam
	• We help you see the complete picture of the syllabus, so that you can answer questions that range across the whole syllabus
	• Our Text covers the syllabus content – no more, no less
Regular review	• We frequently summarise the key knowledge you need
	• We test what you've learnt by providing questions and quizzes throughout the Text
	• Our E2 Passcards summarise what you should know in visual, easy to remember form
	• Our E2 Practice and Revision Kit provides lots more question practice

Our other products

You can purchase the Passcards and Practice and Revision Kit for E2 by visiting www.bpp.com/mybpp

BPP Learning Media also offers these products for the E2 exam:

Success CDs	Covering the vital elements of the E2 syllabus in less than 90 minutes and also containing exam hints to help you fine tune your strategy
i-Pass	Providing computer-based testing in a variety of formats, ideal for self-assessment
Interactive Passcards	Allowing you to learn actively with a clear visual format summarising what you must know
Learn Online	Giving you helpful resources on a fully interactive e-learning site, including tutor support

Features in our Study Text

Section Introductions explain how the section fits into the chapter

KEY TERM

Key Terms are the core vocabulary you need to learn

KEY POINT

Key Points are points that you have to know, ideas or calculations that will be the foundations of your answers

Exam Alerts show you how subjects are likely to be tested

Exam Skills are the key skills you will need to demonstrate in the exam, linked to question requirements

LEARN

Formulae To Learn are formulae you must remember in the exam

EXAM

Exam Formulae are formulae you will be given in the exam

Examples show how theory is put into practice

Questions give you the practice you need to test your understanding of what you've learnt

CASE STUDY

Case Studies link what you've learnt with the real-world business environment

Links show how the syllabus overlaps with other parts of the qualification, including Knowledge Brought Forward that you need to remember from previous exams

Website References link to material that will enhance your understanding of what you're studying

Further Reading will give you a wider perspective on the subjects you're covering

Section Summaries allow you to review each section

BPP
LEARNING MEDIA

Streamlined studying

What you should do	In order to
Read the Chapter and Section Introductions	See why topics need to be studied and map your way through the chapter
Go quickly through the explanations	Gain the depth of knowledge and understanding that you'll need
Highlight the Key Points, Key Terms and Formulae to learn	Make sure you know the basics that you can't do without in the exam
Focus on the Exam Skills and Exam Alerts	Know how you'll be tested and what you'll have to do
Work through the Examples and Case Studies	See how what you've learnt applies in practice
Prepare Answers to the Questions	See if you can apply what you've learnt in practice
Revisit the Section Summaries in the Chapter Roundup	Remind you of, and reinforce, what you've learnt
Answer the Quick Quiz	Find out if there are any gaps in your knowledge
Answer the Question(s) in the Exam Question Bank	Practise what you've learnt in depth

Should I take notes?

Brief notes may help you remember what you're learning. You should use the notes format that's most helpful to you (lists, diagrams, mindmaps).

Further help

BPP Learning Media's *Learning to Learn Accountancy* provides lots more helpful guidance on studying. It is designed to be used both at the outset of your CIMA studies and throughout the process of learning accountancy. It can help you **focus your studies on the subject and exam**, enabling you to **acquire knowledge**, **practise and revise efficiently and effectively**.

Syllabus and learning outcomes

The syllabus comprises:

Topic and Study Weighting

A	Strategic Management and Assessing the Competitve Environment	30%
B	Project Management	40%
C	Management of Relationships	30%

Learning Outcomes				
Lead		**Component**		**Syllabus content**
A		**Strategic Management and Assessing the Competitive Environment**		
1.	Discuss different competitive environments and key external characteristics of these environments	(a)	Discuss the nature of competitive environments;	(i) PEST analysis and its derivatives.
				(ii) The use of stakeholder mapping.
		(b)	Distinguish between different types of competitive environments.	(iii) Qualitative approaches to competitive analysis.
				(iv) Competitor analysis and competitive strategies (both qualitative and quantitative tools of competitor analysis will be used).
				(v) Sources, availability and quality of data for environmental analysis.
				(vi) Porter's Five Forces model and its use for assessing the external environment.
				(vii) Porter's Diamond and its use for assessing the competitive advantage of nations.
2.	Discuss developments in strategic management.	(a)	Discuss concepts in established and emergent thinking in strategic management;	(i) Perspectives on the strategic management of the firm (including transaction cost, resource-based view and ecological perspective).
		(b)	Compare and contrast approaches to strategy formulation;	(ii) Approaches to strategy (eg rational, adaptive, emergent, evolutionary or system-based views).
		(c)	Explain the relationships between different levels of strategy in organisations.	(iii) Levels of strategy (eg corporate, business-level, functional) (Note: candidates are not expected to identify or evaluate options.)

B	Project Management				
1.	Discuss tools and techniques of project management.	(a)	Identify a project, a programme and their attributes;	(i)	The definition of a programme, a project, project management, and the contrast with repetitive operations and line management.
		(b)	Apply suitable structures and frameworks to projects to identify common project management issues;	(ii)	4-D and 7-S models to provide an overview of the project process, and the nine key process areas (PMI) to show what happens during each part of the process.
		(c)	Construct an outline of the process of project management;		
		(d)	Identify the characteristics of each phase in the project process;	(iii)	The benefits and limitations of having a single process for managing projects
		(e)	Apply key tools and techniques, including the evaluation of proposals;	(iv)	Key tools for project managers (eg Work Breakdown Structure, network diagrams (Critical Path Analysis), Gantt charts, resource histograms, gates and milestones).
		(f)	Produce a basic project plan incorporating strategies for dealing with uncertainty, in the context of a simple project;	(v)	Earned Value Management.
				(vi)	Evaluation of plans for projects.
				(vii)	The key processes of PRINCE2 and their implications for project staff.
		(g)	Identify structural and leadership issues that will be faced in managing a project team;	(viii)	Managing scope at the outset of a project and providing systems for configuration management/change control.
		(h)	Compare and contrast project control systems;	(ix)	The production of basic plans for time, cost and quality.
		(i)	Discuss the value of post-completion audit;	(x)	Scenario planning and buffering to make provision for uncertainty in projects, as part of the risk and opportunities management process.
		(j)	Apply a process of continuous improvement to projects.	(xi)	Organisational structures, including the role of the project and matrix organisations, and their impact on project achievement.
				(xii)	Teamwork, including recognising the lifecycle of teams, team/group behaviour and selection.
				(xiii)	Control of time, cost and quality through performance and conformance management systems.
				(xiv)	Project completion, documentation, completion reports and system closedown.
				(xv)	The use of post-completion audit and review activities and the justification of their costs.

2.	Evaluate the relationship of the project manager to the external environment.	(a)	Produce a strategy for a project;	(i)	Determining and managing trade-offs between key project objectives of time, cost and quality.
		(b)	Recommend strategies for the management of stakeholder perceptions and expectations;	(ii)	Stakeholders (both process and outcome), their power and interest, and their needs and expectations, marketing and communications to enhance perceptions.
		(c)	Explain the roles of key players in a project organisation.	(iii)	Roles of support structures, including project management offices, as well as project sponsors (SROs), boards, champions, managers and clients.

C   Management of Relationships

1.	Discuss concepts associated with the effective operation of an organisation	(a)	Discuss the concepts of power, bureaucracy, authority, responsibility, leadership and delegation;	(i)	The concepts of power, authority, bureaucracy, leadership, responsibility and delegation and their application to relationships within an organisation and outside it.
		(b)	Demonstrate the importance of organisational culture;	(ii)	Organisational culture: definition, classification, importance.
		(c)	Identify the nature and causes of conflict;	(iii)	The sources of conflict in organisations and the ways in which conflict can be managed to ensure that working relationships are productive and effective.
		(d)	Discuss alternative approaches to the management of conflict.		

2.	Discuss the activities associated with managing people and their associated techniques.	(a)	Analyse the relationship between managers and their subordinates, including legal aspects affecting work and employment;	(i)	Disciplinary procedures and their operation, including the form and process of formal disciplinary action and dismissal (eg industrial tribunals, arbitration and conciliation).
		(b)	Discuss the roles of negotiation and communication in the management process, both within an organisation and with external bodies;	(ii)	The nature and effect of legal issues affecting work and employment, including the application of relevant employment law (ie relating to health, safety, discrimination, fair treatment, childcare, contracts of employment and working time).
		(c)	Discuss the effectiveness of relationships between the finance function and other parts of the organisation and with external stakeholders;	(iii)	Communication skills (ie types of communication tools and their use, as well as the utility and conduct of meetings) and ways of managing communication problems.
		(d)	Identify tools for managing and controlling individuals, teams and networks, and for managing group conflict;	(iv)	Negotiation skills.
		(e)	Compare and contrast ways to deal effectively with discipline problems;	(v)	Managing the finance function to maximise its value to the organisation through lean operation (eg business process outsourcing, shared service centres) and contribution to other functions (eg embedding finance personnel in business and strategic decision processes).

BPP LEARNING MEDIA

(f)   Explain the process and importance of mentoring junior colleagues;

(g)   Analyse issues of business ethics and corporate governance.

(vi)   Management of relationships with professional advisors (accounting, tax and legal), auditors and financial stakeholders (investors and financiers) to meet organisational objectives.

(vii)   The principles of corporate governance and the CIMA Code of Ethics for Professional Accountants, and their relevance to the role, obligations and expectations of a manager.

(viii)   How to lead and manage a team.

(ix)   The role of a mentor, and the process of mentoring

(x)   Motivating team members.

(xi)   The use of systems of control within the organisation (eg employment contracts, performance appraisal, reporting structures).

Old and new syllabuses

The syllabus for the E2 *Enterprise Management* paper is similar to the syllabus for the old syllabus paper P5 *Integrated Management*. The three main areas are the same for both the old and new syllabus exams. There have been some minor changes to account for new material brought in from old paper P6 and P9 though in both cases at a lower level than these old strategic-level papers.

Therefore you need to read the action verbs carefully for the topics in these chapters, as these will be lower level and more **practical** in their approach. The new material is listed below.

The following topics have been added into the syllabus, with references to the chapter in which they are covered:

- Earned Value Management (8)

- Managing the finance function to maximise its value to the organisation through lean operation (eg business process outsourcing, shared service centres) and contribution to other functions (eg embedding finance personnel in business and strategic decision processes). (3)

- Management of relationships with professional advisors (accounting, tax and legal), auditors and financial stakeholders (investors and financiers) to meet organisational objectives (3)

- PEST analysis and its derivatives (12)

- The use of stakeholder mapping. (12)

- Porter's Diamond and its use for assessing the competitive advantage of nations. (12)

- Qualitative approaches to competitive analysis. (13)

- Competitor analysis and competitive strategies (both qualitative and quantitative tools of competitor analysis will be used). (13)

- Sources, availability and quality of data for environmental analysis. (13)

- Porter's Five Forces model and its use for assessing the external environment. (13)

Studying E2

1 What E2 is about

E2 consists of three fairly distinct areas covering:

(a) Management of Relationships
(b) Project Management
(c) Strategic Management and assessing the competitive environment

1.1 Management of Relationships

This forms Part C of the syllabus, and covers a range of topics in the area of 'people management'. It deals with the nature of management and leadership, and various aspects of the relationship between managers/leaders and their subordinates or team members. It covers key areas of context (such as the nature of managerial authority and the nature of team working); legal aspects (such as equal opportunities); and interpersonal skills (such as conflict resolution, negotiation and communication).

We cover this part of this syllabus first, in Part A of the Study Text, because it gives a good overview of what management is about, and because the skills and concepts covered here can be applied across the rest of the syllabus. You can transfer your learning about teams to project teams, for example, and your learning about conflict resolution to negotiating strategy with organisational stakeholders.

1.2 Project Management

The project management section of the syllabus covers the nature of projects and a wide range of frameworks, tools and techniques for managing projects effectively.

This section of the syllabus carries a slightly higher weighting than the other two. You will need to give close attention to both terminology and concepts *and* to practical skills (such as using planning tools like critical path analysis).

Our coverage is contained in four key chapters, Chapters 6 to 9. These look at the frameworks and concepts, tools and techniques. In addition, you will be able to bring to the project context a great deal of your learning from Part A of the Text. Project control systems, and structural and leadership issues in managing a project team, will already have been covered.

1.3 Strategic Management and assessing the competitive environment

This forms Part A of the syllabus, but it should fall more neatly into place on the foundation of our coverage of organisations, management and leadership.

In simple terms, strategy is about how an organisation gets from where it is now to where it wants to be. We look at various models describing how strategy is formulated. **There is no one view of strategy, and you need to be aware of this**. We look at how organisations decide 'where they want to be', recognising that organisations need to take into account the needs and expectations of a range of stakeholders in formulating their goals. We work through a systematic strategic planning process, explaining some of the tools and techniques used. Finally we study competitive environments using a range of models including the Five Forces and Porter's Diamond.

2 What is required

2.1 Knowledge

Knowledge is a crucial element of this exam. Although scenario-based questions require analysis and application, you are still, basically, being asked to explain, discuss or identify particular concepts and models. **Section A questions** are a further opportunity for the examiner to test factual and theoretical knowledge.

Some theoretical models, or the work of particular writers, are specifically mentioned in the syllabus and others are accepted as part of the body of knowledge on a particular topic. Either way, **you need to know a range of models**, and be able to attribute them to the right thinkers/authors where required.

A frequent complaint in past exam reports from the previous syllabus is that students are simply not adequately prepared. **They lack 'hard' knowledge of the topics set, in the sense of being able to cite and apply factual/theoretical material** – not just common sense and personal experience. Lack of knowledge is guaranteed to sabotage your chances in the exam.

2.2 High level skills

Both sections of the exam are scenario-based, which means that – important as knowledge is – it is not enough to reproduce large tracts of theoretical material, however accurately. You must demonstrate an ability:

(a)   **To analyse the details of the scenario**, in order to identify problems, issues and opportunities which are relevant to the question set

(b)   **To select theoretical concepts and models** which are directly applicable to the scenario and question set (if the question doesn't *tell* you which model to use)

(c)   **To use your theoretical knowledge to structure, inform and support** an answer which is nevertheless focused on the details of the scenario given.

Application does *not* mean repeating chunks of scenario material in your answers. This is a common failing which gains no credit in the exam. **It means selecting those aspects of theoretical concepts and models that are directly relevant** to the problem and circumstances described in the scenario. You may be asked to use a model in relation to a scenario. You'll need to show how each aspect of the model applies to or is illustrated by the scenario. You may be asked to address a problem in a scenario so what model could give you a framework to furnish ideas and structure your answer?

Cultivate these skills as your work through the Study Text and practise exam-style questions.

You must also be aware of the key verbs used in the exam. These are reproduced in full in the exam question and answer bank.

Be aware that in Enterprise Management you are likely to be tested on learning verbs such as 'explain', 'identify' and 'apply'.

3 Passing E2

3.1 Cover the whole syllabus

All of the marks available to you will be for compulsory questions. This means you may be tested in all major areas of the syllabus on *every* paper, but sadly doesn't give you any opportunity to avoid questions you don't like. 50% of the marks are available in Section A of the paper in compulsory questions which require you to write 10 marks worth of material in your answer. Although some of the these marks will be awarded for application to the short scenarios given, you still need a good grasp of factual and theoretical knowledge to apply! The remaining 50% will be awarded for one or two longer scenario-based questions.

3.2 Practise

Our Study Text gives you ample opportunity to practise by providing questions within chapters, quick quiz questions and questions in the exam question bank at the end. In addition, the BPP Learning Media Practice and Revision Kit provides lots more question practice. **It is particularly important to practise questions from both *sections* of the exam, so that you get to grips with the very different answer styles and time management requirements**.

3.3 Develop time management skills

CIMA's feedback has routinely identified time management as being a problem. It is particularly important, therefore, that towards the end of your course, you practise all types of question, only allowing yourself the time you will be given in the exam.

3.4 Develop business awareness

Candidates with good business awareness can score well in a number of areas.

(a)   **Reading articles in CIMA's *Financial Management* magazine and the business press** will help you understand the practical application of many of the theories covered throughout the syllabus.

(b)   **Being aware of the work of different departments in your own organisation** (or others you know about) will help you discuss the practical management issues involved in running a business.

(c)   **Scan the business press for relevant articles**. Most of the case studies in this Study Text come from sources such as these.

This kind of awareness will not only give you ideas on which to model your solutions to the business/management problems passed in exam scenarios. It will also help you to think practically and realistically about the solutions you propose – which is what real-world management is all about.

3.5 Develop your exam technique

Another good reason to practise past and exam-style questions is to get into good habits for the exam, in terms of:

(a)   How to make best use of your reading time

(b)   How to ensure that you obey the instructions in the exam

(c)   How to analyse the precise requirements of each question – and stick to them in your answers

4 Brought forward knowledge

You may be tested on knowledge or techniques learnt in your previous studies. So you may find it useful to go back to your notes for Certificate level or other studies when you start practising questions.

If you have already passed **Paper E1**, some of the topics introduced there, particularly Managing Human Capital, are developed further in this paper.

The exam paper

Format of the paper

		Number of marks
Section A:	Five compulsory questions each worth 10 marks.	50
Section B:	One or two compulsory questions.	50
		100

Time allowed: 3 hours

CIMA guidance

Good answers demonstrate knowledge and show understanding in the application thereof. Reading the scenario should give you clues on what issues or tools to use.

Weaker answers tend to repeat book knowledge without applying it to the question set. Candidates who fail reveal a lack of knowledge or depth in their understanding.

The key to passing this paper is to understand the theories and principles in the syllabus and show you can apply these to whatever situation presents itself in the exam.

Numerical content

This paper can be wholly written. Any numbers are likely to be included in question on project planning tools.

Breadth of question coverage

Questions in **all** sections are likely to cover at least two out of three syllabus areas. The Section A shorter questions will be used to test the **breadth of the syllabus**. Section B questions will be scenario-based and reflect topical management issues. Students will need to apply knowledge often across syllabus areas in one question.

Pilot paper

Section A

1	Project management
2	Corporate appraisal
3	Levels of strategy
4	Sources of power
5	Critical path analysis

Section B

6	Performance measurement and appraisal
7	Stakeholders, resource-based approach

MANAGEMENT OF RELATIONSHIPS

Part A

KEY CONCEPTS IN MANAGEMENT

'Management of relationships' is actually Part C of your syllabus, but we start here for various reasons. Firstly, concepts such as management, leadership and organisation culture underlie all three areas of the syllabus – whether you are managing people, managing a project or developing strategy.

We start by looking at what a manager does. This is fundamental in understanding why there are managers in organisations.

Then we explore the nature of **power and authority relationships** in organisations. These concepts give managers the right to manage – and leaders the ability to lead. They underpin our later discussion of project and stakeholder management, too, because managers need to be able to influence others in contexts where they *don't* necessarily have direct 'line' authority.

We also discuss delegation and responsibility in this section as they are allied to power and authority. These topics introduce the formal relationships and activities in the organisation.

We go on to look at the nature of **leadership**, why it might be different to management, and the different ways in which it can be exercised. You should be able to link this learning to our later coverage of the 'people' aspects of leading projects, and the wider issues of different cultures and how they affect organisations.

Bureaucracy is looked at briefly. You need to understand why bureaucracy developed and why it can be efficient in certain organisations.

Managers need **to manage within the law and** we continue by analysing how managers and subordinates relate in areas as diverse as discipline, grievance, health and safety and equal opportunities.

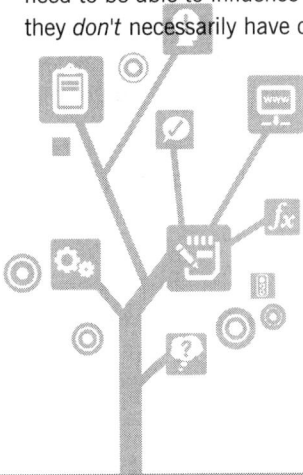

1

topic list	learning outcomes	syllabus references	ability required
1 Role of the manager			Comprehension
2 Power, authority, responsibility and delegation	C1a	C1(i)	comprehension
3 Management and leadership	C1a	C1(i)	comprehension
4 Bureaucracy	C1a	C1(i)	comprehension
5 Discipline	C2a, e	C2(i)	comprehension
6 Grievance	C2a	C2(ii)	comprehension
7 Termination of contract	C2a, e	C2(i)	comprehension
8 Equal opportunities	C2a	C2(ii)	comprehension
9 The practical implications of legislation	C2a	C2(ii)	comprehension
10 Diversity	C2a	C2(ii)	comprehension

1   Role of the manager

1.1 Management

Introduction

Managers manage resources to get things done. In most organisations, it is impossible for one person to do every job and so managers also need to coordinate the actions of others to get things done.

KEY TERM

MANAGEMENT may be defined, most simply, as 'getting things done through other people' (Stewart).

Why is it that organisations have to be managed, and what is the purpose of management?

An organisation has been defined as 'a social arrangement for the controlled performance of collective goals.' This definition suggests the need for management.

(a) **Objectives** have to be set for the organisation.
(b) Somebody has to **monitor progress and results** to ensure that objectives are met.
(c) Somebody has to communicate and sustain **corporate values**, ethics and operating principles.
(d) Somebody has to look after the interests of the **organisation's owners** and other **stakeholders**.

Question 1.1   Management structure

Learning outcome n/a

John, Paul, George and Ringo set up in business together as repairers of musical instruments. Each has contributed £5,000 as capital for the business. They are a bit uncertain as to how they should run the business, and, when they discuss this in the pub, they decide that attention needs to be paid to planning what they do, reviewing what they do and controlling what they do.

Suggest two ways in which John, Paul, George and Ringo can manage the business assuming no other personnel are recruited.

Different organisations have different structures for carrying out management functions. For example, some organisations have separate strategic planning departments. Others do not.

In a **private sector business**, managers act, ultimately, on behalf of shareholders. In practical terms, shareholders rarely interfere, as long as the business delivers profits year on year.

In a **public sector organisation**, management acts on behalf of the government. Politicians in a democracy are in turn accountable to the electorate. More of the objectives of a public sector organisation might be set by the 'owners' – ie the government – rather than by the management. The government might also tell senior management to carry out certain policies or plans, thereby restricting management's discretion.

KEY POINT

Later in the chapter we contrast **management** with **leadership**. The two activities are different. Management broadly focuses on maintaining the 'steady state' in the organisation whilst leadership drives the organisation forward. Leadership also only affects people whilst management deals with all resources.

Section summary

Management is responsible for using the organisation's resources to meet its goals. It is accountable to the owners: shareholders in a business, or government in the public sector.

2 Power, authority, responsibility and delegation

Introduction

We look at four aspects of the relationship between managers and others in the organisation in this section. These aspects cover 'getting the work done'.

Make sure you are clear on the characteristics of each type of relationship, which are covered in the key point here.

KEY POINT

Ensure that you can distinguish clearly between the various terms. **Power and authority** are features of all organisations. They are exercised over others. **Responsibility** falls on any individual to complete their own tasks. **Delegation** is where authority is passed down to make decisions.

2.1 Power

KEY TERM

POWER is the **ability** to get things done.

Power is not something a person 'has' in isolation: it is exercised over other individuals or groups, and – to an extent – depends on their *recognising* the person's power over them.

2.1.1 Types of power

French and *Raven* classified power into six types or sources.

Type of power	
Coercive power	The power of physical force or punishment. Physical power is rare in business organisations, but intimidation may feature, eg in workplace bullying.
Reward (or resource) power	Based on access to or control over valued resources. For example, managers have access to information, contacts and financial rewards for team members. The amount of resource power a person has depends on the scarcity of the resource, how much the resource is valued by others, and how far the resource is under the manager's control.
Legitimate (or position) power	Associated with a particular position in the organisation. For example, a manager has the power to authorise certain expenses, or issue instructions, because the authority to do so has been formally delegated to her.
Expert power	Based on experience, qualifications or expertise. For example, accountants have expert power because of their knowledge of the tax system. Expert power depends on others recognising the expertise in an area which they need or value.
Referent (or personal) power	Based on force of personality, or 'charisma', which can attract, influence or inspire other people.
Negative power (*Handy*)	The power to disrupt operations: for example, by industrial action, refusal to communicate information, or sabotage.

2.1.2 Influence

KEY TERM

INFLUENCE is the process by which one person modifies the behaviour or attitude of another.

Influence, the act of directing or modifying the behaviour of others, may be achieved in a variety of ways.

(a)   The application of force, such as physical or economic power

(b)   The establishment of rules and procedures that are enforced through position and/or resource power

(c)   Bargaining and negotiation, which depend on the relative strengths of each party's position

(d)   Persuasion

2.2 Power centres

The **degree** of power people exercise, and the **types** of power they are able to exploit, differs depending in part on their position in the organisation hierarchy.

2.2.1 Senior management

Senior managers enjoy **high position power**: in theory they take the major decisions and set constraints over the decisions taken by other people. In practice, however, this power is never absolute. Senior managers depend on decisions and information supplied by subordinates, and it is quite possible that the information is shaped at a lower level. Informal leaders may have upward or sideways influence (eg experts, front-line workers).

Senior managers have **high resource powers** which they exercise over budget allocations and strategic direction.

2.2.2 Middle managers

Middle managers have **limited reward power** over their own subordinates; expert power and some decisions; and perhaps **negative power** to delay or subvert decisions taken by senior managers. They need **legitimate power**, hence the need for formal job descriptions, authorisation limits and so on. They may also gain influence from networking: tapping into valued sources of information, or influential mentors and coalitions.

2.2.3 Interest groups

Formal interest groups are groups which represent the interests of their members, in order to wield greater power than their individual members. Examples include trade unions and occupational/professional associations.

2.2.4 Departmental power

Some departments in the organisation exercise power by the use of **functional authority,** for instance, by specifying procedures. Other departments are influential because they deal with **key strategic contingencies:** 'events and activities both inside and outside an organisation that are essential for attaining organisational goals'. They can arise in several ways.

(a)   **Dependency**. A department which depends on another department may not be in a position to exercise power over that department, without support at a higher level. A department may use its resource power to make other departments dependent on it.

(b)   **Financial resources**. This is another sort of dependency, but a department with a larger budget can spend it with more discretion.

(c)   **Centrality**. How critical is the department in the primary activities of the organisation?

(d)   **Non-substitutability**. Some departments cannot easily be broken up and their activities carried out elsewhere. This used to be the case with information systems departments, before the advent of cheap personal computers and software.

(e)   **Uncertainty**. A department which reduces the levels of uncertainty faced by other departments (in dealing with key environmental variables) has a sort of expert power.

> ### Section summary
>
> **Power** is the ability to get things done. There are many types of power in organisations: position or **legitimate power**, expert power, personal power, resource power and negative power are examples.

2.3 Authority

KEY TERM

AUTHORITY is the right to do something, or to ask someone else to do it and expect it to be done. Authority is thus another word for **position or legitimate power**.

Power and influence can be exercised at any level of the organisation, and in any direction – not just 'downwards' (over direct reports and teams), but sideways (over peers and cross-functional colleagues) and even upwards (eg promoting an idea or course of action to your manager).

Authority generally flows downwards through the line or chain of command that is part of the formal organisation structure.

Max Weber (many years before French and Raven's work on power) proposed three ways in which managers exercised what he called legitimate power (or authority).

(a)   **Charismatic authority** arises from the personality of the leader and his or her ability to inspire devotion through, for example, sanctity, heroism or example.

(b)   **Traditional authority** rests on established belief in the importance of immemorial tradition and the status it confers.

(c)   **Rational-legal** authority raises from the working of accepted normative rules, such as are found in organisations and democratic governments.

Managerial authority is exercised in such areas as:

(a)   **Making decisions within the scope of authority** given to the position. For example, a manager's authority is limited to his/her team and with certain limits. For items of expenditure more than a certain amount, say, she may require authorisation from a higher manager.

(b)   **Assigning tasks** to subordinates, and expecting satisfactory performance of these tasks.

2.3.1 Line and staff authority

When analysing the types of authority which a manager may have, the terms **line**, **staff** and **functional authority** are often used.

KEY TERMS

LINE AUTHORITY is the authority a manager has over a subordinate, down the vertical chain (or line) of command.

STAFF AUTHORITY is the authority one manager or department may have in giving specialist advice to another manager or department, over which there is no line authority. Staff authority does not entail the right to make or influence decisions in the advisee department. An example might be the HR department advising the Accounts Manager on selection interviewing methods.

FUNCTIONAL AUTHORITY is a hybrid of line and staff authority, whereby the expert/staff manager has the authority, in certain circumstances, to direct, design or control activities or procedures of another department. An example is where a finance manager has authority to require timely reports from line managers.

Question 1.2   Line and staff authority

Learning outcome C1a

What sort of authority is exercised:

(a)   By the financial controller over the chief accountant?
(b)   By the production manager over the production workforce?
(c)   By the financial controller over the production manager?

There are inevitable tensions involved in asserting staff authority. **Technostructure** here is a term used by *Mintzberg* to describe individuals in the organisation who strive for efficiency and standardise work processes. These are typically planners, HR professionals and analysts.

Problem	Possible solution
The technostructure can **undermine** the **line managers'** authority, by empire building.	Clear demarcations of line, staff and functional authority should be created.
Lack of seniority: middle line managers may be more senior in the hierarchy than technostructure advisers.	Use functional authority (via policies and procedures). Experts should be seen as a resource, not a threat.
Expert managers may **lack realism**, going for technically perfect but commercially impractical solutions.	Technostructure planners should be fully aware of operational issues and communicate regularly with the middle line.
Technostructure experts **lack responsibility** for the success of their ideas.	Technostructure experts should be involved in implementing their suggestions and share accountability for outcomes.

Section summary

Authority is related to position power. It is the right to take certain decisions within certain boundaries.

2.4 Responsibility and accountability

KEY TERMS

RESPONSIBILITY is the **obligation** a person has to fulfil a task which (s)he has been given.

ACCOUNTABILITY is a person's **liability** to be called to account for the fulfilment of tasks (s)he has been given.

The definitions given above are useful because the term 'responsibility' is used in two ways.

(a)   A person is said to be responsible *for* a piece of work when he or she is required to ensure that the work is done.

(b)   The same person is said to be responsible *to* a superior when he or she is given work by that superior: in this sense, the term 'accountable' is often used.

One is thus accountable *to* a superior *for* a piece of work for which one is responsible.

The principle of **delegation** (which we discuss below) is that a manager may make subordinates *responsible for* work, but remains *accountable to* his or her own superior for ensuring that the work is done. Appropriate decision-making authority must be delegated alongside the delegated responsibility.

2.4.1 Responsibility/authority mismatch

In practice, matters are rarely clear cut, and in many organisations responsibility and authority are ambiguous and shifting eg due to departmental 'empire-building' or changes in jobs or structures.

Authority without responsibility is a recipe for arbitrary and irresponsible behaviour: the person has the right to make decisions – without being held accountable for them.

Responsibility without authority places a subordinate in an impossible and stressful position: (s)he is held accountable for results over which (s)he has no control.

Section summary

Responsibility is the obligation a person has to fulfil a task (s)he has been given. Responsibility can be delegated, but the person delegating responsibility still remains accountable to his or her boss for completion of the task

Authority/responsibility mismatch or **ambiguity** is stressful for the individual, and may be risky for the organisation's control over decision-making.

2.5 Delegation

KEY TERM

DELEGATION of authority is the process whereby a superior gives to a subordinate part of his or her own authority to make decisions.

2.5.1 Why delegate?

Delegation has several key benefits.

(a) There are **physical and mental limitations** to the work load of any individual or group in authority.

(b) Managers are freed up to concentrate on **higher-level tasks** (such as planning).

(c) The **increasing size and complexity** of some organisations calls for specialisation, both managerial and technical.

(d) Delegated authority contributes to the job *satisfaction and development* of lower levels of employees. Taking on progressive levels of responsibility supports training, appraisal and management succession planning.

(e) Delegation shortens the chain of decision-making and brings decisions closer to the situations that require them. This is particularly important in fast-changing business environments which require responsiveness to customer demands.

2.5.2 How to delegate

The process of delegation can be outlined as follows.

STEP 1   **Specify performance:** the goals and standards expected of the subordinate, keeping in mind his or her level of expertise.

STEP 2   **Formally assign tasks** to the subordinate, who should formally agree to do them.

STEP 3   **Allocate resources and authority** to the subordinate to enable him or her to carry out the delegated tasks at the expected level of performance.

STEP 4 **Back off** and allow the subordinate to perform the delegated tasks.

STEP 5 **Maintain contact,** to review progress made, make constructive criticism and be available to give help and advice if requested.

KEY POINT

Delegation links to a range of potentially examinable issues, such as team-working and management/leadership style (which, as we will see, is largely about the extent to which managers delegate).

When diagnosing potential 'people problems' in scenarios, don't forget delegation issues: failure to delegate, lack of trust, micro-management, lack of development opportunities etc.

Section summary

Delegation is the process whereby a superior gives a subordinate part of his or her own decision-making authority. It is an important component of time management and employee development

Successful delegation requires that people have the right skills and the authority to do the job, and are given feedback. It also requires a balance of support and trust from the delegator.

2.6 Empowerment

KEY TERM

EMPOWERMENT is the current term for making workers (and particularly work teams) responsible for achieving, and even setting, work targets, with the freedom to make decisions about how they are to be achieved.

Empowerment goes in hand in hand with:

(a) **Delayering**, or cutting the number of levels (and managers) in the chain of command, since responsibility previously held by middle managers is, in effect, being given to operational workers.

(b) **Flexibility**, since giving responsibility to the people closest to the products and customer encourages responsiveness – and cutting out layers of communication, decision-making and reporting speeds up the process.

(c) **New technology**, since there are more '**knowledge workers**'. Such people need less supervision, being better able to identify and control the means to clearly understood ends. Better information systems also remove the mystique and power of managers as possessors of knowledge and information in the organisation.

The argument for empowerment, in a nutshell, is that by empowering workers (or 'decentralising' control of business units, or devolving/delegating responsibility, or removing levels in hierarchies that restrict freedom), not only will the job be done more effectively, but the people who do the job will get more out of it.

'The people lower down the organisation possess the knowledge of what is going wrong with a process but lack the authority to make changes. Those further up the structure have the authority to make changes, but lack the profound knowledge required to identify the right solutions. The only solution is to change the culture of the organisation so that everyone can become involved in the process of improvement and work together to make the changes.' (*Max Hand*)

CASE STUDY

The validity of this view and its relevance to modern trends appears to be borne out by the approach to empowerment adopted by Harvester Restaurants. The management structure comprises a branch manager and a 'coach', while everyone else is a team member. Everyone within a team has one or more 'accountabilities' (these include recruitment, drawing up rotas, keeping track of sales targets and so on)

BPP
LEARNING MEDIA

which are shared out by the team members at their weekly team meetings. All the team members at different times act as 'co-ordinator': the person responsible for taking the snap decisions that are frequently necessary in a busy restaurant. Apparently all of the staff involved agree that empowerment has made their jobs more interesting and has hugely increased their motivation and sense of involvement.

3   Management and leadership

KEY TERM

LEADERSHIP is the ability to get others to follow you willingly. Leadership theories fall under **personality traits**, **situational**, **contingency** and **transformational**. **Leadership** style theories are used to describe places on a continuum of **task** and **relationship** focus.

3.1 Management and leadership

Introduction

The terms 'management' and 'leadership' are often used interchangeably. In some cases, management skills and theories have simply been relabelled to reflect the more fashionable term. However, there have been many attempts to distinguish meaningfully between them.

(a)   *Kotter* (2001) argues that leadership and management involve two distinct sets of action. Management is about coping with **complexity**: its functions are to do with logic, structure, analysis and control, and are aimed at producing order, consistency and predictability. Leadership, by contrast, is about coping with **change**: its activities include creating a sense of direction, communicating strategy, and energising, inspiring and motivating others to translate the vision into action.

(b)   *Yukl* (1998) suggests that while management is defined by a prescribed role and position in the structure of the organisation, leaders are given their roles by the perception of others, through election, choice or influence. Leadership is an interpersonal process. In other words, managers have **subordinates**, but leaders have **followers**.

(c)   *Zaleznik* (1992) suggests that managers are mainly concerned with order and **maintaining the status quo**, exercising their skills in diplomacy and focusing on decision-making processes within the organisation. Leaders, in contrast, direct their energies towards introducing **new approaches and ideas**. They create excitement and vision in order to arouse motivation, and focus with empathy on the meanings of events and actions for people. Leaders search out opportunities for change.

(d)   *Katz and Kahn* (1974) point out that while management aims to secure compliance with stated organisational objectives, leadership aims to secure willingness, enthusiasm and commitment. Leadership is the **influential increment** over and above mechanical compliance with the routine directives of the organisation.

Management can be exercised over resources, activities, projects and other essential non-personal things. Leadership can only be exercised over **people**.

3.2 Transactional and transformational leaders: Burns, Boyd

Some of the values used to distinguish between managers and leaders have also been identified as different styles of leadership (*Burns*).

(a)   **Transactional leaders** see the relationship with their followers in terms of a trade: they give followers the rewards they want in exchange for service, loyalty and compliance.

(b)   **Transformational leaders** see their role as inspiring and motivating others to work at levels beyond mere compliance. Only transformational leadership is said to be able to change team/organisation cultures and create a new direction.

Boyd suggests that the rapid change endemic in the current business environment mandates a new approach to management in order to achieve transformation within the organisation as a response. These transformational leaders will be skilled in areas that contrast with some older prescriptions.

(a)   **Vision**: the leader will use example and persuasion to convince the group to pursue a new purpose.
(b)   **Anticipation**: the leader will possess foresight.
(c)   **Value-congruence**: the leader will understand and empathise with group members' needs.
(d)   **Empowerment**: the leader will empower group members so as to make the group more effective.
(e)   **Self-understanding**: the leader will be aware of his or her own needs and goals.

3.3 Why develop managers as 'leaders'?

Introduction

Whether or not we make the distinction between management and leadership, attempts to define what makes leadership 'special' (such as those outlined above) have suggested some key points about the benefits effective leadership can bring and why it is valuable.

(a)   Leaders energise and support **change**, which is essential for survival in highly competitive and fast-changing business environments. By setting visionary goals, and encouraging contribution from teams, leaders create environments that:

   (i)   Seek out new information and ideas
   (ii)   Allow challenges to existing procedures and ways of thinking
   (iii)   Invite innovation and creativity in finding better ways to achieve goals
   (iv)   Support and empower people to cope with the turbulence

(b)   Leaders secure **commitment**, mobilising the ideas, experience and motivation of employees – which contributes to innovation and improved quality and customer service. This is all the more essential in a competitive, customer-focused, knowledge-based business environment.

(c)   Leaders set **direction**, helping teams and organisations to understand their purpose, goals and value to the organisation. This facilitates team-working and empowerment (allowing discretion and creativity about how to achieve the desired outcomes) without loss of co-ordination or direction.

(d)   Leaders support, challenge and develop **people**, maximising their contribution to the organisation. Leaders use an influence-based, facilitate-empower style rather than a command-control style, and this is better suited to the expectations of empowered teams and the need for information sharing in modern business environments.

Question 1.3   Leadership

Learning outcome C1a

Reflect on your own experience of working under the direction of others. Identify the 'best' leader you have ever 'followed'. Think about how this person behaved and interacted with you and others.

What qualities makes you identify this person as a 'great leader', from your point of view as a follower?

Section summary

There are many different definitions of **leadership**. Key themes (which are also used to distinguish leadership from management) include: interpersonal influence; securing willing commitment to shared goals; creating direction and energy; and an orientation to change.

Leadership offers key **benefits** in a competitive, turbulent environment: activating commitment, setting direction, developing people and energising and supporting change.

4 Bureaucracy

Introduction

Weber saw **bureaucracy** as the ideal form of organisation, because it is impersonal and rational, based on a set pattern of behaviour and work allocation, and not allowing personal issues to get in the way of achieving goals.

KEY TERMS

A BUREAUCRACY is 'a continuous organisation of official functions bound by rules' (Weber).

- CONTINUOUS ORGANISATION. The organisation does not disappear if people leave: new people will fill their shoes.

- OFFICIAL FUNCTIONS. The organisation is divided into areas (eg production, marketing) with specified duties. Authority to carry them out is given to the officials in charge.

- RULES. A rule defines and specifies a course of action that must be taken under given circumstances.

The characteristics of bureaucracy can be summarised as follows.

Characteristic	Description
Hierarchy of roles	An organisation exists even before it is filled with people. Each lower office is under the control and supervision of a higher one.
Specialisation and training	There is a high degree of specialisation of labour.
Professional nature of employment	Officials are full-time employees; promotion is according to seniority and achievement; pay scales are prescribed according to the position or office held in the organisation structure.
Impersonal nature	Employees work within impersonal rules and regulations and act according to formal, impersonal procedures.
Rationality	The jurisdictional areas of the organisation are determined rationally. The hierarchy of authority and office structure is clearly defined. Duties are established and measures of performance set.
Uniformity in the performance of tasks	Procedures ensure that, regardless of who carries out tasks, they should be executed in the same way
Technical competence	All officials are technically competent. Their competence within the area of their expertise is rarely questioned.
Stability	The organisation rarely changes in response to environmental pressures.

4.1 Bureaucracy: good or bad?

It is common to think of bureaucracy as an old-fashioned and dysfunctional form of organisation, but it has some **advantages**.

(a)   Bureaucracies are ideal for **standardised, routine tasks**. For example, processing driving license applications is fairly routine, requiring systematic work.

(b)   Bureaucracies can be very **efficient**. *Weber* considered them the most effective organisational form, in stable environments.

(c)   Rigid adherence to procedures may be necessary for **fairness**, adherence to the **law**, **safety** and **security** (eg procedures for data protection).

(d)   Some people are **suited** to the structured, predictable environment. Bureaucracies tend to be long-lived because they select and retain bureaucratically-minded people.

Stewart suggests that bureaucracy became the dominant organisational model because it was supported by increasing **organisation size and complexity** (requiring formalisation and standardisation) and increasing worker **demands for equitable treatment** (requiring impersonality).

In swiftly-changing environments, however, the **dysfunctions** of bureaucracy become apparent.

(a)   It results in **slow decision-making**, because of the rigidity and length of authority networks and the use of committees.

(b)   Uniformity creates **conformity**, inhibiting the personal development of staff.

(c)   Bureaucracies suppress **innovation**: they can inhibit creativity, initiative and openness to new ideas and ways of doing things.

(d)   Bureaucracies find it hard to **learn** from their mistakes, because of the lack of feedback (especially upwards): control systems are frequently out of date.

(e)   Bureaucracies are **slow to change**. *Crozier* stated that 'a system of organisation whose main characteristic is its rigidity will not adjust easily to change and will tend to resist change as much as possible'. Environmental change therefore causes severe trauma.

(f)   **Communication** is restricted to established channels, ignoring opportunities for networking, upward feedback and suggestions that may contribute to customer service and innovation.

(g)   **Rules** may be functional in their impersonality and consistency, but they can be dysfunctional in encouraging employees to work only to the required minimum level of performance and permitting simplistic decision-making *(Gouldner)*.

CASE STUDY

An example of an administrative change in a professional bureaucracy is the UK's internal market for the National Health Service. This is certainly administrative innovation, creating hospitals as autonomous units, and making (some) general practitioners responsible for their own budgets. Although, in theory, the changes were supposed to direct the resources of the NHS more efficiently, there is no doubt that the structure was imposed 'top-down' in a 'mechanistic way'.

| Question 1.4 | Control |

Learning outcome C1a

Complete the sentence below by inserting one of the words in brackets.

Control in a bureaucracy tends to depend on hierarchy and procedure, while in an organic organisation it depends largely on ....

(Ambiguity, culture, seniority, loyalty)

Section summary

Bureaucracy is 'a continuous organisation of official functions bound by rules' (*Weber*).

5 Discipline

Introduction

We now move on to consider the way relationships in organisations are governed formally, and ultimately by the law. Our discussion here reflects UK legislation but is at a very basic level. You will not need to know all of the names of Acts but make sure you know what they aim to do generally. What matters is the principles used rather than knowing the names of the legislation. So you can use examples from other legal systems if you are more familiar with these.

Disciplinary actions arise for a number of reasons and as such an organisation should prepare itself to deal with them. The **ACAS guidelines** set the benchmark in terms of legal compliance.

5.1 Positive and negative discipline

KEY POINT

The idea of 'positive' and 'negative' discipline makes the distinction between methods of maintaining sensible conduct and orderliness which are technically co-operative, and those based on warnings, threats and punishments.

(a)   **Positive (or constructive)** discipline relates to procedures, systems and equipment in the work place which have been designed specifically so that the employee has no option but to act in the desired manner to complete a task safely and successfully. A machine may, for example, shut off automatically if its safety guard is not in place.

(b)   **Negative discipline** is the promise of sanctions designed to make people choose to behave in a desirable way. Disciplinary action may be punitive (punishing an offence), deterrent (warning people not to behave in that way) or reformative (calling attention to the nature of the offence, so that it will not happen again).

The best discipline is **self-discipline**. Even before they start to work, most mature people accept the idea that following instructions and fair rules of conduct are normal responsibilities that are part of any job. Most team members can therefore be counted on to exercise self discipline.

KEY POINT

Do not confuse 'discipline' with 'punishment'. There is more to it than simply punishing people for 'doing things wrong'. More generally, be aware of the importance of encouraging discipline, and using fair and systematic disciplinary procedures, so that discipline is as 'positive' as possible and compliant with relevant law and codes of conduct.

5.2 Types of disciplinary situations

There are many types of disciplinary situation which require attention by the manager. Internally, the most frequently occurring are these.

(a)   Excessive absenteeism
(b)   Poor timekeeping
(c)   Defective and/or inadequate work performance
(d)   Poor attitudes which influence the work of others or reflect on the image of the firm
(e)   Improper personal appearance or conduct (eg offensive humour or aggression)
(f)   Breaking safety rules
(g)   Other violations of rules, regulations and procedures
(h)   Open insubordination, such as the refusal to carry out a work assignment.

Managers might also be confronted with disciplinary problems stemming from employee behaviour off the job, such as alcohol or drug abuse. In such circumstances, whenever an employee's off-the-job conduct has an impact upon performance on the job, the manager must be prepared to deal with such a problem within the scope of the disciplinary process.

The purpose of discipline is not punishment or retribution. Disciplinary action must have as its goal the improvement of the future behaviour of the employee and other members of the organisation.

5.3 The Employment Act 2002

The **Employment Act 2002** came into effect in October 2004. Among other matters, it aims to encourage internal resolution of workplace disputes, by introducing minimum internal disciplinary and grievance procedures, and encouraging employees to raise grievances with their employer before applying to an employment tribunal. It also requires details of disciplinary and grievance procedures to be included in the 'written particulars' given to new employees.

5.4 The Advisory, Conciliation and Arbitration Service (ACAS)

ACAS's role is (as its name implies):

(a)   **Conciliation**: getting conflicting parties together for informal discussion to resolve a dispute

(b)   **Mediation**: providing a mediator or mediation board which hears arguments and makes proposals and recommendations as a basis for settlement

(c)   **Arbitration**: assisting in the appointment of independent arbitrators who make a binding ruling.

5.5 Disciplinary procedures

The ACAS Code of Practice recommends the following criteria for an effective disciplinary procedure.

Good disciplinary procedures should:

- Be in writing
- Specify to whom they apply
- Be non-discriminatory
- Provide for matters to be dealt with without undue delay
- Provide for proceedings, witness statements and records to be kept confidential
- Indicate the disciplinary actions which may be taken
- Specify the levels of management which have the authority to take the various forms of disciplinary action
- Provide for workers to be informed of the complaints against them and where possible all relevant evidence before any hearing
- Provide workers with an opportunity to state their case before decisions are reached
- Provide workers with the right to be accompanied by a colleague or union representative
- Ensure that, except for gross misconduct, no worker is dismissed for a first breach of discipline
- Ensure that disciplinary action is not taken until the case has been carefully investigated
- Ensure that workers are given an explanation for any penalty imposed
- Provide a right of appeal – normally to a more senior manager – and specify the procedure to be followed

The **statutory disciplinary procedure** providers for the following minimal procedures to be in place.

STEP ① The appropriate manager must write to the employee stating why disciplinary action is being taken and inviting him or her to a meeting to discuss the matter. The employee has the right to be accompanied at the meeting.

STEP ② At the meeting, the manager must explain the problem and allow the employee to respond. After the meeting, the manager should explain his or her decision and inform the employee that he or she has the right to appeal.

STEP ③ The employee may appeal and has the right to be accompanied to the appeal meeting, which should be with a different or more senior manager.

This procedure must be used if the manager is contemplating serious disciplinary action such as dismissal.

5.6 Progressive discipline

KEY POINT

> There are six broad stages of increasing formality and severity in disciplining an employee. These are intended to resolve any problems before they become so serious that dismissal is the only route. We have grouped them into three sets of two in this section so we start with informal action, go on to warnings and end with dismissal.

5.6.1 Informal talk

Many minor cases of poor performance or misconduct are best dealt with by informal advice, coaching or counselling. An **informal oral warning** may be issued. None of this forms part of the formal disciplinary procedure, but workers should be informed clearly what is expected and what action will be taken if they fail to improve.

When the facts of the case have been established, it may be decided that **formal disciplinary** action is needed. The Code of Practice divides this into three stages. These are usually thought of as consecutive, reflecting a **progressive response**. However, it may be appropriate to miss out one of the earlier stages when there have been serious infringements.

5.6.2 Warnings

A *first formal warning* could be either oral or written depending on the seriousness of the case.

(a)   An **oral warning** should include the reason for issuing it, notice that it constitutes the first step of the disciplinary procedure and details of the right of appeal. A note of the warning should be kept on file but disregarded after a specified period, such as six months.

(b)   A **first written warning** is appropriate in more serious cases. It should inform the worker of the improvement required and state that a final written warning may be considered if there is no satisfactory improvement. A copy of the first written warning should be kept on file but disregarded after a specified period, such as twelve months.

If an earlier warning is still current and there is no satisfactory improvement, a **final written warning** may be appropriate.

5.6.3 Lay-off, suspension, demotion, dismissal

The final stage in the disciplinary process is the **imposition of sanctions**.

(a)   **Suspension without pay.** This course of action would be next in order if the employee has committed repeated offences and previous steps were of no avail. Disciplinary lay-offs usually extend over several days or weeks. Some employees may not be very impressed with oral or written warnings, but they will find a disciplinary lay-off without pay a rude awakening. This penalty is only available if it is provided for in the contract of employment.

(b)   **Demotion.** The employee is set back to a lower position and salary. This is not regarded as an effective solution, as it affects the employee's morale and motivation.

(c)   **Dismissal.** Dismissal is a drastic form of disciplinary action, and should be reserved for the most serious offences. For the organisation, it involves waste of a labour resource, the expense of training a new employee, and disruption caused by changing the make-up of the work team. There also may be damage to the morale of the group.

KEY POINT

Think of the disciplinary procedure as a progressive, six stage process as outlined in this section.

5.7 Relationship management in disciplinary situations

Even if the manager uses sensitivity and judgement, imposing disciplinary action tends to generate **resentment**. The challenge is to apply the necessary disciplinary action as constructively as possible.

(a)   **Immediacy (The 'Hot Stove Rule').** Immediacy means that after noticing the offence, the manager proceeds to take disciplinary action as *speedily* as possible, subject to investigations, while at the same time avoiding haste and on-the-spot emotions which might lead to unwarranted actions.

(b)   **Advance warning.** Employees should know in advance (eg in a Staff Handbook) what is expected of them and what the rules and regulations are.

(c)   **Consistency.** Consistency of discipline means that each time an infraction occurs appropriate disciplinary action is taken. Inconsistency in application of discipline lowers the morale of employees and diminishes their respect for the manager.

(d)   **Impersonality.** Penalties should be connected with the act and not based upon the personality involved, and once disciplinary action has been taken, no grudges should be borne.

(e)   **Privacy.** As a general rule (unless the manager's authority is challenged directly and in public) disciplinary action should be taken in private, to avoid the spread of conflict and the humiliation or martyrdom of the employee concerned.

Section summary

Discipline has the same end as **motivation**: to secure a range of desired behaviour from members of the organisation.

ACAS has published a **Code of Practice** for grievance and disciplinary procedures, as well as having a role in helping resolve industrial disputes.

Progressive discipline includes warnings and sanctions of increasing severity, in six broad stages: Informal talk, Oral warning, Written/official warning, Lay-off or suspension, Demotion, Dismissal.

6   Grievance

KEY TERM

A GRIEVANCE occurs when an individual feels that (s)he is being wrongly or unfairly treated by a colleague or supervisor and wishes to assert his or her rights.

Make sure you can distinguish clearly between discipline (when an employee 'does wrong') and grievance (when an employee 'feels wronged'). This is a surprisingly common exam pitfall.

Fairness and equity are vital in ensuring organisations are well-ordered and workers are committed to their work. Read the relevant sections as background for the main topic of grievance.

6.1 Purposes of formal grievance procedure

Introduction

When an individual has a grievance, (s)he should be able to pursue it and ask to have the problem resolved. Some grievances may be capable of solution informally by the individual's manager. However, if an informal solution is not possible, there should be a formal grievance procedure:

(a) To allow **objective grievance handling** – including 'cooling off' periods and independent case investigation and arbitration

(b) To **protect employees** from victimisation – particularly where a grievance involves their immediate superiors

(c) To provide **legal protection** for both parties, in the event of a dispute resulting in claims before an Employment Tribunal

(d) To **encourage grievance airing** – which is an important source of feedback to management on employee problems and dissatisfactions

(e) To **require full and fair investigation** of grievances, enabling the employer-employee relationship to be respected and preserved, despite problems.

6.2 Elements of formal grievance procedures

A formal grievance procedure should:

(a) State the **rights** of the employee for each type of grievance. For example, an employee who is overlooked for promotion might be entitled to a review of his annual appraisal report, or to attend a special appeals promotion/ selection board if he has been in his current grade for at least a certain number of years.

(b) State what the **procedures** for pursuing a grievance should be. The statutory procedure is as follows.

    (i) The individual should state **the grievance** in writing.

    (ii) The **first interview** will be between the immediate manager (unless he is the subject of the complaint, in which case it will be the next level up) and the employee, who has the right to be accompanied by a colleague or representative.

    (iii) If the immediate manager cannot resolve the matter, or the employee is otherwise dissatisfied with the first interview, the case should be **referred upwards** to his superior (and if necessary in some cases, to an even higher authority).

(c) Allow for the involvement of an individual's or group's **trade union or staff association representative**.

(d) State **time limits** for initiating certain grievance procedures and subsequent stages of them (such as communication of decisions, and appeals).

(e) Require **written records** of all meetings concerned with the case to be made and distributed to all the participants.

6.3 Fairness and equity

It should be obvious that most grievances can be avoided if organisations treat their employees fairly, or with equity.

6.3.1 Psychological contracts

A **psychological contract** exists between individuals in an organisation and the organisation itself.

(a)   The individual expects to derive certain benefits from membership of the organisation and is prepared to expend a certain amount of effort in return.

(b)   The organisation expects the individual to fulfil certain requirements and is prepared to offer certain rewards in return.

Three types of psychological contract can be identified.

(a)   **Coercive contract**. This is a contract in which the individual considers that he is being forced to contribute his efforts and energies involuntarily, and that the rewards he receives in return are inadequate compensation.

(b)   **Calculative contract**. This is a contract, accepted **voluntarily** by the individual, in which he expects to do his job in exchange for a readily identifiable set of rewards. With such psychological contracts, motivation can only be increased if the rewards to the individual are improved. If the organisation attempts to demand greater efforts without increasing the rewards, the psychological contract will revert to a coercive one, and motivation may become negative.

(c)   **Co-operative contract**. This is a contract in which the individual identifies himself with the organisation and its goals, so that he actively seeks to contribute further to the achievement of those goals. Motivation comes out of success at work, a sense of achievement, and self-fulfilment. The individual will probably want to share in the planning and control decisions which affect his work, and co-operative contracts are therefore likely to occur where employees participate in decision making.

Employee commitment is secured when the psychological contract is viewed in the same way by the organisation and by the individual and when both parties are able to fulfil their side of the bargain: the individual agrees to work, or work well, in return for whatever rewards or satisfactions are understood as the terms of the 'contract'.

6.3.2 Equitable pay

An important aspect of how employees perceive the equity of their relationship with their employers lies in the way they perceive their material rewards. *Adams* and *Salomon* suggest that this perception will always be coloured by comparisons with other people. Salomon shows the difficulty of achieving equity in a diagram which illustrates the factors on which an equitable relationship can be judged. These will differ between societies, cultures and work groups.

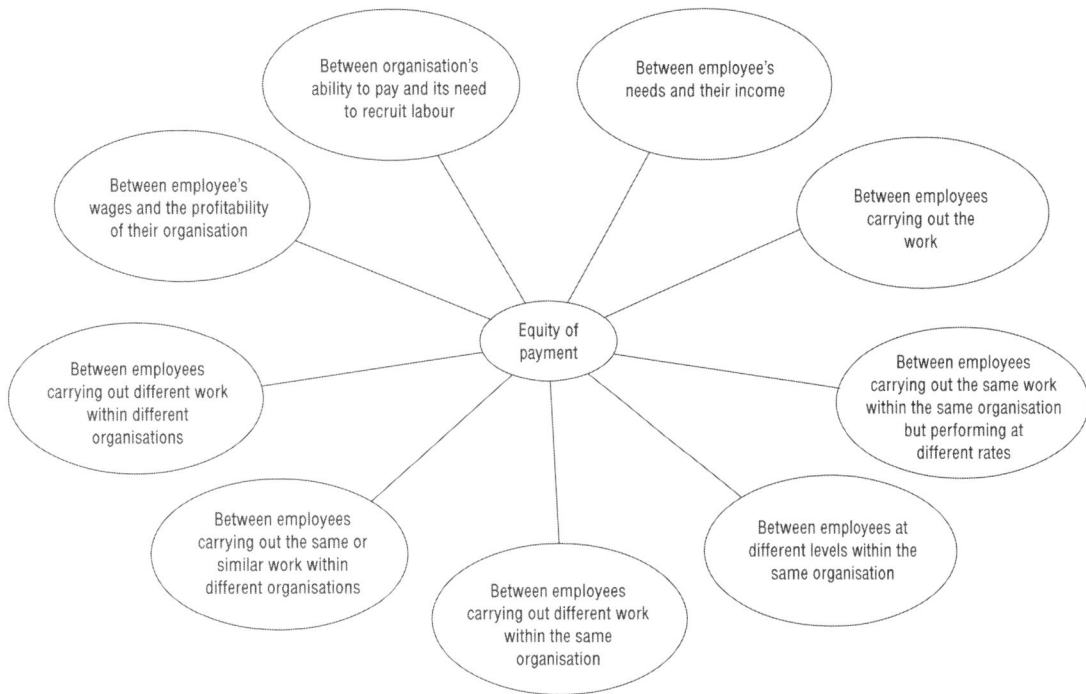

6.3.3 Commitment

KEY TERM

COMMITMENT has been defined as 'the relative strength of an individual's identification with an involvement in a particular organisation'.   (Mowdray)

One of the key reasons to avoid grievance and conflict in an organisation is to secure the commitment of employees, which shows itself in:

(a)   Productivity and time-keeping above the minimal standards set by compliance with rules
(b)   Willingness to exert effort, creativity and initiative on behalf of the organisation's goals
(c)   Positive, co-operative employee relations climate
(d)   Strong morale and esprit de corps
(e)   Lower levels of conflict, grievance and employee stress.

Section summary

Grievance procedures embody employees' right to appeal against unfair or otherwise prejudicial conduct or conditions that affect them and their work.

Any staff **grievances** should be dealt with initially by line managers. Where this cannot be resolved, senior management and HR should be consulted. Most **disputes** arise where the employee feels they have been **treated unfairly**, often in respect of wages, responsibility and status.

---

7   Termination of contract

Introduction

Termination sounds very final and it is indeed the ending of the formal relationship between the employer and the employee. It may come from the employee who hands in their notice, may be required by law or the employer dismisses the employee.

7.1 Retirement

In the UK, many employees are taking **early retirement** perhaps as a result of corporate downsizing, but many people still search for work at an older age and legislation now bans **ageism** in recruitment and retention. Retirement ages for men and women have been **equalised**.

Organisations may encourage early retirement for a variety of reasons.

(a)   Promotion opportunities for younger workers
(b)   Early retirement is an alternative to redundancy
(c)   The age structure of an organisation may become unbalanced
(d)   The cost of providing pensions rises with age

7.2 Resignation

People resign for many reasons, personal and occupational. Employees who are particularly valuable should be encouraged to stay. Particular problems the employee has been experiencing (eg salary) may be solvable, though not always in the short term. In any case, an **exit interview**, when the leaver explains the decision to go, is a valuable source of information.

The **period of notice** required for the employee to leave should be set out in the contract of employment, but some leeway may be negotiated on this.

7.3 Dismissal

There are three forms of termination that constitute dismissal under UK law.

(a)   The termination of an employee's contract **by the employer**

(b)   The ending of a fixed-term contract **without renewal** on the same terms

(c)   Resignation by the employee where the employer's conduct breaches the contract of employment: **constructive dismissal**.

The **statutory minimum** period of notice to be given is determined by the employee's length of continuous service in the employer's service. Longer periods may be written into the contract, at the employer's discretion, and by agreement. Either party may waive his right to notice, or accept payment in lieu of notice. An employee is entitled to a written statement of the **reasons** for dismissal.

7.3.1 Wrongful dismissal

Wrongful dismissal is dismissal that breaches the **contract of employment**. An example would be failure to give the contractual period of notice (assuming the circumstances did not justify summary dismissal).

7.3.2 Unfair dismissal

The legal concept of unfair dismissal gives protection to the employee against **arbitrary** dismissal; that is dismissal without good reason. The basic principle is that any dismissal is potentially unfair: once the employee has proved that he has been dismissed, the onus is on the employer to prove that the dismissal was fair.

Potentially **fair** grounds for dismissal include:

(a)   **Redundancy,** provided that the selection for redundancy was fair.

(b)   **Legal impediment:** the employee could not continue to work in his present position without breaking a legal duty or restriction.

(c)   **Non-capability,** provided adequate training and warnings had been given.

(d)   **Misconduct,** provided warnings suitable to the offence have been given.

(e)   **Other substantial reason:** for example, the employee is married to a competitor.

Dismissal is regarded as **automatically unfair** by reason of:

(a)   Unfair selection for redundancy
(b)   Membership and involvement in a trade union
(c)   Pregnancy
(d)   Insisting on documented payslips and employment particulars
(e)   Carrying out certain activities in connection with health and safety at work

The Conciliation Officer or **Employment Tribunal** to whom a complaint of unfair dismissal is made may order various **remedies**, subject to the circumstances of the case.

(a)   **Re-instatement**: giving the employee the old job back.
(b)   **Re-engagement**: giving the employee a job comparable to the old one.
(c)   **Compensation**: which may include redundancy pay, breach of contract and punitive award.

The order to avoid claims of unfair dismissal, managers must:

(a)   Ensure that **standards of performance and conduct** are set, clearly defined and communicated to all employees

(b)   **Warn** employees where a gap is perceived between standard and performance

(c)   Give a clearly defined and reasonable **period for improvement** - with help and advice where necessary, and clear improvement targets

(d)   Ensure that **disciplinary procedures** are fairly and systematically applied.

If such procedures are formulated, the employee will have been given every chance to redeem the situation, and the organisation will be in a strong position at an Employment Tribunal hearing.

Question 1.5   Dismissal

Learning outcome C2a, e

An employer's treatment of an employee is so bad that eventually she resigns even though she liked her work. This would be an example of:

A   Wrongful dismissal
B   Potentially unfair dismissal
C   Automatically unfair dismissal
D   Constructive dismissal

7.4 Redundancy

Redundancy is defined as dismissal under two circumstances.

(a)   The employer has ceased to carry on the business at all, or in the place where the employee was employed.

(b)   The requirements of the business for employees to carry out work of a particular kind have ceased or diminished, or are expected to.

Compensation is a legal entitlement, and encourages employees to accept redundancy without damage to industrial relations.

The employee is **not entitled** to compensation in three circumstances.

(a)   The employer has made an **offer of suitable alternative employment** and the employee has unreasonably rejected it.

(b)   The employee is of **pensionable age** or over, or has less than two years' continuous employment.

(c)   The employee's conduct merits **dismissal without notice**.

There are certain legal minimums for compensation offered, based on age and length of service.

7.4.1 Procedure for handling redundancies

From a purely humane point of view, it is obviously desirable to consult with employees or their representatives. Notice of impending redundancies is a legal duty for redundancies over a certain number.

The impact of a redundancy programme can be reduced in several ways.

(a)   Retirement of staff over the normal retirement age
(b)   Early retirement to staff approaching normal retirement age
(c)   Restrictions on recruitment to reduce the workforce over time by natural wastage
(d)   Dismissal of part-time or short-term contract staff
(e)   Offering retraining and/or redeployment within the organisation
(f)   Seeking voluntary redundancies

Where management have to choose between individuals doing the same work, the most equitable approach may be to dismiss the less competent (on carefully defined and measured criteria) or require people to re-apply for the job. The LIFO (last-in-first-out) principle may be applied, so that newcomers are dismissed before long-serving employees, but care must be taken that this does not discriminate against women or ethnic minorities, for example.

Many large organisations provide benefits in excess of the statutory minimum, with regard to consultation periods, terms, notice periods, counselling and aid with job search, training in job-search skills and so on. Many firms provide advice and **outplacement** counselling, to help redundant employees find work elsewhere.

Section summary

Termination of the employment relationship is the last resort with alternatives such as **retirement** and **resignation** preferable where possible.

8 Equal opportunities

Introduction

Equal opportunities tend to be preserved via legislation. **Diversity** represents a more positive, voluntary approach to avoid adverse working practices. We look at diversity in Section 10.

Our discussion uses UK legislation but refers to it at a very basic level. Make sure you know what each piece of legislation aims to do generally in terms of age, sex, race, disability or other aspects of equality in the workplace. You need a general awareness that there are laws governing these areas so that when you make decisions as a manager these are taken into account. We look at **codes of practice** in the next section, which are the practical implementation of the law on equality in organisations.

8.1 Equal opportunities

KEY TERM

EQUAL OPPORTUNITIES is an approach to the management of people at work based on equal access and fair treatment, irrespective of gender, race, ethnicity, age, disability, sexual orientation or religious belief.

Equal opportunities employers will seek to redress inequalities (eg of access to jobs, training, promotion, pay or benefits) which are based around differences, where they have no relevance to work performance.

Certain aspects of equal opportunities (such as discrimination on the basis of sex, race or disability) are enshrined in law; others (such as, up to now, discrimination on the basis of age) rely upon models of good practice.

Exam skills

Discrimination and equal opportunities are topics of great importance for managers in real life. We include them in this part of the Study Text because that is where the syllabus puts them. However, you should be aware that they are relevant to all aspects of management and therefore, potentially to *any question* in the examination. Make sure that any strategies or actions you propose, in response to a scenario, are not discriminatory!

8.1.1 Why is equal opportunity an issue for employers?

Sound **business arguments** can be made for equal opportunities policy. Reasons argued for adopting non- or anti-discrimination measures include the following.

(a)   Common decency and fairness, in line with business ethics.

(b)   Good HR practice, to attract and retain the best people for the job, regardless of race or gender.

(c)   Compliance with relevant legislation and Codes of Practice, which are used by employment tribunals.

(d)   Widening the recruitment pool in times of skill shortages.

(e)   Other potential benefits to the business through its image as a good employer, and through the loyalty of customers who benefit from (or support) equality principles.

The Chairman of the Equality and Human Rights Commission, however, has criticised companies that do nothing except use 'equal opportunities designer labels' to make recruitment advertisements look good.

8.2 The legal framework on equality

In Britain, several main Acts have been passed to deal with inequality of opportunity and discrimination at work.

(a)   The **Sex Discrimination Act 1986,** and the **Sex Discrimination and Equal Pay (Miscellaneous Amendments) Regulations 1996**, outlawing certain types of discrimination on the grounds of sex, marital status and sex change.

(b)   The **Race Relations Act 1976** as amended 1996, outlawing certain types of discrimination on grounds of colour, race, nationality, or ethnic or national origin. The **Race Relations (Amendment) Act 2000** added the requirement that larger public organisations (more than 150 employees) must draw up detailed plans for achieving racial equality in all employment practices.

(c)   **Equal pay legislation** is intended to prevent discrimination as regards terms and conditions of employment between men and women and provides that women have the right to equal pay for 'work of equal value' to that of a man in the same establishment (as defined by a job evaluation scheme).

(d)   The **Disability Discrimination Acts 1995 and 2005** give disabled people (including sufferers from HIV, cancer and multiple sclerosis) similar rights against discrimination to those already established in relation to sex and race. In addition, the employer has duty to make 'reasonable adjustments' to working arrangements or premises where these constitute a disadvantage to disabled people.

(e)   The **Employment Equality (Sexual Orientation) (Amendment) Regulations 2003** protects employees from direct and indirect discrimination, harassment and victimization in employment and training on the grounds of sexual orientation.

(f)   The **Employment Equality (Religion or Belief) Regulations 2003** protects employees from direct and indirect discrimination, harassment and victimization in employment and training on the grounds of religion or belief.

(g)   The **Employment Equality (Age) Regulations 2006**, introduced in October 2006, prohibit unjustified age discrimination in employment and vocational training; support later retirement and retirement planning; and remove upper age limits for unfair dismissal and redundancy rights.

8.2.1 Types of discrimination

There are three types of discrimination under the Acts.

KEY TERMS

DIRECT DISCRIMINATION occurs when one interested group is treated less favourably than another (except for exempted cases).

INDIRECT DISCRIMINATION occurs when a policy or practice is fair in form, but discriminatory in operation: for example, if requirements or conditions are imposed, with which a substantial proportion of the interested group cannot comply, to their detriment.

VICTIMISATION occurs when a person is penalised for giving information or taking action in pursuit of a claim of discrimination.

In addition, **harassment** is the use of threatening, intimidatory, offensive or abusive language or behaviour. This is covered by UK law in relation to race, religious belief and sexual orientation: sexual harassment will also be covered in forthcoming legislation.

An employer must, if challenged, justify apparently discriminatory conditions on non-discriminatory grounds. It is often the case that employers are not aware that they are discriminating indirectly, and this concept was a major breakthrough when introduced by the Acts.

| Question 1.6 | Indirect discrimination |

Learning outcome C2a, e

Suggest four examples of practices that would constitute indirect discrimination on the grounds of sex.

Positive discrimination gives preference to a protected person, regardless of comparative suitability and qualification for the job. British legislation does not (except with regard to training) permit positive discrimination. A number of countries in the world do use positive discrimination as an aspect of social policy to correct perceived disadvantages endured by various ethnic and other groups in society. (For example, in India scheduled castes are entitled to a proportion of government jobs.)

Section summary

Discrimination of certain types is illegal in the UK on grounds of:

- Sex and marital status (Sex Discrimination Act 1986)
- Colour, race, nationality and ethnic or national origin (Race Relations Acts 1996 and 2000)
- Disability (Disability Discrimination Acts 1995 and 2005)
- Sexual orientation and religious beliefs (Employment Equality Regulations 2003)
- Age (Employment Equality (Age) Regulations 2006)

Employers should note the implications of the Acts for both:

- **Direct discrimination** – less favourable treatment of a protected group

- **Indirect discrimination** – when requirements or conditions cannot be justified on non-discriminatory grounds and work to the detriment of a protected group.

9 The practical implications of legislation

Introduction

The practical implications of the legislation for employers are set out in **Codes of Practice**, currently issued by the Equality and Human Rights Commission. These do not have the force of law, but may be taken into account by employment tribunals, where discrimination cases are brought before them.

9.1 Formulating an effective equal opportunities policy

Some organisations make minimal efforts to avoid discrimination, paying lip-service to the idea only to the extent of claiming 'We are an Equal Opportunities Employer' on advertising literature. To turn such a claim into reality, the following are needed.

(a) **Support** from the top of the organisation for the formulation of a practical policy.

(b) A **working party** drawn from – for example – management, unions, minority groups, and the HR function and staff representatives. This group's brief will be to produce a draft Policy and Code of Practice, which will be approved at senior level.

(c) **Action plans and resources** (including staff) to implement and monitor the policy, publicise it to staff, arrange training and so on.

(d) **Monitoring**. The numbers of women and ethnic minority staff can easily be monitored

     (i)   On entering (and applying to enter) the organisation

     (ii)   On leaving the organisation

     (iii)   On applying for transfers, promotions or training schemes

(It is less easy to determine the ethnic origins of the workforce through such methods as questionnaires: there is bound to be suspicion about the question's motives, and it may be offensive to some workers.)

(e) **Positive action**: the process of taking active steps to encourage people from disadvantaged groups to apply for jobs and training, and to compete for vacancies. (Note that this is not positive discrimination.) Examples might be: using ethnic languages in job advertisements, or implementing training for women in management skills. In addition, there may be awareness training, counselling and disciplinary measures to manage sexual, racial and religious harassment.

9.2 Recruitment and selection

Introduction

There is always a risk that disappointed job applicants, for example, will attribute their lack of success to discrimination, especially if the recruiting organisation's workforce is conspicuously lacking in representatives of the same ethnic minority, sex or group. The following guidelines should be borne in mind.

(a) **Advertising**

     (i)   Any wording that suggests preference for a particular group should be avoided (except for genuine occupational qualifications).

     (ii)   Employers must not indicate or imply any 'intention to discriminate'.

     (iii)   Recruitment literature should state that the organisation is an Equal Opportunities employer (where this can be justified).

     (iv)   The placing of advertisements only where the readership is predominantly of one race or sex is construed as indirect discrimination. This includes word-of-mouth recruiting from the existing workforce, if it is not broadly representative.

(b) **Recruitment agencies**. Instructions to an agency should not suggest any preference.

(c) **Application forms**. These should include no questions which are not work-related (such as domestic details) and which only one group is asked to complete.

(d) **Interviews**

     (i)   Any non-work-related question must be asked of all subjects, if at all, and even then, some types of question may be construed as discriminatory. (You cannot, for example, ask only women about plans to have a family or care of dependants, or ask – in the most offensive case – about the Pill or PMT.)

     (ii)   It may be advisable to have a witness at interviews, or at least to take detailed notes, in the event that a claim of discrimination is made.

(e) **Selection tests**. These must be wholly relevant, and should not favour any particular group. Even personality tests have been shown to favour white male applicants.

(f) **Records**. Reasons for rejection, and interview notes, should be carefully recorded, so that in the event of investigation the details will be available.

9.3 Other initiatives

Measures such as the following may be used as positive action initiatives.

(a)   Putting equal opportunities **higher on the agenda** by appointing Equal Opportunities Managers (and even Directors) who report directly to the HR Director.

(b)   **Flexible hours** or part-time work, term-time or annual hours contracts (to allow for school holidays) to help women to combine careers with family responsibilities. Terms and conditions, however, must not be less favourable.

(c)   **Career-break or return-to-work** schemes for women.

(d)   **Fast-tracking school-leavers**, as well as graduates, and posting managerial vacancies internally, giving more opportunities for movement up the ladder for groups (typically women and minorities) currently at lower levels of the organisation.

(e)   **Training for women-returners** or women in management to help women to manage their career potential. Assertiveness training may also be offered as part of such an initiative.

(f)   **Awareness training** for managers, to encourage them to think about equal opportunity policy.

(g)   **Counselling and disciplinary policies** to raise awareness and eradicate sexual, racial and religious harassment.

(h)   **Positive action** to encourage job and training applications from minority groups.

Section summary

Recruitment and selection are areas of particular sensitivity to claims of discrimination as well as genuine (though often unintended) inequality.

In addition to responding to legislative provisions, some employers have begun to address the **underlying problems** of discrimination.

---

10 Diversity

Introduction

Diversity in employment, as a concept, goes further than equal opportunities.

The ways in which people meaningfully differ in the work place include not only race and ethnicity, age and gender, but personality, preferred working style, individual needs and goals and so on.

10.1 Managing diversity

A 'managing diversity' orientation implies the need to be proactive in managing the needs of a diverse workforce in areas (beyond the requirements of equal opportunity and discrimination regulations) such as:

(a)   Tolerance of individual differences
(b)   Communicating effectively with (and motivating) ethnically diverse work forces
(c)   Managing workers with increasingly diverse family structures and responsibilities
(d)   Managing the adjustments to be made by an increasingly aged work force
(e)   Managing increasingly diverse career aspirations/patterns, flexible working etc
(f)   Dealing with differences in literacy, numeracy and qualifications in an international work force
(g)   Managing co-operative working in ethnically diverse teams

> **Section summary**
>
> The concept of **'managing diversity'** is based on the belief that the dimensions of individual difference on which organisations currently focus are crude and performance-irrelevant classifications of the most obvious differences between people.

Chapter Roundup

- ✓ **Management** is responsible for using the organisation's resources to meet its goals. It is accountable to the owners: shareholders in a business, or government in the public sector.

- ✓ **Power** is the ability to get things done. There are many types of power in organisations: position or **legitimate power**, expert power, personal power, resource power and negative power are examples.

- ✓ **Authority** is related to position power. It is the right to take certain decisions within certain boundaries.

- ✓ **Responsibility** is the obligation a person has to fulfil a task (s)he has been given. Responsibility can be delegated, but the person delegating responsibility still remains accountable to his or her boss for completion of the task.

- ✓ **Authority/responsibility mismatch** or **ambiguity** is stressful for the individual, and may be risky for the organisation's control over decision-making.

- ✓ **Delegation** is the process whereby a superior gives a subordinate part of his or her own decision-making authority. It is an important component of time management and employee development.

- ✓ **Successful delegation** requires that people have the right skills and the authority to do the job, and are given feedback. It also requires a balance of support and trust from the delegator.

- ✓ There are many different definitions of **leadership**. Key themes (which are also used to distinguish leadership from management) include: interpersonal influence; securing willing commitment to shared goals; creating direction and energy; and an orientation to change.

- ✓ Leadership offers key **benefits** in a competitive, turbulent environment: activating commitment, setting direction, developing people and energising and supporting change.

- ✓ **Bureaucracy** is 'a continuous organisation of official functions bound by rules' (*Weber*).

- ✓ **Discipline** has the same end as **motivation**: to secure a range of desired behaviour from members of the organisation.

- ✓ **ACAS** has published a **Code of Practice** for grievance and disciplinary procedures, as well as having a role in helping resolve industrial disputes.

- ✓ **Progressive discipline** includes warnings and sanctions of increasing severity, in six broad stages: Informal talk, Oral warning, Written/official warning, Lay-off or suspension, Demotion, Dismissal.

- ✓ **Grievance procedures** embody employees' right to appeal against unfair or otherwise prejudicial conduct or conditions that affect them and their work.

- ✓ Any staff **grievances** should be dealt with initially by line managers. Where this cannot be resolved, senior management and HR should be consulted. Most **disputes** arise where the employee feels they have been **treated unfairly**, often in respect of wages, responsibility and status.

- ✓ **Termination of the employment relationship** is the **last resort** with alternatives such as **retirement** and **resignation** preferable where possible.

✓   **Discrimination** of certain types is illegal in the UK on grounds of:

  • Sex and marital status (Sex Discrimination Act 1986)
  • Colour, race, nationality and ethnic or national origin (Race Relations Acts 1996 and 2000)
  • Disability (Disability Discrimination Acts 1995 and 2005)
  • Sexual orientation and religious beliefs (Employment Equality Regulations 2003)
  • Age (Employment Equality (Age) Regulations 2006)

✓   Employers should note the implications of the Acts for both:

  • **Direct discrimination** – less favourable treatment of a protected group

  • **Indirect discrimination** – when requirements or conditions cannot be justified on non-discriminatory grounds and work to the detriment of a protected group.

✓   **Recruitment and selection** are areas of particular sensitivity to claims of discrimination as well as genuine (though often unintended) inequality.

✓   In addition to responding to legislative provisions, some employers have begun to address the **underlying problems** of discrimination.

✓   The concept of '**managing diversity**' is based on the belief that the dimensions of individual difference on which organisations currently focus are crude and performance-irrelevant classifications of the most obvious differences between people.

Quick Quiz

1   Power arising from an individual's formal position in the organisation is called:

  A   Referent power
  B   Legitimate power
  C   Expert power
  D   Resource power

2   Complete the statement below using one of the words in the list given in brackets.

  '................................. authority cuts across departmental boundaries and enables managers to take decisions that affect staff in departments other than their own.'

  (managerial, line, staff, functional, financial, formal)

3   A 'manager' might also be identified as a transformational leader. *True or false?*

4   A grievance occurs when an employee infringes organisational rules or expectations. *True or false?*

5   What is the difference between equal opportunities and diversity?

Answers to Quick Quiz

1   B (or 'position' power)

2   Functional

3   False. Management is identified with 'transactional' leadership

4   False: this is a disciplinary action. (Try and define 'grievance' yourself)

5   Equal opportunities tend to be preserved via legislation. Diversity represents a more positive, voluntary approach to avoiding adverse working practices.

BPP
LEARNING MEDIA

Answers to questions

1.1 Management structure

The purpose of this exercise has been to get you to separate the issues of management functions from organisational structure and hierarchy. John, Paul, George and Ringo have a number of choices. Here are some extreme examples.

(a)   All the management activities are the job of one person.

In this case, Paul, for example, could plan direct and control the work and the other three would do the work.

(b)   Division of management tasks between individuals (eg: repairing drums *and* ensuring plans are adhered to would be Ringo's job, and so on).

(c)   Management by committee. All of them could sit down and work out the plan together etc. In a small business with equal partners this is likely to be the most effective.

1.2 Line and staff authority

(a) and (b) are both examples of line authority.

(c) is staff or perhaps functional authority.

1.3 Leadership

The answer to this is personal. The question was set to get you to think about good leadership.

1.4 Control

Culture.

1.5 Dismissal

D   Little is certain in employment law but on the face of it, this would seem to be a case of constructive dismissal. It may also turn out to be unfair dismissal. Wrongful dismissal is unlikely as the employer may not have actually breached the contract of employment. It may emerge on investigation that the bad treatment of the employee was the result of one of the automatically unfair reasons for dismissal, such as membership of a trade union. However, on the facts we are given, option D is the best answer.

1.6 Indirect discrimination

(a)   Advertising a vacancy in a primarily male environment, where women would be less likely to see it.

(b)   Offering less favourable terms to part-time workers (given that most of them are women).

(c)   Specifying age limits which would tend to exclude women who had taken time out of work for child-rearing.

(d)   Asking in selection interviews about plans to have a family (since this might be to the detriment of a woman, but not a man).

Now try the question below from the Exam Question Bank

Number	Level	Marks	Time
1	Examination	10	18 mins

CONTROL

Control is one of the key functions of management. Control embraces a range of **approaches**, from financial controls (a key part of a management accountant's technical role); to performance management (the use of contracts, performance appraisal, reporting and disciplinary processes to control individual and team performance); to regulatory controls (ensuring compliance with relevant law and regulation); and interpersonal control (the use of values and influence to regulate people's behaviour).

In this chapter, we look at key examples from each type of control. We begin with a model which helpfully highlights different **levels** at which control can be exercised.

This should help you to integrate your learning in this chapter across the syllabus, as you consider the application of controls at a strategic level (in Part A of the syllabus), a tactical level (from which many of the examples here are drawn), and an operational and project level (in Part B of the syllabus).

Aspects related to organisational discipline and the control of conflict are also covered.

The issues of corporate governance and business ethics (an important area of control) are discussed in the context of the business's obligations to its stakeholders.

We look at mentoring which is an aspect of employee development that falls broadly under control.

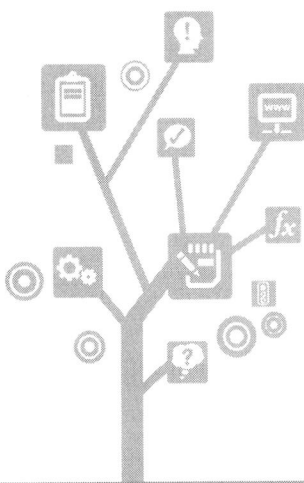

topic list	learning outcomes	syllabus references	ability required
1 Theories of control	C2d	C2(xi)	comprehension
2 Internal control systems	C2d	C2(xi)	comprehension
3 Performance management – controlling the individual	C2d	C2(xi)	comprehension
4 Leading, managing and motivating teams	C2d	C2(viii),(x)	comprehension
5 Controlling health and safety	C2d	C2(ii)	comprehension
6 Mentoring	C2f	C2(ix)	comprehension
7 Business ethics	C2g	C2(vii)	analysis
8 Corporate governance	C2g	C2(vii)	analysis

1 Theories of control

Introduction

Control is used at all levels of the organisation from top-level management down to routine controls over operations. In this section we look at what control systems need to be effective or the 6 'A's. According to *Ouchi,* organisations employ three basic control strategies: market, bureaucratic and clan. *Johnson and Scholes* identify control processes in the organisation according to whether they focus on inputs or outputs and/or are direct or indirect.

1.1 The nature of control

The managers of a business organisation are responsible to its owners and stakeholders for the achievement of its goals. They need to find reliable and systematic ways of ensuring that:

(a) All individuals and units in the business understand their goals and objectives, within the overall direction of the enterprise.

(b) Resources are efficiently mobilised and utilised in pursuit of objectives, without undue risk or waste.

(c) Progress and performance can be continually compared to plans, in order to take corrective action where required.

(d) Performance can be periodically reviewed, in order to derive learning and planned improvements from any strengths and weaknesses identified.

Control is the overall process (or set of processes) whereby goals and standards are defined; performance is monitored and measured against the goals and plans for achieving them; and corrective action is taken, if necessary, to ensure that goals are being accomplished, either in the present planning cycle or in the next (through learning). This can be shown, simply, as follows.

Control system

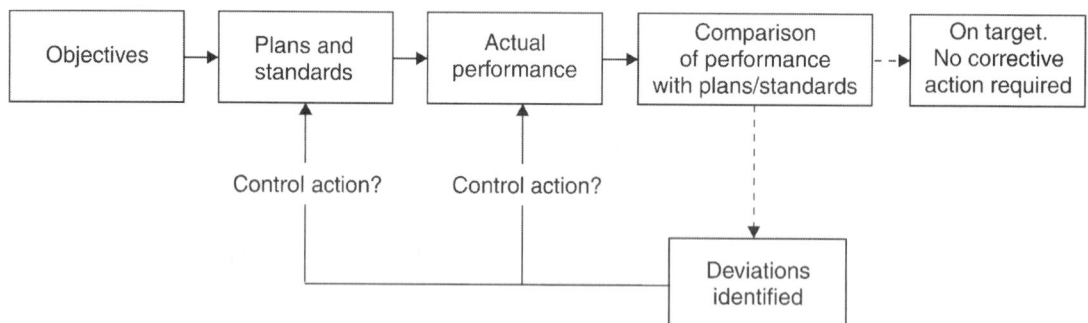

1.2 Levels of control

Robert Anthony classified managerial activity into three basic levels.

(a) **Strategic management** carried out by the strategic apex): concerned with direction-setting, policy making and crisis handling.

(b) **Tactical management** (carried out by the middle line and techno structure): concerned with establishing means to corporate ends, mobilising and controlling resources, and innovating (finding new ways of achieving goals).

(c) **Operational management** (carried out by the operating core): concerned with routine activities to carry out tactical plans.

Managerial level

Top — STRATEGIC — Long-term Planning Decisions

Middle — TACTICAL — Medium-term planning and Management Control Decisions

Lower — OPERATIONAL — Operational/Short-term Decisions. Routine Processing of Transactions

1.2.1 Strategic control

At the strategic level, control involves activities such as:

(a)   **Strategic planning**: setting (and monitoring performance against) key objectives for the organisation as a whole, or organisational direction. This also includes environmental scanning, to identify opportunities and threats.

(b)   Designing (or reviewing and re-designing) **organisational structures**: decisions on downsizing, delayering, acquisition/merger, and divisionalisation and so on.

(c)   Determining **policies** and **codes of conduct**, in a wide range of areas including: HR (recruitment, training, reward, promotion, equal opportunities etc); the environment, ethics and corporate responsibility; risk appetite and risk management measures; sourcing/procurement and so on.

(d)   **Organisation-wide initiatives**, such as Business Process Re-engineering or Total Quality Management.

(e)   Monitoring of progress and performance against strategic plans at a high (non-detailed) level. This includes setting up a framework for management information and reporting.

(f)   Managing **corporate governance**: determining roles of the board of directors; taking board-level decisions; reporting to shareholders and so on.

1.2.2 Tactical control

Tactical control relates to the implementation of board-level decisions by functional managers. It involves activities such as:

(a)   **Tactical planning**. In the case of a marketing manager, for example, this would include product/market planning, media scheduling and so on. In the case of a production manager it may include capacity planning, resource allocation or production scheduling.

(b)   **Budgeting** and budgetary control for the function.

(c)   The development and implementation of **procedures** (to fulfil policy requirements set at the strategic level). These would include recruitment, development and reward of functional staff. Other procedures include administrative procedures and systems, risk management, quality control and so on, within the scope of the function's activity.

(d)   **Monitoring** compliance with plans and procedures within the function.

1.2.3 Operational control

Operational control relates to the control of relatively routine and repetitive activities, to ensure that pre-set plans and targets are met. At this level, little managerial intervention or discretion may be required: operational control systems are often automated, and generate reports only on identified deviations from plan, within pre-set tolerance limits.

Examples of operational control systems include credit controls (in accounting) and order processing, invoicing and delivery scheduling (in sales).

KEY POINT

There are many models of control, but Anthony's three levels gives a basic framework. In the previous syllabus, candidates were asked to identify at which level of control staff appraisal systems are used. You might just as easily be asked to analyse a production or HR system, using the three levels, or to recommend improvements to a specific system in a scenario.

1.3 Effective control systems – the 6 'A's

The effectiveness of any control procedure or system is likely to depend on the extent to which it satisfies six criteria. **We shall call these the 6 'A's.**

(a)   **Acceptability** to the people who will operate it: a fit with their needs and expectations, and the culture of the unit.

(b)   **Accessibility**, in terms of its ease of understanding and operation

(c)   **Adaptability** to changing conditions and demands

(d)   **Action orientation**, so that deviations trigger corrective action or improvements

(e)   **Appropriateness** to the circumstances and skills and needs of the people operating it

(f)   **Affordability** or cost-effectiveness: the cost of operating controls must be *less* than the costs associated with deviation or failure (which will be determined by risk analysis). In other words, prevention costs must be less than failure costs.

1.4 Control strategies and processes

There are various models describing how controls are applied in organisations. We will look briefly at two popular frameworks.

1.4.1 Market, bureaucratic and clan control

William Ouchi identified three basic control strategies used by organisations.

(a)   **Market control** is the use of the price mechanism and related performance measures, internally and externally, to control organisational behaviour. It is used in loose organisational forms such as consortia and alliances and in the construction industry when sub-contractors are employed.

At corporate level, market control is always used: income statement (statement of comprehensive income), cash flow and balance sheet (statement of financial position) information is published, so the organisation's performance can be judged in comparison with other organisations, or with previous years. The market mechanism is provided by the capital markets and competitors.

At divisional level, market control may be relevant if there are separate divisions, which are established as **profit centres**, or **investment centres**.

At operational level, the price mechanism can be used as a means to control activities, for example in the use of target costing, competitive tendering for contracts (as in the UK public sector), or transfer pricing.

(b) **Bureaucratic control** uses an impersonal system of rules and reports to maintain control, as discussed in Chapter 1.

   The main mechanisms of control are policies, standard operating procedures, rules, statistical reports, budgets (and budgetary control), staff performance appraisal and a clear disciplinary framework.

(c) **Clan control** is based on corporate culture. It depends on shared values and standards of behaviour within the organisation, and assumes that employees 'buy in' to the purpose, goals and expectations of the organisation.

Ouchi suggested that all organisations use a mix of these strategies, but took a contingency view as to which control mechanism was likely to predominate in a given set of conditions.

Contingencies	Control strategies
Routine technology Stable environment Large size Functional structure	Mainly **bureaucratic** Some clan control is possible (eg top management, R&D).
Priced internal outputs Competition on price Size – not relevant Product/brand structure	Mainly **market** Bureaucratic or clan control may be used within profit centres.
Non-routine technology Unstable environment Small size Matrix structure	Mainly **clan control** Bureaucratic control may be used in departments dealing with routine matters.

Question 2.1   Control systems

Learning outcome C2d

What type of control would you expect to see in a large international airline?

A   Contingency
B   Market
C   Clan
D   Bureaucratic

1.4.2 Control processes

In their influential work 'Exploring Corporate Strategy', *Johnson and Scholes* suggest that control processes can be classified as:

(a) **Input-focused** (controlling resources input to a given strategy) or **output-focused** (controlling the results and outcomes of a given strategy)

(b) **Direct** (using supervision, monitoring and behaviour-shaping) or **indirect** (creating environmental conditions within which the desired behaviour or results can be achieved).

They outline six controls using this framework. Again, organisations will use a mix of these processes, but some may dominate in a given organisation, depending on its culture, geography, technology and specific strategic challenges.

	Input-focused	Output-focused
Direct	• *Direct supervision* 'The direct control of strategic decisions by one or a few individuals, typically focused on the effort put into the business by employees'. Often the main control process in small organisations. • *Planning systems* Planning resource requirements and allocations, and monitoring their utilisation to identify variance and initiate corrective action. For example, budgetary control, standardisation of work processes, or centralised formulae for calculating resource allocations (eg marketing budget as a percentage of turnover).	• *Performance targets* Focus on outputs such as revenue, profitability, quality standards and other key performance indicators (KPIs). The organisation or Strategic Business Units (SBU) performance is evaluated against defined targets, allowing flexibility as to how they are achieved. Performance targets particularly suit large businesses, since they allow central control over results – without stifling the flexibility or initiative of SBUs in the face of changing 'local' demands
Indirect	• *Social/cultural control* Norms, values and expectations of behaviour become standardised and accepted in the group or organisation, and individuals are 'brought into line' by group influence, education and training, rewards, involvement and so on. This is particularly valuable in dynamic environments, because securing 'buy in' supports change. • *Self-control* Employees are given clear goals, performance feedback, incentives and leadership to support them in maintaining desired standards of conduct and performance without direct intervention. People behave in desired ways because they understand the need to do so, and are willing to commit themselves to the good and goals of the team.	• *Internal market mechanisms* A formalised system of 'contracting' for resources between units in an organisation, as internal market transactions between suppliers/customers. Units are required to earn revenue or achieve results in competition with external providers. Internal markets can foster integration and efficiency by encouraging an 'internal customer' orientation.

Section summary

Control systems exist to support the achievement of organisational objectives. They are of many types, both formal and informal.

Organisations require control at all levels of their operating framework: **strategic, tactical and operational**.

Control systems should be **acceptable, accessible, adaptable, action-oriented, appropriate** and **affordable**.

William Ouchi identified three broad **control strategies**: market control, bureaucratic control and clan control. Strategy gurus *Johnson* and *Scholes* outline a broader framework of **control processes**, both input and output-focused and direct and indirect.

2 Internal control systems

Introduction

Internal controls cover polices, processes, tasks and behaviours (*Turnbull*). These controls enable a business to operate effectively, comply with laws and provide good quality information from reports.

When you think about the **control framework** you need to make a simple distinction between the **control environment** and **control procedures.**

KEY TERM

An INTERNAL CONTROL is any action taken by management to enhance the likelihood that established objectives and goals will be achieved. Management plans, organises and directs the performance of sufficient actions to provide reasonable assurance that objectives and goals will be achieved. Thus, control is the result of proper planning, organising and directing by management. *(Institute of Internal Auditors)*

2.1 Purposes of an internal control system

The UK's *Turnbull Report* provides a helpful summary of the main purposes of an internal control system.

Turnbull comments that internal control consists of 'the **policies**, **processes**, **tasks, behaviours** and other aspects of a company that taken together:

(a)   Facilitate its effective and efficient operation by enabling it to respond appropriately to significant business, operational, financial, compliance and other **risks** to achieving the company's objectives. This includes the safeguarding of assets from inappropriate use or from loss and fraud and ensuring that liabilities are identified and managed.

(b)   Help ensure the quality of internal and external **reporting**. This requires the maintenance of proper records and processes that generate a flow of timely, relevant and reliable information from within and without the organisation.

(c)   Help ensure **compliance** with applicable laws and regulations, and also with internal policies with respect to the conduct of businesses

The Turnbull report goes on to say that a sound system of internal control reduces but does not eliminate the possibilities of poorly-judged decisions, human error, deliberate circumvention of controls, management override of controls and unforeseeable circumstances. Systems will provide **reasonable (not absolute) assurance** that the company will not be hindered in achieving its business objectives and in the orderly and legitimate conduct of its business, but won't provide certain protection against all possible problems.

2.2 The control framework

Organisations need to consider the **overall framework of controls** since controls are unlikely to be very effective if they are developed sporadically around the organisation, and their effectiveness will be very difficult to measure by internal audit and ultimately by senior management.

Perhaps the simplest framework for internal control draws a distinction between:

(a)   **Control environment** – the overall context of control, in particular the attitude of directors and managers towards control. A 'strong' control environment is one in which clear strategies for dealing with risk are supported by policies and codes of conduct; clear definition of authority and responsibility; clear communication of expectations; and senior management commitment to competence, integrity and trust.

(b)   **Control procedures** – the detailed controls in place, including measures such as financial controls, health and safety reporting, quality monitoring and so on.

2.3 Elements of effective internal control

One influential US guidance model (**Committee of Sponsoring Organisations of the Treadway Commission – or COSO**) recommends the following elements for effective internal control.

(a) A strong **control environment**, supportive of business objectives

(b) **Risk assessment** and **risk management** to identify areas of vulnerability and exposure (including a range of business, financial and compliance risks) as a basis for the objectives of the control system.

(c) **A range of control activities**, such as segregation of duties, authorisation procedures, physical security measures, supervision, arithmetical and accounting checks/reconciliations and checking/development of personnel.

(d) **Communication and information processes** to ensure that all levels of management receive appropriate progress reports.

(e) Processes for **monitoring the continuing effectiveness** of the system and taking corrective action where required.

Section summary

Internal controls should help organisations counter risks, maintain the quality of reporting and comply with laws and regulations. They provide reasonable assurance that organisations will fulfil their objectives.

Internal control frameworks include the **control environment** within which **internal controls** operate. Other important elements are the **risk assessment and response processes,** the **sharing of information** and **monitoring** the environment and operation of the control system.

3 Performance management – controlling the individual

Introduction

In this section we cover control as this affects the individual employee. Performance management develops out of the organisation's business plan as this is translated into individual performance targets. Employees are appraised on their performance in accordance with the plan and how they have performed. Employment contracts set out the expectations the organisation has regarding conduct and performance for the employee.

3.1 Human resource strategy

Although personnel control systems typically operate at the tactical level, the purpose of those controls will be to support control at the strategic level via human resource strategies and policies. Human resource policy will be determined with regard to matters such as:

(a) The number and type of skills required by the future plans of the organisation

(b) The organisation's commitment to equality of opportunity and diversity (in regard to recruitment and selection, development, promotion and so on)

(c) Training and development opportunities offered

(d) Promotion and management succession

(e) Flexible working, family-friendly policies, the use of non-standard-contract labour, outsourcing and so on

(f)   Rewards and incentives, and how they are awarded and reviewed

(g)   Codes of conduct, disciplinary and grievance processes and so on

These policy statements can then be translated into procedures at the tactical level.

3.2 Performance management

KEY TERM

PERFORMANCE MANAGEMENT is: 'a means of getting better results…by understanding and managing performance within an agreed framework of planned goals, standards and competence requirements. It is a process to establish a shared understanding about what is to be achieved, and an approach to managing and developing people … [so that it] … will be achieved' (*Armstrong, Handbook of Personnel Management Practice*).

The process of performance management may be outlined as follows.

STEP 1 From the **business plan**, identify the requirements and competences required to carry it out.

STEP 2 Draw up a **performance agreement**, defining the expectations of the individual or team, covering standards of performance, performance indicators and the skills and competences people need.

STEP 3 Draw up a **performance and development plan** with the individual. These record the actions needed to improve performance, normally covering development in the current job. They are discussed with job holders and will cover, typically:

(a)   The areas of performance the individual feels in need of development
(b)   What the individual and manager agree is needed to enhance performance
(c)   Development and training initiatives

STEP 4 **Manage performance continually throughout the year,** not just at appraisal interviews done to satisfy the personnel department. Managers can review actual performance, with more informal interim reviews at various times of the year.

(a)   High performance is reinforced by praise, recognition, increasing responsibility. Low performance results in coaching or counselling.

(b)   Work plans are updated as necessary.

(c)   Performance problems are dealt with: identifying what they are, establishing the reasons for the shortfall, taking control action (with adequate resources) and providing feedback.

STEP 5 **Performance review**. At a defined period each year, success against the plan is reviewed, but the whole point is to assess what is going to happen in future.

Question 2.2   Performance management

Learning outcome C2d

What are the advantages to *employees* of introducing such a system?

3.3 Employment contracts

KEY POINT

As an alternative to negotiated agreements on performance, **contracts of employment** may be used to set out the organisation's expected standards of conduct and performance, as a basis for measurement and discipline/improvement planning.

A **contract of employment** may be written, oral or a mixture of both. There may be a standard form contract, exchange of letters, or terms agreed orally prior to engagement. As long as there is agreement on essential terms, such as hours and wages, a valid contract exists.

Under UK law, an employer must give employees a written statement of **particulars of employment**, within two months of starting work. This statement should identify:

(a)   The names of employer and employee, and the date on which employment began.
(b)   Pay, hours of work, holiday and sick leave entitlements and details of any pension scheme.
(c)   Length of notice of termination to be given on either side.
(d)   Details of disciplinary and grievance procedures and work rules.
(e)   Rules on health and safety at work (by custom)

The purpose of this is to ensure that employees have precise information about the terms on which they are employed. Note that this describes *mutual* expectations, rights and obligations: it can be used to control the performance both of the employee and of the organisation, in case of dispute.

3.4 Performance appraisal

KEY TERM

PERFORMANCE APPRAISAL is the systematic review and assessment of an employee's performance, potential and development or improvement needs.

3.4.1 The purpose of appraisal

The general purpose of any staff appraisal system is to improve the efficiency of the organisation by ensuring that the individuals within it are performing to the best of their ability and developing their potential for improvement. It has a number of aspects.

(a)   **Reward review**. The appraisal should assess whether employees deserve bonuses or pay increases.

(b)   **Performance review.** The appraisal can be used for planning and following-up training and development programmes by identifying training needs and validating training methods.

(c)   **Potential review**. This is an aid to planning career development and succession which attempts to predict the level and type of work the individual will be capable of in the future.

More specific objectives may include:

(a)   **Establishing what the individual has to do** in a job in order that the objectives for the section or department are realised

(b)   **Establishing the key or main results** which the individual will be expected to achieve in the course of his or her work over a period of time

(c)   **Comparing the individual's level of performance against a standard**, to provide a basis for remuneration above the basic pay rate

(d)   **Identifying the individual's training and development needs** in the light of actual performance

(e)   **Identifying potential candidates for promotion**

(f)   **Identifying areas for improvement**

(g)   **Establishing an inventory of actual and potential performance within the undertaking** to provide a basis for manpower planning

(h)   **Monitoring the undertaking's initial selection procedures** against the subsequent performance of recruits, relative to the organisation's expectations

(i)   **Improving communication** about work tasks between different levels in the hierarchy

3.4.2 The process of appraisal

A typical appraisal system will consist of the following processes.

STEP 1   **Identify criteria for assessment**, perhaps based on job analysis, performance standards, and person specifications and so on.

STEP 2   **Prepare an appraisal report**. Traditional approaches focused on appraisal of a subordinate by his or her immediate superior, but modern approaches include:

(a)   *Self assessment*, to encourage self-awareness and learning

(b)   *Upward appraisal*, to gather feedback from subordinates on the managerial style of their superiors

(c)   *360-degree feedback*, to gather a rounded picture though feedback from superior, subordinates, colleagues, customers and other relevant parties.

STEP 3   **Carry out an appraisal interview**, for an exchange of views about the appraisal report, targets for improvement, solutions to problems and so on.

STEP 4   **The assessor's superior reviews the assessment**, so that the appraisee does not feel subject to one person's prejudices. Formal appeals may be allowed, if necessary to establish the fairness of the procedure.

STEP 5   **Prepare and implement an action plan** to achieve improvements and changes agreed.

STEP 6   **Follow-up** the progress of the action plan.

Appraisal can thus be seen in terms of a basic control process, as follows

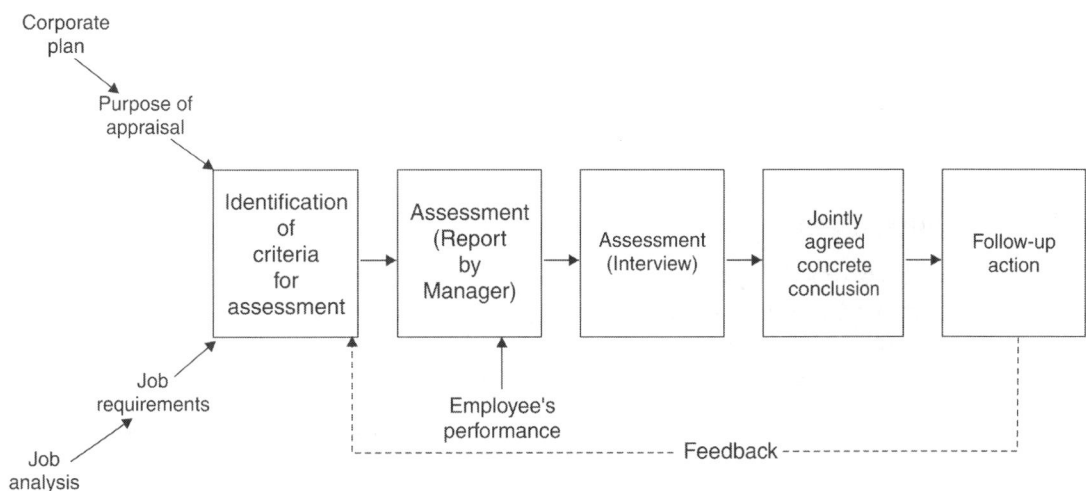

3.4.3 Improving appraisal

Even the most objective and systematic appraisal scheme is subject to **personal** and **interpersonal problems**.

(a) Appraisal is often **defensive on the part of the subordinate**, who believes that criticism may mean a low bonus or pay rise, or lost promotion opportunity.

(b) Appraisal is often **defensive on the part of the superior**, who cannot reconcile the role of judge and critic with the human relations aspect of interviewing and management.

(c) The superior might show **conscious or unconscious bias** in the appraisal or may be influenced by rapport (or lack of it) with the interviewee. Systems without clearly defined standard criteria will be particular prone to the subjectivity of the assessor's judgement.

(d) The manager and subordinate may both **be reluctant to devote time and attention to appraisal**. Their experience in the organisation may indicate that the exercise is a waste of time (especially if there is a lot of form-filling) with no relevance to the job, and no reliable follow-up action.

(e) The organisational culture may **simply not take appraisal seriously**: interviewers are not trained or given time to prepare, appraisees are not encouraged to contribute, or the exercise is perceived as a 'nod' to Human Relations with no practical results.

The appraisal scheme should itself be assessed (and regularly re-assessed) for relevance, fairness, serious intent, co-operative orientation, positive outcomes and cost efficiency. Many of these issues have been addressed by modern approaches which emphasise multi-source feedback, a forward-looking improvement focus, collaborative discussion and problem-solving and results-oriented appraisal criteria.

Question 2.3	Formal appraisal

Learning outcome C2d

List four disadvantages to the individual of *not* having a *formal* appraisal system.

Section summary

Performance management is an approach to controlling the conduct, performance and development of personnel in the organisation. Human resource control systems typically operate at the tactical level of control.

Contracts of employment may be used as the basis for controlling employee conduct and performance, by setting out the organisation's expectations.

There are a number of aspects to **performance appraisal** including reward review, performance review and potential review. Appraisal is an important practical aspect of control in organisations.

4 Leading, managing and motivating teams

Introduction

A team is a form of group with a number of distinguishing features including **common goals**, **norms** and **team loyalty**. Managers are often called on to lead and manage teams. In these circumstances it is useful to know something about how teams work. This helps the manager in **selecting and building teams to make them more effective.**

Part of management is **evaluating the team's performance,** much as individuals are assessed on performance, so we have a section on **evaluation in here.**

It is also essential to motivate teams toward greater achievement so we have included a short section on **team motivation** here.

Finally we look at meetings and how these might be run well for the benefit of all the team attending them.

4.1 Teams

KEY TERM

A TEAM is a 'small number of people with complementary skills who are committed to a common purpose, performance goals and approach for which they hold themselves mutually accountable.'

(Katzenbach and Smith, 1994)

4.1.1 Strengths of team working

Teams are particularly well-adapted to the following purposes.

Type of role	Comments
Work organisation	Teams combine the skills of different individuals.
	Teams are a co-ordinating mechanism: they avoid complex communication between different business functions.
Control	Fear of letting down the team can be a powerful motivator: team loyalty can be used to control the performance and behaviour of individuals.
Ideas generation	Teams can generate ideas, eg through brainstorming and information sharing.
Decision making	Decisions are evaluated from more than one viewpoint, with pooled information. Teams make fewer, but better-evaluated, decisions than individuals.

4.1.2 Limitations and problems of team working

Problems with teams include **conflict** on the one hand, and **groupthink** (excessive cohesion) on the other.

Teams and team working are very much in fashion, but there are potential **drawbacks**.

(a) Teamworking is not suitable for all jobs: it should be introduced because it leads to better performance, not because people feel better or more secure.

(b) Team processes (especially excessive meetings and seeking consensus) can delay decision-making: groups make fewer decisions than individuals.

(c) Social relationships might be maintained at the expense of other aspects of performance or inter-group conflicts may get in the way of effective collaboration.

(d) Group norms may restrict individual personality and flair, or may suppress work output and performance (so that no individual 'shows up' the team by over-producing).

(e) Due to a process called **social facilitation**, performance of simple tasks at which people are relatively confident *improves* in the presence of other people – but performance of new, complex tasks is *hindered* by, the presence of an audience (you may be familiar with this 'flustered' feeling …).

(f) Groups have been found to take **riskier** decisions than individuals on their own.

4.2 Organising team work

Multi-disciplinary teams contain people from different departments, pooling the skills of specialists.

Multi-skilled teams contain people who themselves have more than one skill.

A team may be called together temporarily, to achieve specific task objectives (**project team**), or may be more or less permanent, with responsibilities for a particular product, product group or stage of the production process (a **product or process team**).

There are two basic approaches to the organisation of team work: multi-skilled teams and multi-disciplinary teams. Project teams may be of either type.

4.3 Who should be selected for a team?

Team members should be selected for their potential to contribute to getting things done (**task performance**) and establishing good working relationships (**group maintenance**). This may include:

(a)   **Specialist skills**. A team might exist to combine expertise from different departments

(b)   **Power** in the wider organisation. Team members may have influence

(c)   **Access to resources**. Team members may contribute information, or be able to mobilise finance or staff for the task

(d)   The **personalities and goals** of the individual members of the team. These will determine how the group functions

The blend of the individual skills and abilities of its members will (ideally) **balance** the team.

KEY POINT

You probably have had experience of being put into a group of people you do not know. Many teams are set up this way and it takes some time for the team to become effective. This is a highly relevant issue for project teams, in particular, as they are constantly being formed, disbanded and re-formed.

4.4 Building a team

KEY POINT

Team development can be facilitated by active **team building** measures to support team identity, solidarity and commitment to shared objectives.

Teams may have a natural evolutionary life cycle. However, not all teams develop into mature teams and might be stuck, stagnating, in an ineffective state.

So it often falls to a manager or project team leader to build the team. There are three main issues involved in team building.

Issues	Comments
Team identity	Get people to see themselves as part of the group eg by regular communication, shared mythology and perhaps a separate space (a personalised meeting room or intranet page perhaps).
Team solidarity	Encourage loyalty so that members put in extra effort for the sake of the team. This may require encouraging relationships, controlling competition and perhaps injecting an element of competition with other teams.

Issues	Comments
Shared objectives	Encourage the team to commit itself to shared work objectives and to co-operate willingly and effectively in achieving them. This may involve a range of leader activity. • Clearly setting out the objectives of the team • Allowing the team to participate in setting objectives • Giving regular feedback on progress and results, with constructive criticism • Getting the team involved in providing performance feedback • Offering positive reinforcement (praise etc) for co-operative working and task achievement by the team as a whole (rather than just 'star' individuals) • Championing the success of the team within the organisation

Question 2.4   Group cohesion

Learning outcome C2d

Can you see any dangers in creating a very close-knit group? Think of the effect of strong team cohesion on:

(a)   What the group spends its energies and attention on

(b)   How the group regards outsiders, and any information or feedback they supply

(c)   How the group makes decisions

Question 2.5   Team building

Learning outcome C2d

Why might the following be effective as **team-building exercises**?

(a)   Sending a project team (involved in the design of electronic systems for racing cars) on a recreational day out karting.

(b)   Sending two sales teams on a day out playing 'War Games', each being an opposing combat team trying to capture the other's flag, armed with paint guns.

(c)   Sending a project team on a conference at a venue away from work, with a brief to review the past year and come up with a vision for the next year.

4.5 Evaluating team effectiveness

KEY POINT

The task of the team leader is to build a 'successful' or 'effective' team. The criteria for team effectiveness include:

(a)   **Task performance**: fulfilment of task and organisational goals

(b)   **Team functioning**: constructive maintenance of team working, managing the demands of team dynamics, roles and processes, and

(c)   **Team member satisfaction**: fulfilment of individual development and relationship needs.

Some of the characteristics of **effective** and **ineffective** teams may be summarised as follows.

Factor	Effective team	Ineffective team
Quantifiable		
Labour turnover	Low	High
Accident rate	Low	High
Absenteeism	Low	High
Output and productivity	High	Low
Quality of output	High	Low
Individual targets	Achieved	Not achieved
Stoppages and interruptions to the work flow	Low	High (eg because of misunderstandings, disagreements)
Qualitative		
Commitment to targets and organisational goals	High	Low
Understanding of team's work and why it exists	High	Low
Understanding of individual roles within the team	High	Low
Communication between team members	Free and open	Mistrust
Ideas	Shared for the team's benefit	'Owned' (and hidden) by individuals for their own benefit
Feedback	Constructive criticism	Point scoring, undermining
Problem-solving	Addresses causes	Only looks at symptoms
Interest in work decisions	Active	Passive acceptance
Opinions	Consensus	Imposed solutions
Job satisfaction	High	Low
Motivation in leader's absence	High	'When the cat's away...'

4.6 Motivation and rewarding effective teams

KEY POINT

Team-based rewards and incentives may be used to encourage co-operation and mutual accountability, as well as team performance. The manager needs to consider the desire of individuals to be recognised for their own contribution as well as the performance of the team.

Organisations may try to encourage effective team performance by designing reward systems that recognise team, rather than individual success. Indeed, **individual performance rewards** may act *against* team co-operation and performance.

(a)   They emphasise individual rather than team performance.

(b)   They encourage team leaders to think of team members only as individuals, rather than relating to them as a team.

For team rewards and incentives to be effective, the team must have certain characteristics.

(a)   Distinct roles, targets and performance measures (so the team knows what it has to do to earn the reward)

(b)   Significant autonomy and thus influence over performance (so the team perceives that extra effort will be rewarded)

(c)   Maturity and stability

(d)   Co-operation

(e)   Interdependence of team members (so that the team manages member contribution, everyone 'pulls their weight', no-one feels they could earn higher rewards on their own)

4.7 The purpose of team meetings

KEY POINT

Managers spend a large proportion of their working week in meetings, particularly with the rise of project working. Meetings are thus both a major cost to organisations, and a major context for **decision-making, interpersonal influencing and team collaboration.**

4.7.1 General team meetings

Regular team meetings have particular purposes, over and above problem-solving and decision-making on any particular work-related issue.

(a)   They provide an opportunity to review team working processes and appraise (formally or informally) how well they are working. Team members may raise problems of co-ordination or communication, for example.

(b)   They reinforce the team's sense of itself as a team, drawing them together to focus on their shared goals.

(c)   They allow for goal reinforcement, progress feedback and information sharing, to ensure that team members are 'on the same page' with their efforts – especially if they do not directly work together (eg in dispersed or virtual project teams).

(d)   They allow for all-member involvement and development in team decision-making and information sharing processes. (Discussion leading and research/presentation roles might be rotated, for example, to facilitate this.)

(e)   They allow for informal communication, which is important for working relations, ideas generation and information-sharing. This can be built in at the beginning and end of meeting time.

Question 2.6	Purposeful meetings

Learning outcome C2d

How regularly do you attend team meetings, and for what purpose?

How many of these team meetings do you feel are actually necessary or valuable? What alternative means of communication or decision-making could be used instead of those meetings you feel are a waste of time? What might you *lose* by cutting out these team meetings?

4.7.2 Managing meetings effectively

KEY POINT

Effective meetings depend on: defined purpose; appropriate participants; a planned sequence of business; a well-facilitated process; and continual review and learning.

Whatever the purpose and level of formality of a given meeting, its effectiveness will broadly depend on the following.

(a) There is usually a discussion **leader**, chairperson, or at least an organiser, who guides the proceedings of the meeting and aims to maintain order.

(b) There is often a **sequence of business** or at least a list of items to be covered: topics of discussion or decisions to be reached. It is not essential to formalise this point with an **agenda**, but meetings usually do have one.

(c) The purpose of the meeting is achieved by reaching some **decision or expression of opinion** at the end of the discussion. In some circumstances this may lead to taking a vote to determine what is the majority view. In other circumstances, the discussion may just be **summarised** by the leader and written confirmation of the decisions reached provided later for perusal by the various parties.

4.7.3 Conducting the meeting

Effective facilitation of a team meeting involves the following.

(a) Ensuring that **agreed decisions are accurately recorded** in the notes or minutes of the meeting, ideally with clearly defined responsibility for action. These should be distributed (eg by e-mail) as soon as possible after the meeting.

(b) **Following up on decisions and action points from previous meetings**, to ensure that agreed action has been taken. (In formal meetings, this is done as part of the review of the previous minutes).

Question 2.7	Meeting problems

Learning outcome C2d

What aspects of the following situations might be a problem for an effective team meeting? What might you, in the role of facilitator, do about it?

(a) One person suggests a revision to the agenda, a complex issue which the rest of the team is unprepared to discuss, and which two members are likely to feel is 'targeted' at them.

(b) The team has more items on its agenda than it can handle in a simple meeting.

(c) A team member has called ahead to say that she will be unavoidably late for a scheduled project team meeting.

Section summary

A **team** is more than a group. It has joint **objectives** and **accountability** and may be set up by the organisation under the supervision or coaching of a team leader, although **self-managed teams** are growing in popularity.

5 Controlling health and safety

Introduction

The main UK law governing health and safety is the **Health and Safety at Work Act 1974**. This formalises the obligations of the employer and the employee toward health and safety in the workplace. The Act has been supplemented with regulations addressing individual areas such as VDU regulations and manual handling.

You need to know the main obligations of employer and employee toward health and safety. Also make sure you have a broad awareness of what the individual regulations cover for instance VDU usage though you shouldn't need to know any detail for the exam.

Employers are obliged to report serious accidents under regulations known as RIDDOR and keep accident report books for all accidents which take place in the workplace.

5.1 Why is health and safety important?

Health, safety and well-being at work are important for several reasons.

(a)   Employees should – as human beings – be **protected** from needless pain and suffering!

(b)   Employers and employees have **legal obligations** to take reasonable measures to promote healthy and safe working.

(c)   Accidents, illness and other causes of absence and impaired performance **cost** the organisation money.

(d)   A business' **corporate image** and reputation as an employer (its **employer brand**) may suffer if its health and safety record is bad: this might alienate customers and potential employees.

5.2 The legal framework on health and safety

In 1972, the Royal Commission on Safety and Health at Work reported that unnecessarily large numbers of days were being lost each year through industrial accidents, injuries and diseases, because of the 'attitudes, capabilities and performance of people and the efficiency of the organisational systems within which they work'.

Since 1972, **major legislation** has been brought into effect in the UK, most notably the **Health and Safety at Work Act 1974**, plus Regulations and Codes of Practice under the Act, which implement the provisions of EU directives on health and safety issues.

However, it would be wrong to paint too optimistic a picture of employers' performance on health and safety.

(a)   **Legislation sets bare minimum standards** for (and levels of commitment to) health and safety. ('The law is a floor'). It does not represent satisfactory – let alone best – practice for socially responsible organisations.

(b)   Health and safety are still a **low priority** in some organisation (and even national) cultures. Provisions are costly, and have no immediately quantifiable benefit.

(c)   **Positive discipline** (setting mechanisms and systems which theoretically prevent hazardous behaviour) only goes so far, and irresponsible or ignorant behaviour can still cause accidents.

(d)   **New health and safety concerns** are constantly emerging, as old ones are eradicated.

(i)   New technology and ergonomics may make physical labour less stressful, but it creates new hazards and health risks, such as a sedentary, isolated lifestyle, and problems associated with working long hours at VDUs.

(ii)   New issues in health are constantly arising, such as passive smoking in the workplace or alcohol abuse, with the increasing stress of work in highly competitive sectors.

Question 2.8   Disaster costs

Learning outcome C2d

How many notorious workplace disasters can you think of? What were the main costs to the organisations concerned?

5.3 The legal framework

KEY POINT

Once again, if the UK is not your country of operation, you might like to use this checklist of basic issues and principles, which represent basic standards for ethical employment anywhere.

5.3.1 The Health and Safety at Work Act (HSWA) 1974

In the UK, the Health and Safety at Work Act 1974 provides for the introduction of a system of approved Codes of Practice, prepared in consultation with industry, so that employees, whatever their employment, should find that their work is covered by an appropriate code of practice.

Employers' responsibilities under the HSWA may be summarised as follows.

(a)   To provide **safe systems** (work practices)
(b)   To provide a **safe and healthy work environment** (well-lit, warm, ventilated, hygienic and so on)
(c)   To maintain all **plant and equipment** to a necessary standard of safety
(d)   To **support safe working practices** with information, instruction, training and supervision
(e)   To consult with **safety representatives** appointed by a recognised trade union
(f)   To appoint a **safety committee** to monitor safety policy, if asked to do so
(g)   To **communicate safety policy** and measures to all staff, clearly and in writing

An **employee's responsibilities** under the Act include:

(a)   Taking **reasonable care** of himself and others affected by his acts or omissions at work

(b)   **Co-operating** with the employer in carrying out his duties (including enforcing safety rules)

(c)   **Not interfering** intentionally or recklessly with any machinery or equipment provided in the interests of health and safety.

5.3.2 The Management of Health and Safety at Work Regulations 1992

These regulations impose additional responsibilities on **employers** as follows.

(a)   To carry out **risk assessment**, generally in writing, of all work hazards, on a continuous basis

(b)   To introduce **controls** to reduce risks

(c)   To assess the risks to **anyone else affected** by their work activities

(d)   To **share hazard and risk information** with other employers, including those on adjoining premises, other site occupiers and all subcontractors entering the premises

(e)   To initiate or revise **safety policies** in the light of the above

(f)   To identify employees who are especially **at risk** (other legislation cites pregnant women, young workers, shift-workers and part-time workers)

(g)   To provide **fresh and appropriate training** in safety matters

(h)   To provide **information to employees** (including temporary workers) about health and safety

(i)   To employ competent **safety and health advisors**

Employees have the additional responsibility under the regulations to inform the employer of any situation which may pose a danger to themselves or others.

5.3.3 Health and Safety (Consultation with Employees) Regulations 1996

Employers have the responsibility to consult all employees on health and safety matters, including the planning of health and safety training, changes in equipment and procedures which may substantially affect health and safety at work, or the health and safety consequences of introducing new technology.

Question 2.9	Health, safety and productivity

Learning outcome C2d

What aspects of your studying environment (if any) do you think are:

- A hindrance to your work?
- A source of dissatisfaction?
- A hazard to your health and/or safety?

5.3.4 The Workplace (Health, Safety and Welfare) Regulations 1992

These regulations provide for health and hygiene in work environments, including such aspects as the following.

(a)   **Equipment** must be properly maintained.

(b)   **Ventilation**. Air should be fresh or purified.

(c)   **Temperature** must be 'reasonable' inside buildings during working hours.

(d)   **Lighting** should be suitable and sufficient, and natural, if practicable.

(e)   **Cleaning and decoration**. Floors, walls, ceilings, furniture, furnishings and fittings must be kept clean.

(f)   **Room dimensions and space**. Each person should have at least 11 cubic metres of space.

(g)   **Floors** must be properly constructed and maintained (without holes, not slippery, properly drained and so on).

(h)   **Sanitary conveniences and washing facilities** must be suitable and sufficient.

(i)   **Drinking water**. An adequate supply should be available with suitable drinking vessels.

Question 2.10	Health, safety – and compliance

Learning outcome C2d

Reassess your answer to the previous Question in the light of these specific provisions.

5.3.5 The Manual Handling Operations Regulations 1992

The manual handling regulations cover heavy lifting – a major cause of industrial injury. They require employers, so far as is reasonably practicable, to avoid the need for employees to undertake any manual handling activities which will involve the risk of their becoming injured. However, if the cost of avoiding such risk is unreasonable the employer will be required to carry out an assessment of all manual handling operations, and to take steps to reduce the risks.

5.3.6. The Health and Safety (Display Screen Equipment) Regulations 1992

If you have ever worked for a long period at a VDU you may personally have experienced some discomfort. Backache, eye strain and stiffness or muscular problems of the neck, shoulders, arms or hands are frequent complaints. The common, if somewhat inaccurate, term for this is **Repetitive Strain Injury** or **RSI**. The regulations address areas such as:

(a)   Minimisation of glare and flicker from VDU screens
(b)   Arrangement and flexibility of screens, keyboards, desks and chairs for comfortable working
(c)   The provision of breaks
(d)   Training and consultation to improve work practices

5.4 Accidents and other workplace hazards

5.4.1 Causes of accidents

Many accidents could be avoided by the simple application of common sense and consideration by employer and employee, and by safety consciousness encouraged or enforced by a widely acceptable and well-publicised safety policy.

Common causes of injury in administrative workplaces include falling/tripping, lifting and materials/equipment handling, related to hazards such as:

(a)   Slippery or poorly maintained floors (eg frayed carpets)
(b)   Trailing electric leads
(c)   Obstacles in gangways or staircases
(d)   Standing on chairs (particularly swivel chairs) to reach high shelving
(e)   Lifting heavy items without bending properly
(f)   Incorrect use of electrical machinery (including overloading power sockets)
(g)   Removing the safety guard on a machine to free a blockage
(h)   Incorrect labelling or storage of chemicals (which may burn, cause allergic reactions etc)

5.4.2 The cost of accidents

The costs of accidents to the employer are significant.

(a)   **Time lost by the injured employee** and other employees who choose to, or must of necessity, stop work at the time of or following the accident

(b)   **Time lost by management and technical staff** following the accident

(c)   A proportion of the cost of **first aid materials and officers**

(d)   The cost of **disruption to operations** at work

(e)   The cost of any **damage** to the equipment or any cost associated with the subsequent modification of the equipment

(f)   The costs associated with increased **insurance premiums**

(g)   **Reduced output** from the injured employee on return to work

(h)   The cost of possible **reduced morale**, increased absenteeism, increased labour turnover among employees

(i)   The cost of recruiting and training a **replacement** for the injured worker

(j)   The cost of **compensation payments** if employees sue for damages

Although the injured employee's damages may be reduced if his injury was partly a consequence of his own contributory **negligence**, due allowance is made for ordinary human failings.

(a)   An employee is not deemed to consent to the risk of injury because he is aware of the risk. It is the employer's duty to provide a safe working system.

(b)   Employees can become inattentive or careless in doing work which is monotonous or imposes stress. This factor too must be allowed for in the employer's safety precautions.

(c)   It is not always a sufficient defence that the employer *provided* safety equipment and rules: the employer has some duty to encourage its proper *use*.

(d)   Employees do not work continuously. The employer's duty is to take reasonable care for their safety in all acts which are normally and reasonably incidental to the day's work.

Question 2.11   Responsibility for safe working

Learning outcome C2d

If a person went to wash a tea-cup after use, at his or her office, and slipped on a slippery surface in the kitchen and was injured, who would be at fault?

5.4.3 Preventing accidents

Some steps which might be taken to reduce the frequency and severity of accidents are as follows.

(a)   Developing a **safety consciousness** among staff and workers and encouraging departmental pride in a good safety record: creating a culture of safety.

(b)   Developing effective **consultative participation** between management, workers and unions so that safety and health rules can be accepted and followed.

(c)   Giving **adequate instruction in safety rules** and measures as part of the training of new and transferred workers, or where working methods or speeds of operation are changed.

(d)   **Identified risks** (eg materials handling) to be minimised and designed as far as possible for safe operation.

(e)   Ensuring a **satisfactory standard** for both basic plant and auxiliary fittings (such as safety guards).

(f)   **Proactive maintenance:** apart from making sound job repairs, temporary expedients to keep production going should not prejudice safety.

In general, the appropriate code of practice for the industry/work environment should be implemented in full.

Question 2.12   Workplace hazards

Learning outcome C2d

What hazards can you identify in the following office scene?

5.4.4 Investigation and report of accidents

Safety inspections may be carried out as a comprehensive **audit**, working through a checklist, or by using **random spot checks**, regular checks of **particular risk points** or statutory inspections of particular areas, such as lifts, hoists, boilers or pipelines.

It is essential that checklists used in the inspection process should identify corrective action to be taken, and allocate responsibility for that action. There should be reporting systems and control procedures to ensure that inspections are taking place and that findings are being acted on.

Accident-reporting systems (eg using accident books) will be particularly important, but it must be emphasised to staff that the report is not an exercise in itself but a management tool, designed to:

(a)   Identify problems

(b)   Indicate corrective action

Serious accidents and dangerous occurrences (such as explosions) must be formally reported to the relevant authorities under the **Reporting of Injuries, Diseases and Dangerous Occurrences Regulations** (RIDDOR 1995).

5.5 Working time

The EU Working Time Directive was incorporated into UK law in the **Working Time Regulations 1998**. The regulations limit workers' hours to 48 hours per week (averaged over 17 weeks): individuals may agree in writing to work more than 48 hours per week, and a record of hours should be retained. There are also provisions for entitlement to work breaks and days off (24-hours' rest in every seven days).

This is a health and safety issue, due to the dangers of overwork and inattention due to tiredness and monotony. It is also related to policies supporting work-life balance, and family-friendly working, by ensuring employees' entitlement to rest days.

5.6 Health and safety policy

A comprehensive health and safety policy can be depicted as follows:

Systematic approach to health and safety

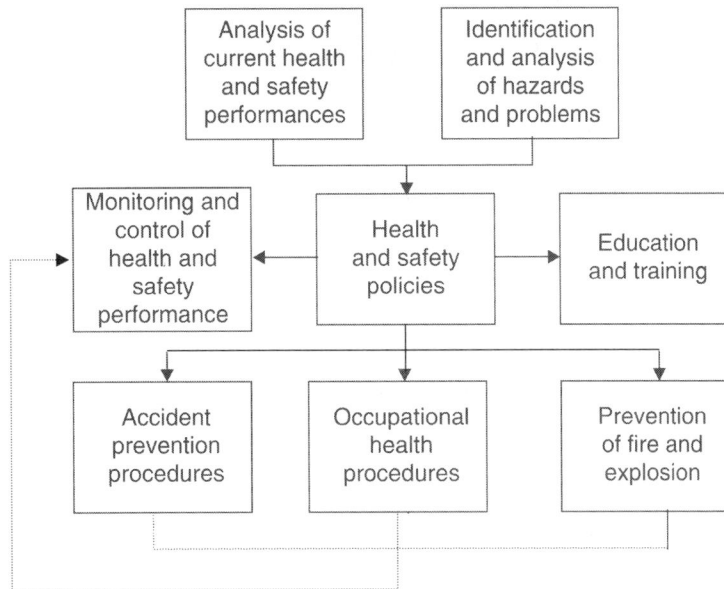

However, there is also a cultural element to health and safety. Staff education and training, appraisal and reward systems and role modelling by management all need to support safety values and compliance with policy and procedures.

CASE STUDY

Charles Hampden-Turner (in his book *Corporate Culture*) notes that attitudes to safety can be part of a **corporate culture**. He quotes the example of a firm called (for reasons of confidentiality) *Western Oil*.

(a)   Western Oil had a bad safety record. 'Initially, safety was totally at odds with the main cultural values of productivity (management's interests) and maintenance of a macho image (the workers' culture) ... Western Oil had a culture which put safety in conflict with other corporate values.' In particular, the problem was with its long-distance truck drivers (who in the US have a culture of solitary independence and self-reliance) who drove sometimes recklessly with loads large enough to inundate a small town. The company instituted *Operation Integrity* to improve safety, in a lasting way, changing the policies and drawing on the existing features of the culture but using them in a different way.

(b)   The **culture** had five dilemmas.

(i)   **Safety-first *vs* macho-individualism**. Truckers see themselves as 'fearless pioneers of the unconventional lifestyle ... 'Be careful boys!' is hardly a plea likely to go down well with this particular group'. Instead of trying to control the drivers, the firm recommended that they become **road safety consultants** (or design consultants). Their advice was sought on improving the system. This had the advantage that 'by making drivers critics of the system their roles as outsiders were preserved and promoted'. It tried to tap their heroism as promoters of public safety.

(ii)   **Safety everywhere *vs* safety specialists**. Western Oil could have hired more specialist staff. However, instead, the company promoted cross functional safety teams from existing parts of the business, for example, to help in designing depots and thinking of ways to reduce hazards.

(iii)   **Safety as cost *vs* productivity as benefit**. 'If the drivers raced from station to station to win their bonus, accidents were bound to occur ... . The safety engineers rarely spoke to the line manager in charge of the delivery schedules. The unreconciled dilemma between safety and productivity had been evaded at management level and passed down the hierarchy until drivers were subjected to two incompatible injunctions, work fast and work safely.' To deal with this problem, safety would be built into the reward system.

(iv)   **Long-term safety *vs* short-term steering**. The device of recording 'unsafe' acts in operations enabled them to be monitored by cross-functional teams, so that the causes of accidents could be identified and be reduced.

(v)   **Personal responsibility *vs* collective protection**. It was felt that if 'safety' was seen as a form of management policing it would never be accepted. The habit of management 'blaming the victim' had to stop. Instead, if an employee reported another to the safety teams, the person who was reported would be free of **official** sanction. Peer presence was seen to be a better enforcer of safety than the management hierarchy.

Section summary

Health and safety are important for both ethical and business reasons.

Legislation is not designed to represent best practice but offers a floor below which standards of conduct cannot drop, for the protection of employees.

Health and safety legislation requires that the systems, environment, equipment and conduct of organisations be such as to minimise the risk to the health and safety of employees and visitors alike.

Employees **share responsibility** for health and safety with employers, although the latter take responsibility for the environment, systems, equipment and training.

Apart from obviously dangerous equipment in offices, there are many **hazards** to be found in the modern working environment.

The **prevention of accidents** requires efforts on the part of employees and management.

Safety inspections should be carried out to locate and define faults in the system that allow accidents to occur.

---

6   Mentoring

Introduction

Both coaching and mentoring have become widely used approaches to continually developing people at work and encouraging learning. We look at mentoring here.

Mentoring is a longer-term relationship, the purpose of which is primarily learning development and support for career development.

6.1 Mentoring

'Mentor' was the name of a character in ancient Greek literature (Homer's *The Odyssey*): an older man who acted as wise counsellor and trusted advisor to a young man, passing on the benefit of his knowledge and experience. The way the team is used in modern business still reflects these roots to an extent.

MENTORING is a long-term relationship in which a more experienced person acts as a teacher, counsellor, role model, supporter and encourager, to foster the individual's personal and career development.

KEY TERM

Exam alert

Mentoring and how a **mentoring system** would aid a junior manager were tested in a previous syllabus exam. This was part of a longer question looking at issues of leadership.

A considerable number of candidates didn't know what mentoring is and couldn't answer this part.

6.1.1 Functions of a mentor

Kram identifies two broad types of function for the mentor.

Career functions include:

(a) Sponsoring within the organisation and providing exposure at higher levels
(b) Coaching and influencing progress through appointments
(c) Protection
(d) Drawing up personal development plans
(e) Advice with administrative problems people face in their new jobs
(f) Help in tackling projects, by pointing people in the right direction

Psychosocial functions include:

(a) Creating a sense of acceptance and belonging
(b) Counselling and friendship
(c) Providing a role model

6.1.2 The mentoring relationship

From an HR practitioner's prospective, *Armstrong* (2003) describes the **function** or **mentors** as giving their allocated protégé(s):

(a) Advice in drawing up self-development programmes or learning contracts
(b) General help with learning programmes
(c) Advice on dealing with administrative, technical and people problems
(d) Information on 'the way things are done around here' (corporate culture and management style)
(e) Coaching in specific skills
(f) Guidance in tackling projects (ie helping protégés to help themselves)
(g) A listening 'ear' for aspirations, concerns and problems

Although every mentoring relationship will be different, depending on the approach followed and the personalities involved, the following may be a handy way of remembering the nature of the role.

> **M**anage the relationship
> **E**ncourage the mentee
> **N**urture the mentee
> **T**each or coach the mentee
> **O**ffer mutual respect
> **R**espond to the mentee's needs

6.2 Strengths of mentoring

Coaching and mentoring have particular strengths as a development approach. Many HR activities help individuals to identify *what they need to change:* appraisal, feedback, training needs analysis and so on. Coaching and mentoring, however, specifically focus on **facilitating and reinforcing actual changes** in a person's work style and habits: transferring learning to the job, putting action plans into practice – and providing on-going support and feedback for lasting change and continuous development.

Zeus and Skiffington (2002) argue that coach/mentors are ideally placed to implement **change**, because of their:

(a) **Communication skills**. Communication is essential to successful change management. Coaching and mentoring provide a trusting, open environment where individuals can share their fears or beliefs about change – and coaches can convey enthusiasm and conviction that the person *can* change, and that barriers can be overcome.

(b) **Orientation**. Change is always more successful where people's needs and goals are taken into account, so that change is seen as a 'win-win' for the individual and the organisation. This is the nature of a coaching/mentoring plan.

(c) **Empathy**. Change agents are most successful when they understand (and show that they understand) the difficulties of change for the individual – as well as being challenging and encouraging. These issues can be explored within the coaching/mentoring relationship.

(d) **Credibility**. Coaches and members are often in the position of role model, and therefore have the power to influence people to change.

Section summary

Mentoring is a development-focused relationship in which a more knowledgeable or experienced person supports the development of another person.

---

7 Business ethics

Introduction

Ethical and **social responsibility** are two key areas in which businesses have adopted non-financial objectives, taking into account stakeholder needs and interests, partly in response to political and consumer pressure. Contemporary thinking is that **shareholders' wealth and ethics need not be mutually exclusive**.

ETHICS are the moral principles by which people act or do business.

KEY TERM

7.1 Business ethics

An organisation may have values to do with non-discrimination, fairness and integrity. It is very important that managers understand:

(a) The importance of ethical behaviour
(b) The differences in what is considered ethical behaviour in different cultures

Theorist *Elaine Sternberg* suggests that two **ethical values** are particularly pertinent for business, because without them business could not operate at all. These are:

(a) **Ordinary decency.** This includes respect for property rights, honesty, fairness and legality.

(b) **Distributive justice**. This means that organisational rewards should be proportional to the contributions people make to organisational ends. The supply and demand for labour will influence how much a person is actually paid, but if that person is worth employing and the job worth doing, then the contribution will justify the expense.

Business ethics in a **global market place** are, however, far from clear cut. If you are working outside the UK, you will need to develop – in line with whatever policies your organisation may have in place – a kind of 'situational' ethic to cover various issues.

(a) **Gifts** may be construed as bribes in Western business circles, but are indispensable in others.

(b) Attitudes to **women** in business vary according to ethnic traditions and religious values.

(c) The use of **cheap labour** in very poor countries (eg through off-shoring) may be perceived as 'development' – or as 'exploitation'.

(d) The expression and nature of **agreements** vary according to cultural norms.

A business may operate on principles which strive to be:

(a) Ethical and legal (eg The Body Shop)
(b) Unethical but legal (eg arms sales to repressive regimes)
(c) Ethical but illegal (eg publishing stolen documents on government mismanagement)
(d) Unethical and illegal (eg the drugs trade, employing child labour)

7.1.1 Applying ethical principles

There are two basic approaches to the **management of ethics** in organisations.

(a) A **compliance based approach** seeks to ensure compliance with law, regulation and rules of behaviour. It is based on the communication of clear rules, procedures and guidelines which must be adhered to in given circumstances. Behaviour is monitored and infringements of ethical codes are subject to disciplinary action.

(b) An **integrity based approach** seeks to support members of the organisation in making their own ethical decisions in any situation they encounter. It is based on the communication and reinforcement of ethical values, and the creation of frameworks within which ethical issues and dilemmas can be freely discussed and resolved.

Using an integrity based approach, a firm can embed ethical values in its culture and systems in the following ways.

(a) Include **value statements** in corporate culture, policy and codes of practice. (Professional staff should also be encouraged to adhere to the ethical codes of their professional bodies).

(b) Ensure that **HR systems** (appraisal, training and rewards) are designed to support ethical behaviour.

(c) Identify ethical objectives in the **mission statement**, as a public declaration of what the organisation stands for.

(d) Establish **ethics committees** and discussion groups to encourage questioning and problem-solving on ethical issues faced by staff.

(e) Provide confidential channels for '**whistle-blowing**' if staff feel that colleagues or the organisation is behaving illegally or unethically.

(f) Ensure that there is **top-down support** for, and modelling of, **ethical behaviour by managers**.

Ethical Reputation Index and business

The latest Ethical Reputation Index survey has shown that simply claiming to be ethical will not necessarily engender positive perceptions of a business.

CASE STUDY

The widening waistlines of the British population and continuing concerns over the rise in childhood obesity has ensured fast-food brands *McDonald's* and *Burger King's* position at the foot of this year's ERI.

At the other end of the scale, *Boots*, which has increased its focus on its beauty and cosmetic offering, has lost its position at the top of the *Index*. It has been replaced by *The Body Shop*, which jumped two places to claim top spot, despite its high-profile acquisition by *L'Oréal*. Meanwhile, *Marks & Spencer* slipped two places, suggesting that its much-publicised 'Plan A' CSR message is failing to reach consumers.

High-profile campaigns by *BP* and *Shell* to trumpet their green credentials have also failed to chime with consumers; both are languishing near the bottom of the table. Ryanair was another toward the bottom of the index, though the lowly position of the brash low-cost airline is perhaps not that surprising. Overall, the research suggested that simply increasing investment in advertising will not repair a brand's reputation, with radio and billboards the least likely media to be trusted.

However, the question remains as to whether a perceived lack of ethics has any impact on consumer purchasing decisions. The research suggests it does; almost eight out of 10 consumers would like to see more ethical brands launched in the next 12 months, and a resounding 91 per cent said they would be more likely to buy ethical brands over the same period.

It is also worth noting, however, that 67 per cent of consumers said that they would switch to more ethical brands only if the cost of purchase were the same as the products that they already buy.

While the marketing community's enthusiasm for all things ethical is showing signs of waning, with the term 'greenwashing' fast taking its place in marketing speak, the consumer market is booming. Just 6 per cent said a brand's ethical reputation had no influence on what they buy, so building a solid green foundation is key to ensuring brand loyalty.

Nicola Clark, Marketing, 29 April 2008

Exam alert

Social responsibility and ethics underpins issues such as corporate governance and also, for example, health and safety, equal opportunity and diversity and employee welfare: organisational policies over and above legal requirements, in areas such as these, fulfil responsibility objectives. Ethics was tested as part of a ten-mark question in a previous syllabus exam.

7.2 CIMA's Code of Ethics for professional accounts

If you are a CIMA registered student, you are subject to CIMA's code of ethics for professional accountants. The preface to the code states that:

> 'As chartered management accountants, CIMA members (and registered students) throughout the world have a duty to observe the highest standards of conduct and integrity, and to uphold the good standing and reputation of the profession. They must also refrain from any conduct which might discredit and profession.'

CIMA's Code of Ethics is based on the International Federation of Accountants (IFAC) Code of Ethics.

Fundamental principles

(a) *Integrity*
A professional accountant should be straightforward and honest in all professional and business relationships.

(b) *Objectivity*
A professional accountant should not allow bias, conflict of interest or undue influence of others to override professional or business judgements.

(c) *Professional competence and due care*
A professional accountant has a continuing duty to maintain professional knowledge and skill at the level required to ensure that a client or employer receives competent professional service based on current developments in practice, legislation and techniques. A professional accountant should act diligently and in accordance with applicable technical and professional standards when providing professional services.

(d) *Confidentiality*
A professional accountant should respect the confidentiality of information acquired as a result of professional and business relationships and should not disclose any such information to third parties without proper and specific authority unless there is a legal or professional right or duty to disclose. Confidential information acquired as a result of professional and business relationships should not be used for the personal advantage of the professional accountant or third party.

(e) *Professional behaviour*
A professional accountant should comply with relevant laws and regulations and should avoid any action that discredits the profession.

Section summary

Business ethics are the values underlying what an organisation understands by socially responsible behaviour.

8 Corporate governance

Introduction

Corporate Governance is an important area of control, and you need to be familiar with the provisions of the **Combined Code**. This prescribes rules covering the conduct of boards and their responsibilities for ensuring the good governance of organisations.

Read the first sections on background to set the scene, but you won't need to write on these in the exam. Consider the section on rules versus principles. Which seems the better approach?

Our discussion focuses on the UK but we have also mentioned the US guidance which is enshrined in the Sarbanes-Oxley Act 2002 and South Africa's King report.

We cover this material at a fairly broad level here as Paper P3 devotes a significant part of its syllabus to covering the issues of corporate governance.

CORPORATE GOVERNANCE is the system by which organisations are directed and controlled.

KEY TERM

Exam alert

The examiner tested corporate governance and ethics in a ten-mark question in a previous syllabus exam. This was generally well answered although some candidates failed to **apply** knowledge to the scenario outlined in the question.

8.1 Driving forces for governance development

Corporate governance issues came to prominence in the USA during the 1970s and in the UK and Europe from the late 1980s. There were several reasons why this happened.

(a) **Increasing internationalisation and globalisation** meant that investors, and institutional investors in particular, began to invest outside their home countries. This lead to calls for companies to operate in an acceptable fashion and to report corporate performance fairly.

(b)   Issues concerning **financial reporting** were raised by many investors and were the focus of much debate and litigation. Shareholder confidence in many instances was eroded and, while focus solely on accounting and reporting issues is inadequate, the regulation of practices such as off-balance sheet financing has led to greater transparency and a reduction in risks faced by investors.

(c)   An increasing number of **high profile corporate scandals** and collapses including Polly Peck International, BCCI, Enron and Maxwell Communications Corporation prompted the development of governance codes in the early 1990s. However the scandals since then have raised questions about further measures that may be necessary.

8.2 Features of poor corporate governance

The scandals over the last 25 years have highlighted the need for guidance to tackle the various risks and problems that can arise in organisations' systems of governance.

(a)   **Domination by a single individual** . A feature of many corporate governance scandals has been boards dominated by a single senior executive with other board members merely acting as a rubber stamp. Sometimes the single individual may bypass the board to action his own interests. The report on the UK *Guinness* case suggested that the Chief Executive, *Ernest Saunders* paid himself a £3 million reward without consulting the other directors.

(b)   **Lack of involvement of board**. Boards that meet irregularly or fail to consider systematically the organisation's activities and risks are clearly weak. Sometimes the failure to carry out proper oversight is due to a **lack of information** being provided.

(c)   **Lack of adequate control function**. An obvious weakness is a lack of internal audit. Another important control is **lack of adequate technical knowledge** in key roles, for example in the audit committee or in senior compliance positions. A rapid turnover of staff involved in accounting or control may suggest inadequate resourcing, and will make control more difficult because of lack of continuity.

(d)   **Lack of supervision**. Employees who are not properly supervised can create large losses for the organisation through their own incompetence, negligence or fraudulent activity. The behaviour of *Nick Leeson*, the employee who caused the collapse of *Barings* bank was not challenged because he appeared to be successful, whereas he was using unauthorised accounts to cover up his large trading losses. Leeson was able to do this because he was in charge of both dealing and settlement, a systems weakness or **lack of segregation of key roles** that featured in other financial frauds.

(e)   **Lack of independent scrutiny**. External auditors may not carry out the necessary questioning of senior management because of fears of losing the audit, and internal audit do not ask awkward questions because the chief financial officer determines their employment prospects. Often corporate collapses are followed by criticisms of external auditors, such as the *Barlow Clowes* affair, where poorly planned and focused audit work failed to identify illegal use of client monies.

(f)   **Lack of contact with shareholders**. Often board members may have grown up with the company but lose touch with the interests and views of shareholders. One possible symptom of this is the payment of remuneration packages that do not appear to be warranted by results.

(g)   **Emphasis on short-term profitability**. Emphasis on short-term results can lead to the concealment of problems or errors, or manipulation of accounts to achieve desired results.

(h)   **Misleading accounts and information**. Often misleading figures are symptomatic of other problems (or are designed to conceal other problems) but in many cases, poor quality accounting information is a major problem if markets are trying to make a fair assessment of the company's value. Giving out misleading information was a major issue in the UK's *Equitable Life* scandal where the company gave contradictory information to savers, independent advisers, media and regulators.

8.3 Benefits of improving corporate governance

A number of benefits can accrue from improved governance.

(a)   **Risk reduction**. Proper corporate governance reduces the risks of financial loss, compliance failure and reputational damage (and ultimately, business collapse) such risks by aligning directors' interests with the company's strategic objectives and by providing for measures to reduce fraud.

(b)   **Performance** should improve if accountabilities are made clear and directors' motivation is enhanced by performance-related remuneration. Also, the extra breadth of experience brought by non-executive directors should improve the quality of decision-making at board level.

(c)   **External support**. External perceptions of the company should be enhanced, leading to: improved ability to raise finance; improved corporate image with public and government; and improved relations with stakeholders such as customers and employees.

8.4 Reports on corporate governance

There were three significant corporate governance reports in the United Kingdom during the 1990s. The **Cadbury and Hampel reports** covered general corporate governance issues, whilst the **Greenbury report** concentrated on remuneration of directors.

The recommendations of these three reports were merged into a **Combined Code** in 1998, with which companies listed on the London Stock Exchange are required to comply. We look at the Combined Code in this section.

Since the publication of the **Combined Code** a number of reports in the UK have been published about specific aspects of corporate governance.

- The **Turnbull report** focused on risk management and internal control
- The **Smith report** discussed the role of audit committees
- The **Higgs report** focused on the role of the non-executive director

8.5 Approaches taken: principles vs. rules

A continuing debate on corporate governance is whether the guidance should predominantly be in the form of principles, or whether there is a need for detailed laws or regulations.

The Hampel report in the UK came out very firmly in favour of a principles-based approach. The committee preferred relaxing the regulatory burden on companies and were against treating the corporate governance codes as sets of prescriptive rules, and judging companies by whether they have complied ('box-ticking'). The report stated that there may be **guidelines** which will normally be appropriate but the differing circumstances of companies meant that sometimes there are valid reasons for exceptions.

However the Hampel report has been criticised for taking this approach. It has been commented that the principles set out in the Hampel report are so broad that they are of very little use as a guide to best corporate governance practice. For example the suggestion that non-executive directors from a wide variety of backgrounds can make a contribution is seen as not strong enough to encourage companies away from recruiting directors by means of the 'old boy network'.

It has also been suggested that the Hampel comments about **box-ticking** are incorrect for two reasons. Firstly, shareholders do not apply that approach when assessing accounts. Secondly, it is far less likely that disasters will strike companies with a 100% compliance record since they are unlikely to be content with token compliance, but will have set up procedures that contribute significantly to their being governed well.

8.6 Stock Exchange Combined Code

8.6.1 Directors

(a) **The board**

All listed companies should be led by an **effective board**. The board should meet regularly and have certain matters reserved for its decision. Directors should be able to obtain independent professional advice and have access to the services of the company secretary. The company secretary is responsible for ensuring that **board procedures and relevant regulations** are followed. The whole board should be responsible for removing the company secretary. Every director should use **independent judgement** when making decisions. Every director should receive appropriate **training.**

(b) **Chairman and Chief Executive**

There are two leading management roles; running the board and running the company. A **clear division of responsibilities** should exist so that there is a balance of power, and no-one person has unfettered powers of decision. Combination of the roles of chairman and chief executive should be justified publicly. There should also be a **strong and independent** body of **non-executive** directors with a recognised senior member other than the chairman.

(c) **Board balance**

The board should have a **balance of executive and non-executive directors** so that no individual or small group is dominant.

(d) **Supply of information**

The board should be **promptly supplied with enough information** to enable it to carry out its duties.

(e) **Appointment of directors**

There should be a **clear, formal procedure** for appointing new directors. A nomination committee should make recommendations about all new board appointments.

(f) **Re-election**

All directors should submit themselves for **re-election regularly,** and at least once every three years.

CASE STUDY

Marks and Spencer sparked a furious reaction from big institutional investors yesterday after announcing that it was **combining the roles of chairman and chief executive** to keep Sir Stuart Rose at the business until 2011. Sir Stuart … said that the move was the best for the business. He said: 'If I was to go it would be hard to identify a successor early.' However, leading institutions said that the **move was a clear breach of corporate governance best practice**.

Source: *The Times Thursday March 11 2008*

8.6.2 Directors' remuneration

(a) **Remuneration policy**

Remuneration levels should be sufficient to attract directors of **sufficient calibre** to run the company effectively, but companies should not pay more than is necessary. A proportion of remuneration should be based on **corporate and individual performance**.

(b) **Service contracts and compensation**

Boards' ultimate objectives should be to **set notice periods at one year or less**. Directors should consider whether to include compensation commitments in the contracts of service.

(c) **Procedure**

Companies should establish a formal and clear procedure for **developing policy on executive remuneration and for fixing the remuneration package of individual directors**. Directors should **not be involved in setting their own remuneration**. A remuneration committee, staffed by independent non-executive directors, should make recommendations about the framework of executive remuneration, and should determine specific remuneration packages. The board should determine the remuneration of non-executive directors.

(d)   **Disclosure**
       The annual report should contain a **statement about remuneration policy** and **details of the remuneration of each director.** The report should give details about **all elements of the remuneration package,** share options, pension entitlements and service contracts or compensation in excess of one year. Shareholders should approve all new long-term remuneration schemes.

8.6.3 Relations with shareholders

(a)   **Institutional shareholders**
       Companies should be prepared to **communicate with institutional shareholders.**

(b)   **Use of the AGM**
       The AGM should be a **means of communication** with **private investors.** Companies should count all proxies and announce proxy votes for and against on all votes on a show of hands. Companies should propose a **separate resolution** on each substantially separate issue, and there should be a resolution covering the **board and accounts**.

8.6.4 Accountability and audit

(a)   **Financial reporting**
       The board should present a **balanced and understandable assessment** of the **company's position and prospects** in the annual accounts and other reports such as interim reports and reports to regulators.

(b)   **Internal control**
       A good system of control should be maintained. The directors should **review effectiveness** annually and report to shareholders that they have done so.

(c)   **Audit committees and auditors**
       There should be **formal and clear arrangements** with the **company's auditors**, and for applying the financial reporting and internal control principles. Companies should have an **audit committee** consisting of non-executive directors, the majority of whom should be independent. The audit committee should review the audit, and the independence and objectivity of the auditors. In particular the committee should keep matters under review if the auditors supply significant non-audit services.

(d)   **Shareholder voting**
       Institutional shareholders should use their votes carefully and **disclose** how they have **voted** to their clients. They should also enter into a dialogue with companies, and should give appropriate weight to all relevant criteria when considering corporate governance arrangements.

8.6.5 Compliance with the Code

The Combined Code requires listed companies to include in their accounts:

(a)   A narrative statement of how they **applied** the **principles** set out in the Combined Code. This should provide explanations which enable their shareholders to assess how the principles have been applied.

(b)   A statement as to whether or not they **complied throughout** the **accounting period** with the provisions set out in the Combined Code. Listed companies that did not comply throughout the accounting period with all the provisions must specify the provisions with which they did not comply, and give **reasons** for **non-compliance.**

8.7 The US framework

Corporate scandals, particularly the Enron scandal, in the United States over the last few years have led to the **Sarbanes-Oxley Act 2002** and consequent changes to the listing rules that companies quoted on Wall Street have to fulfil.

8.8 The South African framework

South Africa's major contribution to the corporate governance debate has been the **King report**, first published in 1994 and updated in 2002 to take account of developments in South Africa and elsewhere in the world.

The King report differs in emphasis from other guidance by advocating an integrated approach to corporate governance in the interest of a wide range of stakeholders – embracing the social, environmental and economic activities of a company's activities. The report encourages activism by shareholders, business and the financial press and relies heavily on disclosure as a regulatory measure.

Exam alert

The US and South African frameworks are not covered in the CIMA syllabus, and are unlikely to be specifically tested in the exams.

Section summary

Corporate governance in the UK is largely defined by the contents of the **Combined Code**. By providing guidance on areas such as **directors, remuneration, shareholder dialogue** and **internal controls** it aims to reduce risk, improve performance and improve public perceptions.

There were three significant corporate governance reports in the United Kingdom during the 1990s. The **Cadbury and Hampel reports** covered general corporate governance issues, whilst the **Greenbury report** concentrated on remuneration of directors.

The recommendations of the three UK reports were merged into a **Combined Code** in 1998, with which companies listed on the London Stock Exchange are required to comply.

Chapter Roundup

✓ **Control systems** exist to support the achievement of organisational objectives. They are of many types, both formal and informal.

Organisations require control at all levels of their operating framework: **strategic, tactical and operational**.

Control systems should be **acceptable, accessible, adaptable, action-oriented, appropriate** and **affordable**.

William Ouchi identified three broad **control strategies**: market control, bureaucratic control and clan control; Strategy gurus *Johnson* and *Scholes* outline a broader framework of **control processes**, both input and output-focused and direct and indirect.

✓ **Internal controls** should help organisations counter risks, maintain the quality of reporting and comply with laws and regulations. They provide reasonable assurance that the organisations will fulfil their objectives.

Internal control frameworks include the **control environment** within which **internal controls** operate. Other important elements are the **risk assessment and response processes,** the **sharing of information** and **monitoring** the environment and operation of the control system.

✓ **Performance management** is an approach to controlling the conduct, performance and development of personnel in the organisation. Human resource control systems typically operate at the tactical level of control.

Contracts of employment may be used as the basis for controlling employee conduct and performance, by setting out the organisation's expectations.

There are a number of aspects to **performance appraisal** including reward review, performance review and potential review. Appraisal is an important practical aspect of control in organisations.

✓ A **team** is more than a group. It has joint **objectives** and **accountability** and may be set up by the organisation under the supervision or coaching of a team leader, although **self-managed teams** are growing in popularity.

✓ **Health and safety** is important for both ethical and business reasons.

Legislation is not designed to represent best practice but offers a floor below which standards of conduct cannot drop, for the protection of employees.

Health and safety legislation requires that the systems, environment, equipment and conduct of organisations be such as to minimise the risk to the health and safety of employees and visitors alike.

Employees **share responsibility** for health and safety with employers, although the latter take responsibility for the environment, systems, equipment and training.

Apart from obviously dangerous equipment in offices, there are many **hazards** to be found in the modern working environment.

The **prevention of accidents** requires efforts on the part of employees and management.

Safety inspections should be carried out to locate and define faults in the system that allow incidents to occur.

✓ **Mentoring** is a development-focused relationship in which a more knowledgeable or experienced person supports the development of another person.

✓ **Business ethics** are the values underlying what an organisation understands by socially responsible behaviour.

✓ **Corporate governance** in the UK is largely defined by the contents of the **Combined Code**. By providing guidance on areas such as **directors**, **remuneration**, **shareholder dialogue** and **internal controls** it aims to reduce risk, improve performance and improve public perceptions.

There were three significant corporate governance reports in the United Kingdom during the 1990s. The **Cadbury and Hampel reports** covered general corporate governance issues, whilst the **Greenbury report** concentrated on remuneration of directors.

The recommendations of the three UK reports were merged into a **Combined Code** in 1998, with which companies listed on the London Stock Exchange are required to comply.

Quick Quiz

1   Complete the table below stating the control strategy most likely to be used in the given contingent cases.

Contingencies	Control strategy mainly
Divisions trading with transfer prices and an overall product structure	
Large size, stable environment, functional structure	
Small entrepreneurial company with no professional managers	

2   Appraisal is an example of what level of control?

   A   Strategic
   B   Tactical
   C   Operational
   D   Clan

3   Performance targets are an example of direct/indirect, output/input-focused control. (Delete words which are not applicable.)

4   When a subordinate rates his or her superior's leadership skills, this is an example of:

   A 360^0 feedback
   B   Performance management
   C   Upward appraisal
   D   Results-oriented appraisal

5   'An employer's responsibilities for health and safety apply solely to employees regularly working on the premises.' Is this statement true or false?

6   What are employees' legal duties in respect of health and safety?

7   Which of the following is a health hazard in the workplace?

   A   Uncollected waste paper
   B   Heavy objects
   C   Frayed carpet
   D   All of the above

8   Outline a policy for accident prevention in the workplace.

Answers to Quick Quiz

1

Contingencies	Control strategy mainly:
Divisions trading with transfer prices and an overall product structure	Market
Large size, stable environment, functional structure	Bureaucratic
Small entrepreneurial company with no professional managers	Personal centralised

2   B: Tactical. (Note that 'clan control' is a type of control strategy: not a level of control).

3   Direct/indirect, output/input-focused

4   C: upward appraisal.

5   False: the employer's responsibilities extend to visitors, contractors, and those on adjoining premises (where relevant)

6   To take reasonable care of themselves and of others. To allow the employer to discharge his duties. Not to interfere with any machinery or equipment

7   D: be aware of the range of common hazards!

8   See Section 5.4.3 for ideas

Answers to questions

2.1   Control systems

D   Bureaucratic control is probably the most likely. Market control might be used for some operations particularly where comparisons could be made with competitors, but the cost structures of aviation are so lacking in transparency that this would be rather rare. There may be some elements of clan control among highly trained specialists such as aircrew and engineers. Option A, 'Contingency', is a red herring.

2.2   Performance management

The key to performance management is that it is forward looking and constructive. Objective-setting gives employees the security of knowing exactly what is expected of them, and this is agreed at the outset with the manager, thus justifying unrealistic expectations. The employee at the outset can indicate the resources needed.

2.3   Formal appraisal

Disadvantages to the individual of not having an appraisal system include: the individual is not aware of progress or shortcomings, is unable to judge whether s/he would be considered for promotion, is unable to identify or correct weaknesses by training and there is a lack of communication with the manager.

2.4   Group cohesion

Problems may arise in an ultra close-knit group because:

(a)   The group's energies may be focused on its own maintenance and relationships, instead of on the task.

(b)   The group may be suspicious or dismissive of outsiders, and may reject any contradictory information or criticism they supply; the group will be blinkered and stick to its own views, no matter what; cohesive groups thus often get the impression that they are infallible: they can't be wrong – and therefore can't learn from their mistakes.

(c)   The group may squash any dissent or opinions that might rock the boat. Close-knit groups tend to preserve a consensus – falsely, if required – and to take risky decisions, because they have suppressed alternative facts and viewpoints.

2.5   Team building

(a)   Recreation helps the team to build informal relationships: in this case, the chosen activity also reminds them of their tasks, and may make them feel special, as part of the motor racing industry, by giving them a taste of what the end user of their product does.

(b)   A team challenge forces the group to consider its strengths and weaknesses, to find its natural leader. This exercise creates an 'us' and 'them' challenge: perceiving the rival team as the enemy heightens the solidarity of the group.

(c)   This exercise encourages the group to raise problems and conflicts freely, away from the normal environment of work and also encourages brainstorming and the expression of team members' dreams for what the team can achieve in the future.

2.7   Meeting problems

Agenda change: Propose the change to the team, and insist on getting a genuine response. If some members do not want to deal with the item, remind the meeting of the ground rules: consensus is required to put a new item on the agenda. It can be included in the next meeting.

Leftover items. The need here is to prevent frustration and loss of focus. You might assign each member an item and ask them to prepare and distribute information before the next meeting. Alternatively, you might keep a legible list of 'other agenda items'. So no-one fears they will be forgotten.

Late attendance. The meeting should start on time, out of respect for the other team members. When the missing member arrives, this would be a good opportunity to summarise the discussion so far. If people are repeatedly late, however, this may need addressing.

2.8   Disaster costs

You may have thought of the Bhopal chemical plant explosion, Chernobyl reactor explosion, Kings Cross station fire, Piper Alpha oil rig disaster, and so on. The main costs are reconstruction, compensation for death and injury, lost production, and loss of reputation.

2.11   Responsibility for safe working

This was a real case. It was held that the employee's injury had occurred in the course of her work, and that the employer had failed in his duty to take reasonable care to provide safe premises.

2.12 Workplace hazards

You may have spotted the following hazards (if not others as well...)

(a) Heavy object on high (secure?) shelf
(b) Standing on swivel chair
(c) Lifting heavy object incorrectly
(d) Trailing wires
(e) Electric bar fire
(f) Open drawers blocking passage and risk toppling cabinet
(g) Unattended lit cigarette – passive smoking AND fire hazard
(h) Over-full waste bin
(i) Overloaded electric socket
(j) Overloaded tray of hot liquids
(k) Dangerous spike and scissors
(l) Frayed carpet

Note: Q 2.6, 2.9 and 2.10 require personal answers, so we have not provided an answer here.

Now try the question below from the Exam Question Bank

Number	Level	Marks	Time
Q2	Examination	25	45 mins

THE FINANCE FUNCTION; CONFLICT

We continue the theme of control by looking at the role of one of the departments principally responsible for financial management, the finance function. A previous syllabus also considered the other department responsible for financial management which is the treasury function. In many organisations, these will only be a single function. However, in larger organisations the responsibilities will be split broadly so that the **finance function** will be responsible for most of the operational issues, and the **treasury function** will be responsible for higher level strategic development plus operational issues involving special skills such as dealing with derivatives.

We then go on to look at conflict which may be seen as a failure of control.

However, some regard conflict as inevitable and useful in moving forward (evolution). Others see it as a symptom of failure in relationships.

We consider both views in the chapter.

It may arise from rivalry between peers, or vertically up and down the hierarchy.

One of management's key roles is managing conflict between parties.

This may divide industrial relations too, when a union is recognised.

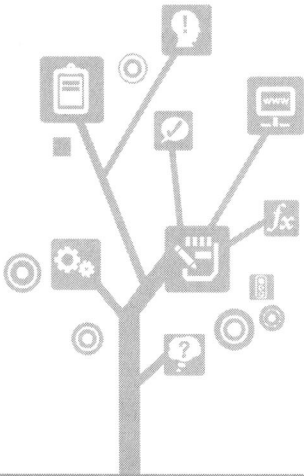

3

topic list	learning outcomes	syllabus references	ability required
1 The role of the finance function	C2c	C2(v), (vi)	analysis
2 The nature of conflict	C1c	C1(iii)	comprehension
3 Causes of conflict	C1c	C1(iii)	comprehension
4 Managing conflict	C1d	C1(iii)	analysis

1 The role of the finance function

Introduction

Although we look at the finance function here, we consider it useful to explain a little of the treasury function as the two are often closely linked. The finance function is more than just reporting on performance and in many organisations has taken on a broader advisory and strategic role.

1.1 Financial control and treasury

Although an organisation may operate a single finance function covering all its financial activities, within this function a distinction can be made between financial control activities and treasury activities.

Financial control activities involve the **allocation and effective use of resources**. This comprises:

(a) Advising on investment appraisal

(b) Analysing performance (management accounting)

(c) Reporting results (financial accounting)

The **treasury function** is involved in **obtaining suitable types of finance.** This includes:

(a) Advising on sources of finance and dividend policy

(b) Financial risk management (hedging)

(c) Liaising with financial stakeholders (banks / key shareholders)

Clearly the two roles have many links. Treasury will use the detailed information prepared by the financial control function, and will in turn set down the parameters, (major assumptions, cost of capital) that the financial control function will use in its detailed calculations.

Examples of interaction between the two functions are:

(a) **Financial control** reports on and identifies currency risk whilst **the treasury function** decides on hedging strategy.

(b) **The treasury function** assesses the cost of capital and **financial control** then applies it to proposed investments.

1.2 The roles of the financial controller

The specific activities and roles that may be expected from a financial control function include:

(a) **Processing** transactions, maintaining accounting records and delivering month-end reports at low cost and efficiently.

(b) **Communicating** results to internal and external stakeholders.

(c) Ensuring the effective operation of **corporate governance and control**. This has become increasingly important in the wake of various financial scandals and the requirements of legislation such as the American Sarbanes-Oxley Act.

(d) Acting as a **business partner** and advisor.

1.2.1 The finance function as business partner

The finance function has faced pressures to become **more actively involved** in business operations. Many finance functions have therefore re-focused their roles as business partners, adopting a more **commercial, action-orientated approach**. This means gaining broad knowledge of the business, participating as full members of operational teams and bringing financial expertise to the management process. They are expected to **integrate management accounting information** with **strategic management accounting data**.

Important areas where the finance function's role has developed have included:

- Providing more useful information on business units, projects, products and customers
- Supplying business cases for new investments
- Giving support in helping operational managers understand the information provided
- Collaborating in strategic planning and budgeting
- Designing information systems that provide greater support for operational managers

One example of where finance functions have been expected to assume a more active role is **investment appraisal**. Accountants are now often required to do more than state that the proposal does not meet financial criteria; they are expected to help develop and refine proposals.

Question 3.1   Sales support

Learning outcome C2c

In what ways can the finance function support the sales function?

1.2.2 Problems with the business partner model

Over the last couple of years the business partner model has in turn faced criticism, due primarily to Enron and other financial scandals. Critics have questioned the **identification** of the finance function with **operational viewpoints** and the **loss of independence** of the finance function that has arisen from finance staff reporting to, and being accountable to, operational managers.

Critics also claim that the finance function has become too greatly diverted from delivering basic controls and safeguards and functions, providing prudent financial management and ensuring the **true and fair view** is given. The finance function has, critics suggest, lost sight of its role in governance and failed to protect shareholder and public interest.

1.2.3 Independent business partner

A new independent business partner model has therefore emerged, not losing sight of co-operation with operational managers, but also having at its heart **strict controls**, **safeguarding of assets** and **effective reporting**.

The independent business partner model stresses that the finance function should seek to **add** value, but its role is not to **create** value. The creation of strategy, ideas and opportunities is the responsibility of the operational departments. Finance's role is to **assess** and **validate** these ideas, taking a commercial view, but also ensuring that business plans and strategy are rigorously reviewed and challenged if necessary. Finance must also **review actual performance** rigorously and be prepared to challenge better than expected as well as worse than expected performance in order to minimise the risks of understatement.

1.3 Assessment of the finance function

There has been increasing emphasis over the last few years on assessment of the contribution made by the finance function. Traditional measures of success have included the following.

1.3.1 Reliable information

A recent survey suggested that about four fifths of chief finance officers rate **reliability of information** as their highest priority. Its importance has been enhanced by the recent financial scandals and the requirement of the American Sarbanes-Oxley legislation for chief finance officers to sign off personally their company's accounts.

As well as fulfilling legal requirements, finance departments must have regard for the information required by different **stakeholders**, the information that is **relevant** to their needs.

Organisations will need to develop processes to ensure that information is reliable. For the finance function this means playing a key role in the development of technology that will **ensure information** is **reliable**, being available to answer queries and resolve problems and **educating** other staff to make sure that they are aware of the information needed, the accounting policies used by the company and the legal framework.

1.3.2 Flexibility

A very important aspect of the finance function's work is how it copes with **new developments and new financial reporting standards**. As well as coping with the technical issues, the finance function also plays a vital role in **educating investors** on the language of new standards and their impact upon the key performance indicators.

The management accounting function also needs to be flexible in **its response to users' requests** for information and reports.

1.3.3 Speed of reporting

The Sarbanes-Oxley legislation has also resulted in tighter reporting deadlines, with companies listed in the USA being required to file quarterly accounts in 35 days rather than 45 days, and annual reports in 60 rather than 90 days. An EU draft directive specifies 60 days for quarterly reports with further reductions towards 35 days.

In addition surveys suggest a possible link between market valuation and speed of reporting, with larger investors in particular viewing shorter reporting times as a sign that the company is well managed.

1.3.4 Efficiency

Pressure on the finance function to reduce costs and make greater use of resources, in particular speeding up basic processing functions, has greatly increased over the last few years. We shall see in Section 1.4 that this has led to pressure to **outsource** the basic functions, and let the finance function concentrate on more 'exciting' work.

Measures of efficiency include:

- The number of transactions processed per transaction processing employee
- The cost of transactions processed as a percentage of revenue per transaction
- The time taken at period-ends to report results

1.3.5 Balanced scorecard approach

As well as the traditional measures discussed above, many organisations have used a balanced scorecard approach to judge the work of the finance function, focusing not just on **traditional financial measures**, but other measures of concern to stakeholders. Whilst many traditional measures focus purely on outcomes, balanced scorecard measures often go a stage back and measure the **factors** that will result in satisfactory outcomes.

(a) **Customer satisfaction.** This focuses on the strength of relationships between the finance function and other stakeholders and whether the finance function is viewed as delivering the right mixture and quality of transaction processing, risk management and decision support.

(b) **Enhancement of internal processes.** These focus on the processes that the finance function must carry out efficiently and effectively in order to report accurately and give customer satisfaction.

(c) **Financial.** Success here could be measured by the frequency of forecasts and the average preparation times for key elements of the business planning process.

(d)   **Learning and growth**. These measures concentrate on the organisation's ability to adapt to change and also the development of finance staff's skills and competencies. Possible measures include turnover of finance staff and what percentage of staff have a recognised financial qualification.

1.3.6 Benchmarking the finance function

One method of measuring the success of the finance function is to benchmark against finance functions elsewhere. With a large group, comparisons can be made of different finance functions within the same group. Alternatively there are organisations who will bring finance directors together to compare best practice, or who offer databases of other departments.

Most benchmarking exercises have suggested that too much time is spent on transaction processing and not enough time on value added activities.

Problems with using benchmarking include the **money and time involved**. If the exercise is to be effective, data has to be collected for an organisation's own finance function as well as obtained for others.

1.4 Outsourcing and shared servicing

1.4.1 Outsourcing the finance function

Even if the finance function has to re-focus towards its more traditional roles, there will still be strong pressures to **outsource basic transaction processing functions**, payroll and expense management.

CASE STUDY

In May 2003 kitchen manufacturer Magnet outsourced accounts payable, credit control, general, accounting, reporting and auditing to Liberata in a seven year deal. However Magnet retained its management accounting function. Marc Bertand, the HR director at Magnet, commented 'Our management accountants produce the monthly figures and forecasts, three-month flashes and financial strategy. This is the sort of thing you need to keep close to the business.'

What Magnet did is typical of many organisations, according to a survey carried out by Accenture. Over 85% of senior executives won't outsource budgeting and forecasting and will also retain policy, strategy, tax planning, merger and acquisition support and economic and financial analysis.

Exam alert

You will have covered outsourcing in other papers, and knowledge from these papers may be relevant.

Outsourcing is introduced in Paper E1 where it is set in the context of the global business environment.

1.4.2 Shared servicing

An alternative to outsourcing is shared servicing, where shared service centres consolidate the **transaction-processing activities** of many operations within a company. Shared service centres are meant to achieve significant cost reductions whilst improving service levels through the use of standardised technology and processes and service level agreements.

Section summary

The financial control function is concerned with the **allocation and effective use of resources.**

The treasury function is concerned with **obtaining finance** and managing relations with financial stakeholders.

Basic processing tasks are now often **outsourced** or **concentrated** in **shared service centres**.

2 The nature of conflict

Introduction

This section considers a range of views on conflict. Some people believe any conflict is bad and that managers should act to eliminate it when it occurs. Others see conflict as inevitable, and even useful in helping the organisation to evolve.

KEY TERM

There are many definitions of CONFLICT. *Huczynski and Buchanan* (2001) usefully reflect the subjective dimensions of conflict (perceptions and values) in their definition:

'Conflict is a process which begins when one party perceives that another party has negatively affected, or is about to negatively affect, something the first party cares about. Typically, conflicts are based upon differences in interests and values, when the interests of one party come up against the different interests of another.' (p. 770)

2.1 Argument, competition and conflict

2.1.1 The 'happy family' view

The happy family view presents organisations as **essentially harmonious**.

(a)   They are co-operative structures, designed to achieve agreed common objectives, with no systematic conflict of interest.

(b)   Management power is legitimate.

(c)   Conflicts are **exceptional** and arise from aberrant incidents, such as misunderstandings, clashes of personality and external influences.

Management literature often attempts to come up with training and motivational techniques for dealing with conflicts which arise in what are seen as potentially conflict-free organisations. Conflict is thus blamed on bad management, lack of leadership, poor communication, or bloody-mindedness on the part of individuals or interest groups that impinge on the organisation. The theory is that a strong culture, good two-way communication, co-operation and motivational leadership will eliminate conflict. **Co-operation is assumed to be desirable and achievable**.

2.1.2 The conflict view

In contrast, there is the view of organisations as **arenas for conflict on individual and group levels**. Members battle for limited resources, status, rewards and professional values. Organisational politics involve constant struggles for control, and choices of structure, technology and organisational goals are part of this process. Individual and organisational interests will not always coincide.

If a **pluralist view** is taken, organisations may be seen as **political coalitions** of individuals and groups which have their own interests. Management has to create a workable structure for collaboration, taking into account the objectives of all the stakeholders in the organisation. A **mutual survival** strategy, involving the control of conflict through compromise, can be made acceptable in varying degrees to all concerned.

2.1.3 The evolutionary view

Conflict may be seen as a useful basis for **evolutionary** rather than revolutionary **change**. Conflict keeps the organisation **sensitive to the need to change**, while reinforcing its essential framework of control. The legitimate pursuit of competing interests can balance and preserve social and organisational arrangements. A flexible society benefits from conflict because such behaviour, by helping to create and modify norms, assumes its continuance under changed conditions.

KEY POINT

This **constructive conflict** view may be the most useful for managers. It neither attempts to dodge the issues of conflict, which is an observable fact of life in most organisations; nor seeks to pull down existing organisational structures altogether.

Managers have to get on with the job of managing and upholding organisational goals with the co-operation of other members. We will therefore look more closely at the idea of **managing conflict**.

2.2 Constructive and destructive conflict

If conflict is inevitable, there are two aspects of conflict which must be dealt with by the manager. They need to manage conflict where it is desirable and seek to eliminate the destructive elements in their workplace.

Conflict can be highly desirable. It can energise relationships and clarify issues. *Hunt* suggests that conflict can have constructive effects.

(a)   It can introduce different solutions to problems.
(b)   Power relationships can be defined more clearly.
(c)   It may encourage creativity and the testing of ideas.
(d)   It focuses attention on individual contributions.
(e)   It brings emotions out into the open.
(f)   It can release hostile feelings.

Conflict can also be **destructive**.

(a)   It may distract attention from the task.
(b)   It can polarise views and affect judgement.
(c)   Objectives may be subverted in favour of secondary goals.
(d)   It encourages defensive or spoiling behaviour, damaging co-ordination and co-operation.
(e)   It may result in disintegration of the group.
(f)   Losers may go into denial, look for scapegoats or withdraw from further participation.

CASE STUDY

Tjosvold and Deerner researched conflict in different contexts. They allocated to 66 student volunteers the roles of foremen and workers at an assembly plant, with a scenario of conflict over job rotation schemes. Foremen were against, workers for.

One group was told that the organisational norm was to '**avoid controversy**'; another was told that the norm was '**co-operative controversy**', *trying* to agree; a third was told that groups were out to **win any arguments that arose**, '**competitive controversy**'. The students were offered rewards for complying with their given norms. Their decisions, and attitudes to the discussions, were then monitored.

(a)   Where **controversy was avoided**, the foremen's views dominated.

(b)   **Competitive controversy** brought no agreement - but brought out feelings of hostility and suspicion.

(c)   **Co-operative controversy** brought out differences in an atmosphere of curiosity, trust and openness: the decisions reached seemed to integrate the views of both parties.

But can real managers and workers be motivated to comply with useful organisational 'norms' in this way?

2.3 Symptoms of conflict

Conflict may result in:

(a)   Poor communications, in all directions
(b)   Interpersonal friction
(c)   Inter-group rivalry and jealousy
(d)   Low morale and frustration
(e)   Widespread use of arbitration, appeals to higher authority, and inflexible attitudes.

The tactics of conflict include:

(a) **Withholding information** from others who need it

(b) **Distorting information**. This will enable the group or manager presenting the information to get their way more easily.

(c) **Empire building**. A group (especially a specialist group such as accounting) which considers its influence to be neglected might seek to impose rules, procedures, restrictions or official requirements on other groups, in order to bolster its own importance.

(d) **Office politics**. A manager might seek to by-pass formal channels of communication and decision-making by establishing informal contacts and friendships with people in positions of importance.

(e) **Fault-finding** in the work of other departments.

Section summary

Argument (resolving differences by discussion) and **competition** can be distinguished from harmful expressions of difference as **conflict**.

Conflict can be constructive, if it introduces new information into a problem, if it defines a problem, or if it encourages creativity. It can be destructive if it distracts attention from the task or inhibits communication. **Conflict** may **manifest** itself in: poor communication; friction between individuals and groups; widespread use of arbitration and other conflict mechanisms; and various political games.

---

3 Causes of conflict

Introduction

Conflict can occur at many different levels:

- Within an individual (eg over two incompatible goals)

- Between two individuals (inter-personal conflict)

- Between groups or teams (eg because of competition for influence or resources, incompatible goals and schedules, or different cultures)

- Between different levels in the organisation hierarchy (eg workers and their trade unions versus management, or 'turf wars' between levels of management)

It may be helpful to distinguish between:

- **Horizontal conflict**, between individuals and groups at the same broad level in the organisation. This is often based, as we will see, on competition for limited influence and resources; and

- **Vertical conflict**, between different levels in the organisation hierarchy. This is often based on conflict of interest and power imbalance.

We will look at the causes of conflict using this distinction.

3.1 Causes of horizontal conflict between departments/teams

It is possible to identify a number of typical sources of conflict between functions and groups in organisations.

(a) **Differences in goals**. Conflict may be caused by differences in the goals of different groups (or individuals). It is a function of management to create a system of planning whereby individual or group goals are formulated within the framework of a strategic plan and to provide leadership, and to encourage individuals to accept the goals of the organisation as being compatible with their personal goals.

(b)   **Different business functions often differ in personality** or culture from those in other functions (eg sales staff and accountants). Different goals, attitudes, job roles, jargon and work styles create potential for lack of understanding and frustration. This effect is worsened as the **size** of the organisation increases: informal interaction between the functions is reduced.

(c)   **Task interdependence**. The dependence of one department on another (eg for resources or information) may be a cause of conflict if the relationship is badly managed. The **technology** in use can have a major influence on task interdependence, as in many manufacturing operations, where products flow from one department to another.

(d)   **Scarcity of resources**. Resources are a source of power: managers fight for them. Departments may be given excessive targets and limited resources. This is another effect that can be amplified by growth and the establishment of specialist departments: staff are loyal to their colleagues and managers struggle to do their best for their staff in such matters as equipment and working conditions.

(e)   **Power distribution.** Conflict may also be caused by disputes about the boundaries of authority. Staff managers may attempt to encroach on the roles of line managers and usurp some of their authority, while departments might start empire building and try to take over the work previously done by other departments.

(f)   **Uncertainty**. Conflict can arise in times of change, where new problems arise. This may be particularly acute in **environments** posing threats through change, competition, resource scarcity and so on.

(g)   The **reward system** can encourage conflict, for instance, if incentives are designed in a way that rewards one department whilst penalising another.

Question 3.2   Conflict

Learning outcome C1c

What kind of conflict issues, based on the same sources of conflict listed above, might arise within a **work or project team**?

3.2 Causes of vertical conflict

Vertical conflict is effectively entrenched in the **power imbalance** between those at higher levels of a hierarchy and those 'below' them. This may be seen (depending on ideology) as inherently inequitable – making conflict both inevitable and desirable, as in a Marxist view – or as a necessary order for the control of organisational performance – making conflict likely, but raising the possibility of compromise for mutual survival and benefit.

Vertical conflict is most visibly reflected in industrial relations (IR): the formal relationship between management and labour representatives. (We will look at IR in more detail later in the chapter.) The desire of employees to join trade unions and staff associations reflects significant sources of vertical conflict.

(a)   **Resource distribution:** how will the value created by the organisation be shared between stakeholders, and in particular, between owners and the workforce?

(b)   **Power:** the lack of power mentioned above can lead to workers joining a union and engaging in trials of strength.

(c)   **Alienation:** many workers have boring, repetitive jobs and do not identify with the organisation. This alienation can be exacerbated by management attitudes.

(d)   **Politics** – in the sense of basic ideas about society and how it should work – is important, with workers seeking security and equality of outcome and managers being concerned to control costs and operate as freely as possible.

3.3 Organisational politics

Organisations are political systems in the sense that they are composed of individuals and groups who have their own interests, priorities and goals. Competition exists for finite resources, power and influence. There are cliques, alliances, pressure groups and blocking groups, centred on values, opinions and objectives which may be opposed by others.

Organisation politics reveals itself in various ways.

(a)   **Individuals** wish to experience victory and avoid defeat. They have their own objectives which are not always reconcilable with those of the organisation.

(b)   There are inevitable **disparities of power and influence** in hierarchical organisations - and despite rational organisation designs, events are in reality decided by dominant individuals or coalitions within and/or outside the organisation. Other individuals tend to want to influence, join or overthrow the dominant coalition.

(c)   Organisations are constantly involved in **compromise**, reconciling or controlling differences, and settling for reality rather than the ideal.

(d)   **Territory** is a useful analogy for the jealousies and rivalries over boundaries of authority, specialisms and spheres of influence.

(e)   Political behaviour might be characteristic of the **informal organisation**, where managers do each other favours in search of influence.

Mintzberg (Power In and Around Organisations) identifies various **political games**, which can be stimulating for the organisation, but can also degenerate into harmful, all-absorbing conflict.

(a)   **Games to resist authority** – to sabotage the aims of superiors

(b)   **Games to counter this resistance** – the imposition of rules and controls by superiors

(c)   **Games to build power bases** – associating with useful superiors, forming alliances among colleagues, gaining the support of subordinates, getting control of information or resources

(d)   **Games to defeat rivals** – inter-group or inter-departmental conflict

(e)   **Games to change the organisation** – higher power struggles, or rebellion

Section summary

It may be helpful to distinguish between:

*   **Horizontal conflict**, between individuals and groups at the same broad level in the organisation. This is often based, as we will see, on competition for limited influence and resources; and

*   **Vertical conflict**, between different levels in the organisation hierarchy. This is often based on conflict of interest and power imbalance.

*   **Political behaviour** is broadly concerned with competition, conflict, rivalry and power relationships in organisations.

4 Managing conflict

> ## Introduction
>
> In this section we look at a model for classifying individual responses to conflict based on assertiveness and co-cooperativeness. This maps five responses to conflict using these two factors. Then we look at ways managers can deal with conflict using a range of techniques. Finally we consider how industrial relations plays a part in resolving conflict.

4.1 Conflict handling styles

Thomas (1976) suggests that individuals' conflict-handling styles can be mapped on two dimensions, according to the **intentions** of the parties involved. He labelled the two dimensions *assertiveness* (trying to satisfy one's own concerns) and *co-operativeness* (trying to satisfy the other party's concerns).

He describes five strategies for resolving conflict but feels however that **compromising** was the optimal solution.

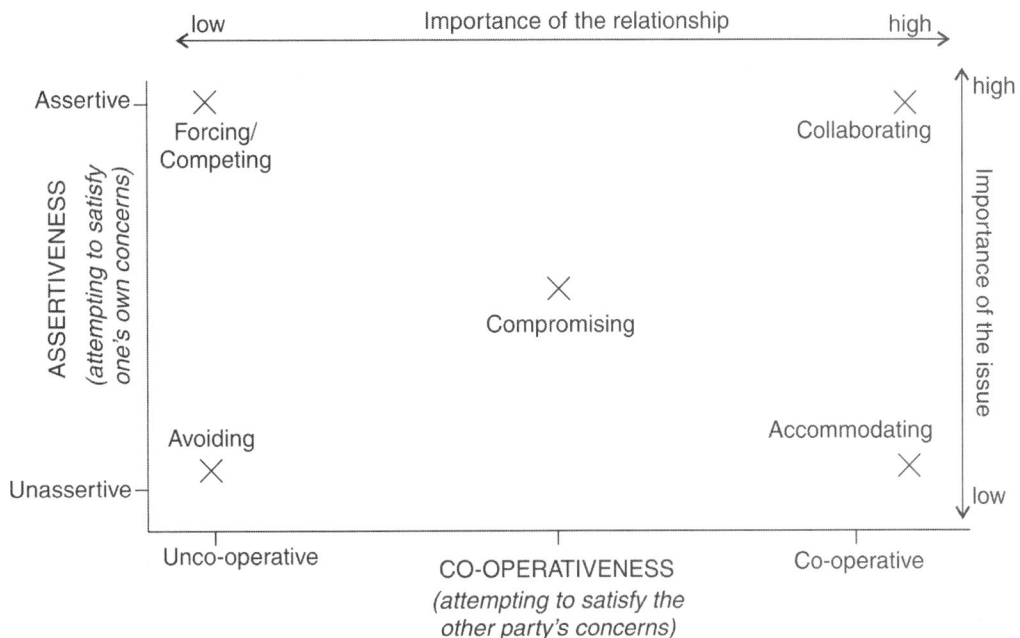

Source: Whetten and Cameron (2002, p. 359)

(a)   **Avoiding**. You withdraw from the conflict or deny/conceal the incompatibility ('sweeping it under the carpet'). This may be appropriate where the issue is trivial: it may simply blow over. Withdrawal is also a legitimate *short-term* response to more serious conflict, allowing tempers to cool and more information to be gathered. However, if underlying causes are not identified and addressed, the conflict may eventually re-emerge or escalate.

(b)   **Accommodating**. You concede the issue to the other person, regardless of your own legitimate concerns. This may be appropriate where the relationship is the most important consideration. It may be the only option where you have relatively low power in the relationship, especially if the time constraints are tight. It may also be appropriate to allow the other person to 'win' (eg allowing a subordinate to learn from his own mistakes). However, your own legitimate interests are not served.

(c)   **Competing/forcing**. You insist on your own concerns at the expense of others. This may be appropriate where the issue is the most important consideration: where it is necessary to solve ideological disputes, break down the inflexibility of others, implement unpopular measures or establish your autonomy. In other words, sometimes you just have to 'stick to your guns'. It is useful in emergencies, when quick, decisive action is required. It is facilitated where you have relatively high power in the relationship. The drawback is that the other person may feel defeated and humiliated, which may affect longer term cooperation.

(d) **Compromising**. You trade concessions through (explicit or implicit) bargaining, negotiating and conciliating, so that each party makes some concessions in order to obtain some gains. This may be appropriate when the issue is not worth disruption of the relationship. It may be necessary where the power is evenly balanced and the parties have mutually exclusive goals which are equally important to them. If the issue is complex, compromise may be a temporary resolution while other options are explored: it may also be a 'fall-back' position if collaborating or forcing are unsuccessful. However, individuals often exaggerate their initial positions (to counteract the effect of compromise) and this may polarise the conflict unnecessarily. Compromise may also be perceived to weaken the value of the decision, perhaps reducing commitment to it on the grounds that 'it wasn't what we wanted'. (And this may be the position of both parties.)

(e) **Collaborating**. You work together with the other party in an attempt to find an outcome in which the assertively-stated needs of both parties are met as far as possible. Conflict-handling is regarded as shared problem-solving. This may be most appropriate when both the issues and the relationship are highly important to you, and time is not pressing: it is worth seeking an integrative solution because both sets of concerns are recognised as being too important to compromise. Collaborating facilitates learning, consensus, the merging of different perspectives and the creation of more options (where these are felt to be desirable). It requires a relative balance of power, if only because of the openness and trust required.

The first three approaches all involve low consideration for the needs of one party or the other: they therefore tend to perpetuate conflict by effectively *legitimising* ill-feeling (on the part of the 'loser') and reinforcing aggression (on the part of the 'winner'). Compromise and collaboration are based on mutual recognition of needs, and therefore have a better chance of reinforcing relationships.

Cornelius and Faire (1989) offer the following story of 'Jane' to illustrate a simple collaborative approach

CASE STUDY

'Not long ago I received a memo from my boss instructing the staff to carry out some new procedures. It was badly phrased and sounded dictatorial to me and many other staff members. I had two choices – to obey or rebel. Either way, I was going to feel terrible about the disharmony. Was there another way?

It wasn't just an internal shift I had to make. It was necessary to take a stand against that memo. I went to my boss with a carefully worded statement: 'I just want you to know that when I read this I felt like doing the opposite of what you asked – and I don't want to be like that. I want to be supportive and co-operative.' My approach wasn't challenging, but factual.

'My boss took it far better than I could have expected. He said, 'That's interesting – which parts made you feel like that?' Then we talked about them. I got a different slant on the situation in this face-to-face friendly discussion. I left feeling I could now freely choose to follow the new procedures. My boss gained some helpful insights about approaching staff to implement his new plan.'

Exam alert

The Thomas model (also sometimes identified as the Thomas-Klinmann model) was specifically tested in a predecessor syllabus. Although the model was not cited by name, and the question avoided the use of the term 'conflict-handling styles', the approaches 'avoiding' and 'collaborating' should have tipped you off to which model was required, together with mention of a diagram with axes. It is unlikely you will be tested in specific models but clients such as those just described may be given in a question. You will then know what general approach to take in answering a question on conflict.

Question 3.3	Conflict handling

Learning outcome C1d

Which would be the most appropriate conflict handling style for a team leader who has given a direct instruction to a team member, in a situation requiring immediate handling in a particular way, and has been challenged in front of other people?

A   Forcing
B   Accommodating
C   Collaborating
D   Avoiding

4.2 Managing inter-group conflict

The conflict behaviour might be reduced in the following ways.

(a)   **Structural separation**. Design the organisation structure so that individuals, groups or departments in conflict have no dealings with each other. This is hardly a long-term solution: in most organisations people need to work together.

(b)   **Bureaucratic authority**. Conflict is controlled from above, by people with position power. Again this is a short-term solution, as it will merely encourage political behaviour by the departments in conflict with each other.

(c)   **Limited communication**. This is a short-term solution in which inter-departmental communications are restricted.

Co-operative behaviour might be encouraged in the following ways.

(a)   **Integration devices,** such as joint problem-solving teams, force people to work together, and, it is hoped, will encourage co-operative attitudes. A co-ordinator may be appointed.

(b)   **Confrontation and negotiation** requires that the members in conflict are forced to hammer out a solution. It is important how the situation is presented to the conflicting parties. A **win-lose strategy** implies that there will be one winner and one loser. Each negotiating party will pursue solely its own interest, will be unwilling to negotiate and will be deceitful and manipulative. A **win-win strategy** presents the conflict as a problem to be solved, not a battle to be won by one of the parties.

(c)   **Consultants** or third-party mediators/arbitrators can be brought in, as objective catalysts for improving communications, exposing group think and stereotyping and acting as an 'honest broker'. In the UK, the government-sponsored *Advisory Conciliation and Arbitration Service* (ACAS) has played this role.

(d)   **Job rotation**. Personnel are seconded to other departments in order to break down communication barriers, eliminate negative stereotypes and create 'ambassadors' when conflict arises.

(e)   **Super-ordinate goals**. Senior managers set shared, corporate objectives, over-arching the agendas of the individual departments.

(f)   **Intergroup training**. People from conflicting departments can be sent on joint training courses to break down barriers, encourage communication and emphasise shared goals and working styles.

(g)   **Organisational adjustments**, such as improved procedures' structures and workflow can be used to minimise the frustration of interdependence, role ambiguity, authority overlaps and so on. One modern approach is to regard workflows in terms of total horizontal business processes, without vertical barriers between functions.

(h)   Specific **issues** can be attacked and minimised by analysing them into components that can be dealt with separately and innovatively.

4.2.1 Environmental and ecological strategies

Charles Handy suggests two types of strategy that may be used to turn conflict into competition or argument, or to manage it in some other acceptable way.

(a)   **Environmental ('ecological') strategies.** Such strategies involve:

         (i)   Agreement of common objectives

         (ii)   Reinforcing the group or 'team' nature of organisational life, via culture

         (iii)   Providing feedback information on progress

         (iv)   Providing adequate co-ordination and communication mechanisms

         (v)   Sorting out territorial/role conflicts in the organisational structure

(b)   **Regulation strategies.** Possible methods include:

         (i)   The provision of arbitration to settle disputes

         (ii)   The establishment of detailed rules and procedures for conduct by employees

         (iii)   Appointing a person to 'manage' the area of conflict – a liaison/co-ordination officer

         (iv)   Using confrontation, or inter-group meetings, to hammer out differences, especially where territorial conflicts occur

         (v)   Separating the conflicting individuals

         (vi)   Ignoring the problem, if it is genuinely likely to 'go away', and there is no point in opening fresh wounds

4.3 Industrial and employee relations

KEY TERM

INDUSTRIAL RELATIONS (IR) can be defined as 'all the rules, practices and conventions governing interactions between managements and their workforces, normally involving collective employee representation and bargaining'.   *(Graham & Bennett)*

Industrial relations typically covers such areas as:

(a)   **Individual and collective procedures for agreeing terms and conditions of work.** (The collective process is known as collective bargaining.)

(b)   **Recognition of trade unions and/or alternative mechanisms for employee representation** and consultation. (This includes joint consultation committees, works councils and partnership agreements.)

(c)   **Machinery for handling individual and collective grievance and disciplinary issues** (including third-party conciliation and arbitration if necessary). Detailed procedural agreements on disputes are generally made during collective bargaining or other non-union negotiated agreements.

4.3.1 Industrial relations orientations

The Industrial Relations Services have identified four approaches to industrial relations (as cited by *Armstrong*, 2003).

(a)   **Adversarial**: the organisation decides what it wants to do and employees are expected to fit in. Employees only exercise power by refusing to co-operate.

(b)   **Traditional**: a good day-to-day working relationship, but management proposes and the workforce reacts through its elected representatives.

(c)   **Partnership**: the organisation involves employees in the drawing up and execution of organisation policies, but retains the right to manage.

(d)   **Power sharing**: employees are involved in both day-to-day and strategic decision-making.

Some companies have taken an aggressive approach to dealing with union power.

(a)   **Avoidance strategies** include complete de-recognition of unions, shifting operations to new non-union sites and only allowing unions a presence in problem solving and not in the settlement of benefits.

(b)   **Human resource management strategies** move away from dealing with staff collectively, establishing instead an individualistic approach to pay and benefits using such mechanisms as single status; appraisal and performance management; profit sharing; enhanced opportunities; and profit-related pay. Other, less confrontational approaches have emphasised problem solving, partnership, teamwork and policies based on a common interest in the success of the firm.

Many unionised firms, however, take a more **co-operative approach**, using mechanisms such as:

(a)   Gain sharing eg profit-related rewards

(b)   Partnership agreements: negotiated agreements in which both parties (management and the trade union) agree to work together to their mutual advantage and to achieve a climate of more co-operation and less adversarial industrial relations' (*Armstrong*). Shared goals may be defined in relation to such matters as: commitment to employment security, quality of working life; information-sharing and consultation; and commitment to the survival and success of the enterprise.

(c)   The use of labour-management teams to increase worker participation and involvement.

CASE STUDY

In 2003, 13 people from and all levels of Marks & Spencer participated in the first meeting of its national business involvement group (Big), the company's body for information and consultation. Their role will be to debate business decisions and HR policies face-to-face with the then chief executive, Roger Holmes.

These types of staff council have been established in companies across the UK in response to the European directive on information and consultation, which came into force in March 2005. But for M&S, the new group is the culmination of a series of measures aimed at improving employee communications.

There have been discussion groups in the stores for some years. But during the firm's financial difficulties in 1999, staff were involved in a consultative process called Clearview, which moved communications up a gear. It involved brainstorming sessions between employees and managers to consider what was wrong with the structure, processes and culture of the business.

M&S recognised the contribution that such a process made to the organisation's recovery. A review of the staff focus groups in Spring 2001 indicated that they wanted a structure that enabled issues to be represented at a more senior level and wanted managers and staff to sit in a combined forum. This led to the creation of Bigs at a local and area level in September 2001.

Local Bigs were set up in 309 shops, head office locations, the financial services unit and its distribution centres. Area Bigs provided a forum for issues that affected more than one store or business area. The company also had a European council, established in 1995 in line with EU legislation. But discussions were confined to issues affecting more than two countries. This was despite the closure of continental European stores in 2001, leaving the European council with members from only the UK and the Republic of Ireland. A review in March 2003 highlighted the need for a national forum.

(Higginbottom)

4.3.2 Employee relations

In line with other modern orientations in human resource management, the view of industrial relations (IR) has shifted. IR has traditionally been adversarial, both in perception ('us and them') and in genuine conflict of interest. However, it has been recognised that employers and employees are interdependent:

employee well-being depends on the continued prosperity of the organisation – and the continued prosperity of the organisation depends on the co-operation of the employees.

It has been argued that HR policies and management styles can capitalise on these shared interests and make traditional IR approaches (based on controlling conflict) largely irrelevant.

Employee relations is defined as all those areas of human resource management that involve general relationships with employees, through collective agreements where trade unions are recognised *and/or* through commonly applied policies for employee involvement and communications' (Armstrong).

Section summary

Thomas's model of conflict suggests individuals' **conflict-handling styles** can be mapped on two dimensions, according to the **intentions** of the parties involved. He labelled the two dimensions *assertiveness* (trying to satisfy one's own concerns) and *co-cooperativeness* (trying to satisfy the other party's concerns).

The solution to inter-group or horizontal conflict might be firstly to deal with the symptoms, by reducing conflict behaviour, and then deal with the causes of the conflict by encouraging co-operative attitudes.

Industrial relations typically covers:

- **Individual and collective procedures for agreeing terms and conditions of work,**

- **Recognition of trade unions and/or alternative mechanisms for employee representation and consultation.**

- **Machinery for handling individual and collective grievance and disciplinary issues**

Chapter Roundup

✓ The financial control function is concerned with the **allocation and effective use of resources.**

The treasury function is concerned with **obtaining finance** and managing relations with financial stakeholders.

Basic processing tasks are now often **outsourced** or **concentrated** in **shared service centres**.

✓ **Argument** (resolving differences by discussion) and **competition** can be distinguished from harmful expressions of difference as **conflict**.

Conflict can be constructive, if it introduces new information into a problem, if it defines a problem, or if it encourages creativity. It can be destructive if it distracts attention from the task or inhibits communication.

Conflict may **manifest** itself in: poor communication; friction between individuals and groups; widespread use of arbitration and other conflict mechanisms; and various political games.

✓ It may be helpful to distinguish between:

- **Horizontal conflict**, between individuals and groups at the same broad level in the organisation. This is often based, as we will see, on competition for limited influence and resources; and

- **Vertical conflict**, between different levels in the organisation hierarchy. This is often based on conflict of interest and power imbalance.

Political behaviour is broadly concerned with competition, conflict, rivalry and power relationships in organisations.

✓   *Thomas's* model of conflict suggests individuals' conflict-handling styles can be mapped on two dimensions, according to the **intentions** of the parties involved. He labelled the two dimensions *assertiveness* (trying to satisfy one's own concerns) and *co-cooperativeness* (trying to satisfy the other party's concerns).

The solution to inter-group or horizontal conflict might be firstly to deal with the symptoms, by reducing conflict behaviour, and then deal with the causes of the conflict by encouraging co-operative attitudes.

Industrial relations typically covers:

Individual and collective procedures for agreeing terms and conditions of work,

Recognition of trade unions and/or alternative mechanisms for employee representation and consultation.

Machinery for handling individual and collective grievance and disciplinary issues

Quick Quiz

1   Assuming an organisation has separate financial control and treasury functions, which is more likely to be responsible for currency management?

2   Which function is more likely to be responsible for preparation of quarterly accounts?

3   Name four measures that have traditionally been used to assess the work of the finance function.

4   Which of the following measures might be used to assess the work of the finance function using a balanced scorecard approach?

    A   Value enhancements
    B   Customer satisfaction
    C   Profits from investments
    D   Learning and growth

5   List four common sources of conflict in organisation.

Answers to Quick Quiz

1   Treasury function

2   Financial control function

3   • Reliability of information
    • Flexibility
    • Speed of reporting
    • Efficiency

4   All of them apart from C, which is most likely to be used to assess the treasury function's work.

5   • Poor relationships
    • Poor communication
    • Competition for power and resources
    • Clashes of personality

Answers to Questions

3.1   Sales support

Support could be provided in the following ways (this is not a definitive list):

(a)   Profitability analysis on sales and discount decisions

(b)   Developing finance deals for customers, such as leasing arrangements

(c)   Planning and analysis of the costs and revenue outcomes of sales promotions and advertising campaigns

(d)   Providing facilities for customers to review products, services and prices

(e)   Setting up deals with other suppliers to provide facilities to simplify customer purchasing

(f)   Developing product and service deals assisting the customer to improve processes and review their costs

(g)   Building relationships and sharing information with customers, and assisting their financial planning

(h)   Dealing with sales administration to enable sales staff to spend more time with customers

3.2   Conflict

Similar conflict issues may arise within a work or project team, due to everyday factors such as:

(a)   Disagreement about goals, priorities and interests, exacerbated by lack of direction and clarity from team leaders.

(b)   Poor communication, leading to negative assumptions, stereotyping and misunderstandings (often the root of so-called 'personality clashes').

(c)   Competition for resources such as recognition, office space, team-based rewards and so on.

(d)   Interpersonal issues, such as aggressive or argumentative communication styles, unfair treatment, or (in extreme cases) bullying or harassment.

(e)   Dissatisfactions with pay and conditions, leadership and so on which create grievances and spill over into interpersonal relations.

3.3   Conflict handling

A   The seriousness of the outcome means that avoiding and accommodating are not options. Collaborating would be a relationship-building long-term approach within a team setting, but in this case the need for compliance is urgent, the leader 'knows best', and his or her authority has been publicly challenged and potentially undermined, (s)he needs to reassert leadership and get the needed outcome quality, so forcing may be the immediate solution.

Now try the question below from the Exam Question Bank

Number	Level	Marks	Time
Q3	Introductory	10	18 mins

NEGOTIATION AND COMMUNICATION

In this chapter, we continue our study into general management and leadership issues, looking at negotiation and communication.

We start with communication which is a key skill of anyone in an organisation. However, it can go wrong and so we need to look at when that happens and how the situation may be improved.

Negotiation is simply the process of meeting to achieve a mutually acceptable outcome. It is used in many workplace contexts including agreeing contracts and trade union issues.

These topics could each be examined from a theoretical or practical point of view. They are also highly relevant to project management (communicating and negotiating with project stakeholders, say) and specific projects (eg change management).

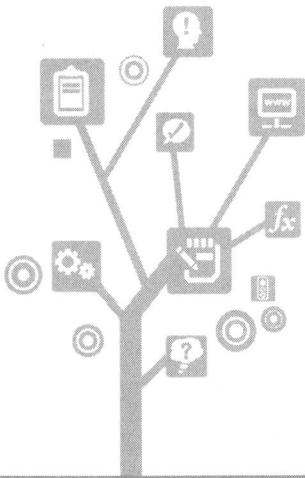

4

topic list	learning outcomes	syllabus references	ability required
1 Communication	C2b	C2(iii)	analysis
2 Negotiation	C2b	C2(iv)	analysis

1 Communication

Introduction

We start this chapter with a run through of communication and how it works. Communication has many forms including non-verbal and written. You need to decide which method is most appropriate to your message and who is receiving it. A little thought and preparation will improve your communication skills. We explain how you can improve your message when it is misunderstood.

1.1 The purpose of communication

In an organisational context, communication has a wide variety of purposes (and specific aims). These can be broadly summarised as:

(a)   Providing information to support managerial decision-making, planning and control.

(b)   Providing information to co-ordinate the plans and activities of different units, functions and individuals.

(c)   Communicating organisational goals, plans and structure to those who will implement them.

(d)   Generating and exchanging ideas and knowledge for learning and innovation.

(e)   Gathering information from the external environment and internal and external stakeholders, in order to shape strategy and managerial responses.

(f)   Providing information to external and internal stakeholders to secure awareness of, and 'buy-in' to, the organisation's plans.

(g)   Developing and maintaining relationships with network partners, stakeholders and employees.

Managers (like management accountants) are a hub of information flow in the organisation.

1.2 Direction of information flows

Formal channels of communication in an organisation may run in three main directions.

(a)   **Vertical**: ie up and down the scalar chain.

(i)   **Downward** communication is very common, and takes the form of instructions, briefings, rules and policies, announcement of plans and so on, from superior to subordinate.

(ii)   **Upward** communication is rarer – but very important for the organisation. It takes the form of reporting back, feedback, suggestions and so on. Managers need to encourage upward communication to take advantage of employees' experience and know-how, and to be able to understand their problems and needs in order to manage better.

(b)   **Horizontal or lateral:** between people of the same rank, in the same section or department, or in different sections or departments. Horizontal communication between 'peer groups' is usually easier and more direct then vertical communication, being less inhibited by considerations of rank.

(i)   **Formally:** to co-ordinate the work of several people, and perhaps departments, who have to co-operate to carry out a certain operation

(ii)   **Informally:** to furnish emotional and social support to an individual

(c)   **Diagonal**. This is interdepartmental communication by people of different ranks. Departments in the technostructure which serve the organisation in general, such as Human Resources or Information Systems, have no clear 'line authority' linking them to managers in other departments who need their involvement. Diagonal communication aids co-ordination, and also innovation and problem-solving, since it puts together the ideas and information of people in different functions and levels. It also helps to by-pass longer, less direct channels, avoiding blockages and speeding up decision-making.

1.3 Barriers to effective communication

General problems which can occur in the communication process include:

(a)   **Distortion**: a process by which the meaning of a message is lost 'in translation'. Misunderstanding may arise from technical or ambiguous language, misinterpretation of symbols etc

(b)   **Noise**: interference in the environment of communication which prevents the message getting through clearly eg due to physical noise, technical interference, or interpersonal differences making communication difficult

(c)   **Misunderstanding** due to lack of clarity or technical jargon

(d)   **Non-verbal signs** (gesture, facial expression) contradicting the verbal message

(e)   Failure to give or to seek **feedback**

(f)   **'Overload'** – a person being given too much information to digest in the time available

(g)   **Perceptual selection**: people hearing only what they want to hear in a message

(h)   **Differences** in social, racial or educational background

(i)   **Poor communication skills** on the part of sender or recipient

Additional difficulties may arise from the **work context**, including:

(a)   **Status** (of the sender and receiver of information)

   (i)   A senior manager's words are listened to closely and a colleague's perhaps discounted.

   (ii)   A subordinate might mistrust his or her superior's intentions and might look for 'hidden meanings' in a message.

(b)   **Jargon.** People from different job or specialist backgrounds (eg accountants, HR managers, IT experts) can have difficulty in talking on a non-specialist's wavelength.

(c)   **Priorities.** People or departments may have different priorities or perspectives so that one person places more or less emphasis on a situation than another.

(d)   **Selective reporting.** Subordinates may give superiors incorrect or incomplete information (eg to protect a colleague, to avoid 'bothering' the superior). A senior manager may, however, only be able to handle edited information because he does not have time to sift through details.

(e)   **Use.** Managers may be prepared to make decisions on a 'hunch' without proper regard to the communications they may or may not have received.

(f)   **Timing.** Information which has no immediate use tends to be forgotten.

(g)   **Opportunity.** Mechanisms, formal or informal, for people to say what they think may be lacking, especially for upward communication.

(h)   **Conflict.** Where there is conflict between individuals or departments, communications will be withdrawn and information withheld.

(i)   **Cultural values** about communication. For example:

   (i)   **Secrecy.** Information might be given on a need-to-know basis, rather than be considered as a potential resource for everyone to use.

   (ii)   **Can't handle bad news.** The culture of some organisations may prevent the communication of certain messages. Organisations with a 'can-do' philosophy may not want to hear that certain tasks are impossible, for example.

Question 4.1   Communication

Learning outcome C2b

Is the statement below true or false?

'A clearly expressed verbal message will always be understood.'

1.4 Improving communication

Depending on the problem, measures to improve communication may be as follows.

(a)   **Encourage, facilitate and reward** communication. Status and functional barriers (particularly to upward and inter-functional communication) can be minimised by improving opportunities for formal and informal networking and feedback.

(b)   **Give training and guidance** in communication skills, including consideration of recipients, listening, giving feedback and so on.

(c)   **Minimise the potential for misunderstanding.** Make people aware of the difficulties arising from differences in culture and perception, and teach them to consider others' viewpoints.

(d)   **Adapt technology, systems and procedures** to facilitate communication: making it more effective (clear mobile phone reception), faster (laptops for e-mailing instructions), more consistent (regular reporting routines) and more efficient (reporting by exception).

(e)   **Manage conflict and politics** in the organisation, so that no basic unwillingness exists between units.

(f)   **Establish communication channels and mechanisms** in all directions: regular staff or briefing meetings, house journal or Intranet, quality circles and so on. Upward communication should particularly be encouraged, using mechanisms such as inter-unit meetings, suggestion schemes, 'open door' access to managers and regular performance management feedback sessions.

Communication between superiors and subordinates will be improved when **interpersonal trust** exists. Exactly how this is achieved will depend on the management style of the manager, the attitudes and personality of the individuals involved, and other environmental variables. *Peters and Waterman* advocate 'management by walking around' (MBWA), and **informality in superior/subordinate relationships** as a means of establishing closer links.

1.5 Communication methods and media

1.5.1 Written communication

A range of written communication media is used in business contexts, for one-to-one and one-to-group communication. Examples include: letters, reports, forms, notice boards, e-mail, information leaflets, manuals and handbooks, the minutes of meetings and so on.

The key advantages of written formats are that:

(a)   They focus the attention of sender and receiver
(b)   They enable subsequent and repeated reference to information and agreements
(c)   They provide legally acceptable evidence of information and agreements exchanged
(d)   They enable both confidentiality (where required) and sharing/copying of information.

1.5.2 Oral and face-to-face communication

Oral and face-to-face verbal media are also widespread in organisations, in forms such as: telephone calls or teleconferencing; discussions, meetings and interviews (and their electronic equivalents in web-casts and video-conferencing); brainstorming sessions, quality circles, team briefings; large-scale public or shareholder meetings; and so on.

These kinds of media are particularly good for:

(a)   Generating new ideas, because of their real-time information sharing and interactivity (as in brainstorming).

(b)   Interactive feedback, exchange of views and questioning (without the lead time required for responses in writing).

(c)   The availability of non-verbal cues (including tone of voice and, in face-to-face communication, body language) to support interpretation of underlying meaning and messages.

(d)   Personal interactions and relationship building (because of the ability to build rapport and be sensitive to the audience's needs and responses).

(e)   Spreading information informally to large groups of people, with opportunities for interactive feedback and questions (as in briefings and public meetings).

Confirmation and reference material can often be provided in writing for, or following, conversations and meetings, in order to support more detailed and repeated reference, where necessary.

1.5.3 Non-verbal communication

Non-verbal communication (often called **body language**) consists of facial expression, posture, proximity, gestures and non-verbal noises (grunts, yawns etc).

Consciously or unconsciously, we send messages through body language during every face to face encounter. We can use it deliberately to **confirm** our verbal message – for example, by nodding and smiling as we tell someone we are happy to help them – or to **contradict** it, if we want to be sarcastic (saying 'How interesting!' with a yawn, for example).

More often, however, our body language contradicts our verbal message *without* our being aware of it, giving a 'mixed message' like your saying you understand an instruction while looking extremely perplexed. Body language can also 'give away' messages that we would – for social or business reasons – rather not send, such as lack of interest, hostility or whatever.

Control and use of body language is needed to:

(a)   Provide 'physical' feedback to the sender of a message (eg a nod of understanding)
(b)   Create a desired impression (eg a confident posture)
(c)   Establish a desired atmosphere or conditions (eg a friendly smile)
(d)   Reinforce spoken messages with appropriate indications (eg nodding 'yes').

Reading other people's body language helps you to:

(a)   Receive feedback from a listener and modify the message accordingly
(b)   Recognise people's real feelings when their words are constrained by formalities
(c)   Recognise existing or potential personal problems
(d)   'Read' situations in order to modify our own communication and response strategy.

1.5.4 Electronic communication

The introduction of personal computer networks facilitates new sorts of communication, of which **e-mail** is probably by far the most prevalent. It is particularly useful in organisations which are widely dispersed over several sites in one or more countries.

Email has many **advantages** over the telephone and paper memos, which explains why it has been so widely adopted.

(a) Emails can be sent to **large numbers of people at the same time** without having to be physically distributed on paper.

(b) Email messages **need not interrupt the recipient's flow of work**, unlike a phone call.

Email also has **drawbacks**, however.

(a) Some people use email when face to face contact is more appropriate.

(b) Although email can feel as informal as a spoken conversation, email records can be used in legal proceedings, eg for former employees suing the company for unfair dismissal. They may also be cited in defamation. *Asda* were successfully sued by a disgruntled customer because untrue rumours that a customer was guilty of fraud had been circulated via the company's email system, for example.

(c) They contribute to information overload: there is a temptation to copy email to people that do not really need to see it.

(d) If email is the main means of communication with external parties, the company's corporate identity may be compromised if people send emails in a variety of formats.

These problems emphasise the need for **internal guidance** on how email should be used. If email is used to communicate with other customers or suppliers, it should be treated in the same way as other business correspondence, including obtaining appropriate authorisation. The guidance should prohibit defamatory or other abusive messages. Above all employees should be made aware that communication by email is permanent and not transitory in nature.

Electronic data interchange (EDI) is a form of direct communication between computers and may be used between organisations. For instance, production scheduling software may send orders directly to a supplier's stock handling computer via a telephone link.

1.5.5 Which medium should be used?

KEY POINT

The choice of medium (letter, memo, e-mail, report, presentation, telephone call) and channel of delivery (telecom system, notice board, postal system, World Wide Web) depends on a number of factors.

(a) **Urgency**: the speed of transmission (eg phone or e-mail as opposed to post)

(b) **Permanency**: the need for a written record for legal evidence, confirmation of a transaction or future reference

(c) **Complexity**: eg the need for graphic illustration to explain concepts

(d) **Sensitivity/confidentiality** (eg a private letter)

(e) **Ease of dissemination**: wide audience (eg a notice board)

(f) **Cost effectiveness** (taking into account all the above)

Question 4.2 Media

Learning outcome C2b

Indicate the most effective way in which the following situations should be communicated.

(a) Spare parts are needed urgently.
(b) A message from the managing director to all staff.
(c) Fred has been absent five times in the past month and his manager intends to take action.
(d) You need information quickly from another department.
(e) You have to explain a complicated operation to a group.

Section summary

Communication in an organisation **flows** downwards, upwards, sideways and diagonally.

Barriers to communication include 'noise' (from the environment), poorly constructed or coded/decoded messages (distortion) and failures in understanding caused by the relative positions of senders and receivers.

A wide range of communication **methods and media** are available for use in organisations, including verbal (oral and written) and non-verbal methods.

Non-verbal communication (including **tone of voice** and **body language**) can support or undermine verbal messages: it needs to be carefully interpreted and managed.

2 Negotiation

Introduction

We now look at negotiation which is a means of communicating with the aim of reaching a mutual agreement. Negotiation is used for more complex communication where there is some uncertainty over the outcome. Professional negotiators work in areas such as government and trade unions where communication takes place over difficult and complex issues.

The process of negotiation follows a number of stages which are illustrated here. Much of the negotiation process is actually preparing before the meeting takes place so that you know exactly what you want to achieve and how you intend to do this.

NEGOTIATION is, simply, a process whereby two parties come together to confer with a view to concluding a jointly acceptable agreement.

KEY TERM

Gennard and Judge (2003) suggest that this process involves two main elements:

(a) **Purposeful persuasion**: whereby each party attempts to persuade the other to accept its case by marshalling arguments, backed by factual information and analysis.

(b) **Constructive compromise**: whereby both parties accept the need to move closer toward each other's position, identifying the parameters of common ground within and between their positions, where there is room for concessions to be made while still meeting the needs of both parties.

KEY POINT

Such an approach can be applied to a number of different situations.

(a) **Conflict resolution**: reducing resentment and preserving relationship, by allowing both parties to obtain at least some of their desired outcomes.

(b) **Group decision-making** and **problem-solving**: integrating different viewpoints and interests so that the decision or solution is high on quality (from diverse relevant input) *and* acceptability (from joint consultation and commitment), enhancing the likelihood of effective implementation. People are increasingly expecting to participate in decisions that affect them, particularly at work.

2.1 Approaches to negotiation

There are two basic approaches to negotiation.

Distributive bargaining	Negotiation is about the distribution of finite resources. One party's gain is another's loss: a 'win-lose' or 'zero sum' equation. If a pay increase of, say, 10% is gained, where the management budget was 5%, the extra has to be funded from elsewhere – shareholders (reduced profits), customers (increased prices), other employee benefits (cuts in training) or whatever.
Integrative bargaining	Negotiation is about joint problem-solving, aiming to find a mutually satisfying (or 'win-win') solution to problems. The aim is not just to get the best outcome for one's own party ('win-lose') or even compromise ('lose-lose') but to fulfil the needs of all parties as far as possible.

It is now generally recognised that integrative bargaining is the most constructive, sustainable and ethical approach to negotiation.

2.2 The negotiation process

The following is a general overview of the negotiation process. Any negotiation will involve the stages illustrated, although the duration and approach of each will vary according to the particular situation.

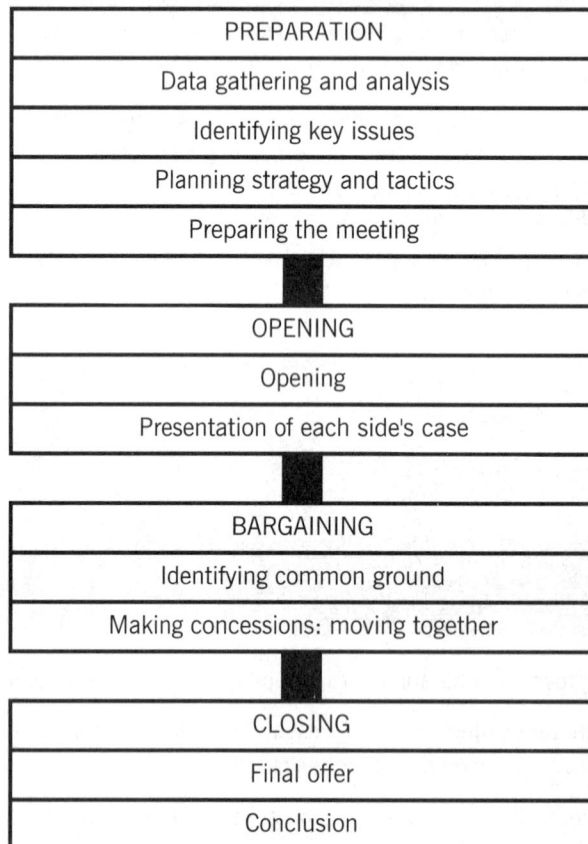

PREPARATION
Data gathering and analysis
Identifying key issues
Planning strategy and tactics
Preparing the meeting

OPENING
Opening
Presentation of each side's case

BARGAINING
Identifying common ground
Making concessions: moving together

CLOSING
Final offer
Conclusion

2.3 Preparing a negotiating strategy

Formal negotiations, as opposed to informal 'arrangements' you may come to, should follow broad guidelines.

(a) **Set objectives for the negotiation**: what you want to get out of it. These should be achievable and consistent with the organisation's policies.

(b) **Gather information** on the issues over which negotiations are going to be conducted: trends in union demands, market pay rates, case studies from similar organisations/sectors, relevant legislation and rules and so on. (Some information will have to be shared with the other party before the negotiation: this is the case in collective bargaining with trade union representatives, for example.)

(c) **Identify potential areas of conflict.** In integrative bargaining, each side accepts that the objectives and viewpoints of the other side are as real and legitimate as their own. Even in distributive bargaining, the outcome will have to be 'sold' to all parties. So recognition of the needs, wants and fears of the other party will help in devising a workable trade-off between different interests. It will also help you to anticipate counter-arguments and counter-proposals to your presentation.

(d) **Identify potential areas of movement**. Each party identifies the key issues or items likely to be on the table, and decides on which of these it will be willing to trade or make concessions. It also tries to anticipate the items on which the *other* party will be willing to trade or make concessions. Some may be amenable to movement on both sides, especially if they are identified as being relatively 'cheap' for one party to give up and relatively valuable for the other party to receive.

(e) **Formulate a negotiating strategy**. There are basically three possible outcomes:

(i)   If we were to achieve all our objectives, what would be the *ideal settlement or outcome*?

'What I would really like is...'

(ii) If we were able to make progress, but being realistic about the bargaining power of the other side, what is a *realistic settlement or outcome?*

'I could live with...'

(iii) If we were to concede, what is an acceptable *fall-back position*: the least favourable outcome that can be accepted without failing to meet our objectives? (This may also represent the limit of our budget or authority.)

'My sticking point is...'

Beyond this point, you cannot afford to concede or agree: the terms are unacceptable, and the only answer is: 'No way...' There may be costs to refusing to agree at this point, including sanctions or penalties which may be imposed by the other party: you should factor these costs in, when you decide where the 'no way!' line is...

A position for each side should be estimated for each of the above options – and areas of agreement concentrated on, as potential middle ground.

2.4 Preparing the meeting

The next part of your preparation focuses on the negotiation meeting itself.

Key elements	Comments
Purpose	What is the purpose or objective of the meeting? Is it about investigation or are you intending to finalise the negotiation?
Plan	Where will the meeting be held? How should the room be laid out? What facilities (eg side meeting rooms, visual aids) will be required?
	How will you structure the meeting? How long will it take?
Pace	About 5% of any meeting time should be given to breaking the ice and making introductions, before 'getting down to business'.
Personalities	With whom are you meeting? Are they experienced negotiators?

2.5 Conducting the negotiation – opening and bargaining

During the conduct of the negotiations themselves, participants should consider the following.

(a) **Opening presentation:** a broad statement of each side's ideal position or opening offer, explaining the rationale (and strength of feeling) behind the proposals, and supporting them with relevant objective data.

(b) **Fact-finding.** Each party should use the other party's presentation as an opportunity for fact finding, rather than point scoring or unconsidered ('knee-jerk') opposition. Negotiators should gain a better understanding of the other party's position *and* its strengths and weaknesses.

(c) **Identifying common ground.** Having established ideal (usually polarised) positions, the emphasis switches to exploring areas where agreement might be reached on realistic and fall-back positions.

(d) **Use of the negotiating strategy and bargaining power.** Items should be linked and packaged to achieve two-way momentum, so that no party gives away anything without getting something in return. Be firm on principles and flexible on details, so that there is room to move without compromising your priority objectives.

(e) **Considering** new proposals or counter proposals. If new proposals are on the table, the meeting should be adjourned to give time for discussion: never do your thinking or strategising aloud in front of the other side!

(f) **Making concessions.** A concession is a 'revision of a position you have held previously and justified publicly' (Guirdham, 1995). Concessions are not easy to make without losing credibility – but they *must* be made in order to bring both parties progressively close together. They should only be made in response to pressure or to offers-in-exchange from the other party – and only in small steps. You can encourage concessions from the other side by negatively reinforcing their present position (eg emphasising that it will not work) and positively reinforcing movement (eg offering options for them to move without losing face).

(g) **The negotiating team.** Members of the same negotiating team should not contradict one another or speak unless asked to do so by their leader. If there is an issue, pass a message to the leader, asking for an adjournment.

(h) **Effective communication skills.** Be brief and to the point: a business-like approach encourages a similar response from the other side. Use language that everyone will be able to understand. Remember that assertiveness (an essential skill) is not the same as aggression: all parties should show respect for one another.

(i) **Leadership.** The meeting should be facilitated by an experienced chairperson, who will ensure that it is conducted in a courteous and effective manner: sticking to the agenda; giving alternating opportunities to speak (rather than a 'free for all') and so on. All relevant details of the discussion should be recorded, in order to furnish minutes which can be used in formulating final agreements.

2.6 Closing the negotiation

Closing a negotiation is similar to closing a sale; it means attempting to bring the process to a conclusion. There are several techniques.

At the conclusion of negotiations, both parties must be satisfied that all issues have been discussed and that they understand exactly what has been agreed: the proceedings should be summarised and agreements 'played back' for confirmation by both sides. If any objectives are raised, negotiations should recommence.

Once there is oral agreement, the points should be written up as a signed 'draft agreement', which will be circulated and checked by both sides. When all clauses have been approved by both sides, the agreement can be printed, formally signed and communicated to those affected by its provisions.

Exam alert

You may be asked to identify the correct sequence of phases in the conduct of negotiation in a longer question. This was tested in the previous syllabus.

2.7 Successful negotiation

John Hunt lists some characteristics of successful negotiators in his book *Managing People at Work*.

(a)   They avoid direct confrontation.
(b)   They consider a wide range of options.
(c)   They hold back counter proposals rather than responding immediately.
(d)   They use emollient verbal techniques: 'would it be helpful if we...'
(e)   They summarise on behalf of all involved.
(f)   They advance single arguments insistently and avoid long winded, multiple reason arguments

Negotiation skills are difficult to learn other than from experience. Role plays and simulations can help, but the best way is to attend live negotiations as a junior member of a team.

Section summary

The process of **negotiation** can be said to involve two main elements: purposeful persuasion and constructive compromise.

Chapter Roundup

✓   **Communication** in an organisation **flows** downwards, upwards, sideways and diagonally.

Barriers to communication include 'noise' (from the environment), poorly constructed or coded/decoded messages (distortion) and failures in understanding caused by the relative positions of senders and receivers.

A wide range of communication **methods and media** are available for use in organisations, including verbal (oral and written) and non-verbal methods.

Non-verbal communication (including tone of voice and body language) can support or undermine verbal messages: it needs to be carefully interpreted and managed.

✓   The process of **negotiation** is said to involve two main elements: purposeful persuasion and constructive compromise.

Quick Quiz

1   Which of the following communication methods is designed to encourage upward communication?

    A   House journal
    B   Organisation manual
    C   Team meetings
    D   E-mail

2   The question 'Did you complete your accountancy qualification?' is:

    A   An open question
    B   A closed question
    C   A leading question
    D   A probing question

3   List the four main stages of the negotiation process.

4   According to Gennard and Judge, negotiation has two main elements. Name them.

5   The choice of communication depends on number of factors. List five.

Answers to Quick Quiz

1   C   Options A and B primarily support downward communication and option D, downward and lateral communication.

2   B.   (You might try to rephrase this question as the other types, for extra practice.)

3   Preparation, Opening, Bargaining, Closing

4   They are purposeful persuasion and constructive compromise.

5   Your list should include five of urgency, permanency, complexity, sensitivity, ease of dissemination, cost effectiveness.

Answers to questions

4.1   Communication

False. 'Clear expression' is a matter of opinion and perception, or in terms of the communications model, of coding and decoding. We must also consider the effect of noise, such as cultural differences.

4.2   Media

Communicating the situations given might best be done as follows.

(a)   Telephone, confirmed in writing (order form, letter)

(b)   Noticeboard, general meeting or email

(c)   Face-to-face conversation. It would be a good idea to confirm the outcome of the meeting in writing so that records can be maintained.

(d)   Telephone, face to face or e-mail.

(e)   Team briefing

Now try the questions below from the Exam Question Bank

Number	Level	Marks	Time
Q4	Examination	10	18 mins

CULTURE

Organisational culture is, broadly, the distinctive way an organisation does things: its particular 'style'. We explore how this reveals itself in the first two sections of this chapter.

Culture is often discussed together with **structure**. Particular structures suit particular cultures (and vice versa). We look at an influential model of this in Section 3.

Then we consider how strategy and culture are linked too. We look at how different organisation cultures affect their approach to strategy.

The impact of **national culture** on organisational culture is important when discussing management in multi-national and cross-cultural contexts. It may be particularly relevant in scenarios where a company is considering strategic options to start overseas operations.

This chapter underpins much of the rest of the syllabus.

Management/leadership style, team-working and relationships, approach to project management and stakeholders, and organisational mission, objectives and strategy will all reflect the organisation's culture: 'the way we do things round here'.

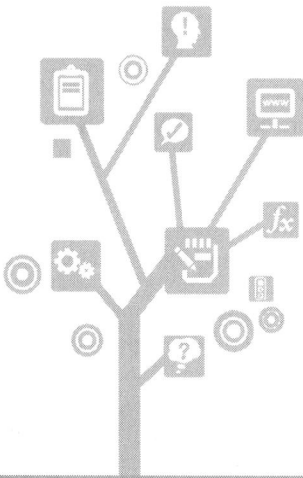

5

topic list	learning outcomes	syllabus references	ability required
1 What is culture?	C1b	C1(ii)	application
2 Organisation culture	C1b	C1(ii)	application
3 Culture and structure	C1b	C1(ii)	application
4 Culture and strategy	C1b	C1(ii)	application
5 Cross-cultural leadership	C1b	C1(ii)	application

1 What is culture?

Introduction

We often think of culture as what you see in a museum but for organisations it is the 'way we do things around here'. Culture is the ways of acting and thinking shared by a group of people. Some of this culture can be hidden but is still influential. You may wish to think of culture in an organisation as an **iceberg** with a large part hidden below the surface.

1.1 Spheres of culture

KEY TERMS

HOFSTEDE (1984) summed up culture as 'the collective programming of the mind which distinguishes the members of one category of people from another'. *Hofstede's* model is explained in more depth later on in this chapter.

CULTURE may therefore be identified as ways of behaving, and ways of understanding, that are shared by a group of people. Schein referred to it as: **'The way we do things round here.'**

Culture can be discussed on many different levels. The 'category' or 'group' of people whose shared behaviours and meanings may constitute a culture include:

(a) A nation, region or ethnic group
(b) Women versus men ('gender culture')
(c) A social class (eg 'working class culture')
(d) A profession or occupation
(e) A type of business (eg 'advertising culture')
(f) An organisation ('**organisational culture**')

If you are a male (or female) accountant in an organisation operating in a given business sector in a particular region of your country of residence (which may not be your country of origin), you may be influenced by all these different spheres of culture!

CASE STUDY

Consider the case of a young French employee of *Disneyland Paris*.

(a) The employee speaks the French language – part of the national culture – and has participated in the French education system etc.

(b) As a youth, the employee might, in his or her spare time, participate in various 'youth culture' activities. Music and fashion are emblematic of youth culture.

(c) As an employee of Disneyland Paris, the employee will have to participate in the corporate culture, which is based on American standards of service with a high priority put on friendliness to customers.

1.2 Elements of culture

Trompenaars (1993) suggested that in fact there are different levels at which culture can be understood.

(a) The **observable**, expressed or 'explicit' elements of culture include:

    (i)   **Behaviour**: norms of personal and interpersonal behaviour; customs and rules about behaviours that are 'acceptable' or unacceptable.

    (ii)   **Artefacts**: concrete expressions such as art and literature, architecture and interior design (eg of office premises), dress codes, symbols and 'heroes' or role models.

    (iii)   **Rituals**: patterns of collective behaviour which have traditional or symbolic value, such as greeting styles, business formalities, social courtesies and ceremonies.

(b)   Beneath these observable phenomena lie **values and beliefs** which give the behaviours, artefacts and rituals their special meaning and significance. For example, the design of office space (artefact) may imply status and honour, or reflect the importance of privacy, or reflect spiritual beliefs (as in feng shui) within a culture: it 'means' more than the observable features. Values and beliefs may be overtly expressed in sayings, mottos and slogans.

(c)   Beneath values and beliefs lie **assumptions**: foundational ideas that are no longer consciously recognised or questioned by the culture, but which 'programme' its ways of thinking and behaving. Examples include the importance of the individual in many Western cultures: this is taken for granted in designing HR (human resources) policies, for example.

1.3 The cultural iceberg

Various writers on culture have used the metaphor of an **iceberg** to describe the levels at which culture operates.

(a)   The **overt** elements of culture are above the surface: differences can be observed, discussed and dealt with openly.

(b)   The **covert** (hidden) elements of culture represent the larger part of the iceberg which is below the water. They exert influence, without necessarily being openly expressed or even acknowledged.

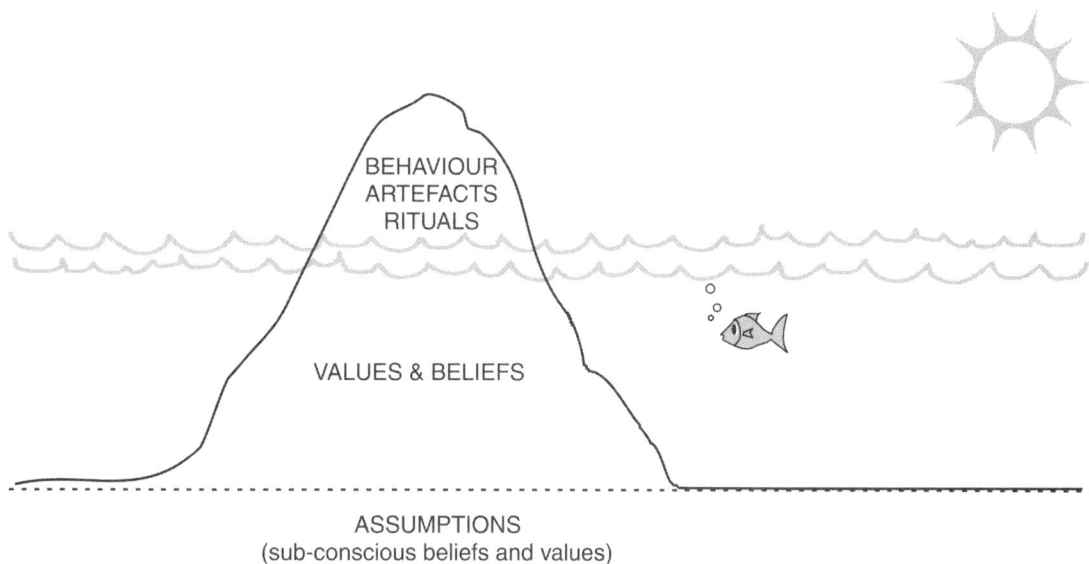

BEHAVIOUR
ARTEFACTS
RITUALS

VALUES & BELIEFS

ASSUMPTIONS
(sub-conscious beliefs and values)

KEY POINT

Cultural assumptions, values and beliefs influence the behaviour of individuals, groups and organisations. They create a shared 'style' of operating within a given culture – but also the potential for misunderstanding and conflict *between* different cultural groups. An important aspect of culture management is to bring covert aspects of culture to the surface where they can be looked at and discussed: differences and influences can then be effectively understood and managed.

Section summary

Culture is 'the collective programming of the mind which distinguishes the members of one category of people from another' (Hofstede). It may be identified as ways of behaving, and ways of understanding, that are shared by a group of people.

Elements of culture include:

- Observable behaviour, artefacts, rituals and symbols
- Underlying values and beliefs which give meaning to the observable elements
- Hidden assumptions which unconsciously shape values and beliefs

2 Organisation culture

Introduction

We continue our study of culture by revisiting the iceberg and behaviour, artefacts and rituals from the last section. How do these explain culture in organisations? How would you as a manager be able to influence and interpret unseen cultural attitudes?

There are other models you can use to explain culture in organisations including the '7S' and cultural web.

Think of these as tools for explaining an organisation if you get a scenario in a question.

KEY TERM

ORGANISATION CULTURE may be defined as:

- 'The collection of traditions, values, policies, beliefs and attitudes that constitute a pervasive context for everything we do and think in an organisation' (Mullins)

- 'A pattern of beliefs and expectations shared by the organisation's members, and which produce norms which powerfully shape the behaviour of individuals and groups in the organisation' (Schwartz & Davies)

- 'The way we do things around here'

2.1 Manifestations of culture in organisations

Examples of organisation culture, following Trompenaars' elements, include the following.

Item	Example
Beliefs and values, which are often unquestioned	'The customer is always right'.
Behaviour	In the City of London, standard business dress is still generally taken for granted and even 'dress down Fridays' have their rules.
Artefacts	Microsoft encourages communication between employees by setting aside spaces for the purpose.
Rituals	Many firms offer awards to outstanding staff members, given at a ceremony.
Symbols	Corporate logos are an example of symbols, but they are directed outwards. Within the organisation, symbols can represent power: dress, make and model of car, office size and equipment and access to facilities can all be important symbols.

Manifestations of culture in an organisation may thus include:

(a)   How formal the organisation structure is
(b)   Communication: are senior managers approachable?
(c)   Office layout
(d)   The type of people employed
(e)   Symbols, legends, corporate myths
(f)   Management style
(g)   Freedom for subordinates to show initiative
(h)   Attitudes to quality
(i)   Attitudes to risk
(j)   Attitudes to the customer
(k)   Attitudes to technology

Question 5.1	Manifestations of culture

Learning outcome C1b

What do you think would differentiate the culture of:

- A regiment in the Army
- An advertising agency?

2.2 The organisational iceberg

French and Bell (among others) apply the iceberg analogy specifically to organisations.

(a)   **Overt aspects** (the tip of the iceberg) are the **formal aspects** of organisation. These are financial resources, products, customers, formal structure, technology, policies, procedures and rules.

   These are overt because they are visible (even to outsiders and new joiners), documented, controlled through formal management processes – and explicitly designed to support the mission of the organisation.

(b)   **Covert aspects** (the larger, hidden part of the iceberg) are the **behavioural aspects** or culture. These include beliefs, assumptions and attitudes. Other covert aspects are informal communication patterns, informal team processes, informal influence and leadership, political behaviour and interpersonal relations.

These are not directly in control of management, not always supportive of the organisation's mission, and not readily visible to outsiders or new joiners.

KEY POINT
> The challenge for managers is to be aware of covert cultural aspects and seek to influence them – as well as the more directly 'manageable' formal processes.

2.3 The McKinsey 7S model

Another model, which depicts the interdependence of formal and cultural/behaviour elements in organisational management, is the McKinsey 7S model.

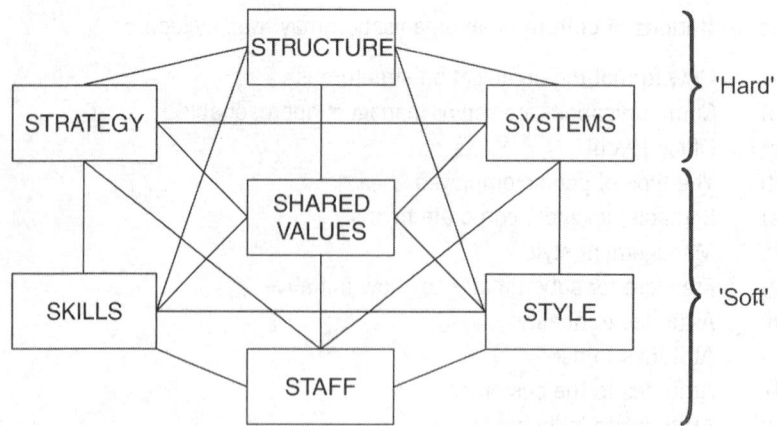

The important points to note here are that:

(a)   Culture occupies a central position in the model, both in terms of style (corporate image, management style, patterns and norms of behaviour) and shared values (the underlying guiding beliefs and assumptions that shape the way the organisation sees itself and its purpose).

(b)   All the elements are inter-linked: altering any one variable will have an effect on the others and on the whole network.

Say you wanted to reposition your organisation by offering unique levels of customer service in your industry (**strategy**). You might have to set up team-working in customer-facing units to increase responsiveness (**structure**). You may have to recruit (**staff**) and train people in customer service skills (**skills**). They will also need new procedures and IT systems for better access to customer data (**systems**). Managers will have to adjust to empowering staff, and a new corporate image will be developed (**style**). But none of this will be sustainable unless there is also a fundamental shift in the organisation's values, to put the customer first (**shared values**).

KEY POINT

You may note from this example that culture (and each of the other elements) may both *shape strategy* – particularly in the resource-based view, where strategy is formulated on the basis of what the organisation is best (most competitive) at – and be *shaped by strategy* – particularly in a positioning view, where internal elements are adjusted to support strategic objectives. We look at resource-based and positioning views later on when we visit strategy.

2.4 The cultural web

Johnson and Scholes also use a 'web' as a way of representing 'the taken-for-granted assumptions, or paradigm, of an organisation, and the behavioural manifestations of organisation culture'.

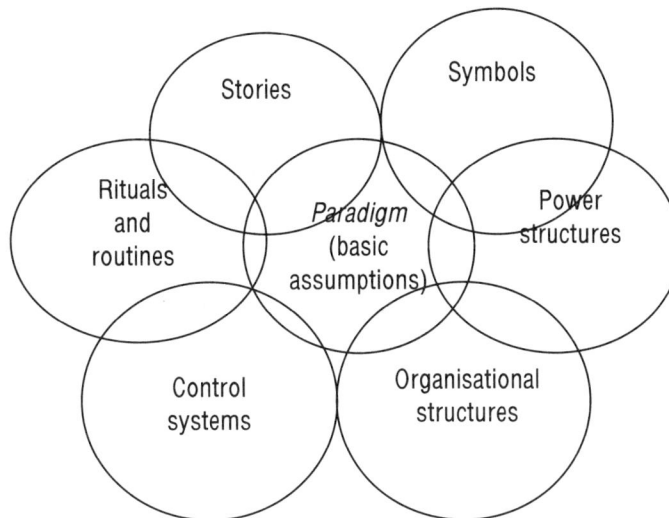

(a)   The **paradigm** (like 'shared-values' in the 7S model) is the guiding set of beliefs, values and assumptions that shape how the organisation sees itself and its purpose.

(b)   **Stories** are the 'mythology' of the organisation: tales of successes and failures, how things got to be the way they are etc.

(c)   **Rituals** are symbolic behaviours (eg business formulation and ceremonies) and **routines** are formal procedures and customs.

(d)   **Control systems** (as discussed in Chapter 2) are ways in which control is exercised: standards, monitoring, supervision etc.

(e)   **Organisational structures** are formal authority/communication channels, departments, teams and so on.

(f)   **Power structures** refer to how power is distributed, and who the influential individuals and groups are.

(g)   **Symbols** include formal logos and corporate identity, as well as things which take on symbolic value to people.

2.5 What shapes organisation culture?

Influences on organisational culture include:

(a)   The organisation's **founder**. A strong set of values and assumptions is set up by the organisation's founder, and even after he or she has retired, these values have their own momentum. Or, to put it another way, an organisation might find it hard to shake off its original culture.

(b)   The organisation's **history**.

    (i)   Culture reflects the era when the organisation was founded.

    (ii)   The effect of history can be determined by stories, rituals and symbolic behaviour. They legitimise behaviour and promote priorities.

(c)   **Leadership and management style**. An organisation with a strong culture recruits and develops managers who naturally conform to it, who perpetuate the culture.

(d)   The **organisation's environment**. As we have seen, nations, regions, occupations and business types have their own distinctive cultures, and these will affect the organisation's style.

2.6 Using and managing organisation culture

2.6.1 Culture and excellence

In 1982, *Tom Peters and Robert Waterman* published *In Search of Excellence.* Using an anecdotal approach, they set about describing and analysing what it was that made successful companies successful.

Excellent companies, according to Peters and Waterman, are good at two things:

(a) Producing commercially viable **new products**
(b) Responding to **changes in their environment**

Their 'excellence' cultural model defined eight characteristics:

(a) **P**roductivity though people. Investment in HR was high.

(b) **A**utonomy and entrepreneurship. Organisations were arranged in small, decentralised units.

(c) **S**tick to the knitting. Competences were built upon.

(d) **S**imple structure within few layers of management,

(e) **C**lose to customers who were listened to.

(f) **A**ction based. They would innovate rather than follow.

(g) **S**imultaneous loose-tight properties so autonomy existed with centralisation.

(h) **H**ands-on and value driven whereby management regularly met workers in the workplace.

These can be remembered by the **PASSCASH** mnemonic.

2.6.2 Cultural strength

Both *Peters and Waterman* and *Deal and Kennedy* argued that **cultural strength** is a powerful factor in shaping the behaviour and success of organisations. A 'strong' culture is one in which:

(a) Key values are widely shared and intensely held by employees.
(b) Employees allow themselves to be guided and motivated by these values.

Strong culture is said to improve overall business performance by:

(a) Replacing restrictive formal control systems. A few strong guiding values focuses attention of strategic goals, empowering employees to take initiative and responsibility in pursuit of those aims. This is turn reduces rigidity, supports change and develops people.

(b) Increasing employee commitment, loyalty and job satisfaction.

You should be aware that while this is an attractive and influential idea, empirical research has failed to show that strong-culture organisations are in fact any more successful in the long run than weak-culture organisations – or that culture is the determining factor in success (compared to other organisational, market or environmental factors).

2.7 Changing corporate culture

So how can an organisation manage its culture, create a positive culture, or change a dysfunctional culture (or one that is unsuited to changing requirements)?

Models such as 7S and the cultural web suggests that any (ideally, all) elements of organisation can be manipulated to support cultural change. The key areas of leverage, however, are:

(a) **Changing the paradigm**: changing underlying values and beliefs, through communication, education and involvement; spreading new values and beliefs and encouraging ownership (through the use of incentives, co-opting people to teach others and so on).

(b)   **Top-down support**: consistent, genuine expression, modelling and rewarding of new values and behaviour by senior management, leaders and influencers.

(c)   **Reinforcement**: by human resource management systems: including new values/behaviours in selection criteria, appraisal/reward criteria, learning/developing planning etc.

Section summary

Organisation culture is **'the way we do things round here'**.

Cultural values can be used to guide organisational processes without the need for tight control. They can also be used to motivate employees, by emphasising the heroic dimension of the task. Culture can also be used to drive change, although – since values are difficult to change - it can also be a powerful force for preserving the *status quo*.

---

3   Culture and structure

Introduction

In this section we look at the idea that culture can shape the structure of an organisation. The simplest example of this is the power culture (what *Handy* calls Zeus) where a strong individual dominates the culture of the organisation as founder. The organisation remains small and informal. There are three other cultural types of organisation described by *Harrison* and later *Handy*.

Remember these are only indications of cultural types matching organisation structures and may indeed only apply in parts of an organisation.

Writing in 1972, *Harrison* suggested that organisations could be classified into four types. His work was later popularised by *Charles Handy* in his book *'Gods of Management'*. The four types are differentiated by their structures, processes and management methods. The differences are so significant as to create **distinctive cultures**, to each of which Handy gives the name of a Greek God.

Zeus Power culture	**Apollo** Role culture
The organisation is controlled by a key central figure, owner or founder. Power is direct, personal, informal. Suits small organisations where people get on well.	Classical, rational organisation: bureaucracy. Stable, slow-changing, formalised, impersonal. Authority based on position and function.
Athena Task culture	**Dionysus** Person culture
Management is directed at outputs: problems solved, projects completed. Team-based, horizontally-structured, flexible, valuing expertise – to get the job done.	The purpose of the organisation is to serve the interests of the individuals who make it up: management is directed at facilitating, administering.

3.1 Power culture

Zeus is the god representing the **power culture** or **club culture**. Zeus is a dynamic entrepreneur who rules with snap decisions. Power and influence stem from a central source, perhaps the owner-directors or the founder of the business. The degree of formalisation is limited, and there are few rules and procedures. Such a firm is likely to be organised on a functional basis.

(a)   The organisation is capable of adapting quickly to meet change.

(b)   Personal influence decreases as the size of an organisation gets bigger. The power culture is therefore best suited to smaller entrepreneurial organisations, where the leaders have direct communication with all employees.

(c)   Personnel have to get on well with each other for this culture to work. These organisations are clubs of 'like-minded people introduced by the like-minded people, working on empathetic initiative with personal contact rather than formal liaison.'

3.2 Role culture

Apollo is the god of the **role culture** or **bureaucracy**. There is a presumption of logic and rationality.

(a)   These organisations have a formal structure, and operate by well-established rules and procedures.

(b)   Individuals are required to perform their job to the full, but not to overstep the boundaries of their authority. Individuals who work for such organisations tend to learn an expertise without experiencing risk; many do their job adequately, but are not over-ambitious.

(c)   The bureaucratic style, as we have seen, can be very efficient in a stable environment, when the organisation is large and when the work is predictable.

3.3 Task culture

Athena is the goddess of the **task culture**. Management is seen as completing a succession of projects or solving problems.

(a)   The task culture is reflected in **project teams** and task forces. In such organisations, there is no dominant or clear leader. The principal concern in a task culture is to get the job done. Therefore the individuals who are important are the **experts** with the ability to accomplish a particular aspect of the task.

(b)   Performance is judged by results.

(c)   Task cultures are expensive, as experts demand a market price.

(d)   Task cultures also depend on variety, and to tap creativity requires a tolerance of perhaps costly mistakes.

3.4 Person culture

Dionysus is the god of the **existential** or **person culture**. In the three other cultures, the individual is subordinate to the organisation or task. An existential culture is found in an organisation whose purpose is to serve the interests of the individuals within it. These organisations are rare, although an example might be a partnership of a few individuals who do all the work of the organisation themselves (with perhaps a little secretarial or clerical assistance): for example, barristers (in the UK) work through chambers.

Management positions in these organisations are often lower in status than the professionals and are labelled secretaries, administrators, bursars, registrars or clerks.

The organisation depends on the talent of the individuals; management is derived from the consent of the managed, rather than the delegated authority of the owners.

3.5 A contingency approach

When thinking about these four types of culture, remember that they do not necessarily equate to specific organisation types, though some styles of organisation culture may accompany particular organisation structures. Also, it is quite possible for different cultures to prevail in different parts of the same organisation, especially large ones with many departments and sites. In other words, as the contingency approach says: 'it all depends'.

CASE STUDY

Handy cites a pharmaceutical company which at one time had all its manufacturing subcontracted, until the turnover and cost considerations justified a factory of its own. The company hired nine talented individuals to design and run the factory. Result:

(a)   The *design team* ran on a task culture, with a democratic/consultative leadership style, using project teams for certain problems. This was successful while the factory was being built.

(b)   After its opening, the *factory*, staffed by 400, was run on similar lines. There were numerous problems. Every problem was treated as a project, and the workforce resented being asked to help sort out 'management' problems. In the end, the factory was run in a slightly more autocratic way. Handy states that this is a classic case of a task culture (to set something up) being superseded by a role culture (to run it). Different cultures suit different businesses.

Handy also matched appropriate cultural models to *Robert Anthony's* classification of managerial activity.

(a)   **Strategic management** (carried out by senior management) is concerned with direction-setting, policy making and crisis handling. It therefore suits a **power culture**.

(b)   **Tactical management** (carried out by middle management) is concerned with establishing means to the corporate ends, mobilising resources and innovating (finding new ways of achieving goals). It therefore suits a **task culture**.

(c)   **Operational management** (carried out by supervisors and operatives) is concerned with routine activities to carry out tactical plans. It therefore suits a **role culture**.

Question 5.2   Classifications of culture

Learning outcome C1b

Review the following statements. Ascribe each of them to one of Harrison/Handy's four corporate cultures.

People are controlled and influenced by:

(a)   The personal exercise of rewards, punishments or charisma

(b)   Impersonal exercise of economic and political power to enforce procedures and standards of performance

(c)   Communication and discussion of task requirements leading to appropriate action motivated by personal commitment to goal achievement

(d)   Intrinsic interest and enjoyment in the activities to be done, and/or concern and caring for the needs of the other people involved

---

Section summary

Harrison classified four types of culture, to which Handy gave the names of Greek deities.

*   **Power** culture (Zeus) is shaped by one individual
*   **Role** culture (Apollo) is a bureaucratic culture shaped by rationality, rules and procedures
*   **Task** culture (Athena) is shaped by a focus on outputs and results
*   **Existential** or person culture (Dionysus) is shaped by the interests of individuals.

4 Culture and strategy

Introduction

If culture is the way things are done, perhaps it is not surprising that it can be aligned with the strategy an organisation adopts. *Miles and Snow* describe four types of culture in an organisation and how these exhibit certain strategies. *Denison* takes a different approach by classifying organisations according to internal/external strategic orientation and environmental stability/dynamism. He uses this classification to describe organisations as one of four cultural types.

Finally, *Deal and Kennedy* describe four cultures that arise out of a combination of risk-taking and speed of feedback.

Use these models if you want to illustrate how strategy may be linked to the individual organisation and its culture. We discuss strategy in more detail in later chapters.

4.1 Miles and Snow

Miles and Snow characterised four cultural types, and the kinds of strategies they are likely to expose.

(a) **Defenders** like low risks, secure niche markets, and tried and trusted solutions. These companies have cultures whose stories and rituals reflect historical continuity and consensus. Decision-taking is relatively formalised. (There is a stress on 'doing things right' ie efficiency.) Personnel are drawn from within the industry.

(b) **Prospectors** are organisations where the dominant beliefs are more to do with results (doing the right things ie effectiveness). They seek to expand and increase market presence, and move into new areas.

(c) **Analysers** try to balance risk and profits. They use a core of stable products and markets as a source of earnings, like defenders, but move into areas that prospectors have already opened up. Analysers follow change, but do not initiate it.

(d) **Reactors** do not have viable strategies, other than living from hand to mouth: they simply respond to external demands and changes.

CASE STUDY

Miles and Snow's analysis was applied to the responses by the **regional electricity companies (RECs)** to takeover bids in the Autumn of 1995. (The RECs are responsible for supplying and distributing electricity.)

At privatisation they 'shared a common heritage and hence ... greater similarities than would be found in more well-established private sector market places'.

(a) The largest REC, Eastern Group, 'embraced' the possibility of an alliance with Hanson. Eastern exhibits the characteristics of a 'prospector'. Its chief executive is 'non-REC' 'with a North American corporate pedigree and a greater interest in activities outside the traditional REC field'.

(b) Norweb and Midlands were 'cautious prospectors' which allow significant degrees of decentralisation, and a 'willingness to bring in executives with experience external to the industry'. They countenance 'strategic alliances'.

(c) Many of the RECs 'have demonstrated classical defender strategies'. They have specific features.

   (i)   Hierarchical company structures

   (ii)   Board membership drawn from within the industry

   (iii) Incremental growth, rather than more rapid growth by entering new business areas; little enthusiasm for diversification

4.2 Denison

Denison's model uses a grid to assess the relationship of culture, strategy and the environment. There are two dimensions.

(a)   How orientated is the firm to the environment rather than to its internal workings? (An internal orientation is not always a bad thing, eg maintaining the safety of a nuclear installation.)

(b)   To what extent does the environment offer stability or change?

		Organisation's strategic orientation	
		Internal	*External*
Environmental responses required	*Stability*	Consistency	Mission
	Change/flexibility	Involvement	Adaptability

In Denison's analysis there are thus four possible cultures.

(a)   **Consistency culture.** This exists in a stable environment, and its structure is well integrated. Management are preoccupied with efficiency. Such cultures are characterised by formal ways of behaviour. Predictability and reliability are valued. This has some features in common with the Apollonian culture.

(b)   **Mission culture.** The environment is relatively stable, and the organisation is orientated towards it (eg 'customers'). A mission culture, whereby members' work activities are given meaning and value, is appropriate. For example, hospitals are preoccupied with the sick: inevitably their values are 'customer' orientated. A church is concerned with saving souls.

(c)   **Involvement culture.** The basic premise is that the satisfaction of employees' needs is necessary for them to provide optimum performance. An example might be an orchestra, whose performance depends on each individual. Involvement and participation are supposed to create a greater sense of commitment and hence performance. For example, if you train people well enough, it is assumed that they will perform well. An involvement culture might take a 'human relations' approach to management.

(d)   **Adaptability culture.** The company's strategic focus is on the external environment, which is in a state of change. Corporate values encourage inquisitiveness and interest in the external environment. Fashion companies are an example: ideas come from a variety of sources. Customer needs are fickle and change rapidly.

Question 5.3	Contrasting cultural models

Learning outcome C1b

(a)   What do you think is the most significant contrast between Denison's model and Harrison's model?

(b)   Which is better?

4.3 Deal and Kennedy

Deal and Kennedy (*Corporate Cultures*) consider cultures to be a function of the willingness of employees to take **risks**, and how quickly they get **feedback** on whether they got it right or wrong.

High risk

BET YOUR COMPANY CULTURE ('Slow and steady wins the race') Long decision-cycles: stamina and nerve required eg oil companies, aircraft companies, architects	**HARD 'MACHO' CULTURE** ('Find a mountain and climb it') eg entertainment, management consultancy, advertising
PROCESS CULTURE ('It's not what you do, it's the way that you do it') Values centred on attention to excellence of technical detail, risk management, procedures, status symbols eg banks, financial services, government	**WORK HARD/PLAY HARD CULTURE** ('Find a need and fill it') All action - and fun: team spirit eg sales and retail, computer companies.

Slow feedback (left side)   *Fast feedback* (right side)

Low risk

Deal and Kennedy suggest that some companies blend elements of all four cultural types and that this can enable them to respond well to environmental change. The stronger the culture, the more successful the company is likely to be, as discussed earlier.

Section summary

A model of culture which focuses specifically on a firm's approach to strategy was suggested by **Miles and Snow**, who outlined three strategic cultures, and a fourth 'non-strategic' culture.

Denison analysis cultural types on two axes: internal/external strategic orientation and environmental stability/dynamism.

Deal and Kennedy plot cultural types on two dimensions: willingness to take risks and speed of feedback on results.

5 Cross-cultural leadership

Introduction

Different countries have different ways of doing business, and different cultural values and assumptions which influence business and management styles.

Ouchi studied US and Japanese companies and concluded that there was a 'third way' of management that combined the best of both cultures. He named this Theory Z.

Hofstede researched offices in a large multinational organisation in over 60 countries. From this he identified four characteristics that differed according to the country and which affected the culture of the organisation in that country.

5.1 Ouchi: Theory Z

When the Japanese economy was performing well, a generation ago, it became fashionable to study Japanese management methods and promote them as a solution to the West's then seemingly intractable industrial problems. Profiling American management culture as 'Theory A' and typical Japanese management as 'Theory J', *William Ouchi* sought to synthesise the two, to propose a form of Japanese-style management that could be successfully applied in Western contexts. Ouchi called these methods 'Theory Z'.

The characteristics of a **Theory Z** organisation offer some interesting contrasts with the Western way of doing things, notably in key Japanese values such as consensus decision-making and mutual loyalty in the employment relationship.

Ouchi described the Theory Z organisation as being characterised by:

(a)   **Long-term employment, with slow-progressing managerial career paths** (as in the Japanese system, but with a more Western specialisation of skills).

(b)   **Broad concern for employee welfare**, both inside and outside the work context (not just work performance, as in the Western system): commitment to the 'organisation family'.

(c)   **Implicit informal controls** (such as guiding values) alongside explicit, formal measures.

(d)   **Collective consensus decision-making processes** (Japanese), but with individual retention of ultimate responsibility for defined areas of accountability (Western).

(e)   **Industrial relations characterised by trust, co-operation and mutual adjustment**, rather than unionisation, demarcation and artificial status barriers.

Theory Z was welcomed as a more human and therefore more effective way of managing employee relations: Marks and Spencer in the UK has been cited as an organisation operating on principles akin to Theory Z. Elements of the approach have been incorporated into the 'Human Resource Management' (HRM) orientation to management, which regards committed people as the key resource of a business. However, it is less easy to transfer cultural values to foreign contexts than it is to apply methods and techniques: employee development programmes and quality circles have been adopted without necessarily being underpinned by Theory Z values.

5.2 The Hofstede model

Hofstede (1984) carried out cross-cultural research at 66 national offices of IBM and formulated one of the most influential models of work-related cultural differences.

The Hofstede model describes four main dimensions of difference between national cultures, which impact on all aspects of management and organisational behaviour: motivation, team working, leadership style, conflict management and HR policies.

(a)   **Power distance**: the extent to which unequal distribution of power is accepted.

  (i)   *High* **PD cultures** (as in Latin, near Eastern and less developed Asian countries) accept greater centralisation, a top-down chain of command and closer supervision. Subordinates have little expectation of influencing decisions.

  (ii)   *Low* **PD cultures** (as in Germanic, Anglo and Nordic countries) expect less centralisation and flatter organisational structures. Subordinates expect involvement and participation in decision-making. (Japan is a medium PD culture.)

(b)   **Uncertainty avoidance**: the extent to which security, order and control are preferred to ambiguity, uncertainty and change.

  (i)   *High* **UA cultures** (as in Latin, near Eastern and Germanic countries and Japan) respect control, certainty and ritual. They value task structure, written rules and regulations, specialists and experts, and standardisation. There is a strong need for consensus: deviance and dissent are not tolerated. The work ethic is strong.

  (ii)   *Low* **UA cultures** (as in Anglo and Nordic countries) respect flexibility and creativity. They have less task structure and written rules; more generalists and greater variability. There is more tolerance of risk, dissent, conflict and deviation from norms.

(c)   **Individualism**: the extent to which people prefer to live and work in individualist (focusing on the 'I' identity) or collectivist (focusing on the 'we' identity) ways.

     (i)   *High* **Individualism cultures** (as in Anglo, more developed Latin and Nordic countries) emphasise autonomy and individual choice and responsibility. They prize individual initiative. The organisation is impersonal and tends to defend business interests: task achievement is more important than relationships. Management is seen in an individual context.

     (ii)   *Low* **Individualism (or Collectivist) cultures** (as in less developed Latin, near Eastern and less developed Asian countries) emphasise interdependence, reciprocal obligation and social acceptability. The organisation is seen as a 'family' and tends to defend employees' interests: relationships are more important than task achievement. Management is seen in a team context. (Japan and Germany are 'medium' cultures on this dimension.)

(d)   **Masculinity**: the extent to which social gender roles are distinct. (Note that this is different from the usual sense in which the terms 'masculine' and 'feminine' are used.)

     (i)   *High* **Masculinity cultures** (as in Japan and Germanic and Anglo countries) clearly differentiate gender roles. Masculine values of assertiveness, competition, decisiveness and material success are dominant. Feminine values of modesty, tenderness, consensus, focus on relationships and quality of working life are less highly regarded, and confined to women.

     (ii)   *Low* **Masculinity (or Feminine) cultures** (as in Nordic countries) minimise gender roles. Feminine values are dominant – and both men and women are allowed to behave accordingly.

Question 5.4   National culture and management style

Learning outcome C1b

According to the Hofstede model, what issues might arise in the following cases?

(a)   The newly-appointed Spanish (more developed Latin) R & D manager of a UK (Anglo) firm asks to see the Rules and Procedures Manual for the department.

(b)   A US-trained (Anglo) manager attempts to implement a system of Management by Objectives in Thailand (less developed Asian).

(c)   A Dutch (Nordic) HR manager of a US (Anglo) subsidiary in the Netherlands is instructed to implement downsizing measures.

Exam alert

In the previous syllabus the model was tested by asking for a discussion of how Hofstede's research could be used to assess the compatibility of a corporation's intended *strategy* with the culture of a country in which it wanted to start to do business. It could equally well be used, as in our example, to analyse how a *project manager's* style would work with a cross-culture team. When revising, don't forget to test-run major concepts against: (a) general people management; (b) project management and (c) strategic management – to get into the 'integration' habit!

KEY POINT

Apart from these models, a manager operating in a cross-cultural or international environment will need to be **sensitive** to potential cultural assumptions and differences, and **flexible** in adapting to their demands. This will particularly be the case when working in *virtual teams* (geographically dispensed but collaborating using information and communications technology links). Project teams may now be global – and team leaders may have to deal with:

(a)   Differences in cultural values (eg about seniority or the role of women)

(b)   Differences in social and business customs (eg business gifts, religious observances)

(c)   Differences in communication, negotiating and conflict resolution styles (eg different tolerance for challenging authority or displays of emotion)

(d)   Language barriers

(e)   Difference in education/qualifications

(f)   Different time zones for communicating with team members.

CASE STUDY

'French managers see their work as an intellectual challenge, requiring the remorseless application of individual brainpower. They do not share the Anglo-Saxon view of management as an interpersonally demanding exercise, where plans have to be constantly "sold" upward and downward using personal skills.

'Selection interviewers need to allow for cultural influences on interviewees' behaviour. For instance, Chinese applicants in Singapore tend to defer to the interviewer, whom they treat as "superior", and to focus on the group or family, besides avoiding self-assertion... Hence, applicants from a Chinese background may be disadvantaged when being interviewed for jobs with multi-national companies that are heavily influenced by Anglo-American culture.' (*Guirdham*)

Section summary

National culture (and other factors in the international environment) poses a challenge for managers working in **cross-cultural and international contexts**.

Ouchi combined the American and Japanese ways of management in an ideal 'Theory Z' approach.

National culture influences organisation culture in various ways. One model of these effects is the 'Hofstede model' which describes four dimensions on which cultures differ:

*   Power distance
*   Uncertainty avoidance
*   Individuality/collectivity
*   Masculinity/femininity

Chapter Roundup

✓   **Culture** is 'the collective programming of the mind which distinguishes the members of one category of people from another' (Hofstede). It may be identified as ways of behaving, and ways of understanding, that are shared by a group of people.

Elements of culture include:

- Observable behaviour, artefacts, rituals and symbols
- Underlying values and beliefs which give meaning to the observable elements
- Hidden assumptions which unconsciously shape values and beliefs

✓   Organisation culture is **'the way we do things round here'**.

Cultural values can be used to guide organisational processes without the need for tight control. They can also be used to motivate employees, by emphasising the heroic dimension of the task. Culture can also be used to drive change, although – since values are difficult to change - it can also be a powerful force for preserving the status quo.

✓   Harrison classified four types of culture, to which Handy gave the names of Greek deities.

- **Power** culture (Zeus) is shaped by one individual
- **Role** culture (Apollo) is a bureaucratic culture shaped by rationality, rules and procedures
- **Task** culture (Athena) is shaped by a focus on outputs and results
- **Existential** or person culture (Dionysus) is shaped by the interests of individuals.

✓   A model of culture which focuses specifically on a firm's approach to strategy was suggested by **Miles and Snow**, who outlined three strategic cultures, and a fourth 'non-strategic' culture.

Denison analysis cultural types on two axes: internal/external strategic orientation and environmental stability/dynamism.

Deal and Kennedy plot cultural types on two dimensions: willingness to take risks and speed of feedback on results.

✓   National culture (and other factors in the international environment) poses a challenge for managers working in **cross-cultural and international contexts**.

Ouchi combined the American and Japanese ways of management in an ideal 'Theory Z' approach.

National culture influences organisation culture in various ways. One model of these effects is the 'Hofstede model' which describes four dimensions on which cultures differ:

- Power distance
- Uncertainty avoidance
- Individuality/collectivity
- Masculinity/femininity

Quick Quiz

1   What are the elements of culture, according to Trompenaars?

2   In the McKinsey 7S model, the three 'hard' elements are:

    A   Strategy, skills, systems
    B   Structure, skills, systems
    C   Strategy, skills, staff
    D   Strategy, systems, structure

3   'Bureaucracy' is another name for a:

    A   Power culture
    B   Role culture
    C   Task culture
    D   Existential culture

4   A project team is most likely to be a role culture. *True or false?*

5   Identify the seven elements of the cultural web.

6   Whose cultural analysis identified defenders, prospectors, analysers and reactors?

    A   Miles and Snow
    B   Deal and Kennedy
    C   Denison
    D   Handy

Answers to Quick Quiz

1   Observable phenomena (behaviour, artefacts, rituals), values and beliefs, assumptions.

2   The answer is D.

3   B

4   False: it is most likely to be a task culture.

5   Paradigm, symbols, stories, rituals and routines, control systems, organisation structures, power structures.

6   The answer is A.

Answers to questions

5.1 Manifestations of culture

Here are some hints. The Army is very disciplined. Decisions are made by officers; behaviour between ranks is sometimes very formal. The organisation values loyalty, courage and discipline and team work. Symbols and artefacts include uniforms, medals, regimental badges and so on. Rituals include corporate expressions such as parades and ceremonies.

An advertising agency, with a different mission, is more fluid. Individual flair and creativity, within the commercial needs of the firm, is expected. Artefacts may include the style of creative offices, awards or prizes, and the agency logo. Rituals may include various award ceremonies, team meetings and social gatherings.

5.2 Classifications of culture

(a) Zeus/power culture
(b) Apollo/role culture
(c) Athena/task culture
(d) Dionysus/person culture

5.3 Contrasting cultural models

(a) Harrison's model places much more emphasis on organisation structure and systems, which both determine and are determined by culture. Harrison's model describes actual cultures. Denison's model describes *ideal* cultures, and is more concerned with the environment and a firm's external orientation than its structure. Denison suggests that if the environment is stable *and* the business is most effective with an internal orientation, *then* a consistency culture will be *best* and so on.

(b) It depends on what you wish to use each model for.

5.4 National culture and management style

(a) A high-UA manager, expecting to find detailed and generally adhered-to rules for everything, may be horrified by the ad-hocracy of a low-UA organisation: if (s)he attempts to impose a high-UA culture, there may be resistance from employees and management.

(b) A high-individuality manager may implement MbO on the basis of individual performance targets, results and rewards: this may fail to motivate collectivist workers, for whom group processes and performance is more important.

(c) A low-masculinity manager may try to shelter the workforce from the effects of downsizing, taking time for consultation, retraining, voluntary measures and so on: this may seem unacceptably 'soft' to a high-masculinity parent firm.

Now try the question below from the Exam Question Bank

Number	Level	Marks	Time
Q5	Examination	10	18 mins

PROJECT MANAGEMENT

Part B

PROJECT MANAGEMENT

This chapter will introduce the subject of project management, explain what project management is and outline what a **project manager** does.

We outline the widely-used **PRINCE2** methodology for project management. We will look in more detail at specific tools and techniques for planning and controlling projects in later chapters.

Finally we briefly visit projects and structure in a short section which you should read as it links projects to the wider theme of organisations in this syllabus.

Remember that this paper covers **integrated management** so much of the material covered in Part A of this Study Text can be directly applied to project working. So, for example, you need to think about leadership, and conflict in the context of a *project* team. We won't be repeating ourselves here and you can simply recap earlier chapters if you need to.

In the following chapters we look at the different phases of the project life cycle, how a **project team** should be put together, and examine the **stakeholders** of a project and the relationships between them. (Our main coverage of stakeholder analysis and management is kept for later when we look at the wider context of organisational stakeholders.)

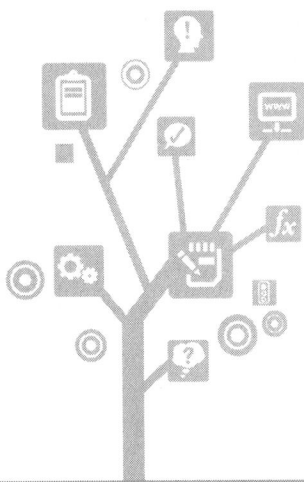

6

topic list	learning outcomes	syllabus references	ability required
1 The nature of project management	B1a,b	B1(i), (ii)	comprehension and application
2 The project manager	B1c, g	B1(i)	analysis
3 Identifying projects	B1a,2a	B1(i), (vi)	comprehension and application
4 PRINCE2	B1b,c	B1(vii),(viii)	analysis and application
5 Projects and organisational structure	B1b,g	B1(xi)	comprehension and application

1   The nature of project management

Introduction

Welcome to project management! This section outlines how projects differ from ordinary work within the organisation. Projects tend to have their own deadlines, staff (at least temporarily), and resources and are intended to be one-offs. A typical project in an organisation would be installing a new IT system. This usually involves people from many departments and has its own dedicated staff and resources running alongside the ordinary activities in the organisation.

The '7S' model is a useful framework for managing a project. This is very similar to the model explained in the earlier chapter on culture. The role of the project manager is explained in the next section so this is merely an overview.

Exam alert

The syllabus awards 40% to project management generally, so you should expect something in the exam testing projects. In the predecessor syllabus, projects were tested in every exam usually in a longer 25-mark question. Much of the material covered is equally relevant to other aspects of management (and is covered elsewhere in this Study Text) but you can expect plenty of questions that are connected in some way to project management.

For example, in the previous syllabus November 2007 exam, the role of the project manager was examined as well as the purposes and types of controls needed in a project. This question was well answered although weaker candidates referred to skills and problems rather than addressing responsibilities. Very few candidates were able to explain the project controls relating to each stage and also referred to tools but didn't put these into the **control** context.

1.1 What is a project?

To understand project management it is necessary to first define what a project is.

KEY TERMS

A PROJECT is 'an undertaking that has a beginning and an end and is carried out to meet established goals within cost, schedule and quality objectives'. (Haynes, *Project Management*)

RESOURCES are the money, facilities, supplies, services and people allocated to the project.

1.1.1 How does project working differ from 'business as usual'?

In general, the work which organisations undertake involves either **operations** or **projects**. Operations and projects are planned, controlled and executed. So how are projects distinguished from 'ordinary work'?

Projects	Operations ('business as usual')
Have a defined beginning and end	On-going
Have resources allocated specifically to them, although often on a shared basis	Resources used 'full-time'
Are often unique or intended to be done only once	Many recurring tasks
Follow a plan towards a clear intended end-result	Goals and deadlines are more general
Often cut across organisational and functional lines	Usually follows the organisation or functional structure

An activity that meets the first four criteria above can be classified as a project, and therefore falls within the scope of project management. Whether an activity is classified as a project is important, as projects should be managed using **project management techniques**.

Common examples of projects include:

(a)   Producing a new product, service or object
(b)   Changing the structure of an organisation
(c)   Developing or modifying a new information system
(d)   Implementing a new business procedure or process

Maylor has described a project in **systems** terms as a process of conversion. This provides a useful overview of the concept.

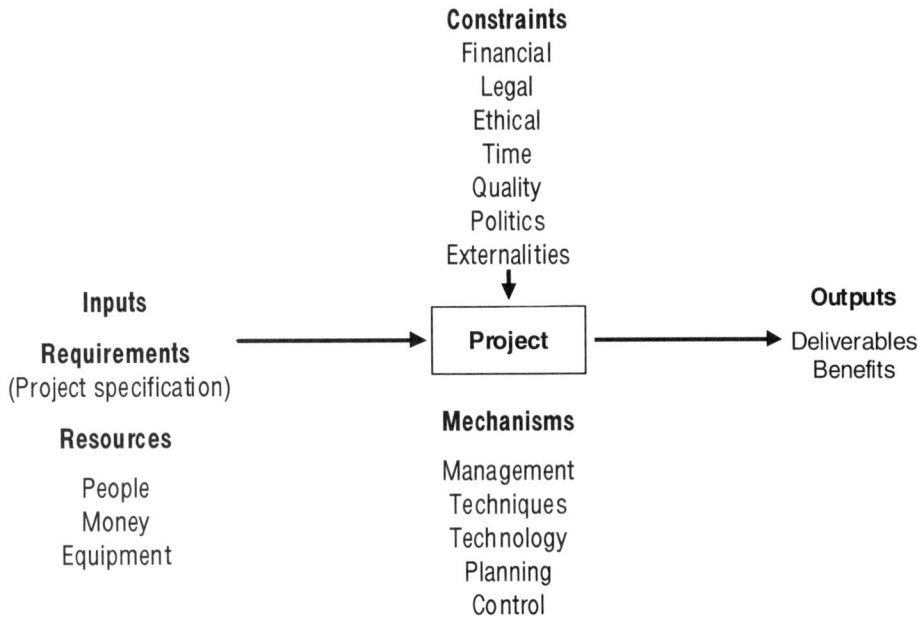

1.2 A framework for project management: the 7S model

Project management differs in scope from on-going operational management and employs its own specialised and distinctive techniques. However, it is embedded in the wider management environment and depends for its success on a range of considerations that will be familiar to you in general terms. These considerations are referred to by *Maylor* as **7S**, an adapted version of the *McKinsey* 7S model covered earlier.

- Staff
- Skills
- Style
- Structure

- Stakeholders (in McKinsey: Shared Values)
- Strategy
- Systems

> **KEY POINT**
>
> Be careful to distinguish between the McKinsey 7S model and the Maylor model. The McKinsey model is applied to strategic management: Maylor's model is adapted specifically for project management setting. Useful warning of the need to learn terms and models – and to read exam questions – carefully.

1.2.1 Staff and stakeholders

The most important member of the project staff is the **project manager**, whose skills are crucial. Then there are the members of the project team, both permanent allocated staff and those who have a temporary or part-time commitment alongside other responsibilities.

Stakeholders are people who have an interest in or are affected by the operation of the project or its outcomes. Their attitudes, perceptions and influence will vary and they must all be properly identified and dealt with if the project is to be a success.

We consider staff and stakeholders in more detail in a later chapter.

1.2.2 Structure

Several aspects of structure are important in project management.

(a)   The **structure of the project** itself must be considered. This is basically a matter of the **project lifecycle**, discussed later, but other structural matters may arise, as when, for instance a project involves new development work and the systems development lifecycle may be relevant.

(b)   **Project planning** is to some extent a structure matter, as is the control of progress, approval and hand over.

(c)   Structure as a concept is also relevant to the **building of project teams** and their internal and external relationships.

(d)   **Processes**, both within the project and outside it are an important aspect of structure. Project management often demands a kind of **matrix structure**, which can be particularly challenging in larger, traditionally operated organisations.

(e)   The degree of structure present in the project and its environment have an influence on **risk**.

(f)   The higher management structure of the project is important. It will be usual for the project manager to report to some higher authority, such as a project committee or board that is set up to represent the interests of the major stakeholders. The **PRINCE2** project management system, dealt with later, incorporates such a management structure.

1.2.3 Systems

The project may be regarded as a system in itself, with its own inputs and outputs or, probably more usefully, as a subsystem of the overall system that is the organisation. The importance of an awareness of this idea is that it implies the inevitability of interaction between the project and other organisational subsystems. These interactions are obviously of great importance and have the potential to cause project failure.

The **project control system** is also an important consideration. We discussed control systems in Chapter 2 of this Study Text and you should refer back to that chapter if you need to revise the basics of this topic. Specific project planning and control techniques are dealt with in the next chapter.

1.2.4 Strategy

CIMA's definition of strategy is: 'a course of action, including the specification of resources required, to achieve a specific objective'. This definition is equally applicable to a project strategy.

Just as the project system must mesh with the wider organisational system, so the strategy employed to bring the project to a successful conclusion must mesh with and support the organisation's overall strategic assumptions and practices. In particular, the object of the project must support the organisation's strategy.

1.2.5 Style

Here, as in the McKinsey 7S model, **style** effectively means culture, discussed in an earlier chapter this Study Text. Culture is an important area of potential distinction between project operations and continuing operations and, likewise, a potential source of conflict.

1.2.6 Skills

Specific project management **skills** are dealt with in later chapters. Remember, however, that **people management** skills are equally important; they must be appropriate to the project environment.

Question 6.1   7S

Learning outcome B1a,b

Which of the following is not made up entirely of elements of the project 7S model?

A   Staff, style, skills, strategy
B   Systems, stakeholders, structure, style
C   Skills, style, strategy, shared values
D   Structure, stakeholders, style, staff

1.3 What is project management?

KEY TERM

PROJECT MANAGEMENT: Integration of all aspects of a project, ensuring that the proper knowledge and resources are available when and where needed, and above all to ensure that the expected outcome is produced in a timely, cost-effective manner. The primary function of a project manager is to manage the trade-offs between performance, timeliness and cost.   *(CIMA Official Terminology)*

The objective of project management is a successful project. A project will be deemed successful if it is completed at the **specified level of quality, on time** and **within budget**. We revisit these project objectives in Chapter 9 when we look at how these are balanced as competing objectives. This is known as the Time/Cost/Quality or Iron Triangle.

Constraint	Comment
Quality	The end result should conform to the project specification. In other words, the result should achieve what the project was supposed to do.
Budget	The project should be completed without exceeding authorised expenditure.
Timescale	The progress of the project must follow the planned process, so that the 'result' is ready for use at the agreed date. As time is money, proper time management can help contain costs.

Quality, cost and **time** are normally regarded as the yardsticks against which project success is measured. It is possible to add a fourth constraint: **scope** or **functionality**. This means that all the work that was specified has been done and all the deliverables have, in fact, been delivered. Under this analysis, the quality constraint is restricted to a slightly narrower meaning and the difference between scope and quality becomes the difference between doing a job and doing it well – or badly.

1.3.1 Management challenges of project working

Projects present some management challenges.

Challenge	Comment
Teambuilding	The work is carried out by a team of people often from varied work and social backgrounds. The team must 'gel' quickly and be able to communicate effectively with each other.
Expected problems	Expected problems should be avoided by careful design and planning prior to commencement of work.

Challenge	Comment
Unexpected problems	There should be mechanisms within the project to enable these problems to be resolved quickly and efficiently.
Delayed benefit	There is normally no benefit until the work is finished. The 'lead in' time to this can cause a strain on the eventual recipient who is also faced with increasing expenditure for no immediate benefit.
Specialists	Contributions made by specialists are of differing importance at each stage.
Potential for conflict	Projects often involve several parties with different interests. This may lead to conflict.

Project management ensures responsibilities are clearly defined and that resources are **focussed** on specific objectives. The **project management process** also provides a structure for communicating within and across organisational boundaries.

All projects share similar features and follow a similar process. This has led to the development of **project management tools and techniques** that can be applied to all projects, no matter how diverse. For example, with some limitations similar processes and techniques can be applied whether building a major structure (eg The Millennium Dome) or implementing a company-wide computer network.

All projects require a person who is ultimately responsible for delivering the required outcome. This person (whether officially given the title or not) is the **project manager**.

1.3.2 Why do projects go wrong?

Many projects go wrong: this is usually manifested as a **failure to complete on time**, but this outcome can arise for a variety of reasons.

(a)   **Unproven technology**

Then use of **new technological developments** is likely to be a feature of any project. The range of such developments extends from fairly routine and non-critical improvements, through major innovations capable of transforming working practices, costs and time scales, to revolutionary techniques that make feasible projects that were previously quite impracticable. As the practical potential of a technical change moves from minor to major, so too moves its potential to cause disruption if something goes wrong with it. A classic example is *Rolls Royce's* attempt to use carbon fibre in the design of the *RB211* engine in the early 1970s. Not only did the project fail to meet its objectives, its failure led to the company's financial failure, which necessitated its rescue by government.

(b)   **Changing client specifications**

It is not unusual for clients' notions of what they want to evolve during the lifetime of the project. However, if the work is to come in on time and on budget, they must be aware of what is **technically feasible**, reasonable in their **aspirations**, prompt with their **decisions** and, ultimately, prepared to **freeze the specification** so that it can be delivered. The failure of the *TSR2* aircraft project forty years ago was in large part caused by major, unrealistic changes to specification.

Note that the term 'client' includes *internal* specifiers.

(c)   **Politics**

This problem area includes politics of all kinds, from those internal to an organisation managing its own projects, to the effect of national (and even international) politics on major undertakings. **Lack of senior management support** is an important political problem. This may be partly caused by:

(i)   Lack of processes to evaluate potential projects and define a business case for the project

(ii)   Reliance on informal measurement of project costs and benefits, rather than rigorous feasibility analysis and subsequent review and control

(d)   **Poor project management**

This comes in several guises

(i)   **Over optimism**. This can be particularly troublesome with new technology. Unrealistic deadlines may be accepted, for instance, or impossible levels of performance promised.

(ii)   **Over-promotion of technical staff**. It is common for people with a high level of technical skill to be promoted. Only then is it made clear that they lack management and leadership ability. This is a particular problem with IT projects.

(iii)   **Poor planning**. Realistic timescales must be established, use of shared resources must be planned and, most fundamental of all, jobs must be done in a sensible sequence.

(iv)   **Poor control**. Progress must be under continuous review and control action must be taken early if there are problems. The framework of control must provide for review at all levels of management and prompt reporting of problems. Communication and relationship skills must be deployed to a high standard by the project manager.

1.3.3 Project success factors

KEY POINT

An article in *Financial Management* (June 2006) helpfully summarises the factors that contribute to successful project delivery as follows.

(a)   Proper planning with regard to time, cost and resource constraints

(b)   The involvement of users (among other key stakeholders) in development and delivery processes, to ensure that their needs are met (without subsequent changes)

(c)   Competent and committed project staff, with the right skills

(d)   Ownership by senior managers on the basis of a clear business case

(e)   Careful management of constraints: control procedures for monitoring the pace, money/resource usage and conformance of the project

(f)   Risk assessment and management, allowing for risk reduction and contingency planning

(g)   Clear criteria for business case and precise measurements of performance, so that project success can be evaluated and lessons learned.

Section summary

A **project** is an undertaking that has a beginning and an end and is carried out to meet established goals within cost, schedule and quality objectives. It often has the following characteristics:

*   A defined beginning and end
*   Resources allocated specifically to it
*   Intended to be done only once (although similar separate projects could be undertaken)
*   Follows a plan towards a clear intended end-result
*   Often cuts across organisational and functional lines

Crucial aspects of the project management environment are listed in the **7S model**.

Project management is the combination of systems, techniques, and people used to control and monitor activities undertaken within the project. It will be deemed successful if it is completed at the specified level of **quality**, **on time** and within **budget**.

2 The project manager

> **Introduction**
>
> The project manager is dedicated to the running of the project so long as it is in existence. They have significant responsibilities covering task and people management. Often large projects employ professional project managers who have experience in running projects as their skills are transferrable and they do not have to be a technical specialist.
>
> The US Project Management Body of Knowledge or PMBOK is a guide to the successful management of projects in **nine key knowledge areas**.

Some project managers have the job title 'Project Manager'. These people usually have one major responsibility: the project. Most people in business will have 'normal work' responsibilities outside their project goals – which may lead to conflicting demands on their time. Anybody responsible for a project (large or small) is a project manager.

KEY TERM

The person who takes ultimate responsibility for ensuring the desired result is achieved on time and within budget is the PROJECT MANAGER.

The role a project manager performs is in many ways similar to those performed by other managers. There are however some important differences, as shown in the table below.

Project managers	Operations managers
Are often 'generalists' with wide-ranging backgrounds and experience levels	Usually specialists in the areas managed
Oversee work in many functional areas	Relate closely to technical tasks in their area
Facilitate, rather than supervise team members	Have direct technical supervision responsibilities

A person should only take on the role of project manager if they have the time available to do the job effectively. Also, if somebody is to be held responsible for the project, they must be given the resources and authority required to complete project tasks.

2.1 Duties of a project manager

The duties of a project manager are summarised below.

Duty	Comment
Outline planning	Project planning (eg targets, sequencing) <ul><li>Developing project targets such as overall costs or timescale needed (eg project should take 20 weeks).</li><li>Dividing the project into activities and placing these activities into the right sequence, often a complicated task if overlapping.</li><li>Developing a framework for procedures and structures needed to manage the project (eg decide, in principle, to have weekly team meetings, performance reviews and so on).</li></ul>
Detailed planning	Work breakdown structure, resource requirements, network analysis for scheduling.

Duty	Comment
Obtain necessary resources	Resources may already exist within the organisation or may have to be bought in. Resource requirements unforeseen at the planning stage will probably have to be authorised separately by the project board or project sponsor.
Teambuilding	Build cohesion and team spirit.
Communication	The project manager must let superiors know what is going on, and ensure that members of the project team are properly briefed.
Co-ordinating project activities	Between the project team and users, and other external parties (eg suppliers of hardware and software).
Monitoring and control	The project manager should estimate the causes for each departure from the standard, and take corrective measures.
Problem-resolution	Even with the best planning, unforeseen problems may arise.
Quality control	There is often a short-sighted trade-off between getting the project out on time and the project's quality.

Project management as a discipline developed because of a need to co-ordinate resources to obtain desired results within a set timeframe. Common project management tasks include establishing goals and objectives, developing a work-plan, scheduling, budgeting, co-ordinating a team and communicating.

The project management process helps project managers maintain control of projects and meet their responsibilities.

2.2 The responsibilities of a project manager

A project manager has responsibilities to both management and to the project team.

Responsibilities to management:

(a)   Ensure resources are used efficiently – strike a balance between cost, time and results

(b)   Keep management informed with timely and accurate communications

(c)   Manage the project to the best of his or her ability

(d)   Behave ethically, and adhere to the organisation's policies

(e)   Maintain a customer orientation (whether the project is geared towards an internal or external customer) – customer satisfaction is a key indicator of project success

Responsibilities to the project and the project team:

(a)   Take action to keep the project on target for successful completion

(b)   Ensure the project team has the resources required to perform tasks assigned

(c)   Help new team members integrate into the team

(d)   Provide any support required when members leave the team either during the project or on completion

2.3 The skills required of a project manager

To meet these responsibilities a project manager requires a wide range of skills. The skills required are similar to those required when managing a wider range of responsibilities. Some of the skills required are described in the following table.

Type of skill	How the project manager should display the type of skill
Leadership and team building	A participative style of leadership is appropriate for much of most projects, but a more autocratic, decisive style may be required on occasion
	Be **positive** (but realistic) about all aspects of the project
	Understand where the project fits into the **big picture**
	Delegate tasks appropriately – and not take on too much personally
	Build team spirit through **co-operation** and recognition of achievement
	Do not be restrained by organisational structures – a high tolerance for ambiguity (lack of clear-cut authority) will help the project manager
Organisational	Ensure all project **documentation** is clear and distributed to all who require it
	Use project **management tools** to analyse and monitor project progress
Communication and negotiation	**Listen** to project team members
	Use **persuasion** to coerce reluctant team members or stakeholders to support the project
	Negotiate on funding, timescales, staffing and other resources, quality and disputes
	Ensure management is kept **informed** and is never surprised
Technical	By providing (or at least providing access to) the **technical expertise** and experience needed to manage the project
Personal qualities	Be **flexible**. Circumstances may develop that require a change in plan
	Show **persistence**. Even successful projects will encounter difficulties that require repeated efforts to overcome
	Be **creative**. If one method of completing a task proves impractical a new approach may be required
	Patience is required even in the face of tight deadlines. The 'quick-fix' may eventually cost more time than a more thorough but initially more time-consuming solution.
Problem solving	Only the very simplest projects will be without problems. The project manager must bring a sensible approach to their solution and **delegate** as much responsibility as possible to team members so that they become used to **solving their own problems.** By the nature of a project there is always uncertainty and risk. The project manager needs to be able to react to these situations fast, and adopt an efficient problem solving attitude so as not to hold up the project at key moments.
Change control and management	Major projects may be accompanied by the kind of far-reaching **change** that has wide-ranging effects on the organisation and its people. Here, however, we are concerned with **changes to the project itself**. Changes can arise from a variety of sources (not least the intended end-users) and have the potential to disrupt the progress of the project. They must be properly authorised, planned and resourced and records kept of their source, impact and authorisation if the project is not to become unmanageable. **Change control** is one of the components of the **PRINCE2** project management system.

2.4 Leadership styles and project management

As in other forms of management, different project managers have different styles of leadership. There is no 'best' leadership style, as individuals suit and react to different styles in different ways.

The leadership style adopted will affect the way decisions relating to the project are made. Although an autocratic style may prove successful in some situations (eg 'simple' or 'repetitive' projects), a more consultative style has the advantage of making team members feel more a part of the project. This should result in greater **commitment**.

Not all decisions will be made in the same way. For example, decisions that do not have direct consequences for other project personnel may be made with no (or limited) consultation. A **balance** needs to be found between ensuring decisions can be made efficiently, and ensuring adequate consultation.

The type of people that comprise the project team will influence the style adopted. For example, professionals generally dislike being closely supervised and dictated to. Some people however, prefer to follow clear, specific instructions and not have to think for themselves.

Project management techniques encourage **management by exception** by identifying, from the outset, those activities which might threaten successful completion of a project.

2.5 The Project Management Body of Knowledge

The US Project Management Institute has published a guide to what it calls the **Project Management Body of Knowledge (PMBOK)**. This divides the process of project management into nine **key knowledge areas**.

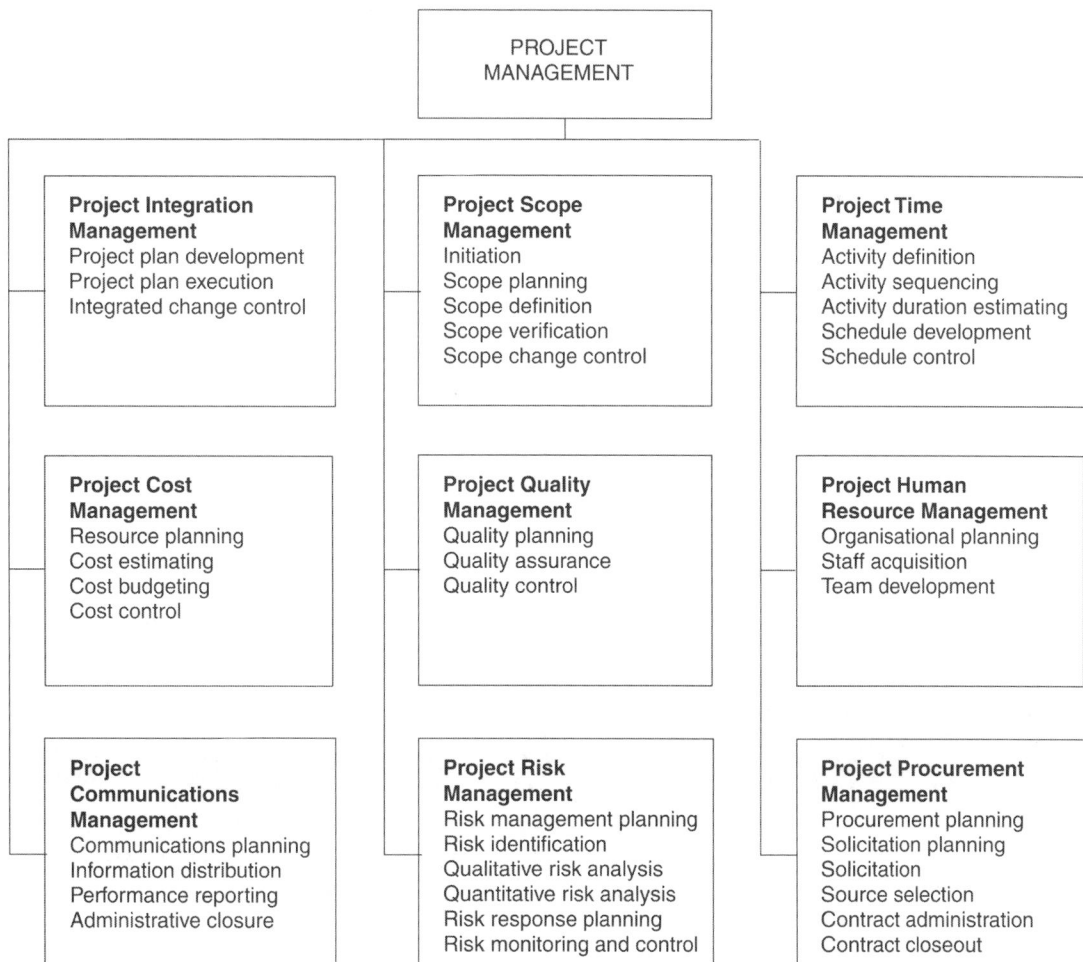

```
                         ┌─────────────────┐
                         │     PROJECT     │
                         │   MANAGEMENT    │
                         └─────────────────┘
```

Project Integration Management Project plan development Project plan execution Integrated change control	**Project Scope Management** Initiation Scope planning Scope definition Scope verification Scope change control	**Project Time Management** Activity definition Activity sequencing Activity duration estimating Schedule development Schedule control
Project Cost Management Resource planning Cost estimating Cost budgeting Cost control	**Project Quality Management** Quality planning Quality assurance Quality control	**Project Human Resource Management** Organisational planning Staff acquisition Team development
Project Communications Management Communications planning Information distribution Performance reporting Administrative closure	**Project Risk Management** Risk management planning Risk identification Qualitative risk analysis Quantitative risk analysis Risk response planning Risk monitoring and control	**Project Procurement Management** Procurement planning Solicitation planning Solicitation Source selection Contract administration Contract closeout

Project Management Knowledge Areas and Project Management Processes

These key knowledge areas between them support **five project management process areas**. These process areas and the relationships between them are shown in the diagram below. You should be able to remember them using the mnemonic **IPECC**.

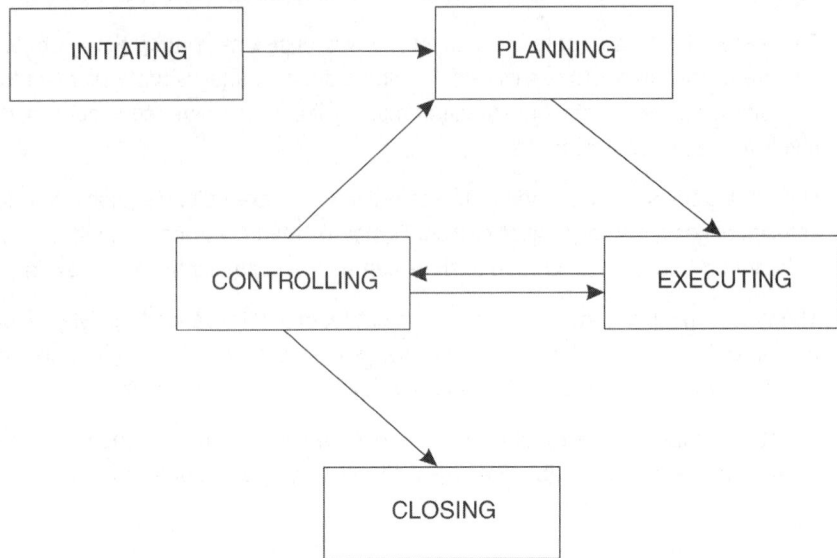

Section summary

The person who takes ultimate responsibility for ensuring the desired result is achieved on time and within budget is the **project manager**.

Duties of the project manager include: planning, team building, communication, co-ordinating project activities, monitoring and control, problem-resolution and quality control.

Project managers require the following **skills**: leadership and team building, organisational ability, communication skills (written, spoken, presentations, meetings), some technical knowledge of the project area and inter-personal skills.

3 Identifying projects

Introduction

Projects should fit in with the strategies of the organisation. Once these have been drawn up and objectives identified then a project may be the means by which an objective is achieved. A **feasibility study** will establish whether a project can achieve its objective in a cost-effective manner.

KEY POINT

A project will be initiated when an **objective** is identified that can only be achieved in this way. Where the objective is of **strategic importance**, a project set up to achieve it will amount to a **strategy** in the sense we will explore in Part C of this Study Text. Of course, not all strategic effort consists of projects, nor do all projects have strategic significance.

If an organisational objective emerges that can only be achieved by undertaking a project, this is often called the project **requirement**. (This is distinguished from the **project specification**: a detailed account of the nature of the project or the outcomes it is intended to deliver.)

Like all potential strategies, project proposals should be assessed for suitability, acceptability and **feasibility**. Feasibility will be particularly important when the project objective is innovative, complex or difficult to achieve, since such projects are likely to entail a high risk of failure or excessive expense. The mechanism employed for this area of assessment is the **feasibility study**.

3.1 The feasibility study

The purpose of the feasibility study is not so much to find out if a proposed project can achieve its objective as to establish whether or not it can do so in a **cost-effective** manner. Given sufficient resources, most proposals that lie outside the realms of fantasy can be implemented but not all are worth undertaking. The feasibility study is the mechanism by which the organisation filters out proposed projects that would cost too much, because too much disruption, make excessive demands on human and other resources or have side effects whose undesirability outweighs their advantages. The assessment of feasibility can be broken down into a number of areas.

3.1.1 Technical feasibility

The assessment of technical feasibility will depend on the nature of the technology involved in the project: software would be a major part of an IS project, for example, while materials and structures would be fundamental to a civil engineering project.

(a)   Does all the necessary technology exist or is significant **innovation** required?
(b)   Is the technology mature enough to use or is further **development** likely to be required?
(c)   How **specialised** is the required technology and is **the expertise** to make use of it available?

Technical feasibility also includes **technical matters that do not relate to technology**; that is to say, matters of technical expertise, such as marketing, financial strategy and human resource management. We might wish to know, for example, whether it were feasible to communicate effectively with a particular identified market segment.

In this category of technical feasibility assessment we would include **features analysis**, which is the process of identifying and prioritising those features of the project requirement that are critical to its success. This process can help to guide the allocation of project resources so that the importance of deliverable features is reflected in the resources expended on achieving them.

3.1.2 Social feasibility

Any project is likely to have effects upon people, both those in the organisation concerned and those outside it. The social feasibility of a project depends on the nature and extent of those effects. There are obvious human resource management implications to most projects, in the area of forming, leading and motivating the project team. The progress and outcome of a project may also have important consequences for employees outside the team, such as increased demand for certain categories of staff, redundancies, training requirements and changed work patterns.

Outside the organisation, the undertaking of projects and their outcomes may have **wider social consequences**, such as the drain of public funds and disruption of transport systems confidently expected as a result of the staging of the 2012 Olympic games in London.

3.1.3 Financial feasibility

It is appropriate to submit proposed projects to **cost-benefit analysis**, though this can be very difficult when the benefits are largely in intangible form. Part of the difficulty lies in identifying the benefits and part in assigning monetary values to them. Dealing with intangible or qualitative benefits is likely to be particularly important in the public and voluntary sectors, where objectives such as improved road safety or education are common.

The usual analysis of costs should be made.

(a)   **Capital costs** are incurred in the purchase of assets.
(b)   **Finance costs** are the charges made for the use of loan capital.
(c)   **Revenue costs** are all other costs.

The financial feasibility of a project is assessed using the common techniques such as net present value, **payback period** and **accounting rate of return**.

Exam alert

Make sure when you are asked for an **explanation** of the purpose of a project feasibility study, to refer to the types of feasibility to be considered. In a previous syllabus exam, a number of candidates referred to types of feasibility without explaining these correctly.

3.2 Risk

Risk differs from **uncertainty** in that risk can be quantified and managed.

Risk management is an important aspect of project management and we will discuss it in more detail later, when we consider management tools and techniques. However, the assessment of risk is also important at the project appraisal stage.

(a)   The risk may be so high as to make it imprudent to continue with the project.

(b)   The process of **risk management** can begin straight away, with appropriate steps being taken to mitigate the level of risk involved. Suitable strategies include **avoidance**, **transference**, **acceptance** or **reduction**.

3.3 SWOT analysis

We will look briefly at the assessment of strengths, weaknesses, opportunities and threats in the corporate appraisal stage of the rational model of strategy (in a later chapter). This can also be used to evaluate and compare projects, particularly when there are a number of potential projects contending for funds. The strengths and weaknesses of each could be considered in relation to the opportunities and threats the organisation was facing at the time and likely to face in the future. An assessment of project strengths and weaknesses would include consideration of the deliverables and the factors revealed by the investigation of feasibility.

3.4 Selecting projects – a summary

STEP 1   **List potential projects** and for each one establish:

(a)	Need or opportunity	(d)	Approximate duration
(b)	Financial and other resource requirements	(e)	Risk profile
(c)	Overall feasibility		

STEP 2   Eliminate projects which are unsuitable, inappropriate and unfeasible.

STEP 3   Prioritise the remaining projects.

Question 6.2   Projects

Learning outcome B1a, 2a

Give six examples of work you would consider suitable for a project management approach.

> **Section summary**
>
> Projects may have **strategic significance**. As strategies, they should be subjected to the same **evaluation** for suitability, feasibility and acceptability as other strategies. SWOT should be used. Even where they do not constitute strategic action, proposed projects must be appraised for their value before they are started. **Feasibility studies** are a common approach; technical, social, environmental and financial feasibility are all assessed. An assessment of risk must also be made.

4 PRINCE2

> **Introduction**
>
> PRINCE2 is mentioned in the syllabus and has been tested in previous syllabus exams. It is a model built on eight components and eight processes. We suggest that you learn what is in each as you are likely to have to use these in any question based on PRINCE2.

The acronym **PRINCE** stands for **PR**ojects **IN** **C**ontrolled **E**nvironments and is a registered trademark of the Office for Government Commerce (OGC). However, OGC has adopted the principles of public domain for its guidance and no licence is required to use its material. Specific tools, training and services are developed and provided by companies on a commercial basis.

The latest version of PRINCE, **PRINCE2** is now the *de facto* UK standard for Information Systems (IS) project management and is widely used in other countries. The wide acceptance PRINCE has achieved is itself an important advantage to its use for managing projects, since it provides a common language for all participants.

4.1 Main features of PRINCE2

(a) PRINCE2 may be used to manage any project of any size or complexity, since the system is **scaleable**.

(b) A clear **management structure** of roles and responsibilities within the system is defined; this may be adapted according to the skills available within the organisation and the nature of the project.

(c) The system focuses on **delivering results** (called 'products') rather than on the technical processes of project management. The users of the final end-product are actively involved in the project.

(d) It is a fundamental aspect of PRINCE2 that a project is driven by its **business case**; the continuing viability of the project is checked at regular intervals.

4.2 The PRINCE2 approach to project management

PRINCE2 uses its own terminology to describe its constituent parts; this terminology is not intuitive and can be difficult to grasp. However, it is precise in its meaning. The PRINCE2 methodology is built up mainly from **components** and **processes**.

4.3 Components

Components are rather conceptual in nature, being matters to which proper consideration must be given if the project is to succeed, but also varying widely in actual nature from project to project. There are **eight components.**

(a)	**Business case**	(e)	**Risk**
(b)	**Organisation**	(f)	**Quality**
(c)	**Plans**	(g)	**Configuration management**
(d)	**Controls**	(h)	**Change control**

4.3.1 Business case

A business case is not something that is confined to commercial organisations. The term may be understood as meaning a **reasoned account of what is to be achieved and why it will be of benefit**. As already mentioned, it is fundamental that a project is driven by its business case. Occasions when the business case must be referred to should be specified at the outset. This is to ensure focus on what the project is really supposed to be about. The business case may require updating as the project progresses.

4.3.2 Organisation

Management implies a structure of authority and accountability. PRINCE2 recognises four layers of management responsibility, though levels may be combined or eliminated if appropriate. A major project of strategic significance will be of interest to the organisation's **strategic apex**, or top level decision makers, which may appoint one of its members or form a **steering committee** to set policy to support business objectives. An **executive committee** below strategic apex level may have the job of translating policies into specific projects that support them.

The top level of management for an individual project is the **project board**, chaired by the **Executive**. This person provides overall guidance and must represent the business interests of the organisation. Two other constituencies may also be represented.

(a)   The **senior user** represents the interests of those who are affected by the introduction of the new system and is accountable for the quality of the specification.

(b)   The **senior supplier/senior technical** person represents those charged with implementing the project. This role may be filled by an external prime contractor or a person within the organisation such as the purchasing officer or, in the case of an IT project, for example, the senior IT person appointed to the project.

Day to day management of the project is the responsibility of the **project manager**, who is supported by one or more **stage managers** or **team managers**. The roles of project manager and stage or team manager may be combined. The **project team** reports to the stage manager. Also working for the project manager, but with a responsibility to the project board and representing the same three interests, is the **project assurance team**.

4.3.3 Plans

Clearly, projects must be planned if they are to succeed; we have already noted that PRINCE2 planning is based on products rather than processes. Planning is therefore based on **product breakdown structure** rather than work breakdown structure.

4.3.4 Controls

Control is built into PRINCE2, using the normal cybernetic feedback control action approach discussed elsewhere in this Study Text. The project board restricts authorisation to one stage at a time and manages by exception.

4.3.5 Risk

Risk is analysed and managed throughout the project's life and reviewed at pre-determined intervals.

4.3.6 Quality

Quality management is built into the management of the project, though PRINCE2 is not itself a quality management system, despite the prominence of quality products in the product breakdown. Further quality procedures may need to be introduced into a project if it is to satisfy ISO 9000, for example.

4.3.7 Change control

Any project may be subject to changed conditions or requirements, such as failure to deliver by a supplier or new legislation. Changes to the project itself must be dealt with in a comprehensive and rational way, so that all concerned know what is going on and what the new plan is.

4.3.8 Configuration management

A **configuration** is a technical description, a complete specification of everything that is needed to bring a project to a successful conclusion. With complex projects, it is likely that frequent technical changes will be made: all of these changes must be approved and documented. **Configuration management** controls the processes by which projects evolve.

4.4 Processes

Project processes are more concrete than components, being essentially groups of linked activities. They are largely identifiable as approximately equivalent to stages of the project lifecycle (see Chapter 7), though they also relate to aspects of continuing project management activity. There are eight processes.

(a)	**Directing a project**	(e)	**Controlling a stage**
(b)	**Starting up a project**	(f)	**Managing stage boundaries**
(c)	**Initiating a project**	(g)	**Managing product delivery**
(d)	**Planning**	(h)	**Closing a project**

4.4.1 Directing a project

Directing a project is the responsibility of the senior management team or project board. This process continues throughout the life of the project but is limited to higher aspects of control and decision-making.

4.4.2 Starting up a project

Starting up a project is a short scene-setting pre-project process concerned with fundamentals such as the project's aims and the appointment of the project board and project manager.

4.4.3 Initiating a project

Initiating a project is an initial planning process that includes quality planning, setting up project controls and creating the **Project Initiation Document**, which sets fundamental progress and success criteria. The first productive stage of the project is planned during this process.

4.4.4 Planning

Planning is a process that may be carried out at any time in order to satisfy the requirements of other processes. The PRINCE2 hierarchy of plans has up to four levels.

(a)   The **project plan** is the overall plan and is produced at the beginning of the project. It will probably be in summary form.

(b)   A **stage plan** is produced for each stage of the project.

(c)　**Detailed plans** are produced if more detail is needed at any point in a stage.

(d)　**Individual work plans** guide the activity of each team member.

Much past project planning has been based on the ideas embodied in **work breakdown structure (WBS)**, in which the processes required to complete the project are analysed into discrete, manageable units. PRINCE2, however, uses a **product-based** approach. This has the advantage of directing management attention to *what* is to be achieved rather than *how* to do it, thus providing an automatic focus on achieving the product goals. Also, it can be helpful in complex projects, where the processes involved may be unclear initially.

Under this approach, work breakdown is preceded by **product breakdown**. PRINCE2 starts this analysis by dividing the **project products** into three groups.

(a)　**Technical products** are the things the project has been set up to provide to the users. For an IT system, for example, these would include the hardware, software, manuals and training.

(b)　**Quality products** define both the quality controls that are applied to the project and the quality standards the technical products must achieve.

(c)　**Management products** are the artefacts used to manage the project. They include the project management organisation structure, planning documentation, reports and so on.

Each of these groups of products is then broken down into manageable components as part of the planning process, using the traditional work breakdown structure approach if the complexity of the project requires it. Project and stage plans may make use of the normal planning tools such as CPA, Gantt charts and resource histograms.

Plan text describes the plan, its assumptions, constraints and reporting structure. Cumulative costs and the status of major products are shown on the **resource plan graphical summary**.

An interesting feature of the PRINCE2 management approach is the use of **tolerances**. Project and stage managers may be authorised to make variations to the plan within stated tolerances of **time**, **cost** and **quality**, thus providing them with some flexibility of implementation. However, if it seems likely that the stated tolerances will be exceeded, the further approval of the project board must be sought for an **exception plan**.

4.4.5 Controlling a stage

Controlling a stage is the process undertaken by the project manager to ensure that any given stage of the project remains on course. A project might consist of just one stage, of course.

PRINCE2 project control includes a structure of reports and meetings.

(a)　A **project initiation** meeting agrees the scope and objectives of the project and gives approval for it to start.

(b)　The completion of each project stage is marked by an **end stage assessment**, which includes reports from the project manager and the project assurance team. The next stage does not commence until its plans have been reviewed and approved.

(c)　**Mid stage assessments** are optional and may arise if, for example, a stage runs for a particularly long time or it is necessary to start a new stage before the current one is complete.

(d)　**Highlight reports** are submitted regularly to the project board by the project manager. These reports are the main overall routine control mechanism and their frequency (often monthly) is agreed at project initiation. They are essentially progress reports and should include brief summaries of project schedule and budget status.

(e)　The **checkpoint** is the main control device used by the project team itself. Meetings are held more frequently than highlight reports are prepared (possibly weekly) and provide a basis for continuing progress review by team leaders and members.

4.4.6 Managing stage boundaries

Managing stage boundaries is the process that must be undertaken when a project has more than one stage. This process ensures that one stage is properly completed before the next one begins.

4.4.7 Managing product delivery

Managing product delivery is the process that controls work done by specialist teams by agreeing what work is to be done and ensuring that it is carried out to the proper standard.

4.4.8 Closing a project

Closing a project is the process by which the project manager brings the project to a conclusion. It consists of checking and reporting on the extent that the project has been a success. The completion of the project is formally marked by the **project closure meeting**. This is held to ensure that all planned work has been carried out, including any approved variations to the plan, and that the work has been accepted.

4.5 Alternatives to PRINCE2

We have already mentioned the US **Project Management Institute** and the **Guide to the Project Management Body of Knowledge** (PMBOK). This is widely used by specialists. There is a good article which compares PRINCE2 with PMBOK. This is 'Comparing PRINCE2 with PMBOK' by *R Max Wideman,* which can be found on the Internet.

Six Sigma was original a scheme of improvement for quality in manufacturing but it has been adapted to project management.

The **Carnegie Mellon Software Engineering Institute** has developed management processes and methodologies for improving the quality of new software, such as **IDEAL** and **INTRO**.

We revisit these in Chapter 8 when we compare and contrast project control systems.

Section summary

PRINCE2 is a widely accepted, standard method of project management. It offers clear management structures and planning and control methods and is noteworthy for its focus on **outputs** rather than processes.

The PRINCE2 method is based on **eight components** and **eight processes**.

5 Projects and organisational structure

Introduction

Projects are better suited to flatter, organisational structures where individuals opt in and out of the project as they are needed. The project can employ people as they are needed which means they are a flexible labour force or it can use existing employees co-opted into the project for the time their skills are needed.

Traditional organisational structures are hierarchical with layers of management. Many modern organisations have undergone restructuring to cut out layers of management. These flatter structures are claimed to simplify decision-making and will therefore affect how projects are managed in the organisation.

Project managers usually have to work within the structure that exists. Depending on their influence, they may have input in determining the structure in which the project is managed.

We outline a few organisational structures used in project management here.

5.1 Pure project organisation

This structure is described by *Maylor* in *Project Management 2003*.

It is typical in the construction industry where the workforce is flexible and changes over the project lifecycle depending on the needs of the project. The project organisations consists of a project board which is permanent and made up of managers, directors and administration staff.

This board oversees the work of the project manager who co-ordinates the project team over the life of the project. The team will be ad hoc, brought together to compete tasks at certain stages in the project.

The organisation has **advantages** including:

(a)   **A flexible labour force drafted in as needed**. So lawyers and architects would be engaged at the planning stage. Contractors would be used during the construction phase.

(b)   **A saving on employment costs** as the workforce is only engaged and paid at certain points in the project.

There are also **disadvantages** including the **temporary nature of the team** which means there may be little commitment to success. Members of the team may not be able to pass on what they have learnt once they leave and there is little continuity over the life of the project.

5.2 Matrix management

Maylor (ibid) notes that 'matrix management was invented as a way of achieving some of the benefits of the project organisation without the disadvantages'.

He describes three styles of matrix organisations used for project management. The advantages and disadvantages of each style are outlined. These stages represent a progression from an outline project team to a fully engaged project team.

5.2.1 Lightweight matrix

The **project manager co-ordinates the project and chairs meetings between the departments involved**. Responsibility for the success of the project is shared by the departments. **This structure has its disadvantages** including a lack of commitment from the departments and the relative weakness of the project manager compared to departmental managers. These disadvantages may lead to the project being led off course or being neglected in departments with conflicting priorities.

5.2.2 Balanced model

This style of matrix organisation seeks to redress the relative powerlessness of the project manager described above. This is achieved by making part of the income earned by the department dependent on their involvement in the project.

However, the dual responsibilities of departmental managers to the project and their own department may lead to a conflict in loyalties.

Another disadvantage arises from there being a second line of command exercised by department managers in addition to the project manager.

5.2.3 Heavyweight matrix

Departmental members are **seconded to the project on a full-time basis**. They can then devote their time to the project without distraction. The project benefits from drafting in expertise as and when needed.

One disadvantage, however, is clearly to the sponsoring department which loses its staff for their duration in the project team.

Section summary

Project managers must normally manage projects within the existing structure of their organisation. Certain organisational structures are more suited to project success than others.

Chapter Roundup

✓   A project is an undertaking that has a beginning and an end and is carried out to meet established goals within cost, schedule and quality objectives. It often has the following **characteristics**:

- A defined beginning and end
- Resources allocated specifically to it
- Intended to be done only once (although similar separate projects could be undertaken)
- Follows a plan towards a clear intended end-result
- Often cuts across organisational and functional lines

Crucial aspects of the project management environment are noted in the **7S model**.

Project management is the combination of systems, techniques, and people used to control and monitor activities undertaken within the project. It will be deemed successful if it is completed at the specified level of **quality**, **on time** and within **budget**.

✓   The person who takes ultimate responsibility for ensuring the desired result is achieved on time and within budget is the **project manager**.

Duties of the project manager include: planning, team building, communication, co-ordinating project activities, monitoring and control, problem-resolution and quality control.

Project managers require the following skills: leadership and team building, organisational ability, communication skills (written, spoken, presentations, meetings), some technical knowledge of the project area and inter-personal skills.

✓   Projects may have **strategic significance**. As strategies, they should be subjected to the same **evaluation** for suitability, feasibility and acceptability as other strategies. SWOT should be used. Even where they do not constitute strategic action, proposed projects must be appraised for their value before they are started. **Feasibility studies** are a common approach; technical, social, environmental and financial feasibility are all assessed. An assessment of risk must also be made.

✓   **PRINCE2** is a widely accepted, standard method of project management. It offers clear management structures and planning and control methods and is noteworthy for its focus on **outputs** rather than processes.

The PRINCE2 method is based on **eight components** and **eight processes**.

✓   Project managers must normally manage projects within the existing structure of their organisation. Certain organisational structures are more suited to project success than others.

Quick Quiz

1   What is a successful project?

2   Which of the following is most likely to be a success factor for project delivery?

     A   Clear business case
     B   Loose control and encouragement of initiative
     C   Strong leadership without interference from users
     D   Appointment of technical specialists as project managers

3   List four areas a project manager should be skilled in.

   1   ....

   2   ....

   3   ....

   4   ....

4   'Project management techniques encourage management by exception.'

   True   ☐

   False   ☐

5   Which of the following is **not** one of the nine key knowledge areas of the PMBOK?

   A   Project scope management
   B   Project risk management
   C   Project configuration management
   D   Project communications management

6   'An investigation into whether a project can be successfully implemented given the organisational structures, expertise and tools available is likely to focus on .... feasibility?'

   Which type of feasibility most accurately completes this statement?

7   What is the term given to the most frequent progress review meetings of a project team, in the PRINCE2 methodology?

   A   End stage assessments
   B   Milestones
   C   Highlight reports
   D   Checkpoints

Answers to Quick Quiz

1   One that is completed on time, within budget and to specification.

2   A   Business case encourages ownership/support by senior management. The other options reflect common problems in project management. (Poor control, lack of stakeholder involvement, over-promotion of technical staff.)

3   [Four of] Leadership, team building, organisational, communication, technical, personal.

4   True.

5   C   Although configuration management would be included in Project Integration Management.

6   Technical

7   D   (Note that 'milestones' is general project management terminology for key points at which progress is reviewed for control: it is not unique to PRINCE2.)

Answers to questions

6.1   7S

The answer is C. There is only one difference between the project 7S model and the McKinsey 7S model: the former includes stakeholders while the latter includes shared values. Staff, style, strategy, systems, structure and skills are common to both models.

6.2   Projects

Common examples of projects include:

- Building a new national football stadium
- Producing a new product, service or object
- Changing the structure of an organisation
- Implementing a new service style
- Streamlining the company's ordering service
- Reorganising the company car park to maximise parking

Now try the question below from the Exam Question Bank

Number	Level	Marks	Time
Q6	Examination	25	45 mins

PROJECT LIFECYCLE AND PLANNING

This is the second chapter in the part of the syllabus that covers project management. We move on now to look at the different phases of the project life cycle. Be aware that other books may refer to **project stages** with different names or may include more or fewer stages: the principles behind the process and techniques are more important than the labels used.

Then, we consider what happens when projects don't go according to plan. This is the area of **project risk** and project managers need to assess risk and make plans to accommodate it in their running of a project.

We will look in more detail at specific tools and techniques for planning and controlling projects in Chapter 8.

The chapter finishes with an explanation of the main parties or stakeholders involved in a project.

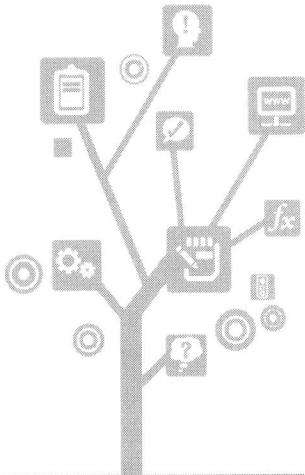

topic list	learning outcomes	syllabus references	ability required
1 The project life cycle	B1d	B1(i), (ii),	comprehension
2 Managing project risk	B1f	B1 (x)	analysis
3 Roles and management of project stakeholders	B2b,c	B2(ii),(iii)	evaluation, comprehension

1 The project life cycle

Introduction

Projects are conventionally seen as having a **life cycle and** this is particularly true of larger projects. The life cycle concept can be useful in the management of projects, since it breaks the whole down into more easily manageable parts. This is applicable to the **allocation and management of resources**, since their type and quantity vary from phase to phase.

A useful description of the stages of a project is the **4D model** where the stages are definition, design, delivery and development.

The project life cycle can be seen as having **four main phases**. These can be shown diagrammatically.

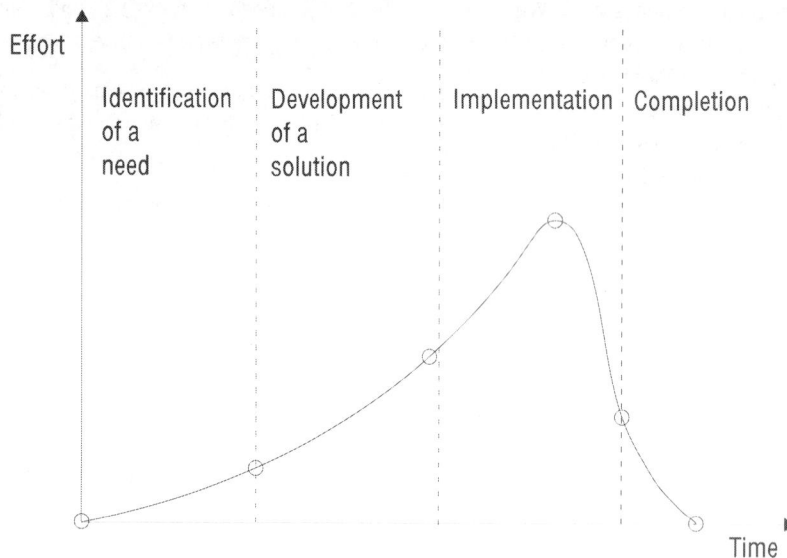

Identification of a need, a problem or an opportunity. This may lead to a **feasibility study**, possibly carried out internally to the organisation or possibly by external contractors in response to an invitation to tender or a request for proposal. If this process shows that the project has merit, a **project initiation document** is written and a **project team** established.

Development of a solution. There must be agreement on what is to be done. This may be through the medium of competitive bidding or by an internal process of iterative development.

Implementation. The proposed outcome must be delivered. This may involve further detailed planning and the achievement of agreed progress stages and, where contractors are involved, stage payments.

Completion. The success or otherwise of the project is assessed, documentation is completed and final payments are made.

KEY POINT

It is unlikely that there will be clear boundaries between the phases and the various aspects may run in parallel to some extent.

Field and Keller suggest that uncertain requirements and the need to integrate a range of ideas may make an **iterative process** appropriate, with scope, plans, solutions and methods all being developed more or less simultaneously. Where contractors are involved this has the advantage of involving the customer in the process of development. The process would aim at the development of a 'predictive model' that can be tested and revised in a simulated environment until a solution emerges. This approach helps in the management of risk and contributes to the development of project methods and system integration.

Maylor, in his book *Project Management*, also describes four phases or stages: this is the **4D model**.

Stage in project life cycle	Component Title	Activities
Define the project	Conceptualisation	Produce a clear and definitive statement of needs
	Analysis	Identify what has to be done and check its feasibility
Design the project	Planning	Show how the needs will be met
	Justification	Compute costs and benefits
	Agreement	Obtain sponsor agreement
Deliver the project (Do it!)	Start up	Assemble resources and people
	Execution	Carry out planned project activities
	Completion	Success or abandonment
	Handover	Output passed to sponsor/user
Develop the process	Review	Identify outcomes for all stakeholders
	Feedback	Document lessons and improvements for future use

Exam alert

Exam questions may refer to the '**project lifecycle**' or **PLC**, or they may simply refer to '**stages**' in a project. Either way, they are asking for the same thing, and will generally refer specifically to a four-stage model (although there are alternative models).

1.1 Define the project

Exam alert

Under the previous syllabus, candidates were asked to describe the **initiation** stage of a project and explain what should be included in a project initiation document for rebuilding a school.

The feedback given commented that there were some very good answers but some candidates **did not confine themselves to the specific project stage requested**.

Projects start when someone becomes aware of the need for one. This can occur at any level and in any context, though more formal business projects of management significance will normally be originated within the area of responsibility of the sponsoring manager. Larger projects are likely to involve the creation of a **project brief** or **terms of reference** for discussion. A **project initiation document** may be prepared, if it is decided to continue with the project. This will include a **statement of requirements**, a **statement of the vision** for the project and a **business case**.

KEY POINT

At this early stage, one of the most important things to get under control is the **scope of the project**; that is, just what is included and what is not. A firm grasp of the agreed scope of the project must be maintained throughout its life.

Planning will start in this phase, but is unlikely to be completed until the end of the project. The aim should be to do enough planning to achieve three things.

(a)   Avoid the chaos of unplanned activity

(b)   Provide a basis for accepting or rejecting the project

(c)   Identify problems in advance.

More complex projects will have a greater requirement for detailed plans. **Work breakdown structure** (WBS) is the traditional method of planning a project. WBS is dealt with in the next chapter.

Larger projects will benefit from being broken down into phases. This assists the planning process and enhances the ability of those responsible to control progress. The boundary between one phase and the next is a suitable place to impose a review of progress, with the option of closing down the whole thing if it is proving unsatisfactory in any way. Established project management methods such as PRINCE2 incorporate review procedures for ensuring that phases are completed on time.

1.1.1 Identifying requirements

Project scope is all the things that have to be achieved if the project is to succeed: essentially it is all of the work that has to be done. There are several ways of determining what has to be done if a project is to succeed. This is a necessary stage whatever approach is taken overall, be it iterative or linear.

(a)   **Gap analysis**. Where a replacement or an upgrade is needed a comparison can be made between what currently exists and what is desired. This is a common approach in IS projects.

(b)   **Reverse engineering** identifies the features of an existing product or system by taking it apart.

(c)   **Functional decomposition** is a process of analysis that starts with the desired end state and establishes what must be done to achieve it. The process starts in broad brush terms and continues in ever-finer detail until manageable tasks and elements are established.

1.2 Design the project

There are several aspects to detailed project planning. *Maylor* categorises the various techniques used for scheduling, such as network analysis and Gantt charts as **time planning**. He also deals with the need to plan for **cost**, **quality** and **risk**.

1.2.1 Project planning

Exam alert

Remember to answer the question! In a previous syllabus exam, candidates were asked to explain the potential problems that could result from poor project planning. The feedback given was that many students answered this point by **writing about project planning rather than the problems where there is no planning**.

The project manager will be responsible for producing plans and documentation for the project.

(a)   The project charter or project initiation document

(b)   Plan for time

(c)   Plan for cost

(d)   Plan for quality

(e)   Plan for risk and contingencies

These aspects of planning are dealt with in a later chapter.

It may also be necessary to produce further plans.

(a)   A **resource plan** specifies the resources of all types that are needed and how they will be used. The aim is to match resources smoothly to workload.

(b)   A **communication plan** may be necessary when there are many and varied stakeholders needing different amounts and types of information.

1.3 Deliver the project

This is the **operational** phase of the project. Planning will continue as required in order to control agreed changes and to deal with unforeseen circumstances, but the main emphasis is on getting the work done.

There are several important themes.

(a)   **Management and leadership**: people management assumes a greater importance as the size of the project work force increases.

(b)   **Control**: time, cost and quality must be kept under control, as must the tendency for changes to proliferate.

(c)   **Supply chain**: all the aspects of logistics management must be implemented, especially with projects involving significant physical output.

(d)   **Problems and decisions**: problems are bound to arise and must be solved sensibly and expeditiously. Complex problems will require careful analysis using the scientific tools of decision theory.

1.4 Develop the process

Because project management is episodic in nature, it is difficult to improve. The lack of continuous operation means that the skills and experience developed during a project are likely to fragment and atrophy after it is complete. This is especially true of organisations that do not have many projects or manage them on an *ad hoc* basis. Managers move around, projects are sponsored in different departments from time to time and the pressure of normal work inhibits organisational learning. Even in project-based organisations, there can be a reluctance to devote resources to improving the corporate body of project management knowledge.

The completion and review phase involves a number of important but often neglected activities.

(a)   **Completion** itself is often neglected. All activities must be properly and promptly finished; care must be taken that contractors do not either leave small things undone or, if paid by time, spin things out for as long as possible.

(b)   **Documentation** must be completed. This is important on any project but it is vital if there are quality certification issues or it is necessary to provide the user with operating documentation. Indeed, these two types of documentation should be specified as deliverables at the outset. Contracts, letters, accounting records and so on must be filed properly.

(c)   **Project systems** must be closed down, but in a proper fashion. In particular, the project accounts and any special accounting systems must remain in operation and under control until all costs have been posted but must then be closed down to avoid improper posting.

(d)   **Handover** must take place where the project has been managed for a client under contract. At some point the client must formally accept that the contract is complete and take responsibility for any future action that may be required, such as the operation and maintenance of a system.

(e)   **Immediate review** is required to provide staff with immediate feedback on performance and to identify short-term needs such as staff training or remedial action for procedure failures.

1.4.1 The review process

A thorough review is the organisation's opportunity to make significant improvements in how it manages its projects. The review should cover all aspects of the project, possibly organised on a functional basis, and have clear **terms of reference** for each. This cannot be done on the cheap: appropriate quantities of management time and attention must be allocated to the review process and to the assimilation of its results and recommendations.

1.4.2 The project management maturity model

The concept of project management maturity (*Maylor*; *Buttrick*) suggests that some organisations have more developed capabilities to implement projects than others.

Different models focus on the **levels of development** or the **pace of improvement and learning**, but broadly:

(a)   **Level 1 organisations** have little or no organisational processes or methodologies for project management. The delivery of cost, time and quality objectives depends on the efforts of the project manager and team.

(b)   **Level 2 organisations** have developed an **agreed project methodology**, based on accumulated experience: new projects can now follow defined paths rather than individual initiative. Outcomes are more predictable.

(c)   **Level 3 organisations** are not only able to implement projects successfully, but to realise significant **benefits** at the end. The focus has shifted from quality/cost/time objectives to intended benefits.

(d)   **Level 4 organisations** integrate projects with **overall corporate strategy**. The entire project portfolio is selected and managed to support organisational strategy and add value to the organisation as a whole.

Project maturity models are used as a project control tool, to evaluate where the organisation has reached in the maturing process – and what steps might be needed to take it to the next stage.

In Chapter 9, we look at *Kerzner's* five level project maturity model. This sees project development in terms of *continuous improvement*.

1.5 Another 4D model

Your syllabus simply mentions the '4-D' model. We believe that Maylor's model is the most useful, but there is another, very different (and rather vague) model that may be useful in projects involving cultural change or those that are highly innovative. This is sometimes called **appreciative inquiry**.

(a)   **Discover**: What is best about the current state? What gives the system life?
(b)   **Dream**: What might be? What positive outcome do we seek?
(c)   **Design**: What should be? How should the elements be put together?
(d)   **Deliver**: Implement the design and build on it.

Section summary

Projects may be perceived as having a **life cycle**. This is commonly seen as commencing with the identification of a need and progressing through the development of a solution, implementation and closure. *Maylor* suggests that the four phases of the project life cycle are **definition**, **design**, **delivery** and **development**. These phases constitute the **4D model**.

The definition phase includes consideration of the **scope** of the project and the production of initial plans. Detailed planning continues in the **design phase**.

The **operational management** of the project involves attention to people management, control requirements, logistics and problem solving.

The final phase of project management is **completion and review**. Work must be finished, documentation completed, systems closed down, deliverables handed over and proper review undertaken so that skills may be improved.

2 Managing project risk

Introduction

Projects don't always go according to plan. There is always a risk of something going wrong. Risk is the probability of an unwanted outcome happening.

Projects and other undertakings carry an element of risk, for example the risk of an inappropriate system being developed and implemented. Risk management is concerned with identifying such risks and putting in place policies to eliminate or reduce these risks. The identification of risks involves an overview of the project to establish what could go wrong, and the consequences.

2.1 Types of risk

Risk is, broadly, 'the *probability* of an *unwanted* outcome happening'.

(a) Some risks are **quantifiable**: probability can be established by statistical analysis of past occurrences. The probability of a given loss can then be multiplied by its likely cost.

(b) Some risks are **unquantifiable**: this takes them into the area of **uncertainty**, which makes them difficult to manage. However, it may be possible to assign some estimation of probability and magnitude of loss to them.

(c) Attention must be given to **socially constructed risk**, which is an aspect of human psychology. People tend to be poor at the rational assessment of risk, downplaying some (particularly those they are familiar with) and being over-concerned about others. Since stakeholder views must be taken into account, **perceived** as well as **actual** risk must be managed: this may make it necessary to take precautions in some areas that are greater than are really warranted.

(d) Other classifications of risk include: **internal** (within the project process) and **external** (arising from the environment); and business, commercial, operational, environmental, compliance, technical and reputational (depending on which aspect of the process and outcomes is likely to be affected).

2.2 Risk management

KEY POINT

Risk management may be viewed as a five-stage process.

Stage 1	Identify and record risks, for example in a **risk register**.
Stage 2	Assess risks and record this assessment.
Stage 3	Plan and record risk strategies.
Stage 4	Carry out risk management strategies.
Stage 5	Review and monitor the success of the risk management approach.

2.3 Risk analysis and assessment

Risk assessment is the process of assessing the likelihood and impact of a given risk event on the organisation.

The likelihood and consequences of risks can be plotted on a **matrix**. This approach allows unquantifiable risks to be considered alongside those to which a numerical value can be given.

Risk Assessment Matrix

High	M	H	VH
Med	L	M	H
Low	VL	L	M
	Low	**Med**	**High**

Potential impact (vertical axis)

Threat likelihood

Developing a risk **contingency plan** that contains strategies for risks that fall into the VH quadrant should have priority, followed by risks falling into the two H quadrants. Following the principle of **management by exception**, the most efficient way of dealing with risks outside these quadrants may be to do nothing unless the risk presents itself. Extra time and finance should be held in reserve for dealing with likely contingencies.

2.4 Responses to risk

KEY POINT

There are four basic responses to risk.

(a)   **Avoidance**: the factors which give rise to the risk are removed, or the project is not undertaken

(b)   **Reduction** or **mitigation**: measures taken to reduce the likelihood and / or the consequences of the risk event.

(c)   **Transference**: the risk is passed on to or shared with, another party (eg an insurer).

(d)   **Absorption**: the potential risk is accepted in the hope or expectation that the incidence and consequences can be coped with if necessary.

These are sometimes re-labelled as Four Ts: **Terminate, Treat, Transfer and Tolerate.**

Risk management is a continuous process. Procedures are necessary to regularly review and reassess the risks documented in the risk register. Each project risk should have an allocated '**owner**' to monitor and manage the risk.

> **Section summary**
>
> Projects, being one-off activities are particularly subject to risk. Risks must be identified in advance, recorded and managed using one of four strategies: **avoidance**, **reduction**, **transference** and **absorption**.

Exam alert

A compulsory ten-mark question was set in a previous syllabus paper, asking you to explain the concept of risk and how it can be managed in a project. This is a key area of project and business management: ensure that you grasp the basic principles.

3   Roles and management of project stakeholders

> **Introduction**
>
> One of the key roles a project manager has is to keep stakeholders informed and involved in a project. Some stakeholders are hands-off whereas others are deeply involved in a project. See if you can work out which is which from the list below.
>
> Ensure you are clear about the differences between **process** and **outcome** stakeholders.
>
> **Mendelow's matrix** provides a tool for **mapping** stakeholders and suggests strategies for managing them.

KEY TERM

PROJECT STAKEHOLDERS are the individuals and organisations who are involved in or may be affected by project activities.

Project stakeholders may be:

(a)   **Process stakeholders**, with an interest in how the project process is conducted (eg those involved in it, those who want a say in it, and those who need to evaluate and learn from it)

(b)   **Outcome stakeholders** with an interest in the outcomes, results or deliverables of the project (eg users of the new system)

We will look at the role of the **Project Manager** and the **Project Team** later on. Other key stakeholders are defined as follows.

KEY TERMS

The PROJECT OWNER. The project owner is the person for whom the project is being carried out (eg a client or senior manager) and is primarily interested in the deliverables achieved

The PROJECT SPONSOR provides and is accountable for the resources invested into the project and is responsible for the achievement of the project's business objectives.

The PROJECT BOARD is the body to which the project manager is accountable for achieving the project objectives. It represents the interests of the project owner and sponsor.

The PROJECT CHAMPION represents the project to the rest of the organisation, communicating its vision and objectives and securing commitment and resources.

PROJECT SUPPORT TEAM is a term used to designate the personnel working on a project who do not report to the project manager administratively.

USERS are the individuals or group that will utilise the end product, process (system), or service produced by the project.

RISK MANAGER. For large projects it may be necessary to appoint someone to control the process of identifying, classifying and quantifying the risks associated with the project.

QUALITY MANAGER. For large projects it may be necessary to appoint someone to write the quality plan and develop quality assurance and control procedures.

VENDORS. In any project, many of the components of the solution may be bought in from suppliers or vendors.

SPECIALISTS. Many complex projects will use specialists from within the organisation eg specialists from human resources, engineering and so on.

Project stakeholders should all be **committed towards a common goal** – successful project completion. The project plan should be the common point of reference that states priorities and provides cohesion.

3.1 Differing stakeholder interests

However, the individuals and groups that comprise the stakeholders all have different roles, therefore are likely to have different points of view and perhaps also conflicting objectives (eg user needs v cost reduction). There is therefore the potential for disagreements between stakeholder groups. The project manager should seek to manage stakeholder expectations and perceptions. Stakeholders must be identified and their interests assessed so that critical relationships may be managed. This is especially important when things go wrong.

The **Mendelow matrix** may be used to assist risk management and focus attention. We cover this briefly below.

KEY POINT

The project manager should be aware of the following matters for each stakeholder or stakeholder group.

(a)   Goals
(b)   Past attitude and behaviour
(c)   Expected future behaviour
(d)   Reaction to possible future developments

Exam alert

You should be able to *identify* project stakeholders and what their role is, state *why* it is important to consider the needs of different stakeholders in a project and suggest ways of *communicating* with stakeholders and securing their support for a project.

3.1.1 Managing stakeholder disputes

The first step is to establish a **framework** to predict the potential for disputes. This involves **managing risk**, since an unforeseen event (a risk) has the potential to create conflict, and **dispute management**: the managing of dispute procedures with minimum impacts on costs, goodwill and progress.

We have already discussed negotiation and resolution techniques in the context of general conflict in Chapter 3. Many of the principles discussed previously can be applied to stakeholder conflicts, although the relative positions of the stakeholders involved can complicate matters. Conflict between project stakeholders may be resolved by:

(a)   **Negotiation**: the parties discuss the issue with a view to finding mutually acceptable solutions.

(b)   **Mediation** (or assisted negotiation): a third party facilitates the negotiation process.

(c)   **Partnering**: creating communication links between project participants with the intention of directing them to a common goal – the project outcome – ahead of their own self-interest.

(d)   **Arbitration**: a third party may be asked to intervene to impose a solution.

On very large projects a **Disputes Review Board** (DRB) may be formed. This may comprise persons directly involved in the project engaged to maintain a 'watching brief' to identify and attend upon disputes as they arise. Usually there is a procedure in place which provides for the DRB to make an 'on the spot' decision before a formal dispute is notified so that the project work can proceed, and that may be followed by various rights of review at increasingly higher levels.

Question 7.1 — Project board

Learning outcome B2b,c

What is the role of the project board?

A   To represent the interests of the project to the rest of the organisation
B   To represent the interests of the project sponsor
C   To provide the resources needed to undertake the project
D   To implement the project

3.2 Stakeholder power

How stakeholders relate to the management of the company depends very much on what **type** of stakeholder they are – internal, connected or external – and on the level in the management hierarchy at which they are able to **apply pressure**. In the case of projects, internal stakeholders will be employed by the company and so they have a strong interest in the success of the project. Vendors are probably connected stakeholders who would hope for repeat business if the project is successful.

We revisit stakeholders and stakeholder mapping in Paper E3.

Specific factors that influence stakeholders' power

(a) Seniority (managers)
(b) Reputation
(c) Social status
(d) Shareholding (directors)
(e) Volume of sales (customers)
(f) Volume of purchases (suppliers)
(g) Formal representation (eg trades union staff)
(h) Legal status

The way in which the relationship between company and stakeholders is conducted is a function of the character of the relationship, the parties' relative bargaining strength and the philosophy underlying each party's objectives. This can be shown as a spectrum.

Spectrum of relationship between organisation and stakeholders

	Weak			Stakeholders' bargaining strength		Strong
Company's conduct of relationship	Command/ dictated by company	Consultation and consideration of stakeholders' views	Negotiation	Participation and acceptance of stakeholders' views	Democratic voting by stakeholders	Command/ dictated by stakeholders

3.3 Managing stakeholders – stakeholder mapping

Mendelow classifies stakeholders on a matrix whose axes are **power held** and **level of interest** in the organisation's activities. These factors will help define the type of relationship the project manager should seek with the project stakeholders.

Level of interest

	Low	High
Low	A	B
High	C	D

Power

(a)   **Key players** are found in segment D: strategy must be *acceptable* to them, at least. These stakeholders may **participate** in decision-making.

(b)   Stakeholders in segment C must be treated with care. While often passive, they are capable of moving to segment D. They should, therefore be **kept satisfied.**

(c)   Stakeholders in segment B do not have great ability to influence strategy, but their views can be important in influencing more powerful stakeholders, perhaps by lobbying. They should therefore be **kept informed.**

(d)   **Minimal effort** is expended on segment A.

It is not possible to produce a single, definite map: stakeholders are likely to move about the map as different issues are considered.

Stakeholder mapping is used to assess the significance of stakeholders. This in turn has implications for the organisation.

(a)   The framework of **corporate governance** should recognise stakeholders' levels of interest and power.

(b)   It may be appropriate to seek to **reposition** certain stakeholders and discourage others from repositioning themselves, depending on their attitudes.

(c)   Key **blockers** and **facilitators** of change must be identified.

3.4 Conflicting stakeholder objectives

Since their interests may be widely different, conflict between stakeholders can be quite common. Project managers must take the potential for such conflict into account when setting policy and be prepared to deal with it if it arises in a form that affects the organisation.

Section summary

Project stakeholders are the individuals and organisations who are involved in, or may be affected by, project activities.

Chapter Roundup

✓ Projects may be perceived as having a **life cycle**. This is commonly seen as commencing with the identification of a need and progressing through the development of a solution, implementation and closure. *Maylor* suggests that the four phases of the project life cycle are **definition**, **design**, **delivery** and **development**. These phases constitute the **4D model**.

The **definition phase** includes consideration of the **scope** of the project and the production of initial plans. Detailed planning continues in the design phase.

The **operational management** of the project involves attention to people management, control requirements, logistics and problem solving.

The final phase of project management is **completion and review**. Work must be finished, documentation completed, systems closed down, deliverables handed over and proper review undertaken so that skills may be improved.

✓ Projects, being one-off activities are particularly subject to risk. Risks must be identified in advance, recorded and managed using one of four strategies: **avoidance**, **reduction**, **transference** and **absorption**.

✓ **Project stakeholders** are the individuals and organisations who are involved in, or may be affected by, project activities.

Quick Quiz

1   List four ways a dispute between project stakeholders could be settled.

    1 ....

    2 ....

    3 ....

    4 ....

2   List five typical phases of a project.

    1 ....

    2 ....

    3 ....

    4 ....

    5 ....

3   Who is the project sponsor?

Answers to Quick Quiz

1   Negotiation
     Partnering
     Mediation
     Arbitration

2   Defining, planning, implementing, controlling, completing.

3   The project sponsor may be the owner, financier, client etc, or their delegate. The sponsor is accountable for the resources invested into the project and responsible for the achievement of the project's business objectives

Answers to Questions

7.1.   Project board

The answer is B. Option A is the role of a project champion, option C that of the project sponsor and option D is that of the project manager.

Number	Level	Marks	Time
Q7	Examination	25	45 mins

PROJECT IMPLEMENTATION

In the last chapter we looked at the phases of a project. Now we explore the key tools and techniques used in managing projects.

Project software is then explained and its usefulness particularly with large projects and processing data. Then we move on to review the documentation and reports used in projects.

Next, we look at leadership and structural issues involved in managing project teams.

The chapter concludes with a brief review of different project control systems.

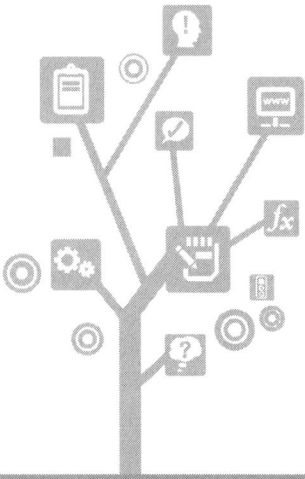

8

topic list	learning outcomes	syllabus references	ability required
1 Management tools and techniques	B1e	B1(iv),(v),(x), (xiii)	application
2 Project management software	B1e	B1(iv)	application
3 Documentation and reports	B1e	B1(vii),(ix)(xiv)	application
4 The project team	B1g	B1(xii)	comprehension
5 Compare and contrast project control systems	B1h	B1(iv)	analysis

1　Management tools and techniques

Introduction

The tools for managing projects in this chapter measure the **time required** and **resources needed** to complete the project successfully. If you remember that, it will be easier to grasp what each tool is meant to do. They have two purposes then: **planning and control** of the project process.

Network analysis was tested frequently in the previous syllabus so we advise you to practise drawing the network diagrams and work through the examples here carefully.

Exam alert

In a previous syllabus exam, candidates were asked for an explanation of how different tools and techniques could assist in project planning. The feedback given was that the question was generally well answered though **candidates must not just rely on writing about PRINCE2.**

The techniques we discuss in this section are concerned with the fundamentals of planning projects and controlling their progress. As with most activities, it is difficult to separate the process of planning a project from that of controlling it: planning is likely to continue throughout the life of the project. A **baseline plan** will show the following.

(a)　Start and end dates for the project and its major phases or activities
(b)　The resources needed and when they are required
(c)　Estimates of cost for the project and the major phases or activities

1.1 Work breakdown structure

Work breakdown structure (WBS) is fundamental to project planning and control. Its essence is the **analysis** of the work required to complete the project into **manageable components**. These are also known as **work packages** which have defined outcomes and responsibilities.

A good way to approach WBS is to consider the **outputs** (or '**deliverables**') the project is required to produce. This can then be analysed into physical and intangible components, which can in turn be further analysed down to whatever level of simplicity is required. Working backwards in this way helps to **avoid preconceived ideas** of the work the project will involve and the processes that must be undertaken.

Example

For example, a simple domestic project might be to create a vegetable plot in a garden. The output would be a plot of cultivated, well-drained soil that was free of weeds, of a suitable level of fertility and with suitable exposure to sun and rain, together with protection from strong winds. This has obvious implications for what must be done. A plot must be selected; existing vegetation must be cleared; weeds must be dug out; the soil must be improved if necessary, by liming and composting; and a physical boundary or kerb must be provided to prevent invasion by creeping weeds such as grass.

The WBS can allow for several levels of analysis, starting with major project phases and gradually breaking them down into major activities, more detailed sub-activities and individual tasks that will last only a very short time. There is no standardised terminology for the various levels of disaggregation, though an **activity** is sometimes regarded as being composed of **tasks**.

The delivery phase of many projects will break down into significant stages or sub-phases. These are very useful for control purposes, as the completion of each stage is an obvious point for reviewing the whole plan before starting the next one.

1.1.1 Dependencies and interactions

A very important aspect of project planning is the determination of **dependencies** and **interactions**. At any level of WBS analysis, some tasks will be dependent on others; that is to say, **a dependent task cannot commence** until the task upon which it depends is completed.

Example again

In our vegetable plot example, it is quite obvious that thought must be given to selecting the site of the plot in order to achieve the necessary sun, rain and shelter *before* seizing a spade and starting to dig. Similarly, it would be physically impossible to apply fertiliser if it had not already been positioned at the site.

Careful analysis of dependencies is a major step towards a workable project plan, since it provides an **order in which things must be tackled**. Sometimes, of course, the dependencies are limited and it is possible to proceed with tasks in almost any order, but this is unusual. The more complex a project, the greater the need for analysis of dependencies.

Interactions are slightly different; they occur when tasks are linked but not dependent. This can arise for a variety of reasons: a good example is a requirement to share the use of a scarce resource.

Example again

If we only possessed one spade to prepare our vegetable plot, we could not use it simultaneously both to cultivate the plot itself and to dig the trench in which we wish to place the kerbstones. We could choose to do either of these activities first, but we could not do them both at the same time.

The output from the WBS process is a list of tasks, probably arranged hierarchically to reflect the disaggregation of activities. This then becomes the input into the planning and control processes described in the rest of this Section.

1.2 The project budget

KEY TERM

PROJECT BUDGET. The amount and distribution of resources allocated to a project.

Building a project budget should be an orderly process that attempts to establish a realistic estimate of the cost of the project. There are two main methods for establishing the project budget; **top-down** and **bottom-up**.

Top-down budgeting describes the situation where the budget is imposed 'from above'. Project Managers are allocated a budget for the project based on an estimate made by senior management. The figure may prove realistic, especially if similar projects have been undertaken recently. However the technique is often used simply because it is quick, or because only a certain level of funding is available.

In **bottom-up budgeting** the project manager consults the project team, and others, to calculate a budget based on the tasks that make up the project. WBS is a useful tool in this process.

It is useful to collate this information on a **Budgeting Worksheet**.

Budgeting Worksheet				
Project Name: _____			**Date worksheet completed:** _____	
Project Manager: _____				
Task (code)	Responsible staff member or external supplier	Estimated material costs	Estimated labour costs	Total cost of task

Estimates (and therefore budgets) cannot be expected to be 100% accurate. Business **conditions may change**, the project plan may be amended or estimates may simply prove to be incorrect.

Any **estimate** must be accompanied by some **indication of expected accuracy**.

KEY POINT

Estimates can be **improved** by:

(a) **Learning** from past mistakes
(b) Ensuring sufficient design **information**
(c) Ensuring as **detailed a specification as possible** from the customer
(d) Properly **analysing the job** into its constituent units

The overall level of cost estimates will be influenced by:

(a) **Project goals**. If a high level of quality is expected costs will be higher.

(b) **External vendors**. Some costs may need to be estimated by outside vendors. To be realistic, these people must understand exactly what would be expected of them.

(c) **Staff availability**. If staff are unavailable, potentially expensive contractors may be required.

(d) **Time schedules**. The quicker a task is required to be done the higher the cost is likely to be – particularly with external suppliers.

The budget may express all resources in monetary amounts, or may show money and other resources - such as staff hours. A monetary budget is often used to establish the current cost variance of the project. To establish this we need:

(a) **The Actual Cost of Work Performed (ACWP)**. This is the amount spent to date on the project.

(b) **The Budgeted Cost of Work Scheduled (BCWS)**. The amount that was budgeted to be spent to this point on scheduled activities.

(c) **The Budgeted Cost of Work Performed (BCWP)**. This figure is calculated by pricing the work that has actually been done – using the same basis as the scheduled work.

BCWP – ACWP = The **cost variance** for the project.

BCWP – BCWS = The **schedule variance** for the project.

During the project, actual expenditure is tracked against budget on either a separate **Budget Report,** or as part of a regular **Progress Report**.

Budgets should be presented for approval and **sign-off** to the stakeholder who has responsibility for the funds being used.

Before presenting a budget for approval it may have to be revised a number of times. The 'first draft' may be overly reliant on rough estimates, as insufficient time was available to obtain more accurate figures.

On presentation, the Project Manager may be asked to find ways to cut the budget. If he or she agrees that cuts can be made, the consequences of the cuts should be pointed out - eg a reduction in quality.

It may be decided that a project costs more than it is worth. If so, scrapping the project is a perfectly valid option. In such cases the budgeting process has highlighted the situation before too much time and effort has been spent on an unprofitable venture.

1.3 Gantt charts

A **Gantt chart**, named after the engineer *Henry Gantt* who pioneered the procedure in the early 1900s, is a horizontal bar chart used to plan the **time scale** for a project and to estimate the **resources** required.

The Gantt chart displays the time relationships between tasks in a project. Two lines are usually used to show the time allocated for each task, and the actual time taken.

A simple Gantt chart, illustrating some of the activities involved in a network server installation project, follows.

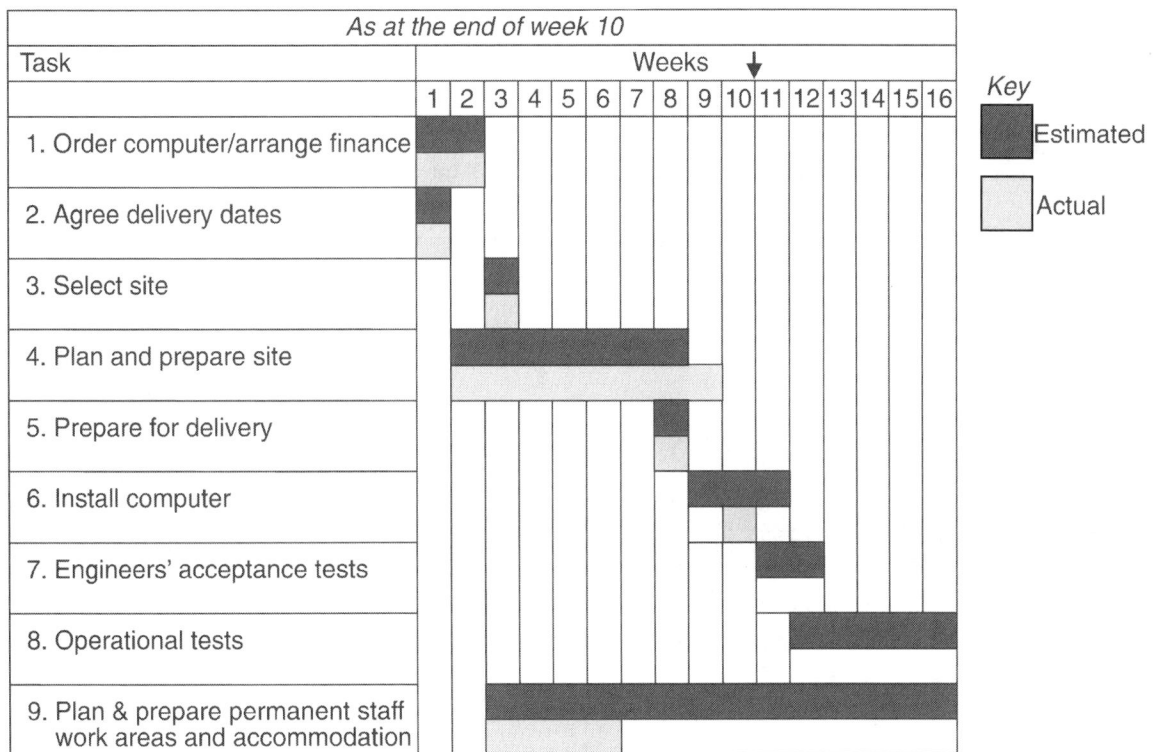

The chart shows that at the end of the tenth week Activity 9 is running behind schedule. More resources may have to be allocated to this activity if the staff accommodation is to be ready in time for the changeover to the new system.

Activity 4 had not been completed on time, and this has resulted in some disruption to the computer installation (Activity 6), which may mean further delays in the commencement of Activities 7 and 8.

A Gantt chart does not show the interrelationship between the various activities in the project as clearly as a **network diagram** (covered later in this chapter). A combination of Gantt charts and network analysis will often be used for project planning and resource allocation.

Question 8.1

Learning outcome B1e

What is the surname of the man who invented the resource planning chart a century ago?

A   Gannt
B   Gantt
C   Ganntt
D   Gant

1.4 Network analysis or Critical Path Analysis (CPA)

Network analysis, also known as **Critical Path Analysis** (CPA), is a useful technique to help with planning and controlling large projects, such as construction projects, research and development projects and the computerisation of systems.

KEY TERMS

NETWORK ANALYSIS requires breaking down the project into tasks, arranging them into a logical sequence and estimating the duration of each.

This enables the series of tasks that determines the minimum possible duration of the project to be found. These are the CRITICAL ACTIVITIES.

Exam alert

Network analysis is very easy to set practical questions on and lends itself particularly well to shorter part-questions. There was a good example of this type of question in a previous syllabus exam for ten marks. Expect something on networks in all exams. You may be required to analyse a critical path diagram (to identify critical path, project duration, earliest start/end times and floats). You may also be required to draw a network, either to help you identify critical path etc or as a task in its own right.

KEY POINT

CPA aims to ensure the progress of a project, so the project is completed in the **minimum amount of time**. It pinpoints the tasks which are **on the critical path**, ie those parts which, if delayed beyond the allotted time, would **delay the completion** of the project as a whole. The technique can also be used to assist in **allocating resources** such as labour and equipment.

Critical path analysis is quite a simple technique. The events and activities making up the whole project are represented in the form of a **diagram**. Drawing the diagram or chart involves the following steps.

STEP 1   Estimating the time needed to complete each individual activity or task that makes up a part of the project.

STEP 2   Sorting out what activities must be done one after another, and which can be done at the same time, if required.

STEP 3   Representing these in a network diagram.

STEP 4   Estimating the critical path, which is the longest sequence of consecutive activities through the network.

The duration of the whole project will be fixed by the time taken to complete the longest path through the network. This path is called the **critical path** and activities on it are known as **critical activities**. Activities on the critical path **must be started and completed on time**, otherwise the total project time will be extended. The method of finding the critical path is illustrated in the example below.

Network analysis shows the **sequence** of tasks and how long they are going to take. The diagrams are drawn from left to right. To construct a network diagram you need to know the activities involved in a project, the expected duration of each and the order (or precedences, or dependencies) of the activities.

For example:

Activity	Expected duration (days)	Preceding activity
A	3	-
B	5	-
C	2	B
D	1	A
E	6	A
F	3	D
G	3	C, E

1.4.1 Activity on arrow presentation

Here is a network diagram showing our example in the form known as **activity on arrow**.

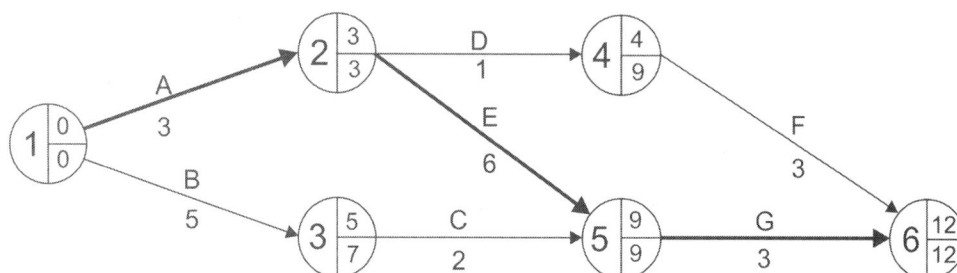

(a)   The network is made up of **events and activities, represented by circles and arrows respectively**. The diagram is laid out to show the dependencies that exist between the activities, working from left to right. The first event is the start of the overall sequence of activities (or the project). Each subsequent event marks the beginning of at least one activity and, therefore, the end of any activities upon which it is dependent. In the network diagram above, for example, event 5 marks the completion of activities E and C and the start of activity G.

(b)   **Events are numbered, working from left to right** and the numbers are entered in the left hand halves of the event circles. Also by convention, the events are numbered so that the event at the end of any activity has a higher number than the one at its start.

(c)   **Activities are lettered, again working from left to right**. The duration of each activity is shown by a number entered against its identifying letter.

(d)   When the basic information has been entered on to the network, it becomes possible to determine the **critical path** through it: this is the sequence of activities that takes the longest time and which therefore determines the overall expected duration of the project.

(e)   A **forward pass** is made through the network and the **earliest event time** (EET) is entered in the upper right quadrant of each event circle. This time depends on the duration of any sequence of activities leading to the event in question and therefore reflects the dependencies involved. In the diagram, event 5, for example, cannot occur (and activity G therefore cannot begin) until the sequences A-E and B-C are both complete. B-C takes (5 + 2) days, while A-E takes (3 + 6) days. The *earliest* event time for event 5 is therefore 9 days. This is a general rule: the EET for any event shows the **longest duration sequence of activities leading to it**.

(f)   When the forward pass is complete, a **rearward pass** is made, starting at the final event and working back to establish the **latest event time** (LET) for each event. The LET for an event is entered in the lower right quadrant of its symbol. Like the EET, the LET depends on the longest sequence of activities involved, but this time it is the sequences of events that follow the event in question that are relevant rather than the ones that precede it. In the example network diagram, event 2 is followed by sequences D-F and E-G with durations (1 + 3) days and (6 + 3) days respectively. If there is to be time to complete the longer sequence E-G, the LET for event 2 must be 3 days.

(g)   When both forward and rearward passes are complete, the **critical path** is identifiable as the route through the network that links all the events that have LET equal to EET: there is no **float** on this path. We discuss float times later in this section. The critical path activities are highlighted on the diagram in some way, such as by using double lines or hash marks.

The **critical path** in the diagram above is AEG. Note the **float time** of five days for Activity F. Activity F can begin any time between days 4 and 9, thus giving the project manager a degree of flexibility.

(h)   Sometimes it is necessary to use a **dummy activity** in a network diagram. Dummies indicate dependency, but they take no time. The need for them arises from the convention that activity arrows are always straight. Thus, if an activity, C, depends on both activity A and activity B, the presentation below is not used:

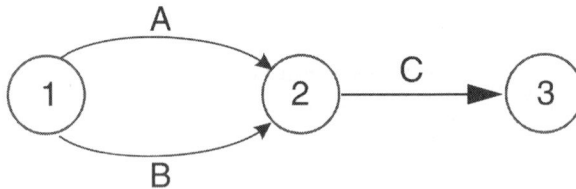

Instead, an extra event and a dummy are inserted:

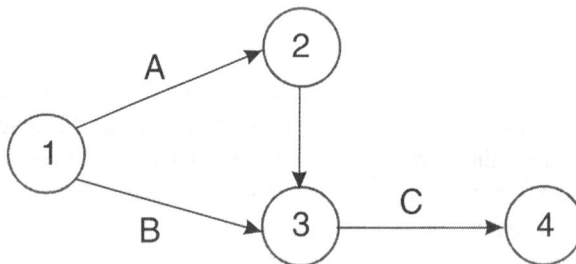

The dummy activity is shown as a broken line. Note also how the dummy starts at an event with a lower number than the one it ends at. Sometimes it is necessary to use a dummy activity not just to comply with the convention, but to **preserve the basic logic** of the network.

Question 8.2

Dummy activity

Learning outcome B1e

Consider the following example of a project to install a new office telephone system.

Activity	Preceding Activity
A: buy equipment	–
B: allocate extension numbers	–
C: install switchboard	A
D: install wiring	B, C
E: print office directory	B

The project is finished when both D and E are complete.

Identify why there may be a need for a dummy activity, and draw the basic network showing it.

Dummy activities are not required when the **activity on node** technique (discussed below) is used for drawing the network.

In our earlier example, if activity G had depended on activity D as well as on activities C and E, this would have been shown as a dummy running from event 4 to event 5.

1.4.2 Activity-on-node presentation

Network diagrams may also be drawn using **activity-on-node** presentation which is similar in style to that used by the **Microsoft Project** software package.

1.5 Example: Activity-on-node

Suppose that a project includes three activities, C, D and E. Neither activity D nor E can start until activity C is completed, but D and E could be done simultaneously if required.

This would be represented as follows.

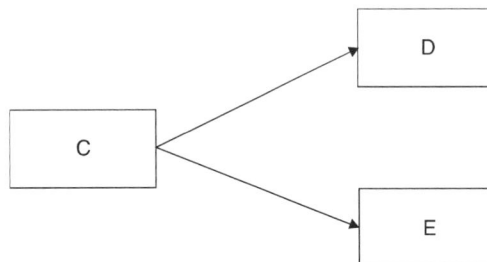

Note the following.

(a)   An **activity** within a network is represented by a rectangular box. (Each box is a **node.**)
(b)   The **flow** of activities in the diagram should be from **left to right**.
(c)   The diagram clearly shows that **D and E must follow C.**

A second possibility is that an activity cannot start until two or more activities have been completed. If activity H cannot start until activities G and F are both complete, then we would represent the situation like this.

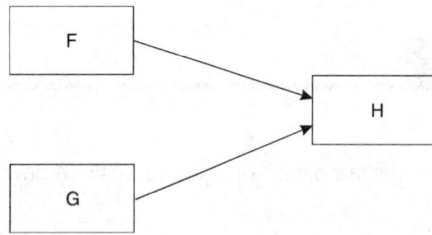

In some conventions an extra node is introduced at the start and end of a network. This serves absolutely no purpose (other than to ensure that all the nodes are joined up), so we recommend that you do not do it. Just in case you ever see a network presented in this way, both styles are shown in the next example.

1.6 Example: starts and ends

Draw a diagram for the following project. The project is finished when both D and E are complete.

Activity	Preceding activity
A	–
B	–
C	A
D	B & C
E	B

Solution

Microsoft Project style

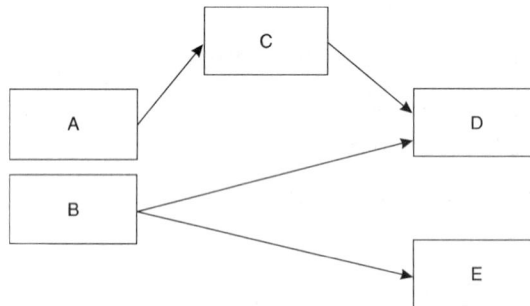

With start and end nodes

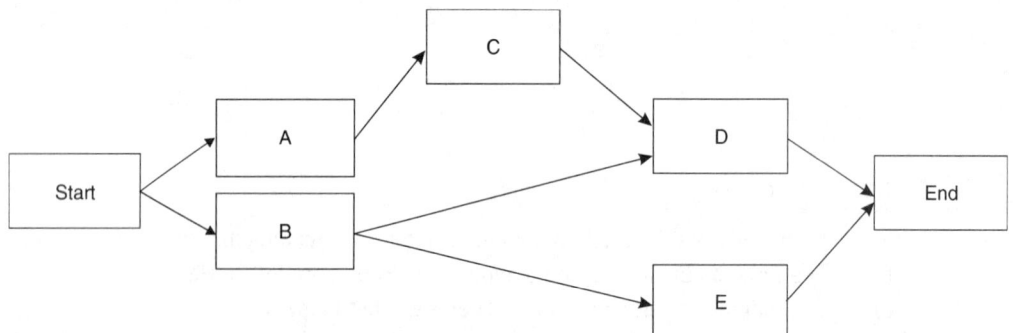

Any network can be analysed into a number of different paths or routes. A path is simply a sequence of activities which can take you from the start to the end of the network. In the example above, there are just three routes or paths.

(a)   A C D.

(b)   B D.

(c)   B E.

The time needed to complete each individual activity in a project must be estimated. This duration is shown within the node as follows. The reason for and meaning of the other boxes will be explained in a moment.

Task A		
	6 days	

1.7 Example: the critical path

Activity	Immediately preceding activity	Duration (weeks)
A	–	5
B	–	4
C	A	2
D	B	1
E	B	5
F	B	5
G	C, D	4
H	F	3
I	F	2

(a)   What are the paths through the network?

(b)   What is the critical path and its duration?

Solution

The first step in the solution is to draw the network diagram, with the time for each activity shown.

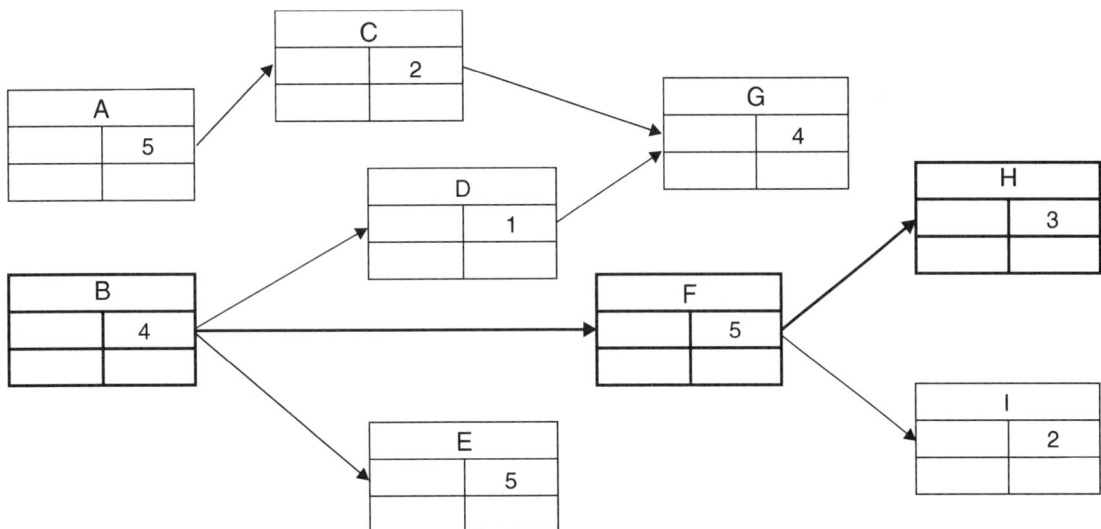

We could list the paths through the network and their overall completion times as follows.

Path	Duration (weeks)	
A C G	(5 + 2 + 4)	11
B D G	(4 + 1 + 4)	9
B E	(4 + 5)	9
B F H	(4 + 5 + 3)	12
B F I	(4 + 5 + 2)	11

The critical path is the longest, BFH, with a duration of 12 weeks. This is the minimum time needed to complete the project.

The critical path is indicated on the diagram by drawing thick (or double-line) arrows, as shown above. In Microsoft Project the arrows and the nodes are highlighted in red.

Listing paths through the network in this way should be easy enough for small networks, but it becomes a long and tedious task for bigger and more complex networks. This is why software packages are used in real life.

Project management software packages offer a much larger variety of techniques than can easily be done by hand. **Microsoft Project** allows each activity to be assigned to any one of a variety of types: 'start as late as possible', 'start as soon as possible', 'finish no earlier than a particular date', 'finish no later than a particular date', and so on.

In real life, too, activity times can be shortened by working weekends and overtime, or they may be constrained by non-availability of essential personnel. In other words with any more than a few activities the possibilities are mind-boggling, which is why software is used.

Nevertheless, a simple technique is illustrated in the following example.

1.8 Find the critical path

The procedure for finding the critical path is essentially the same as we used with the activity on arrow example earlier.

One way of showing earliest and latest **start** times for activities is to divide each event node into sections. This is similar to the style used in **Microsoft Project** except that Project uses real dates, which is far more useful, and the bottom two sections can mean a variety of things, depending what constraints have been set.

These sections record the following things.

(a) The **name** of the activity, for example Task A. This helps us to understand the diagram.

(b) An **ID number** which is unique to that activity. This helps computer packages to understand the diagram, because it is possible that two or more activities could have the same name. For instance two bits of research done at different project stages might both be called 'Research'.

(c) The **duration** of the activity.

(d) The **earliest start time**. Conventionally for the first node in the network, this is time 0.

(e) The **latest start time**.

(*Note*. Don't confuse start times with the **'event'** times that are calculated when using the **activity-on-arrow** method, even though the approach is the same.)

Task D	
ID number: 4	Duration: 6 days
Earliest start: Day 4	Latest start: Day 11

1.8.1 Earliest start times

To find the earliest start times, always start with activities that have no predecessors and give them an earliest starting time of 0. In the example we have been looking at, this is week 0.

Then work along each path from **left to right** through the diagram calculating the earliest time that the next activity can start, just as with activity on arrow.

For example, the earliest time for activity C is week 0 + 5 = 5. The earliest time activities D, E and F can start is week 0 + 4 = 4.

To calculate an activity's earliest time, simply look at the box for the *preceding* activity and add the bottom left figure to the top right figure.

If *two or more* activities precede an activity take the *highest* figure as the later activity's earliest start time: it cannot start before all the others are finished!

1.8.2 Latest start times

The latest start times are the latest times at which each activity can start **if the project as a whole is to be completed in the earliest possible time**, in other words in 12 weeks in our example.

Work backwards from **right to left** through the diagram calculating the latest time at which the activity can start, if it is to be completed at the latest finishing time. For example the latest start time for activity H is 12 - 3 = week 9 and for activity E is 12 - 5 = week 7.

Activity F might cause difficulties as two activities, H and I, lead back to it.

(a)   Activity H must be completed by week 12, and so must start at week 9.
(b)   Activity I must also be completed by week 12, and so must start at week 10.

Activity F takes 5 weeks so its latest start time is either 9 − 5 = week 4 or 10 − 5 = week 5. However, if it starts in week 5 it will not be possible to start activity H on time and the whole project will be delayed. We therefore take the *lower* figure.

The final diagram is now as follows.

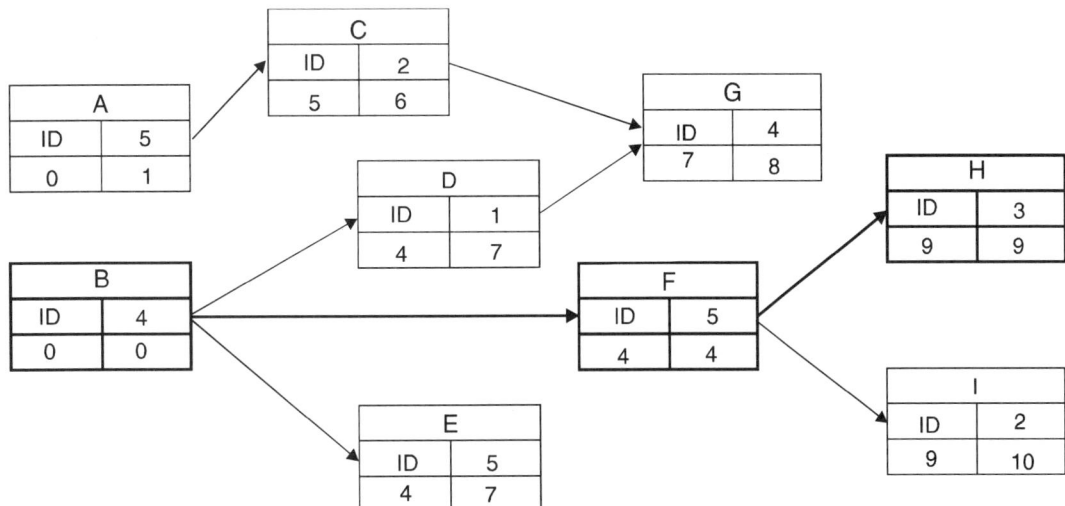

Critical activities are those activities which must be started on time, otherwise the total project time will be increased. It follows that each event on the critical path must have the same earliest and latest start times. The critical path for the above network is therefore B F H.

1.9 Float times

Float time is the time available for unforeseen circumstances.

(a)   **Total float** on an activity is the time available (earliest start date to latest finish date) *less* time needed for the job. If, for example, job A's earliest start time was day 7 and its latest end time was day 17, and the job needed four days, total float would be:

(17 − 7) − 4 = 6 days

(b)   **Free float** is the delay possible in an activity on the assumption that all preceding activities start as early as possible and all subsequent activities also start at the earliest time.

(c)   **Independent float** is the delay possible if all preceding jobs have finished as late as possible, and all succeeding jobs are to start as early as possible.

By definition there is no float time on the critical path.

1.10 Criticisms of critical path/network analysis

KEY POINTS

(a)   It is not always possible to devise an effective WBS for a project.

(b)   **It assumes a sequential relationship** between activities. It assumes that Activity B starts after Activity A has finished. It is not very good at coping with the possibility that an activity 'later' in the sequence may be relevant to an earlier activity.

(c)   There are **problems in estimation**. Where the project is completely new, the planning process may be conducted in conditions of relative ignorance.

(d)   Although network analysis plans the use of resources of labour and finance, it does not appear to develop plans for contingencies, other than crashing time.

(e)   CPA **assumes a trade-off between time and cost.** This may not be the case where a substantial portion of the cost is **indirect overheads** or where the direct labour proportion of the total cost is limited.

1.11 Example: Using Gantt charts and CPA

This example consolidates what we have learnt so far in this section, in a short example on Gantt Charts and CPA.

A company is about to undertake a project about which the following data is available.

Activity	Preceded by activity	Duration	Workers required
		Days	
A	–	3	6
B	–	5	3
C	B	2	4
D	A	1	4
E	A	6	5
F	D	3	6
G	C, E	3	3

There is a multi-skilled workforce of nine workers available, each capable of working on any of the activities.

Draw the network to establish the duration of the project and the critical path. Then draw a Gantt chart, using the critical path as a basis, assuming that jobs start at the earliest possible time.

Solution

Here are the diagrams.

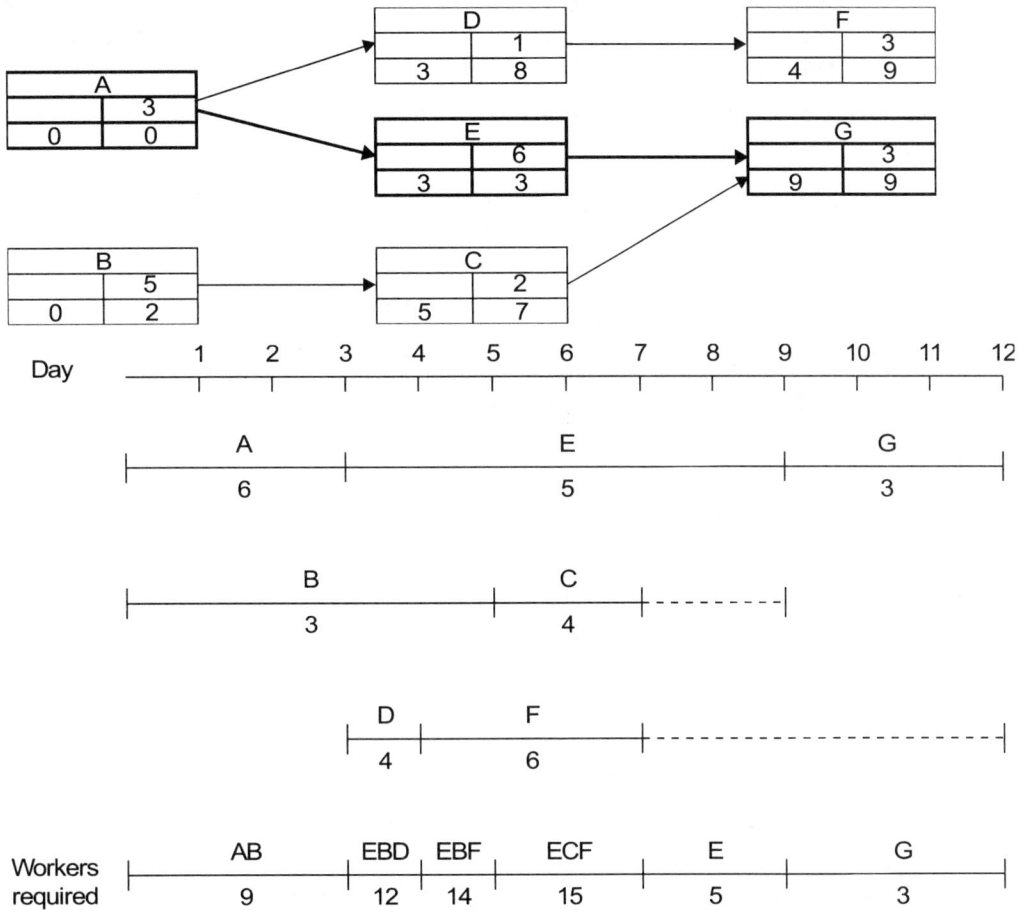

Day: 1 2 3 4 5 6 7 8 9 10 11 12

(First Gantt chart)

A — 6
E — 5
G — 3

B — 3
C — 4

D — 4
F — 6

Workers required:
AB — 9
EBD — 12
EBF — 14
ECF — 15
E — 5
G — 3

It can be seen that if all activities start at their earliest times, as many as 15 workers will be required on any one day (days 6-7) whereas on other days there would be idle capacity (days 8-12).

The problem can be reduced, or removed, by using up spare time on non-critical activities. Suppose we **deferred the start** of activities D and F until the latest possible days. These would be days 8 and 9, leaving four days to complete the activities by the end of day 12.

The Gantt chart would be redrawn as follows.

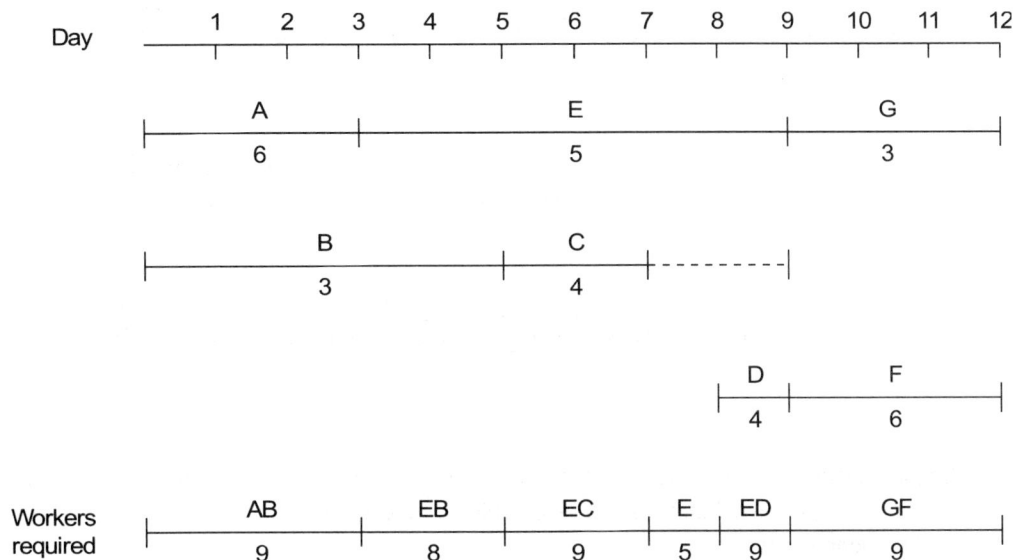

Day: 1 2 3 4 5 6 7 8 9 10 11 12

A — 6
E — 5
G — 3

B — 3
C — 4

D — 4
F — 6

Workers required:
AB — 9
EB — 8
EC — 9
E — 5
ED — 9
GF — 9

1.12 Uncertainty: Project evaluation and review technique (PERT)

Project evaluation and review technique (PERT) is a modified form of network analysis designed to account for **uncertainty**. For each activity in the project, **optimistic**, **most likely** and **pessimistic** estimates of times are made, on the basis of past experience, or even guess-work. These estimates are converted into a mean time and also a standard deviation.

Once the mean time and standard deviation of the time have been calculated for each activity, it should be possible to do the following.

(a)   Establish the duration of the critical path using **expected times**.
(b)   Calculate a **contingency time allowance**.

1.12.1 Expected times

The **probable** time estimate is based on the assumption that **all relevant conditions are normal**. The **expected** time is a different concept: like an **expected value** it is an estimate based on the use of probability.

$$\text{Expected time} = \frac{o + 4m + p}{6}$$

where

o = optimistic estimate
m = probable estimate
p = pessimistic estimate

1.12.2 Contingency time allowances

The standard deviation of the time required for the critical path activities is calculated.

STEP 1   Calculate the standard deviation for each critical activity time using the formula $\frac{p - o}{6}$

STEP 2   Square the standard deviations to obtain the **variances**.

STEP 3   Sum the variances to give the total variance for the critical path.

STEP 4   Find the square root of the total variance to give the standard deviation of the duration of the critical path.

A contingency time allowance stated in terms of a number of **standard deviations** will indicate the probability of completion within the total time allowed, including contingency.

1.12.3 Costs

A similar approach may be employed to deal with uncertainty over costs.

1.12.4 Further analysis

Similar, slightly more complex statistical processes may be used to establish the probability that any given activity or sequence of activities will be completed by a given time. This is useful when **staged payments** or **time penalties** are involved.

Exam alert

PERT is not specifically mentioned in the syllabus, so we have not included a worked example. Be aware that it exists and that it is designed to build in allowances for uncertainty.

1.13 Critical chain project management (CCPM)

Critical chain project management (CCPM) is a relatively new approach which attempts to address some of the problems of time scheduling which arise with network analysis and work breakdown structure.

(a)   Sequential scheduling (eg by CPA) tends to 'pad' the schedule. Safety margins are included in time estimates for tasks – but these are rarely used constructively, so that if a task is finished 'early', the next task can begin early. The safety margin often encourages people to begin tasks at the last moment – and then if problems occur, the task over-runs! Moreover, as Parkinson's Law states, 'work expands to fill the time available for it'.

(b)   Delays in one task are passed on to the next – but time gains are usually wasted (eg to avoid appearing a poor estimator or to set harder standards for future timings).

CCPM overcomes these problems by:

(a)   Allowing **no padding of time estimates**. The agreement of all estimates is sought for this, and the project manager accepts the likelihood that some tasks will be underestimated, leading to over-runs.

(b)   A **margin of safety** is built in at the final stages of the project, to counter the accumulated over-run – *not* at individual tasks, where they are likely to be wasted.

(c)   Precedence relationships (the planned task sequence) is only regarded as a helpful overview: the emphasis is on **responding flexibly** to changes, constraints and problems as they occur.

When time becomes critical on a project, the traditional management approach is based on 'crashing' float activities: reducing their durations by injecting extra resources. The CCPM approach instead uses **buffers** defined quantities of time applied to a project schedule to protect the promised due date from slippage.

(a)   A **feeding buffer** is added to non-critical tasks where they feed into critical tasks, so that the critical task can begin on time.

(b)   A **capacity buffer** is used in a multi-project programme, so that one project is not affected by variations in resource usage by another project.

(c)   A **resource buffer** is added to key resources, so that they will not be in short supply when needed.

1.14 Resource histogram

A RESOURCE HISTOGRAM shows a view of project data in which resource requirements, usage, and availability are shown against a time scale.

KEY TERM

A simple resource histogram showing programmer time required on a software development program is shown below.

Programmer Time Required

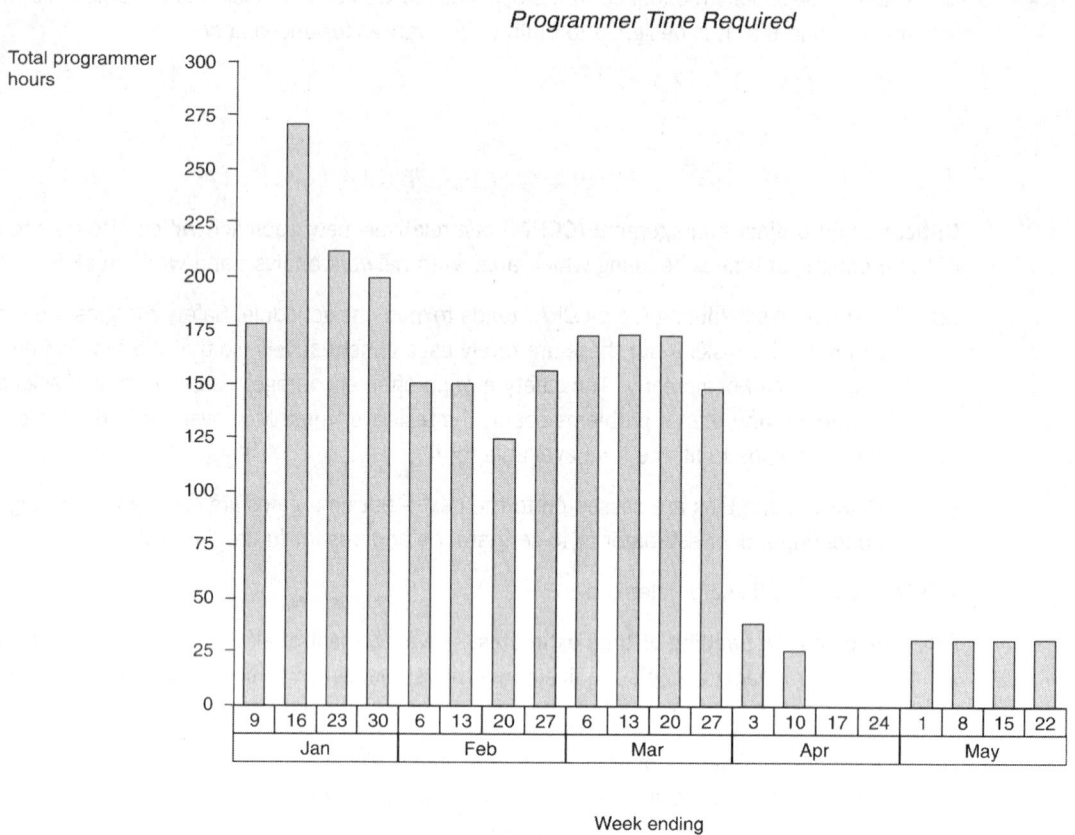

Week ending

Some organisations add another bar (or a separate line) to the chart showing resource availability. The chart then shows any instances when the required resource hours exceed the available hours. Plans should then be made to either obtain further resource for these peak times, or to re-schedule the work plan. Alternately the chart may show times when the available resource is excessive, and should be re-deployed elsewhere. An example follows.

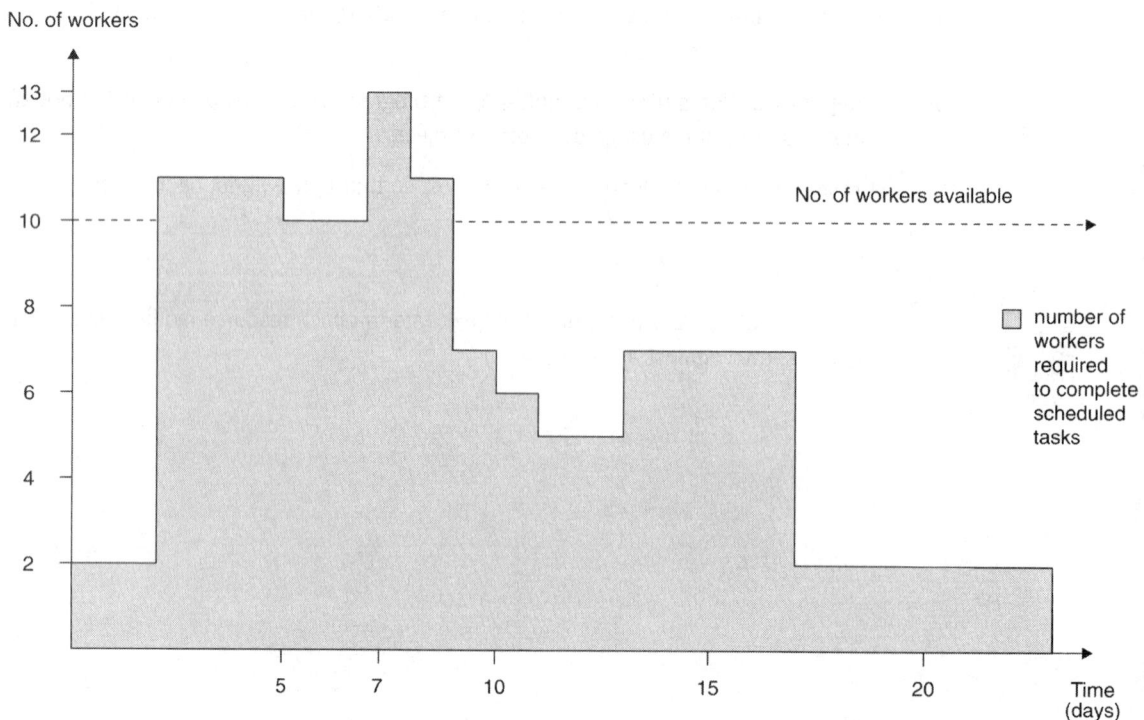

The number of workers required on the seventh day is 13. Can we re-schedule the non-critical activities to reduce the requirement to the available level of 10? We might be able to re-arrange activities so that we can make use of the workers available from day 9 onwards.

1.15 Earned Value Management

Earned value management (EVM) is a means of measuring the progress of a project by **comparing performance on cost and time**. So variances arise from costs not matching budget and also work not being done by the scheduled time for its completion. The following explanation is based on a paper by David Christensen in the *Acquisition Review Quarterly* Fall 1998 entitled 'The Costs and Benefits of the Earned Value Management Process'.

To implement EVM successfully, management must have in place a good management and control system that allows planning and control to be carried out effectively. In other words, EVM can only be used successfully if there are already systems for measuring and controlling projects. EVM enhances these systems by requiring each element of work in the project to have a budget and a time schedule. One of the main measures used in EVM is the **cumulative cost performance index (CPI)** which is the earned value to date/cost to date. This measure can be used to estimate the likely final cost of a contract or estimate at completion.

There are other criteria for EVM, 32 in all, which cover five categories relating to major project management activities. These are:

- Organisation
- Planning and budgeting
- Accounting
- Analysis
- Revisions

EVM was originally adopted in the defence industry but has spread to other large projects. It has benefits and criticisms.

Benefits include the following:

It integrates work, schedule and cost data using a **work breakdown structure**

The CPI provides an early warning signal.

Among the **criticisms** are that the cost-schedule reporting required is 'too detailed, repetitive and voluminous to be used effectively as a management tool' (Coopers and Lybrand/TASC cited in Christensen.)

Section summary

Work breakdown structures are useful tools for **scheduling**, **costing** and **control**. They work by breaking down the project into individual elements and allocating responsibility for these to individuals.

The **project budget** plans the allocation of resources to the project and forms a basis for their control. Budgeting may be top-down or bottom-up.

Gantt charts are a **visual** planning tool useful for projects but are limited in their use as they do not recognise the interrelations between tasks.

Network analysis illustrates interactions and dependencies. It is used to plan the sequence of tasks making up project scope and to determine the **critical path**. **PERT** uses probabilities to make estimates of likely completion and milestone dates.

A **resource histogram** is a useful planning tool that shows the amount and timing of the requirement for a resource (or a range of resources).

Earned value management is a tool that combines **cost** and **time measurement** to monitor large projects. It covers five main categories of project activity which are organisation, planning and budgeting, accounting, analysis and revisions.

2 Project management software

Introduction

Project software is useful when projects become complex. Computer programmes allow project managers to calculate outcomes more quickly than manually and produce standardised reports. Beware of drawbacks though which include human error in inputting and interpreting data.

Project management techniques are ideal candidates for computerisation. Inexpensive project management software packages have been available for a number of years. *Microsoft Project* and *Micro Planner X-Pert* are two popular packages.

Software might be used for a number of purposes.

(a) **Planning and scheduling**

Calendars, **network diagrams** (showing the critical path) and Gantt charts (showing resource use) can be produced automatically once the relevant data is entered. Packages also allow a sort of 'what if?' analysis for initial planning, trying out different levels of resources, changing deadlines and so on to find the best combination.

(b) **Estimating and controlling costs**

As a project progresses, actual data will become known and can be entered into the package and collected for future reference. Since many projects involve basically similar tasks (interviewing users and so on), actual data from one project can be used to provide more accurate estimates for the next project. The software also facilitates and encourages the use of more sophisticated estimation techniques than managers might be prepared to use if working manually.

(c) **Monitoring**

Actual data can also be entered and used to facilitate monitoring of progress and automatically updating the plan for the critical path and the use of resources as circumstances dictate.

(d) **Reporting**

Software packages allow standard and tailored progress reports to be produced, printed out and circulated to participants and senior managers at any time, usually at the touch of a button. This helps with co-ordination of activities and project review.

Most project management packages feature a process of identifying the main steps in a project, and breaking these down further into specific tasks.

A typical project management package requires four **inputs**.

(a) The length of **time** and the resources required for each activity of the project.
(b) The **logical relationships** between each activity.
(c) The **resources** available.
(d) **When** the resources are available.

The package is able to analyse and present this information in a number of ways. The views available within Microsoft Project are shown in the following illustration – on the drop down menu.

The advantages of using project management software are summarised in the following table.

Advantage	Comment
Enables quick re-planning	Estimates can be **changed many times** and a new schedule produced almost instantly. Changes to the plan can be reflected immediately.
Document quality	Outputs are accurate, well presented and easy to understand.
Encourages constant progress tracking	Actual times can be captured, enabling the project manager to be able to compare **actual** progress against **planned** progress and investigate problem areas promptly.
What if? analysis	Software enables the effect of various scenarios to be calculated quickly and easily. Many project managers conduct this type of analysis using **copies** of the plan in separate computer files – leaving the actual plan untouched.
Complexity	Software can handle projects of size and complexity that would be very difficult to handle using manual methods.

The software also has several **disadvantages**, some of which also apply to manual methods.

(a)   **Focus**. Some project managers become so interested in software that they spend too much time producing documents and not enough time managing the project. Entering actual data and producing reports should be delegated to an administrator.

(b)   **Work practices**. The assumptions behind work breakdown structure are not always applicable: people tend to work in a more flexible way rather than completing discrete tasks one by one.

(c)   **Estimates**. Estimation is as much an art as a science and estimates can be wildly wrong. They are subject to the **experience** level of the estimator; influenced by the **need to impress clients**; and based on **assumptions** that can easily change.

(d)   **Human factors**. Skill levels, staff turnover and level of motivation can have profound effects on performance achieved. Also, human variation makes rescheduling difficult since putting more people on to an activity that is running late may actually slow it down at first, while the newcomers are briefed and even re-trained.

Section summary

Project management software can be used to produce detailed project planning documentation, to update plans and to produce reports. These will be faster and more accurate than non-automated tools. They will also suffer from a **lack of intelligence** and human error.

Exam alert

Perhaps the most likely questions on project software are how it might be used, and how it might help the project manager to successfully carry out a project. You are unlikely to have to describe detailed technical specifications.

3   Documentation and reports

Introduction

We will now look at the main **documents and reports** used in project management. The name allocated to documents will vary across different organisations. What is constant is the need for clear and relevant documentation that helps monitor and control the project.

Remember that reports are not a substitute for **face-to-face communication**. Too many (or too lengthy) reports will result in **information overload**.

When outlining possible content of documents some **duplication** of items occurs. This does not mean that information should be repeated, but that the information may appear in one or other of the documents depending on the format adopted by the organisation.

3.1 Project charter

KEY TERMS

The PROJECT CHARTER or PROJECT BRIEF or PROJECT AUTHORISATION or PROJECT INITIATION DOCUMENT is approved by the project board and provides the project manager with the authority to apply resources to project activities. It also defines the terms of reference for the project.

The Project Charter is presented at the **Project Initiation Meeting**. This meeting agrees the project organisation structure and the initial project plans, which may then be incorporated into the Project Charter. The aim of the meeting is to ensure that everyone knows their role; all agree on what job is to be done; there are good business reasons for the project; and that any risks involved have been assessed.

It is likely that the Charter will evolve as the project develops, until it is ultimately incorporated into the Project Management Plan.

The Project Charter defines the **terms of reference** for the project. The charter should contain the statements of project manager, team, stakeholders and sponsors about:

(a)   Overview of the project including key dates
(b)   The **scope** of the project – what it is intended to cover and what it is not
(c)   The objectives for the team during the project, and for the completed project
(d)   Project team organisation, roles and responsibilities

The charter is not likely to give many specifics about how the team and the project are to proceed. The **Project Management Plan** will do that.

3.2 Project Management Plan

The project manager should also develop a **Project Management Plan**. (In some organisations what is described here as the Project Management Plan would simply be called the Project Plan. In other organisations the Project Plan refers only to the project schedule, usually in the form of a network diagram.)

KEY TERM

The PROJECT MANAGEMENT PLAN is used as a reference tool for managing the project. The plan is used to guide both project execution and project control. It outlines how the project will be planned, monitored and implemented.

KEY POINT

The **project management plan** should include:

(a)   Project objectives and how they will be achieved and verified
(b)   How any **changes** to these procedures are to be **controlled**
(c)   The **management and technical procedures**, and **standards**, to be used
(d)   The **budget** and **time-scale**
(e)   **Safety**, health and environmental policies
(f)   Inherent **risks** and how they will be managed

An example of a simple **Project Plan/Project Management Plan** is shown below. This plan was produced by an American organisation, the Project Management Institute (PMI), to manage a project to produce formal project management principles.

The Project Plan **evolves** over time. A high-level plan for the whole project and a detailed plan for the current and following stage is usually produced soon after project start-up. At each subsequent stage a detailed plan is produced for the following stage and, if required, the overall project plan is revised.

Project Management Plan	
Project Name	The full name of this project is 'Project Management Principles.'
Project Manager	The project manager is Joe Bloggs. The project manager is authorised to (1) initiate the project, (2) form the project team and (3) prepare and execute plans and manage the project as necessary for successful project completion.
Purpose/Business Need	This project addresses a need for high-level guidelines for the project management profession through the identification and presentation of project management principles. The project sponsor and accepting agent is the Project Management Institute (PMI) Standards Program Team (SPT). The principal and beneficial customer is the membership of PMI. Principles are needed to provide high-level context and guidance for the profession of project management. These Principles will provide benefit from the perspectives of practice, evaluation, and development.

Project Management Plan	
Product Description and Deliverables	The final deliverable of this project is a document containing a statement of project management Principles. The text is to be fully developed and ready for publication. As a research and development project, it is to be approached flexibly in schedule and resource requirements, with an initially proposed publication date of June 20X1.
Project Management	The project team will use project methodology consistent with PMI Standards. The project is to be managed with definitive scope and acceptance criteria fully established as the project progresses and the product is developed.
Assumptions, Constraints and Risks	The project faces some increased risk that without a clearly prescribed definition of a Principle, standards for product quality will be more difficult to establish and apply. To mitigate this risk, ongoing communication between the project team and the project sponsor on this matter will be required.
Resources	The PMI Standards Program Team (SPT) is to provide the project team with the following.
	Financial. SPT will provide financial resources as available. The initial amount for the current year is $5,000. The project manager must not exceed the allocated amount, and must notify the SPT when 75% of the allocation has been spent.
	Explanation of Standards Program. SPT will provide guidance at the outset of the project, updates as changes occur, and clarifications as needed.
	Personnel/Volunteers. SPT will recruit volunteer team members from within the membership of PMI through various media and liaisons. The project team is to consist of no less than ten members, including the project manager. General qualifications to be sought by SPT in recruiting will be:
	Mandatory
	• Acceptance of project plan
	• Demonstrated capability for strategic, generalised or intuitive thinking
	• Capability to write clearly on technical subject matter for general audiences
	• Capability to work co-operatively with well-developed interpersonal skills
	• Be conversant in English and be able to use telephone and Internet email telecommunications
	As possible
	• **Time availability** (Team members may contribute at different levels. An average of approximately five to ten hours per month is desired.)
	• **Diversity** (Team members collectively may represent diverse nationalities, types of organisations or corporate structure, business sectors, academic disciplines, and personal experience).
	• **Travel** (As determined mutually by the project sponsor and manager, some travel for face-to-face meetings may be requested).
Approach	The project will progress through the following phases.
	Phase 1: Team formation – Recruit and orient volunteer team members. Establish procedures and ground rules for group process and decision making.
	Phase 2: Subject Matter Clarification – Identify and clarify initial scope and definitions of project subject matter.
	Phase 3a: Exploration – Begin brainstorming (through gathering, sharing, and discussion) of data and views in unrestricted, non-judgmental process.
	Phase 3b: Selection – Conclude brainstorming (through evaluation and acceptance

Project Management Plan

	or rejection) of collected data and views. As the conclusion to this phase, the SPT will review as an interim deliverable the selection made by the project team.

Phase 4: Development – Conduct further research and discussion to develop accepted subject matter.

Phase 5: Articulation - Write a series of drafts to state the accepted and developed subject matter as appropriate for the project business need and product description.

Phase 6: Adoption – Submit product to SPT for the official PMI standards approval and adoption process. Revise product as needed.

Phase 7: Closeout – Perform closure for team and administrative matters. Deliver project files to SPT.

Communication and Reporting

The project manager and team will communicate with and report to the PMI Standards Program Team as follows.

Monthly Status Reports – Written monthly status and progress reports are to include:

- Work accomplished since the last report
- Work planned to be performed during the next reporting period
- Deliverables submitted since the last report
- Deliverables planned to be submitted during the next reporting period
- Work tasks in progress and currently outside of expectations for scope, quality, schedule or cost
- Risks identified and actions taken or proposed to mitigate
- Lessons learned
- Summary statement for posting on PMI website

Monthly Resource Reports – Written monthly resource reports are to include:

Financial resources

- Total funds allocated
- Total funds expended to date
- Estimated expenditures for the next reporting period
- Estimated expenditures for entire project to completion

Human resources

- List of all volunteer team members categorised by current involvement (ie, active, new (pre-active), inactive, resigned)
- Current number of new and active volunteer team members
- Estimated number of volunteer team members needed for project completion

Milestone and Critical Status Reports – Additional status reports are to be submitted as mutually agreed upon by SPT and the project manager and are to include at least the following items.

- Milestone Status Reports are to include the same items as the Monthly Status Reports, summarised to cover an entire project phase period since the last milestone report, or entire project to date.
- Critical Status Reports are to focus on work tasks outside of expectations and other information as requested by SPT or stipulated by the project manager.

Project Management Plan	
Acceptance	The project manager will submit the final product and any interim deliverables to the Standards Program Team (SPT) for formal acceptance. The SPT may (1) accept the product as delivered by the project team, or (2) return the product to the team with a statement of specific requirements to make the product fully acceptable. The acceptance decision of the SPT is to be provided to the project manager in writing.
Change Management	Requests for change to this plan may be initiated by either the project sponsor or the project manager. All change requests will be reviewed and approved or rejected by a formal proceeding of the Standards Program Team (SPT) with input and interaction with the project manager. Decisions of the SPT will be documented and provided to the project manager in writing. All changes will be incorporated into this document, reflected by a new version number and date.

Plan acceptance	Signature and date
By PMI Standards Program Team	_____ 12 July 20X0 Fred Jones – PMI Technical Research & Standards Manager
By Project Manager	_____ 20 July 20X0 Joe Bloggs – PMI Member

The format and contents of a Project Management Plan will **vary** depending on the organisation involved and the complexity of the project. The contents page and introduction from a detailed Project Management Plan relating to a software implementation project at a call centre follow.

Call centre software implementation - Project Management Plan

CONTENTS		Page
1	INTRODUCTION	
2	PROJECT ROLES	
3	COMMUNICATIONS PLAN	
4	TRAINING PLAN	
5	CHANGE MANAGEMENT PLAN	
6	QUALITY MANAGEMENT	
7	PROJECT DOCUMENTATION	
8	FINANCIAL MANAGEMENT	
9	PROGRAMME MANAGEMENT	

SECTION 1

INTRODUCTION

1.1 Purpose of the Project Management Plan

The purpose of this Plan is to define the working relationship between Project Team (PT) and the Manager, Customer Centres Group (MCCG). It details the level of service to be provided by Project Team to the client and the associated cost. If the nature of the project changes, or if situations develop which indicate a need for modification, then this plan will be altered accordingly in consultation with the Client. This Plan details key milestones, the methods for delivering these milestones, and responsibilities of the project manager, project owner and the project team representatives.

1.2   Project Objective

To develop and fully support a call centre environment that promotes the achievement of '80% of all incoming calls resolved at the first point of contact.'

1.3   Project Deliverable

To deliver to the MCCG, fully commissioned and operational system upgrades as defined within this project plan, including an appropriately skilled call centre team, by 15 April 20X0 at an estimated Project Team cost of $123,975.

Note: Only the contents page and introduction of this comprehensive plan are reproduced here.

3.3 Progress report

A PROGRESS REPORT shows the current status of the project, usually in relation to the planned status.

The frequency and contents of progress reports will vary depending on the length of, and the progress being made on, a project.

The report is a **control tool** intended to show the discrepancies between where the project is, and where the plan says it should be.

A common form of progress reports uses two columns – one for **planned** time and expenditure and one for **actual**.

Any additional content will depend on the format adopted. Some organisations include only the 'raw facts' in the report, and use these as a basis for discussion regarding reasons for variances and action to be taken, at a project review meeting.

Other organisations (particularly those involved in long, complex projects) produce more comprehensive progress reports, with more explanation and comment.

The report should monitor progress towards key **milestones.**

A progress report may include a milestone slip chart which compares planned and actual progress towards project milestones. Planned progress is shown on the X-axis and actual progress on the Y-axis. Where actual progress is slower than planned progress **slippage** has occurred.

Milestone slip chart

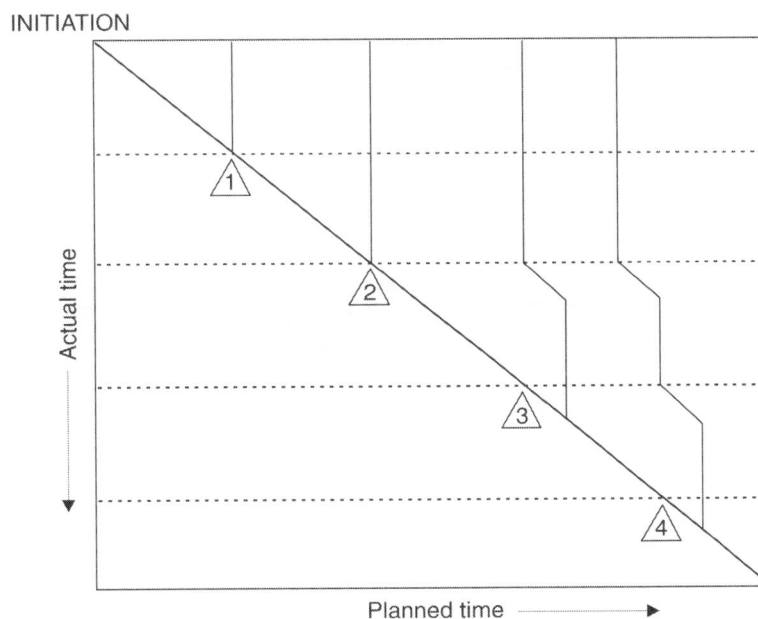

On the chart above milestones are indicated by a triangle on the diagonal planned progress line. The vertical lines that meet milestones 1 and 2 are straight – showing that these milestones were achieved on time.

At milestone 3 some slippage has occurred. The chart shows that no further slippage is expected as the progress line for milestone 4 is the same distance to the right as occurred at milestone 3.

We look at ways of dealing with slippage later in this chapter.

The progress report should also include an updated budget status – such a report could adopt the format shown in the following example.

CASE STUDY

PROJECT STATUS REPORT

Project title: Software Implementation   **To date:**   **11 May 200X**

OVERALL STATUS	Behind __XX__ days	On target	Ahead........days

KEY MILESTONES

	Plan	Actual
1. Project scope and plans signed off		
2. SLA / contract signed off		
3. Acceptance criteria signed off		
4. Training plan signed off		
5. Business processes signed off		
6. User training complete (on existing 'test' system)		
7. Pilot system established		
8. Pilot system reviewed		
9. Go live date confirmed		
10. Go live		

IMPACT OF SLIPPAGES

M/s	Details / planned remedial action	Date

KEY RISKS

Ref	Description	Management actions	Date

KEY ISSUES

Ref	Description	Resolve by date

FINANCIAL STATUS

$ 000's	(a) Initial budget	(b) Current budget (inc approved changes)	(c) Actual spend to date	(d) Forecast spend to complete	(e) Variance	Reason
Capital						
Fixed						
Variable						
Ongoing						
Fixed						
Variable						
Total						

Note: Variance = (c+d) – b

Other comments (notable achievements / major changes / planned absences etc):

Project Manager..

Project Sponsor..

3.4 Completion report

The COMPLETION REPORT summarises the results of the project, and includes client sign-off.

KEY TERM

On project completion the project manager will produce the **Completion Report.** The main purpose of the completion report is to document (and gain client sign-off for) the end of the project.

The report should include a **summary** of the project outcome. The completion report should contain:

(a)   Project objectives and the outcomes achieved.

(b)   The final project budget report showing expected and actual expenditure (If an external client is involved this information may be sensitive - the report may exclude or 'amend' the budget report).

(c)   A brief outline of time taken compared with the original schedule.

The completion report will also include provision for any **on-going issues** that will need to be addressed after completion. Such issues would be related to the project, but not part of the project. (If they are part of the project the project is not yet complete!) An example of an on-going issue would be a procedure for any 'bugs' that become apparent *after* a new software program has been tested and approved.

Responsibilities and procedures relating to any such issues should be laid down in the report.

The manager may find it useful to distribute a provisional report and request **feedback**. This should ensure the version presented for client sign-off at the completion meeting is acceptable to all parties.

A more detailed review of the project follows a few months after completion, the post-completion audit.

3.5 The post-completion audit

The POST-COMPLETION AUDIT is a formal review of the project that examines the lessons that may be learned and used for the benefit of future projects.

KEY TERM

The audit looks at all aspects of the project with regard to two questions. We look at this in detail in the next chapter.

3.6 Project meetings

The multi-disciplinary nature of most larger projects makes frequent meetings unavoidable: they are essential for the proper management of project progress. There will be both scheduled, regular meetings and occasional meetings as required. They will be concerned with three main areas of project management.

(a)   **Project design review meetings** are held to air technical problems and possible solutions and to gain approval for design features and changes.

(b)   **Project status review meetings** are held regularly to monitor progress and gain approval for schedule changes.

(c)   **Problem-solving meetings** are held as required to investigate, define and solve (and gain approval for the solutions to) problems as they arise.

Section summary

A variety of **reports** and other **documentation** is used in project management. The **project charter** authorises the work and cost; various **planning documents** are produced; regular **progress reports** are submitted by the project manager and a **completion report** is produced when the objective has been realised. The post-completion audit should generate a report and recommendations.

4   The project team

Introduction

One of the key tasks the project manager has is to build a team to carry out the project. This team needs a range of skills and may include people drafted in for a specific task as well as long-term members. Team building was covered in Chapter 2 for teams in general but we have tailored our review to project teams in particular in this section.

Notice the particular features of team structures which are set up for the purpose of running the project.

4.1 Teams and teamworking

We discussed the way groups and teams function in Chapter 2. That was a general coverage, applicable to all work groups and, therefore, relevant to project teams as well: recap that material if you need to.

In this section, we offer some notes on aspects of teamworking and leadership that are particularly relevant to the project environment.

4.2 Building a project team

KEY TERM

The PROJECT TEAM comprises the people who report directly or indirectly to the project manager.

Project success depends to a large extent on the team members selected. The ideal project team achieves project completion on time, within budget and to the required specifications – with the minimum amount of direct supervision from the project manager.

The team will comprise individuals with **differing skills and personalities**. The project manager should choose a balanced team that takes advantage of each team member's skills and compensates elsewhere for their weaknesses.

The project team will normally be drawn from existing staff, but highly recommended **outsiders with special skills** may be recruited. When building a team the project manager should ask the following questions.

(a)   **What skills** are required to complete each task of the project? This list will be based on the project goals established previously.

(b)   **Who** has the talent and skills to complete the required tasks, whether inside or outside the organisation?

(c)   Are the people identified **available**, **affordable**, and able to join the project team?

(d)   What level of **supervision** will be required?

This information should be **summarised in worksheet format**, as shown in the following example.

Project Skill Requirements		
Project Name: **Project Manager:**	**Date worksheet completed:**	
Task	Skill needed	Responsibility

The completed worksheet provides a document showing the skills required of the project team. Deciding who has the skills required for each task and if possible seconding those identified to the project team, should be done **as early as possible**. Team members should then be able to **participate** in the planning of schedules and budgets. This should encourage the acceptance of agreed deadlines, and a greater commitment to achieve project success.

The individuals selected to join the team should be told **why they have been selected**, referring both to their technical skills and personal qualities. This should provide members with guidance as to the role they are expected to play.

Although the composition of the project team is critical, project managers often find it is not possible to assemble the ideal team, and have to do the best they can with the personnel available. If the project manager feels the best available team does not possess the skills and talent required, the project should be **abandoned or delayed.**

Once the team has been selected each member should be given a (probably verbal) project briefing, outlining the overall aims of the project, and detailing the role they are expected to play.

4.3 Managing the project team

Group cohesiveness is an important factor for project success. It is hoped that team members will **develop and learn from each other**, and solve problems by drawing on different resources and expertise.

The performance of the project team will be enhanced by the following.

(a)   Effective communication
(b)   All members being aware of the team's purpose and the role of each team member
(c)   Collaboration and creativity among team members
(d)   Trusting, supportive atmosphere in the group
(e)   A commitment to meeting the agreed schedule
(f)   Innovative/creative behaviour
(g)   Team members highly interdependent, interface effectively
(h)   Capacity for conflict resolution

(i)   Results orientation

(j)   High energy levels and enthusiasm

(k)   An acceptance of change

Collaboration and interaction between team members will help ensure the skills of all team members are utilised, and should result in 'synergistic' solutions. Formal (eg meetings) and informal channels (eg e-mail links, a bulletin board) of **communication** should be set up to ensure this interaction takes place.

Refer back to Part A of this Study Text. We have already discussed many aspects of people management that can be applied to project working, including:

(a)   Methods for developing and building teams

(b)   Methods for managing conflict and negotiating solutions

(c)   Supporting communicating development and ideas generation.

CASE STUDY

BUSINESS DAY SURVEY – PROJECT MANAGEMENT – STAFF ARE THE KEY TO SUCCESS

People who have left the comfort of their traditional management environment are often the most important ingredient in successful project management.

You can have the best tools and techniques, the most advanced systems and methods and most innovative structure, but ultimately it is the committed project team of people who choose to make it happen, says Mark Wright, MD of Scott Wilson's project management division. The faster the markets change and the technology advances, the greater need there will be for successful project management implementation to satisfy goals.

As the project management profession continues to evolve, globalisation is often seen as a threat. But it need not be seen as such, says David Sparrow, managing partner of global operations for EC Harris, an international capital project and facilities consultancy company. The reality is that through globalisation, various world-class processes are exposed to the local market. Similarly, clients are globalising and changing to remain competitive, he says.

Project managers need to be focused on client needs and thus the technical consultancy skill is now just a mere tool that needs to be applied in innovative ways. Trevor Lowen, GM of business development for Axis Interim Management, says the problem most organisations have is the lack of project management experience within their ranks. He says the use of interim management is creating a growing project management resource for business.

Interim management is the provision of short-term senior managers, industry or functional specialists to companies to undertake an assignment which they lack the resources to undertake themselves. The launch of a new product is an example of project work undertaken by interim managers.

Business Day (South Africa) Nov 1999

4.4 Project team meetings

There are three basic types of meeting used in project management.

(a)   **Status review meetings** used to control progress and maintain stakeholder communication. The purpose of such meetings, which may be held periodically and/or at defined project milestones and end of stages, is to:

   (i)   Keep the team, project manager and key stakeholders informed about progress and current status (where the project is 'up to' in terms of planned schedule, cost and deliverables).

   (ii)   Identify any problems, issues or changes that need to be resolved.

   (iii)   Develop action plans for the next period or stage of the project, and/or authorise changes to the existing project plan in response to deviations or contingencies.

(b)   **Problem-solving meetings**, which may be called at any time an issue emerges in the course of the project. The meeting should involve those with a stake, competence and/or authority to make decisions and take corrective action (eg re-allocate resources to the problem).

(c)   **Post-project evaluation meetings**, used to review and derive learning from the project. Such a meeting should involve all relevant participants and stakeholders, to cover a range of issues: how effective was the project in attaining its objectives; How effectively was the project planned, managed and controlled; Are stakeholders satisfied with the deliverables and the process?; What 'unfinished business' needs to be followed up?; What lessons can be learned for future projects?; and so on.

4.5 Project team structure

There are three broad ways of structuring a project within an organisation. We looked at these in Chapter 6 when we considered how projects fit in with certain organisational structures.

(a)   **Functional structure**: the project is 'housed' within a particular function (eg a marketing research project within the marketing department), alongside the on-going work of the function. This takes advantage of the shared resources and pooled expertise of the function. It also provides continuity when individuals leave the project, and when the project ends. It is common in organisations where most of the work is project based, such as construction companies. However, there is the risk that the project/client may take lower priority than the on-going work of the 'host' function. There may also be restricted access to needed resources and expertise in other functions.

(b)   **Matrix structures**: team members in different functions report both their departmental manager (for on-going work in that function) and to a project manager (for work pertaining to the project). It is perhaps the most common modern approach to project working for organisations which undertake projects on an occasional basis. It is relatively efficient approach to genuine cross-functional collaboration.

(c)   **Process (pure project) structure**: The whole organisation structures permanently for project work. There are soft, or no, boundaries between functions: work is seen from a horizontal business process or value chain perspective. Project management is built into the line management structure, so that the project manager has full line authority over the process and involved personnel. This may be reflected in advertising agency and management consultancy project groups, for example.

This structure has the advantage of direction, co-ordination, control and accountability (via the central authority of the project manager). It gives each project a distinct identity and visibility, and helps to develop project management knowledge (since there is a more or less permanent group of experts in place for successive projects).

However, it can also cause duplication if each project is fully staffed on a permanent basis, and isolation of the project team from the rest of the organisation.

Section summary

Project success depends to a large extent on how the **project team** is selected, led/managed and structured.

5   Compare and contrast project control systems

Introduction

Organisations use a range of systems to control projects. We have already met **PMBOK and PRINCE2**. In this section we also consider **Six Sigma** and end with a quick review of other systems.

5.1 PMBOK and PRINCE2

We have already mentioned the US **Project Management Institute** and the **Guide to the Project Management Body of Knowledge** (PMBOK). This is widely used by specialists. There is a good article which compares PRINCE2 with PMBOK. This is 'Comparing PRINCE2 with PMBOK' by *R Max Wideman*, which can be found on the Internet.

5.2 Six Sigma

5.2.1 The search for perfection

Six Sigma was original a scheme of improvement for quality in manufacturing but it has been adapted to project management.

'Sigma' is a measure of statistical variation. Six Sigma indicates near perfection. It is a rigorous operating methodology aimed to ensure complete customer satisfaction by ingraining a culture of excellence, responsiveness and accountability within an organisation.

Six Sigma requires the delivery of **defect-free products or services** 99.9997 percent of the time. Thus, only 3 out of a million products or services offered would fail to meet the customer's expectations. The average company runs at around Three Sigma, or 66,800 errors per million.

This superior target for operations and product designs requires **Six Sigma programs** that constantly measure and analyse data on the variables in any process. These then use statistical techniques to understand what improvements will drive down defects.

These programs also incorporate a system for gathering customer feedback.

5.2.2 The five key steps

Six Sigma entails five key steps. These can be memorized as an acronym **DMAIC.** These are the steps an organisation should take when looking at **improving processes.**

STEP 1   **Define.** Identify the customer requirements, clarify the problem and set goals.

STEP 2   **Measure.** Select what needs to be measured, identify information sources and gather data.

STEP 3   **Analyse.** Develop hypotheses, identify the key variables and root causes.

STEP 4   **Improve.** Generate solutions and put them into action, either modifying existing processes or developing new ones. Quantify costs and benefits.

STEP 5 **Control.** Develop monitoring processes for continued high-quality performance.

Organisations can also apply Six Sigma to **new processes** and the steps here are define, measure, analyse, design and verify or **DMADV**.

5.2.3 The benefits

Benefits claimed for Six Sigma include:

(a) **Making processes more rigorous** by using hard, timely data, not opinions or gut feel, to make operating decisions

(b) **Cultivating customer loyalty** by delivering superior value

(c) **Strengthening and rewarding teamwork** by aligning employees around complex processes whose performance can still be easily, clearly and empirically measured

(d) **Accustoming managers to operating in a fast-moving internal business environment** that increasingly mirrors marketplace conditions outside the company

(e) **Achieving quantum leaps** in product performance

(f) **Reducing variation in service processes**, such as the time from order to delivery, or offering a consistent, high-quality service experience

(g) **Improving financial performance**, through cost savings from projects, increased revenue from improved products and expanded operating margins

5.3 Other control systems

The **Carnegie Mellon Software Engineering Institute** has developed management processes and methodologies for improving the quality of new software, such as **IDEAL** and **INTRO**.

Chapter Roundup

✓   **Work breakdown structures** are useful tools for **scheduling**, **costing** and **control**. They work by breaking down the project into individual elements and allocating responsibility for these to individuals.

The **project budget** plans the allocation of resources to the project and forms a basis for their control. Budgeting may be top-down or bottom-up.

Gantt charts are a **visual** planning tool useful for projects but are limited in their use as they do not recognise the interrelations between tasks.

Network analysis illustrates interactions and dependencies. It is used to plan the sequence of tasks making up project scope and to determine the **critical path**. **PERT** uses probabilities to make estimates of likely completion and milestone dates.

A **resource histogram** is useful planning tool that shows the amount and timing of the requirement for a resource (or a range of resources).

Earned value management is a tool that combines cost and time measurement to monitor large projects. It covers five main categories of project activity which are organisation, planning and budgeting, accounting, analysis and revisions.

✓   **Project management software** can be used to produce detailed project planning documentation, to update plans and to produce reports. These will be faster and more accurate than non-automated tools. They will also suffer from a **lack of intelligence** and human error.

✓   A variety of **reports** and other **documentation** is used in project management. The **project charter** authorises the work and cost; various **planning documents** are produced; regular **progress reports** are submitted by the project manager and a **completion report** is produced when the objective has been realised. The post-completion audit should generate a report and recommendations.

✓   Project success depends to a large extent on how the **project team** is selected, led/managed and structured.

Quick Quiz

1   What would you expect a Project Initiation Document to contain?

2   What is Work Breakdown Structure?

3   What is the purpose of a Gantt chart?

4   What is the Project Quality Plan used for?

5   Why do many project managers prefer to use project management software?

6   An approach to project management which uses buffers to flexibly respond to the uncertainties of time estimating is:

     A   Critical Path Analysis
     B   Project Management Maturity
     C   Critical Chain Project Management
     D   PERT

Answers to Quick Quiz

1   Contents could include: project objectives, the scope of the project, overall budget, final deadlines, the ultimate customer, resources, risks inherent in the project, a preliminary project plan (targets, activities and so on) and details of how the project is to be organised and managed.

2   Work Breakdown Structure (WBS) is the process of breaking down the project into manageable tasks.

3   A Gantt chart displays the time relationships between tasks in a project. It is a horizontal bar chart used to estimate the amount and timing of resources required.

4   The Project Quality Plan is used to guide both project execution and project control. It outlines how the project will be planned, monitored and implemented.

5   A project management software package saves time and produces high quality output. As with all software, it is dependent on the quality of the data fed into the package - the length of time required for each activity of the project, the logical relationships between each activity, the resources available and when the resources are available.

6   C   (PERT has a similar orientation, in accounting for uncertainty, but is a very different approach.)

Answers to Questions

8.1 Terminology

The answer is B: Gantt. Some people find this extremely difficult to get right.

8.2 Dummy activity

The problem arises because D can only start when both B and C have been finished, whereas E is only required to follow B. The only way to draw the network is to use a dummy activity.

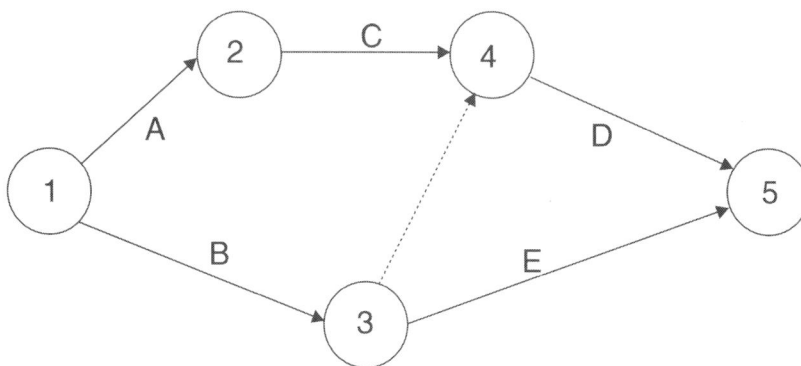

Now try the question below from the Exam Question Bank

Number	Level	Marks	Time
Q8	Introductory	10	18 mins

PROJECT CONCLUSION

We are now at the end of our study of this part of the syllabus. In this chapter we wrap up what we need to know abut projects by looking into the **post completion audit**. This is a formal review of the project after it has finished which aims to learn from the project for the benefit of future projects.

Project troubleshooting is a separate topic and here we consider what happens when problems arise in the project. Remember that the project manager must balance time, cost and quality (**The Iron Triangle**) which can clash with each other.

Project managers should also look at **continuous improvement** especially where projects are frequently carried out in an organisation so that they improve their management building up an expertise in this area.

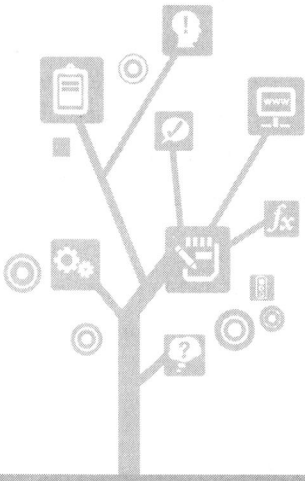

9

topic list	learning outcomes	syllabus references	ability required
1 Post-completion audit	B1i	B1(xv)	analysis
2 Project troubleshooting	B1j	B2(i)	application
3 Projects and continuous improvement	B1j	B1(xv)	application

1   Post-completion audit

Introduction

This section looks at what happens when the project comes to an end. The project needs to be signed off and delivered to the client. In common with any contract, the project completion report should ensure the parties both agree what has been delivered and sign when they do agree.

The post-completion audit is a formal review of the project that examines the lessons that may be learned and used for the benefit of future projects.

1.1 Completion report

KEY TERM

The COMPLETION REPORT summarises the results of the project, and includes client sign-off.

We looked at project completion and the Completion Report in the last chapter. As the topic is relevant here, we will just update the main points covered again.

KEY POINT

The report should include a **summary** of the project outcome. The completion report should contain:

(a)   Project objectives and the outcomes achieved.

(b)   The final project budget report showing expected and actual expenditure (If an external client is involved this information may be sensitive - the report may exclude or 'amend' the budget report).

(c)   A brief outline of time taken compared with the original schedule.

The completion report will also include provision for any **on-going issues** that will need to be addressed after completion. Such issues would be related to the project, but not part of the project. (If they are part of the project the project is not yet complete!) An example of an on-going issue would be a procedure for any 'bugs' that become apparent *after* a new software program has been tested and approved.

Responsibilities and procedures relating to any such issues should be laid down in the report.

The manager may find it useful to distribute a provisional report and request **feedback**. This should ensure the version presented for client sign-off at the completion meeting is acceptable to all parties.

A more detailed review of the project follows a few months after completion, the post-completion audit.

1.2 The post-completion audit

KEY TERM

The POST-COMPLETION AUDIT is a formal review of the project that examines the lessons that may be learned and used for the benefit of future projects.

KEY POINT

The audit looks at all aspects of the project with regard to two questions.

(a)   Did the end result of the project meet the **client's expectations**?

    (i)   The actual **design** and **construction** of the end product
    (ii)   Was the project achieved **on time**?
    (iii)   Was the project **completed within budget**?

(b)   Was the **management of the project** as successful as it might have been, or were there bottlenecks or problems? This review covers two things.

    (i)   Problems that might occur on future projects with similar characteristics
    (ii)   The performance of the team individually and as a group

In other words, any project is an opportunity to learn how to manag[...] should be clear that the audit thus has the potential to reduce the cost[...] Where senior management are reluctant to incur the expense involved in a[...] may be carried out to demonstrate the likely effect on future costs.

The post-completion audit should involve **input from the project team**. A simple q[...] developed for all team members to complete, and a reasonably informal meeting held[...] on what went well (and why), and what didn't (and why).

KEY POINT

This information should be formalised in a report. The **post-completion audit report** should con[...] following.

(a) A **summary** should be provided, emphasising any areas where the structures and tools used to manage the project have been found to be **unsatisfactory**.

(b) A **review** of the end result of the project should be provided, and compared against the results expected. Reasons for any significant **discrepancies** between the two should be provided, preferably with suggestions of how any future projects could **prevent these problems recurring**.

(c) A **cost-benefit review** should be included, comparing the forecast costs and benefits identified at the time of the feasibility study with actual costs and benefits.

(d) **Recommendations** should be made as to any steps which should be taken to **improve** the project management procedures used.

Section summary

Lessons learnt that relate to the way the **project was managed** should contribute to the smooth running of future projects.

A starting point for any new project should be a **review** of the documentation of any **similar projects** undertaken in the past.

2 Project troubleshooting

Introduction

This is where project managers really earn their money, dealing with problems!

Project managers need to manage any number of conflicting requirements and trade-offs. These trade-offs concern time, cost and quality. One of the major problems a project manager must cope with is slippage where project targets begin to fall behind.

2.1 Project management problems

Project managers are often appointed from the ranks of technical experts. Technical ability is no guarantee of management skill – an individual might be highly proficient technically, but not a good manager.

The project manager has a number of **conflicting requirements**.

(a) The project sponsor wants the project **delivered on time**, to specification and within budget.

(b) **User** expectations may be misunderstood, ignored or unrealistic.

(c) The project manager has to plan and supervise the work of **experts** in fields about which he may have little knowledge.

velop an **appropriate management style**. What he or she should
project will fail if users are not consulted, or if the project team is
needs to encourage participation from users, an excessively

an unrealistic deadline - the timescale is fixed early in the
may be accepted as deadlines before sufficient consideration is

a recipe for disaster. Unrealistic deadlines would be identified
process was undertaken.

s, resulting in costly changes to the system as it is being

2.2 Trade-offs in project objectives: the Iron Triangle

The relationship between key project objectives an be shown as a triangle.

The Time/Cost/Quality Triangle

TIME

'Competitive edge' project

Low-budget project

Safety-critical project

COST   QUALITY

All three objectives are important: we would like our projects to finish on time, within budget *and* to the
level of quality/performance required. However:

(a)   The **relative importance** of each objective may depend partly on the type of project. Where a
        project is aiming to beat a competitor to market, or has a non-negotiable deadline (eg organising
        an event that has been advertised for a particular date) time will be a priority. In a low-budget or
        fixed-grant project, cost is a priority: once resources run out, the project ceases – complete or not!
        In a safety-critical project (such as building or aircraft construction) quality is a priority.

(b)   This inevitably requires **trade offs** between the three objectives. Schedule slippage could be
        brought back on track by extra expenditure, for example, or cost slippage could be brought back on
        track by 'cutting corners' on quality. Ideally, such decisions should be taken within a framework of
        stakeholder expectations and consultation.

The balance of time, cost and quality will influence decision making throughout the project – for example
whether to spend an extra $5,000 to fix a problem completely or only spend $1,000 on a quick fix and
implement a user work-around?

2.3 Dealing with slippage

When a project has slipped behind schedule there is a range of options open to the project manager.
Some of these options are summarised in the following table.

Action	Comment
Do nothing	After considering all options it may be decided that thin; continue as they are.
Add resources	If capable staff are available and it is practicable to ad(it may be possible to recover some lost ground. Could soʀ...
Work smarter	Consider whether the methods currently being used are the most suitable – for example could prototyping be used.
Replan	If the assumptions the original plan was based on have been proved invalid a more realistic plan should be devised.
Reschedule	A complete replan may not be necessary – it may be possible to recover some time by changing the phasing of certain deliverables.
Introduce incentives	If the main problem is team performance, incentives such as bonus payments could be linked to work deadlines and quality.
Change the specification	If the original objectives of the project are unrealistic given the time and money available it may be necessary to negotiate a change in the specification.

2.4 Controlling project changes

Some of the reactions to slippage discussed above would involve changes that would significantly affect the overall project. Other possible causes of changes to the original project plan include:

(a)   The availability of new technology
(b)   Changes in personnel
(c)   A realisation that user requirements were misunderstood
(d)   Changes in the business environment
(e)   New legislation eg Data protection

The **earlier** a change is made the **less expensive** it should prove. However, changes will cost time and money and should not be undertaken lightly.

When considering a change **an investigation** should be conducted to discover:

(a)   The consequences of **not** implementing the proposed change
(b)   The impact of the change on **time, cost** and **quality**
(c)   The expected costs and benefits of the change
(d)   The risks associated with the change, and with the *status quo*

The process of ensuring that proper consideration is given to the impact of proposed changes is known as **change control**.

Changes will need to be implemented into the project plan and communicated to all stakeholders.

WHY CAN'T WE BUILD SOFTWARE LIKE WE BUILD BUILDINGS?

Introduction

CASE STUDY

The software development industry has a reputation for poor project performance. This makes many organisations reluctant to undertake large development projects.

The Project Manager's Responsibility

The project manager plays the same role within a software development as they would in a construction project: their aim is to finish the job within time and cost to the quality required.

Get the Right Person for the Job

Just imagine that you have built a garden shed and a passer-by compliments you on your achievement. The passer-by then asks since you've made such a good job of the shed would you build a new three-bedroom house. After all, it will utilise the same materials, just more of them. It's not very likely is it?

Yet many people learned how to use a PC-based database development application such as Microsoft Access, Dbase, or Paradox, and then went on to build 'commercial' systems. In many cases these were not designed to be commercial systems, they just started as a useful place to store information, then grew until they became a vital source of information.

Appropriate Methodology

Every size of building project requires its own set of processes to most cost effectively complete. Software is no different. Applying skyscraper standards to a house will be expensive and result in over-engineering. When setting up a software development project the same rules apply. Select the right methodology and ensure that your developer is experienced with this methodology.

Reusable Components

When building, there is little point in designing non-standard sizes into a building then trying to fit standard components into the design. These components are often as simple as the garage or interior doors, but could well include items which cannot easily be built on site, such as sealed unit double glazing.

In the software industry, the reuse of code or objects is a relatively recent development. As with buildings, if you are going to use existing components, the design must be created in such a way as to accommodate them. In the early years of software development these components would be simple subroutines which could be copied into the code to perform simple tasks such as date verification. More recently the advent of commercially successful component infrastructures such as CORBA, the Internet, ActiveX or Java Beans, has triggered a whole industry of off-the-shelf components for various domains, allowing you to buy and integrate components rather than developing them all in-house. Reusability shifts software development from programming software (a line at a time) to composing software (by assembling components) just as a modern builder does not fabricate their own material but assembles the delivered components.

Responsibility of the Project Manager

The project manager is key to the success of any project and must be able to manage both people and other resources. The key role of the manager is not simply in monitoring progress but is in fixing things when they go wrong. This is the case in both industries.

Create the Environment

The project manager can create a little bit of 'project magic' by establishing a project environment which allows project participants to operate effectively and co-operatively. This type of project environment is significantly more effective than an aggressive environment.

Issue Resolution

In the building industry, the issues that arise are more likely to be physical in nature. If a team is gathered around a hole in the ground or a piece of building which doesn't quite fit, they can start to suggest solutions by measuring, drawing or simply explaining what they think will fix it.

In the software industry, the issues that arise are more likely to be abstract. However, the need for the sponsor to understand the problem is just as important. Any explanation that can be given in terms which mere mortals can understand is worth far more than the exact technical definition, especially if the sponsor is required to make a decision on how to resolve the issue.

Conclusion

The use of modern methodologies and modelling techniques allows much of the risk of software development to be reduced. The rigorous use of CASE tools applies standards which are as close to regulations the software industry has at present. The development environments, frameworks and object libraries of software developers are gaining in sophistication to a point where many of the risks are already written out of a new development.

It may take a few years to come to terms with the international implications of electronic commerce over the Internet. The changes in taxable revenue of having a business process independent of location will have far-reaching effects. This is likely to be the next challenge for the technology industry.

Adapted from a paper prepared by Synergy International 1999

Section summary

Common problems in project management include conflicting requirements for time, cost and quality at the outset; changing user requirements; the need to supervise experts; poor planning; and poor control.

3 Projects and continuous improvement

Introduction

Continuous improvement applies to projects especially where they become a routine means of working in organisations. In that case project managers must think about how they might improve the way they run projects.

Project management can be a **core strategic competence** for companies working in such industries as consulting and construction. Such companies must ensure that they maintain and improve their project management abilities if they are to continue to be commercially successful. We have already looked at the project management maturity model as a framework for assessing project competence and improvement.

KEY POINT

Kerzner describes a five level **project management maturity model,** in terms of continuous organisational improvement in methodology. Organisations should aspire to progress to the highest level, which is a state of **continuous improvement**. The five levels need not necessarily follow one another in a linear fashion: they may overlap, but the degree of overlap allowed is reflected in the risk associated with the overall process.

Kerzner's Five Levels

1 **Common knowledge**
   The importance of project management to the organisation is understood and training in the basic techniques and terminology is provided.

2 **Common processes**
   The processes employed successfully are standardised and developed so that they can be used more widely, both for future projects and in concert with other methodologies such as total quality management.

3 **Singular methodology**
   Project management is placed at the centre of a single corporate methodology, achieving wide synergy and improving process control in particular. A separate methodology may be retained for Information Systems matters.

4   **Benchmarking**
Competitive advantage is recognised as being based on process improvement and a continuing programme of benchmarking is undertaken.

5   **Continuous improvement**
Benchmarking information is critically appraised for its potential contribution to the improvement of the singular methodology.

Models such as *Kerzner's* are a guide to progress; in particular they indicate corporate training needs and career development routes for project managers.

Section summary

Kerzner suggests that where project management is a core competence, **a continuous improvement** approach should be taken to developing and consolidating the methodology.

Chapter Roundup

✓ Lessons learnt that relate to the way the **project was managed** should contribute to the smooth running of future projects.

✓ A starting point for any new project should be a **review** of the documentation of any **similar projects** undertaken in the past.

✓ **Common problems** in project management include conflicting requirements for time, cost and quality at the outset; changing user requirements; the need to supervise experts; poor planning; and poor control.

✓ *Kerzner* suggests that where project management is a core competence, **a continuous improvement** approach should be taken to developing and consolidating the methodology.

Quick Quiz

1   Briefly outline the relationship between quality, cost and time in the context of an information systems project.

2   What actions could a project manager take to improve the accuracy of his or her budget estimates?

3   You are a project manager, and milestone reports indicate that your project is beginning to fall behind schedule. Brainstorm some of your options for dealing with this slippage.

4   What should a completion report on a project include?

5   What should the risk management process achieve?

Answers to Quick Quiz

1   The **quality** of information system produced is dependent upon (among other things) the **time** available to develop the system and the **resources** (ie cost) available to the project. Insufficient time and / or resources will have an adverse effect on the quality of system produced.

2   Estimates can be **improved** by:

- **Learning** from past mistakes and using past (adjusted/real) figures
- Ensuring sufficient design **information** to cost all project/product elements
- Ensuring as **detailed a specification as possible** from the customer
- Properly **analysing the job** into its constituent units (using a work breakdown structure)
- Using **accurate labour budgets and costs** (eg realistic time requirements, pay rates etc)

3

Action	Comment
Do nothing	After considering all options it may be decided that things should be allowed to continue as they are.
Add resources	If capable staff are available and it is practicable to add more people to certain tasks it may be possible to recover some lost ground. Could some work be subcontracted?
Work smarter	Consider whether the methods currently being used are the most suitable – for example could prototyping be used.
Replan	If the assumptions the original plan was based on have been proved invalid a more realistic plan should be devised.
Reschedule	A complete replan may not be necessary – it may be possible to recover some time by changing the phasing of certain deliverables.
Introduce incentives	If the main problem is team performance, incentives such as bonus payments could be linked to work deadlines and quality.
Change the specification	If the original objectives of the project are unrealistic given the time and money available it may be necessary to negotiate a change in the specification.

4   The completion report should contain:

(a)   Project objectives and the outcomes achieved.

(b)   The final project budget report showing expected and actual expenditure (If an external client is involved this information may be sensitive - the report may exclude or 'amend' the budget report).

(c)   A brief outline of time taken compared with the original schedule.

5   The risk management process should identify and quantify the risks associated with the project, and decide as how the risks should be managed.

Now try the question below from the Exam Question Bank

Number	Level	Marks	Time
Q9	Examination	25	45 mins

STRATEGIC MANAGEMENT AND ASSESSING THE COMPETITIVE ENVIRONMENT

Part C

INTRODUCTION TO STRATEGY

We now turn to Part A of the syllabus which covers strategic management.

Strategy deals with how an organisation **achieves its objectives**. We look at contrasting ways in which different researchers consider that strategy *should be* made and how strategy *is* made.

- In the **rational model** (Section 2), decisions are made by logical analysis of the environment and the organisation. This is followed by the generation of alternative strategies, which are then evaluated objectively on their merits. The aim might be to secure a 'fit' with the environment, or a **positioning** approach.

- The emergent **strategies** model (Section 3) argues that strategy can be generated from the 'bottom up' as well as from the 'top down'. Strategic management can mean 'crafting strategies as they emerge'.

- The **muddling through or adaptive approach** (Section 4) suggests that strategies in many organisations are small-scale adjustments, which react to events.

- The **bounded rationality** and **logical incrementalist** (Section 4) models seek a middle ground between these two extremes.

- **Chandler** identified the evolution of structure as organisations mature and their strategies change. This is covered in Section 5.

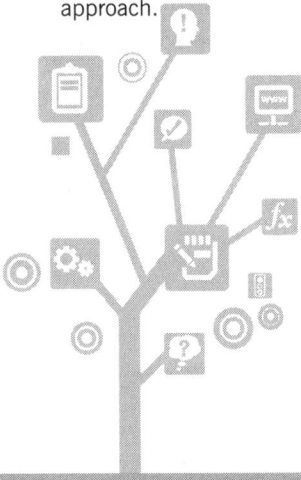

10

topic list	learning outcomes	syllabus references	ability required
1 What is strategy – background	–	–	comprehension
2 Planned strategies: the rational model	A2b	A2(ii)	analysis
3 Crafting emergent strategies	A2b	A2(ii)	analysis
4 Other approaches to strategy	A2b	A2(ii)	analysis
5 Strategy and structure	A2b	A2(ii)	analysis

1   What is strategy – background

STRATEGY: A course of action, including the specification of resources required, to achieve a specific objective.

STRATEGIC PLAN: Statement of long-term goals along with a definition of the strategies and policies which will ensure achievement of these goals.

POLICY: Undated, long-lasting and often unquantified statement of guidance regarding the way in which an organisation will seek to behave in relation to its stakeholders.

CIMA Official Terminology

KEY TERMS

Introduction

Strategy can be quite a difficult idea to grasp. Make sure you understand the definitions here and how strategic decisions differ from others.

Strategy is about the higher direction of an enterprise. In organisations it is the concern of top management. In less exalted contexts it might be a simple technique.

An organisation's objective is the desired outcome of the organisation's activities. The strategy specifies in broad terms how this should be achieved. (**Tactics** are the 'most efficient deployment of resources in an agreed strategy'.) This can be summarised in a diagram.

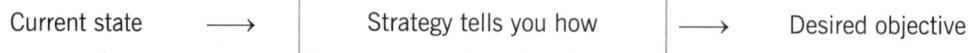

Current state $\longrightarrow$ | Strategy tells you how | $\longrightarrow$ Desired objective

An overall **objective** of a government's road safety policy might be to reduce deaths and injuries. There might be several **strategies** to achieve this objective: more stringent law enforcement, advertising, speed limits and so on.

CIMA's *Official Terminology* suggests the following example for a company. If the primary objective is 25% return on capital, and the secondary objective is to increase market share a **strategy** would be to 'sell on the basis that a 20% increase in sales and production capacity will reduce unit costs by 25%. Use £10m capital'.

1.1 Strategic decisions

What distinguishes strategy from other types of organisation decision? *Johnson and Scholes* have summarised the characteristics of **strategic decisions** for an organisation.

(a)   **Scope.** Strategic decisions will be concerned with the **overall, long-term direction** of activities.

(b)   **Environment.** Strategy involves the matching of an organisation's **activities** to the **environment** in which it operates.

(c)   Strategy also involves the matching of an organisation's activities to its **resource capability.** Strategic decisions include the allocation or re-allocation of resources.

(d)   Strategic decisions will **affect operational decisions**, because they will set off a chain of lesser decisions and operational activities, involving the use of resources.

(e)   Strategic decisions will be affected by the **values and expectations of the people in power** within the organisation.

(f)   Strategic decisions have implications for **change** throughout the organisation, and so are likely to be **complex** in nature.

It is possible to think of strategy under three headings.

(a)   **Financial strategy** is about raising capital and satisfying the requirements of providers of capital for income and capital appreciation. It encompasses capital structure, dividend policy, investor relations, risk management and hedging.

(b)   **Investment and resource strategy** uses capital to provide resources of strategic value, such as premises, new products and brands and to finance growth by acquisition.

(c)   **Competitive strategy** is about how the business makes its market offering and seeks to out-perform its commercial rivals. Competitive strategy generates the earnings needed by financial strategy. There is thus a flow of value linking the three elements together.

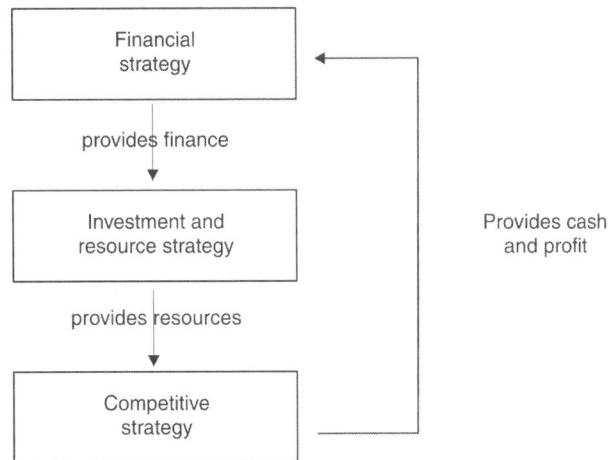

1.2 Competitive advantage

So far, we have discussed organisations in general terms. Business organisations differ from other types of organisation in that their fundamental objective is **financial**. Smaller, owner-managed businesses may be content to jog along without making too much effort or achieving significant success, but for most businesses, the aim of strategy will be to achieve a **competitive advantage** that leads to **superior profitability and Return on Investment**. In economic terms, they are seeking **supernormal profit**, a phrase you may recall if you have studied economics previously.

This is only possible where conditions of **perfect competition** do not apply: that is to say, supernormal profit would normally be associated with firms operating under monopoly, oligopoly or monopolistic competition, any of which should give them some degree of **market power**. All of these market forms are based on the idea of making it difficult for potential competitors to erode that market power through effective competition. You should keep this idea in mind when we come to discuss the means by which firms typically seek to achieve competitive advantage.

Section summary

Strategic decisions affect the scope of an organisation's activities, the environment, resource capability and allocation, and the organisation's long-term direction.

2 Planned strategies: the rational model

KEY TERM

RATIONAL MODEL. Rational models can be set up to solve most problems. In the context of management, 'rational model' usually means a comprehensive and systematic system of strategic planning.

Introduction

The rational model is likely to be the model that comes to mind when you think about strategy. It is a planned and methodical way of looking at strategy in the organisation. It has three main steps: **analysis, choice and implementation.** According to the model, strategies are made at the top of the organisation and flow down to the operational level (**remember Anthony's levels of managerial activity in Chapter 2**). At each level supporting strategies are devised which cover activities at those levels. So for instance, the marketing director would have a strategy for each market and there would be operational strategies for issues such as pricing and personnel.

2.1 Plans

A plan is a consciously intended course of action. Many early books on business strategy supposed that strategy making was necessarily a planning process. Often, this involved delegating the task of strategic planning to a separate department.

Drucker defines strategic planning as having three aspects.

(a)   'The continuous process of **making present risk-taking decisions** systematically and with greatest knowledge of their futurity' (ie their future effect)

(b)   '**Organising systematically** the efforts needed to carry out these decisions'

(c)   '**Measuring the results** of these decisions ... through organised, systematic feedback'

2.2 The need for planning

KEY POINT

Characteristics of strategic plans:

(a)   They are written down.
(b)   They are circulated to interested parties in the organisation.
(c)   They specify the outcomes (eg where the business wishes to be in five years' time).
(d)   They specify how these are going to be achieved.
(e)   They trigger the production of operational plans lower down the hierarchy.

Advantages of having a plan:

(a)   It helps the organisation to take a long view and avoid short-termism while at the same time providing a sensible approach to the uncertainty of the future.

(b)   It guides the allocation of resources.

(c)   It co-ordinates the activities of the various parts of the organisation, ensuring the integration of operational management decisions into the higher strategy, the wider organisational context and longer term goals.

(d)   It sets a standard by which the actual performance of the organisation is measured and controlled.

(e)   It comforts providers of finance in particular and encourages suppliers and employees to think in terms of a long-term relationship.

(f)   The process of forming strategy requires wide and complex input so it can have a beneficial effect on managers' personal development and awareness and can assist with management succession planning.

2.3 The rational model

The rational model represents the **planned approach** to strategy development. Through a sequence of logical steps it will allow the development, appraisal, choice, implementation and control of strategies that allow for both **internal** and **external factors**.

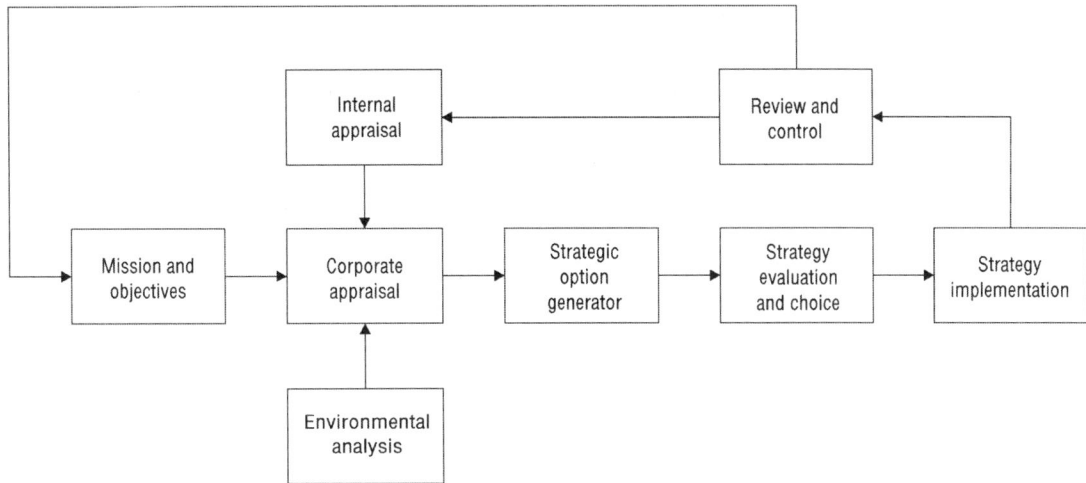

The rational model

2.3.1 Strategic analysis

Strategic analysis is concerned with understanding the strategic position of the organisation in the widest terms.

(a)   The organisation operates within its **environment**. This has political/legal, economic, social and technological (**PEST**) aspects. The environment contains both **threats** and **opportunities.**

(b)   The **resources** of the organisation (its **strengths** and **weaknesses**), how it adds value and its **distinctive competences** (what it does best or uniquely) must be matched to opportunities.

(c)   **Mission and objectives**. The firm sets goals. The expectations of **stakeholder groups** must be considered. For example, if the organisation is financed by venture capitalists, a strategy might require sufficient growth generation to allow them to recover their investment.

(d)   **Corporate appraisal** assesses the overall importance of strengths, weaknesses, opportunities and threats (SWOT) in the light of the organisation's mission and objectives. We revisit corporate appraisal in Chapter 13 when we consider how the organisation appraises its internal strengths and weaknesses and external environment.

2.3.2 Strategic choice

Strategy development has three phases.

(a)   **Strategic options generation**. A variety of options can be set up for consideration. The aim is to build on the firm's capabilities to exploit market opportunities.

(b)   **Strategic options evaluation**. Each option is then examined on its merits.

   (i)   Is it **feasible**?
   (ii)   Is it **suitable**, considering the firm's existing position?
   (iii) Is it **acceptable** to stakeholders?

   A variety of techniques is used to assess and value strategies. Some will be assessed on financial criteria such as net present value. Where this is not possible, or where the uncertainty in the environment is great, other models are used. For instance, **scenario building** postulates a number of possible futures based on different assumptions about such things as world-wide economic growth, interest rates and competitors.

(c)   **Strategy selection**. A strategy is chosen, according to the evaluation above. This process is strongly influenced by the **values** of the managers concerned.

2.3.3 Implementation of strategy

The chosen strategy is embodied in a corporate plan. From this, plans for operations are developed. The diagram below relates the corporate strategy to the activities of the sales force.

KEY POINT

In this case what is defined as 'strategic' is in part determined by where you are, and your own relation to the plan. Similar cascades will relate corporate strategy to the plans of other departments such as production and HRM.

2.4 Problems with planning

The concept of formal processes for strategy generation and their limited success in practice has led to criticisms of both the rational model and the very idea of strategic planning as a separate business activity.

(a)   The formal approach encourages a sense of **omniscience and control** among planners: this is dangerous because of the **inherent unpredictability of the business environment**. In practice, strategic thinking tends to be iterative and even muddled, with the various processes and stages being undertaken on an *ad hoc* basis. Moreover, as we shall see later, many developments of strategic significance, or information about them, occur at **operational** level. Environmental uncertainty also tends to lead managers to adopt an approach of **bounded rationality**, satisfying themselves with solutions that are acceptable rather than ideal.

(b)   There is an associated problem of **detachment**: planners tend to assume that strategy can be divorced from operations and this is inappropriate. Planners rarely have to implement the strategies they devise and feedback occurs too late or is badly filtered. Similarly, more junior managers, not directly involved in the planning process may misunderstand or resist the plans they are required to implement.

(c)   The idea of the **learning organisation** has been applied to strategy on the basis that an organisation's strengths and weaknesses can be in constant flux and strategy should reflect current developments as a kind of learning process itself.

(d)   The formal approach is usually couched in terms of a **planning cycle**: this may extend for up to five years; even a one year cycle is not responsive enough to changing circumstances.

(e)   The **expense and complexity** of the formal approach are inappropriate for smaller businesses.

(f)   There has been much comment on the place of **strategic objectives**. A sociological perspective, such as that of *Cyert and March*, views the emergence of strategic objectives as the result of a

political or **bargaining process** involving a variety of priorities and interest groups. Today the capitalist, free market philosophy seems more strongly established than ever and most Western business organisations acknowledge the creation of shareholder value as their primary objective.

(g)   There is a view that great strategies should not really be rational at all, but should emerge from **inspiration and entrepreneurial talent**. *Brunsson* argues for the selection of a reasonable course of action from among a small number of choices, while *Ohmae* finds that good strategy is made by practical people who 'have an intuitive grasp of the basic elements of strategy'.

The criticisms are directed less at planning in principle, than at the assumption that **planning can create strategies** as opposed to supporting strategic decisions, co-ordinating them and mobilising resources.

2.5 A strategic planning system

The rational model of strategy-making, or any other formal system, has distinct **organisational implications**. Indeed, it is really only where strategy develops over time (as is often the case in smaller businesses), that there is no requirement for systems to support the strategy process. Even then, it seems likely that such an approach to strategy would be more effective if some of the features outlined below were incorporated.

(a)   A **system to collect strategic information** should be established. This would have dedicated human resources (which might be as little as a few hours per week for one or more individuals) and Information Systems to support them. Information about the environment and internal matters could be accumulated on a routine basis *via*, for example, data service subscriptions and management accounting reports. These could be **supplemented by specific investigations**, perhaps using consultants to do the work.

(b)   A **strategic planning committee** or team formed at the strategic apex, but with staff support and advice from subordinate managers. Such a team should meet regularly to direct information-gathering, consider reports and liaise with consultants. It would also have the task of debating and agreeing future strategy: even where strategic decisions are taken by a single person, they are likely to be improved by such a process of consideration.

(c)   A **system to implement and control the chosen strategy** might include a written summary plan; live or video presentations to stakeholders; detailed plans and budgets developed to support the overall plan; and the establishment of financial and non-financial targets for managers and staff. Suitable reports should be made and control action taken.

It would also be necessary to renew existing strategy regularly as a kind of **double loop control**, checking that current objectives, methods and plans were still relevant.

Section summary

Strategic plans are formal statements of direction. The planning process suggests a sequence of strategic analysis (of the environment and the organisation), strategy generation and evaluation (several options are weighed up and compared) and strategic choice of the best alternative.

3 Crafting emergent strategies

Introduction

Johnson, Scholes and Whittington describe **emergent strategies** as those that develop out of the day to day and routine activities of the organisation. These strategies are not drawn up as a separate activity unlike the rational strategies we have just read.

Mintzberg refers to 'crafting' strategies. Even though strategies are emergent, they are guided and moulded by managers.

3.1 Types of strategy

The case example below shows how a spectacularly successful strategy developed, *against* managers' conscious intentions.

CASE STUDY

Honda

Honda is credited with identifying and targeting an untapped market for small 50cc bikes in the US, which enabled it to expand, trounce European competition and severely damage indigenous US bike manufacturers. By 1965 Honda had 63% of the US market.

In practice, there was no clearly thought-out strategy at all. Honda had wanted to compete with the larger European and US bikes of 250ccs and over. These bikes had a defined market, and sold through dedicated motor bike dealerships. Disaster struck when Honda's larger machines developed faults - they had not been designed for the hard wear and tear imposed by US motorcyclists. Honda was unable to sell the larger machines.

Honda had made little effort to sell the small 50cc motorbikes - its staff rode them on errands around Los Angeles. Sports goods shops, ordinary bicycle and department stores had expressed an interest, but Honda did not want to confuse its image in the target market of men who bought the larger bike.

The faults in Honda's larger machines meant that reluctantly Honda had to sell the small 50cc bike. It proved very popular with people who would never have bought motor-bikes before. Eventually the company adopted this new market with enthusiasm with the slogan: 'You meet the nicest people on a Honda'. Effectively, the strategy had emerged, against the conscious 'planned' intentions of management. However, Honda exploited the new market and crafted a strategy to deal with it.

KEY TERM

EMERGENT STRATEGIES arise from *ad hoc* or even uncontrolled responses to circumstances. If they work and have potential, the quick solutions may be developed into strategies.

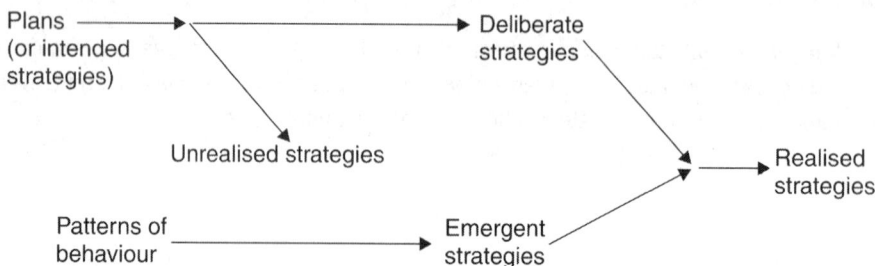

Intended strategies are plans. Those plans or aspects of plans which are actually realised are called **deliberate strategies**.

Emergent strategies are those which develop out of patterns of behaviour. 'Because big strategies can grow from little ideas ... almost anyone in an organisation can prove to be a strategist.' A sales person may sell to some new customers, with the result that the company enters a whole new market.

Question 10.1   Deliberate strategy

Learning outcome A2b

'Deliberate strategies are always based upon earlier planning.' Is it true or false?

The task of strategic management is to control these emergent strategies in the light of a broader insight into the business's capabilities.

CASE STUDY

Emergent strategies can be driven by new business. BPP began life as a training company. Lecturers had to prepare course material. This was offered for sale in a bookshop in the BPP building. Owing to the demand, BPP began offering its material to other colleges, in the UK and world-wide. BPP's publishing and e-learning activities, which began as a small offshoot of BPP's training activities, now lead the market for targeted study material for the examinations of several professional bodies. It is unlikely that this development was anticipated when the course material was first prepared.

3.2 Crafting strategy

There will come a point when even an emergent strategy will need some conscious direction, perhaps to change its course. Alternatively, senior managers, when faced with an emergent strategy, might favour some aspects of it over others. For example a company might pride itself on the high quality of its products, even though this involves expensive labour costs. If the quality strategy is favoured, management might try to develop practices which reduce the cost of this given quality.

Mintzberg uses the phrase **crafting strategy** to help understand this idea. The planning approach encountered already implies rational control and systematic analysis of competitors and markets, and of company strengths and weaknesses. However, the idea of strategy as a **craft** evokes an idea of 'skill, dedication, perfection, through mastery of detail.' More importantly, forming a strategy and implementing it are 'fluid processes of **learning** through which creative strategies evolve'.

Mintzberg uses the image of a potter's wheel. The clay is thrown, and through shaping the clay on the wheel, the potter gives shape to the clay lump through a gradual process. *Mintzberg* believes this is a good analogy of how strategies are actually developed and managed.

(a) The potter can introduce innovations during the process of shaping. The potter is both the producer and consumer of the vase. The gap between thinking and doing is short.

(b) A sales representative who discovers a new way of providing customer satisfactions may have to convince large numbers of people within the organisation of the idea's merits. The gap between insight and execution is a long one.

The trouble with the long **feedback** loop is that there is a separation between 'thinking' and 'doing' when it comes to strategy. This has the following results.

(a) A **purely deliberate strategy prevents learning** (once the formulators have stopped formulating). For example, it is hard with deliberate strategies to learn from mistakes, or stumble by accident into strategic growth.

(b) A **purely emergent strategy defies control**. It may in fact be a bad strategy, dysfunctional for the organisation's future health.

Deliberate strategies can introduce strategic change as a sort of quantum leap in some organisations. In this case, a firm has only a few strategic changes in a short period but these are very dramatic.

CASE STUDY

Mercedes-Benz, having concentrated on large expensive cars, has recently changed its strategy. Its head recently stated that the company's strategy of expecting customers to pay premium prices for 'over-engineered' cars is no longer tenable. The company intends to produce a much wider range of cars, including small cars, than hitherto. This is a major, planned change of direction.

In other organisations, however, strategic change can be *haphazard*. Mintzberg mentions the example of the *Canadian National Film Board*. This used to make short documentaries but ended up by chance with a feature film. This forced it to learn the marketing of such films, and so it eventually became much more involved in feature length productions than before - 'strategy by accident'.

3.2.1 How to craft strategy

Mintzberg mentions a number of essential activities in strategic management.

(a) **Managing stability.** Most of the time, managers should be effectively implementing the strategies, not planning them: formal planning is the detailed working out of the agreed strategy. Obsessions with change are dysfunctional: **knowing when to change** is more important.

(b) **Detecting discontinuity.** Environments do not change regularly, nor are they always turbulent. Strategists should realise that some small environmental changes are much more significant than others, though guessing which these are is a problem.

   (i) **Technological developments** are hard to assess. *Drucker* quotes the example of *Hoffmann-LaRoche*, a Swiss based pharmaceutical company, which began as a small firm making dyes. It acquired the patents to vitamins when no one else wanted them, and invested and borrowed all it could into producing and selling them. It is now an industry leader. Other technologies, combined with cheap production processes, can revolutionise certain industries (eg the motor car revolutionised transportation).

   (ii) International developments are frequent causes of uncertainty. Spotting international trends which are important to the organisation (which markets are likely to grow and so forth) must be supplemented by assessments of commercial and political risks.

(c) **Knowing the business.** Strategic management involves an intimate feel for the business. This has to include an **awareness and understanding of operations**.

(d) **Managing patterns.** 'A key to managing strategy is the ability to detect emerging patterns and to help them take shape'. Some emergent strategies must be uprooted, others nurtured.

(e) **Reconciling change and continuity.** 'Crafting strategy ...... requires a natural synthesis of the future, present and past'. Obsessions with change and or continuity can both be counterproductive.

Question 10.2   Plan or vision

Learning outcome A2b

Britannia Hospital has just appointed a new director, Florian Vole, imported from the private sector, where he had run 'Hanky House' a niche retail operation specialising in handkerchiefs and fashion accessories. The recession put the business into receivership, but Mr Vole was sought out to inject his private sector expertise in running a public sector institution. He calls a meeting of the hospital's senior managerial, medical and nursing staffs. 'What the public sector has been missing too long is vision, and when you're eyeball-to-eyeball with change, it's vision you need, not planning documents and statistics. We need to be nimble and quick to adapt to our customers' ever changing needs. That is our strategy!'

What do you think of Florian Vole's approach?

> **Section summary**
>
> **Emergent strategies** are those which develop out of patterns of behaviour, which is not consciously thought out, but which eventually has a long-term, 'strategic' effect. Emergent strategies need to be crafted by managers and shaped to the organisation's advantage.

4 Other approaches to strategy

> **Introduction**
>
> Incrementalism is taking **small steps** or 'muddling through'. This is the opposite of rational planning and its **long-term approach** to making strategy. There is a middle way, of course, and **logical incrementalism** refers to managers taking small steps and testing strategies as they go along.

4.1 Incremental/adaptive strategy

> **KEY POINT**
>
> **Rationalism** and **incrementalism** are the two models which are generally represented as occupying opposite ends of the spectrum of approaches to strategy-making.

When an organisation appears to be '**muddling through**' then it is likely to be adopting the **incrementalism** approach involving developing the business through a series of **small logical steps**. Management's role will be to provide information, overcome change and plan future developments whilst building support and awareness for those.

Lindblom argued that comprehensive rational planning was impossible, and likely to result in disaster if actively pursued. Strategy making involving small scale extensions of past practices was more likely to be successful: it would avoid major errors, and was more likely to be acceptable, because consultation, compromise and accommodation were built into the process. This **incrementalist** approach was referred to by Mintzberg as the **adaptive** mode of strategy making.

Critics argued that such muddling through was not a good prescriptive model.

(a) **Muddling through** does not work where radical new approaches are needed, and it has a built-in conservative bias. Lindblom denied the accusation of conservative bias, and suggested that it was possible to achieve a radical shift in policy over a period as a result of a series of incremental shifts. But he partially conceded the case for some forward planning in later versions of his model.

(b) Even as a descriptive model of the **public sector**, it does not always fit. Some changes do not seem incremental, but involve dramatic shifts. Examples include the reorganisation of the UK National Health Service.

4.2 A middle way? Logical incrementalism

> **KEY TERM**
>
> LOGICAL INCREMENTALISM was identified by *James Brian Quinn*. Logical incrementalism is not just muddling through: 'it is a purposeful, effective, proactive management technique for integrating both the analytical and behavioural aspects of strategy formation.'

(a) **Strategy is best described as a learning process**, by which managers have to deal with major internal or external events. One of the problems is that it is impossible to predict the long term consequences of decisions made in those situations of crisis or change. For example, the ramifications of a radical new technology may not be foreseen.

(b) **Managers have some notion as to where the organisation should be.** They 'may be able to predict the broad direction but not the precise nature of the strategy that will result'.

(c)   **Managers deliberately keep their decisions small scale**, so that they can be *tested* in small steps, as there is so much uncertainty. However, unlike muddling through which appears simply reactive, the logical incremental model suggests a *conscious* process of decision making.

The implications of the rational model and incrementalism can be expressed in diagrammatic form.

(a)   **Rational planning model**

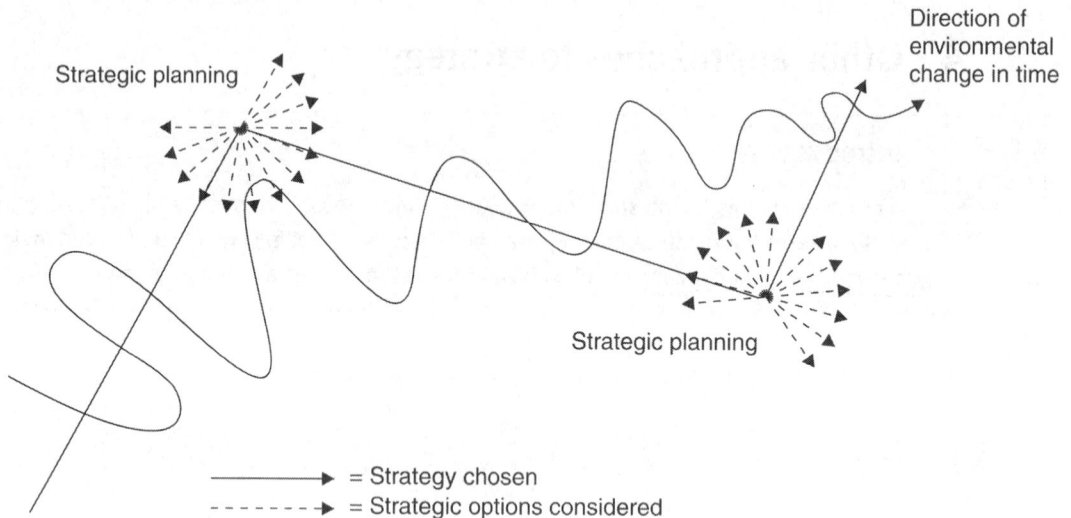

The dangers of the rational model are that the environment may change too quickly for the planning processes to react. All directions are considered, however.

(b)   **Incremental model**

As we can see, the advantage of incrementalism is that it can map the environment closely. However, incremental change may not be enough as the number of strategic options considered may be insufficiently radical in terms of their ability to cope with environmental shift.

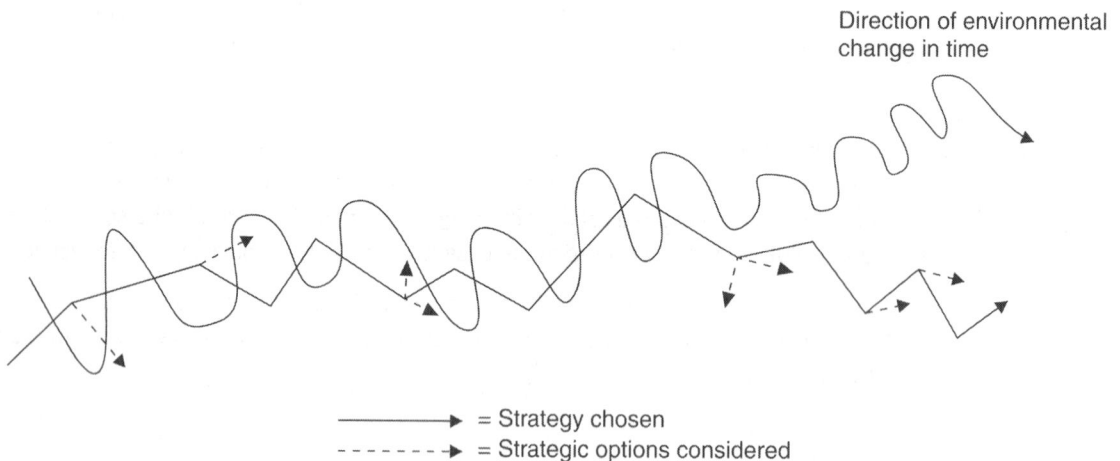

The two models are not mutually exclusive.

(a)   The **rational model** may be appropriate where the change in the environment is significant or where incrementalism is not enough.

(b)   **Incrementalism** may be appropriate where there is significant uncertainty, so that the organisation follows, rather than pre-empts, changes in the environment.

Both the rational model and logical incrementalism contrast with the idea of emergent strategies, in that they hold that strategy is made by managers, whereas in the emergent strategy model it can grow from the lower levels of the organisation.

Question 10.3   Incrementalism

Learning outcome A2b

The logical incrementalist approach to strategy differs from the rational model in that it:

A   Is less bound by formal medium-term forecasting
B   Is more concerned with the company's resources
C   Can be based on *ad hoc* practices introduced by junior staff
D   Is based on solutions that are good enough rather than ideal

4.3 Strategic issues of small businesses

Small organisations have specific strategic problems.

(a)   **Lack of economies of scale**: a small business will not qualify for the best purchasing terms from suppliers; will probably have to pay a higher rate of interest on its bank borrowings; and will not be able to afford to employ specialist staff, instead having to buy in their services at very high hourly rates.

(b)   **External factors**. It is a constant complaint from businesses in the UK that there is an ever-increasing **burden of regulation and compliance** upon them. To the extent that this is true, this burden is likely to weigh most heavily on the small, owner managed business, with its very limited administrative capacity.

(c)   Over reliance on a few key individuals can produce catastrophe if one of them leaves or is sick for a prolonged period.

(d)   **Small market areas or a restricted range of products** mean that small businesses are particularly vulnerable to environmental changes. They tend to have all their eggs in one basket.

(e)   **Cannot raise money**. Many small businesses complain they are unable to raise finance and rely heavily on bank loans. (Many proprietors, however, are unwilling to sacrifice control in order to raise bank finance.)

4.4 Strategic issues of start-ups

In addition to the problems that can affect small businesses generally, the **start-up** business has its own particular weaknesses.

(a)   **Lack of profit**. A new venture is unlikely to turn an accounting profit for two to three years because significant investment has to be made in such things as premises, stocks, recruitment and business development before turnover starts to build up. It is essential, therefore, that start-ups have the financial resources to run at a loss for several years.

(b)   **Poor cashflow**. Managing cashflow is a demanding job: many owner managers do not possess the necessary skills. The problem is exacerbated when the business is under-capitalised, which is often the case with start-ups. A further problem is that large firms often fail to pay their small business suppliers on time.

(c)   New owner managers are often **deficient in other skills** besides financial ones. New businesses are often founded by a person, or group of people, with expertise in only one or two business disciplines. Typically, these will be selling and/or technological expertise. Knowledge of procurement, logistics, personnel management, production engineering, marketing techniques and the essential detail of administration will often be missing. As a result, the aspiring sole trader or partnership is likely to find that unforeseen problems arise and consume an inordinate amount of time, hampering the deployment of the skills the managers do possess.

(d)   **Marketing expertise** is a particularly crucial requirement for the new business. Where the business is founded to exploit a new technical development, there is a long journey from the initial idea to market success. A fertile target market must be discovered by market research or created by promotional techniques; distribution systems must be set up and, perhaps most important of all, a suitable price must be set. Where distribution is to be through agents or wholesalers, as will often be the case, important discounts must be conceded without undermining either immediate cash flow or ultimate profitability.

(e)   Another important area of skill that is frequently lacking in new businesses is **personnel management**. Information technology applications have reduced the requirement for staff in terms of overall numbers but have increased the requirement for staff with a high level of specialised skills. Whether staff are engaged in large or small numbers, they must be managed carefully if they are to be motivated to support the firm's efforts. All too frequently, staff are taken for granted, poorly organised and even abused.

(f)   The effect of the **business cycle** should not be overlooked. A business starting up at the peak of the cycle is likely to have only three or four years in which to establish itself and secure its position before the economic trend starts to decline. When times are hard, it will be difficult for most businesses even to maintain turnover, and expansion will be a remote dream. Larger customers are likely to be merciless in their exploitation of small business's unwillingness to press them for payment, while suppliers will be equally merciless in demanding payment. During the trough of the cycle, larger businesses will cut costs by reducing their headcounts. The option of self-employment is likely to be quite attractive to some of those made redundant, but their prospects are not good: they will be starting up in a sluggish market and in the face of increased competition – from each other.

Section summary

Logical incrementalism makes strategy in a series of incremental changes rather than big leaps. It suggests practical limits to the rational model. People make strategic decisions on the basis of precedent, accepting satisfactory rather than ideal solutions.

5   Strategy and structure

Introduction

Chandler's study of US corporations revealed that they developed their structures to accommodate the strategies they pursued. The large corporations he looked at had all ended up with a decentralised structure. *Chandler* believed this was a structure designed to cope with the problems of growth and control brought about by the strategic choices of these corporations.

Structure is an important aspect of the implementation of strategy and must be optimised to support it although the relationship may not be straight forward.

5.1 Chandler

Alfred Chandler conducted a detailed historical study of the development of four major US corporations: *Du Pont, General Motors, Standard Oil of New Jersey* and *Sears Roebuck*. He found that all four had evolved a decentralised structure based on operating divisions, though by different routes. In order to reach this final stage, the businesses typically grew through four structural stages.

You will study these in greater detail when you take Paper E3 so we won't go into detail here.

(a) Entrepreneurial structure
(b) Functional structure
(c) Holding company structure
(d) Divisionalised structure

This would seem to be a normal evolutionary process for a business organisation to experience as it expands.

Chandler suggested that during the period 1850 to 1920 (which he describes as the formative years of modern capitalism), the development of high volume production to serve mass markets forced the replacement of entrepreneurial, owner management by innovative professional managers. Ultimately, these managers created the modern, multi-unit corporation as the best response to the administrative problems associated with growth. The **divisionalised organisation** is thus a response to strategy in its broadest sense.

Chandler discerned two main types of strategy, positive and negative. **Positive strategy** is aggressive, seeks new markets and leads to growth by product diversification. **Negative strategy** seeks to defend a current position and leads to growth by vertical integration based on mergers and acquisitions. In both cases, the initial structural response is likely to be centralised control based on functional departments. Both Du Pont and Sears Roebuck went through this stage.

Unfortunately, this approach has important disadvantages, especially where there is geographic dispersion. Du Pont therefore created an innovative decentralised structure of largely autonomous product-based business units co-ordinated rather than controlled by the corporate headquarters. General Motors copied the idea to overcome a lack of overall control in its loose federation of operating units. Standard Oil of New Jersey followed suit after a series of *ad hoc* responses to crises of control; its particular problem was the need to allocate and co-ordinate resources. Sears Roebuck went through essentially the same process as Du Pont.

The creation of the **multi-unit structure** was thus a logical managerial response to the problems associated with strategies that create very large organisations.

Chandler described four levels of management activity typical of this structure.

(a) The **general office** is the headquarters, responsible for overall performance. It allocates resources to the divisions and controls their performance by setting targets. Divisions are responsible for a product line or sales region.

(b) The **divisional central office** is responsible to the general office. Divisions are organised internally on a functional basis.

(c) Each function, such as production or sales has a **departmental headquarters, which** manages **field units** such as manufacturing plants or a sales team. Only at field unit level do managers carry out day-to-day operational work.

It has been argued that an established and well-functioning structure can influence strategy, as, for instance, when two retail organisations merge because the geographical pattern of their branches is complementary. Similarly, **value chain analysis** and **activity-based management** will tend to take existing structures as given factors, though they may lead to structural improvements. However, these are really aspects of organisational strengths and weaknesses analysis. Structure should, if necessary, be adjusted to suit the chosen strategy.

5.2 Organisational consistency

It is often difficult to identify a single best solution to the problem of organisation structure, particularly when the considerations point in different directions. For example, departmentation by geography or by function is often a difficult decision to take and usually produces a range of possible solutions. *Child* has shown that when the contingency approach seems to allow several different outcomes, it is important to ensure **internal consistency** in the measures adopted. For example, if a decentralised solution is chosen, leadership and control mechanisms based on centralisation will be inappropriate. Intangible aspects, such as culture and management philosophy, must also be considered.

Section summary

Strategy and structure must be in harmony and it will normally be appropriate to regard organisation structure as an aspect of strategic implementation. **Chandler** believed that structure should follow strategy and charted the development of structures from **entrepreneurial** through **functional** to **divisional**.

Exam alert

A previous syllabus tested knowledge of a variety of ways in which strategy could be developed in an organisation. Candidates were expected to consider whether the rational model suited all organisations or if emergent and incremental strategies were better in certain cases.

Chapter Roundup

✓ **Strategic decisions** affect the scope of an organisation's activities, the environment, resource capability
   and allocation, and the organisation's long-term direction.

✓ **Strategic plans** are formal statements of direction. The planning process suggests a sequence of strategic
   analysis (of the environment and the organisation), strategy generation and evaluation (several options are
   weighed up and compared) and strategic choice of the best alternative.

✓ **Emergent strategies** are those which develop out of patterns of behaviour, which is not consciously
   thought out, but which eventually has a long-term, 'strategic' effect. Emergent strategies need to be
   crafted by managers and shaped to the organisation's advantage.

✓ **Logical incrementalism** makes strategy in a series of incremental changes rather than big leaps. It
   suggests practical limits to the rational model. People make strategic decisions on the basis of precedent,
   accepting satisfactory rather than ideal solutions.

✓ **Strategy and structure** must be in harmony and it will normally be appropriate to regard organisation
   structure as an aspect of strategic implementation. **Chandler** believed that structure should follow strategy
   and charted the development of structures from **entrepreneurial** through **functional** to **divisional**.

Quick Quiz

1   Define business strategy in fewer than 20 words.

2   Strategic decisions affect operational decisions because:

    A   Operational level managers will always participate in the making of strategy
    B   Strategy is concerned with short-term concerns
    C   Operational decisions relate to the environment
    D   Operational decisions are based upon assumptions that flow from prior strategic decisions

3   Complete the statement below using one of the phrases in the list in brackets:

    'In the rational model, mission and objectives; environmental analysis; and internal appraisal lead directly
    to ....'

    (strategic options generation; corporate appraisal; strategy selection; stakeholder expectations)

4   Is the statement below true or false?

    'Corporate strategy differs from business strategy in that the former relates to a given market, while the
    latter is about what kind of business the company should be in.'

5   Which of the following statements is not true of the emergent strategy approach?

    A   It prevents learning
    B   It defies control
    C   It requires an awareness and understanding of operations
    D   It requires no detailed planning

6   Is the statement below true or false?

    'Centralised control and functional departmentation are essential to the management of large diversified
    businesses.'

7   The two diagrams below are diagrammatic expressions of which models?

(a)

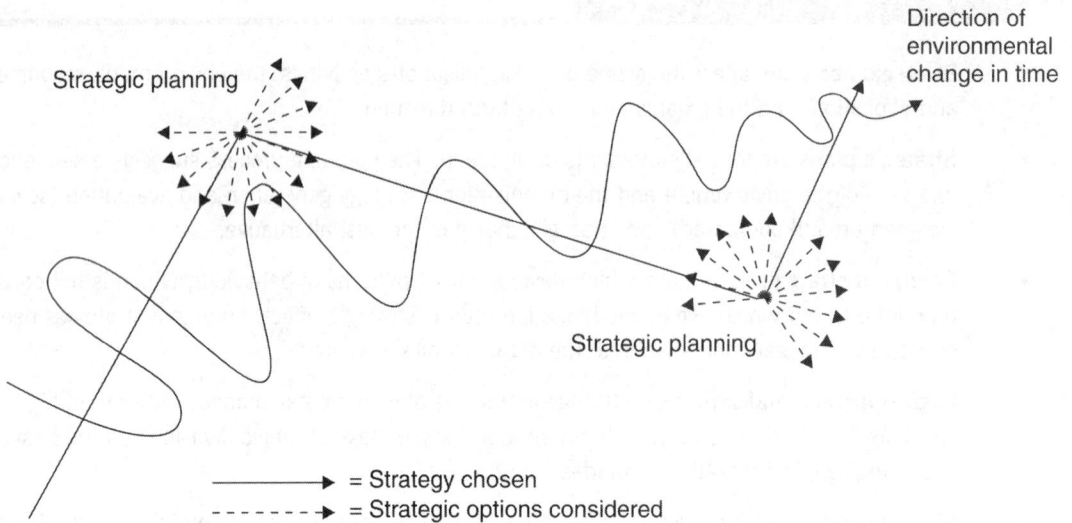

(b)

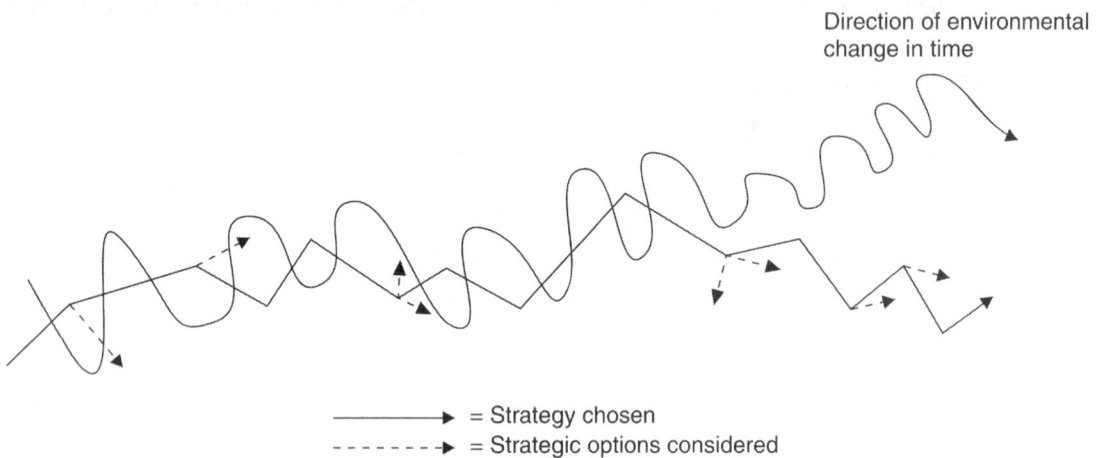

Answers to Quick Quiz

1   A course of action, including the specification of resources required, to achieve a specific objective.

2   D   A and B are untrue. C is irrelevant.

3   Corporate appraisal.

4   False. The opposite is true.

5   A   It depends on learning.

6   False. Such a business is almost certainly best organised into product-based autonomous divisions.

7   (a)   Rational planning model
     (b)   Incremental model

Answers to Questions

10.1 Deliberate strategy

The statement is true and is really a point of definition.

10.2 Plan or vision

Mr Vole hasn't quite made the transition from the fashion industry, where desire for silk handkerchiefs is relatively fickle, to an institution like Britannia Hospital. Here planning *is* necessary. Resources must be obtained to cope with future needs. 'Customer needs' are likely to be fairly basic (ie security, comfort, medical attention, stimulation). However, in the actual delivery of care and services, Florian Vole has a point: experimentation with new care techniques might improve the hospital's service to its patients. In this case, pursuing his 'vision' rather than simply following old procedures might be a good approach.

10.3 Incrementalism

A   B is untrue, C is true of emergent strategy, D is a description of bounded rationality.

Now try the question below from the Exam Question Bank

Number	Level	Marks	Time
Q10	Examination	25	45 mins

LEVELS AND CONCEPTS OF STRATEGY

We have just looked at different ways of making strategies. Now we turn to the ways in which strategies relate at different levels in the organisation. In the last chapter we looked at this briefly when we studied the **rational model.**

This chapter also considers ideas in established and emergent thinking in strategic management. By this we mean views such as transaction costs, resource-based view and the ecological perspective.

- **Transaction costs** consider how organisations arrange production on either a market or hierarchy basis.

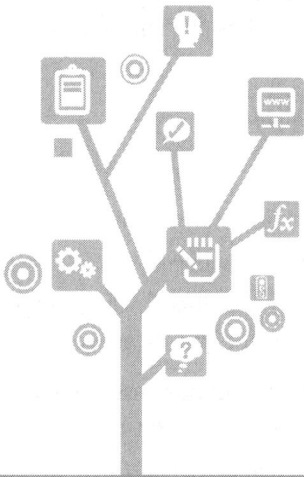

- The **resource based** approach argues that rather than fitting strategy to the external environment (positioning), an organisation should seek to exploit its distinctive internal competences and resources.

- The **ecology model** suggests that as an organisation's environment changes, it will only survive if it **adapts** and **evolves**.

We conclude the chapter by briefly running through **vision, mission, goals and objectives**. So we look at how the organisation's **strategic intent or vision** becomes reality throughout the organisation.

11

topic list	learning outcomes	syllabus references	ability required
1 Levels of strategy	A2c	A2(iii)	comprehension
2 Concepts in established and emergent thinking in strategic management	A2a	A2(ii)	analysis
3 The transaction cost approach	A2a	A2(i)	analysis
4 Mission	A2c	A2(iii)	comprehension
5 Goals, aims and objectives	A2c	A2(iii)	comprehension
6 Implementation	A2c	A2(iii)	comprehension

1   Levels of strategy

In the previous chapter we looked at the implementation of strategy throughout the organisation by cascading strategies down the organisation. *Hofer and Schendel* take this further and make the following distinction.

(a) **Corporate strategy** is the most general level of strategy in an organisation. (In the words of Johnson and Scholes, corporate strategy is 'concerned with what types of business the company as a whole should be in and is therefore concerned with decisions of **scope'**. An example would be choosing between diversifying and limiting the activities of the business.

(b) **Business strategy** defines how an organisation approaches a particular **market**, or the activity of a particular **business unit**. For example, this can involve decisions as to whether, in principle, a company should segment the market and specialise in particularly profitable areas or compete by offering a wider range of products.

(c) **Operational and functional strategies** involve decisions of strategic importance, but which are made or determined at operational levels. These decisions include product pricing, investment in plant, personnel policy and so forth. The contributions of these different functions determine the success of the strategy as, effectively, a strategy is only implemented at this level.

Question 11.1   Levels of strategy

Learning outcomes A2c

Ganymede Co is a company selling widgets. The finance director says: 'We plan to issue more shares to raise money for new plant capacity – we don't want loan finance – which will enable us to compete better in the vital and growing widget markets of Latin America. After all, we've promised the shareholders 5% profit growth this year, and trading is tough.'

Identify the corporate, business and functional strategies in the above quotation.

CASE STUDY

Goold and Quinn (in Strategic Control) cite Ciba-Geigy, a Swiss-based global firm with chemicals and pharmaceuticals businesses as an example of formal strategic control and planning processes.

(a) Strategic planning starts with the identification of strategic business sectors, that is, identifiable markets where profit, management and resources are largely independent of the other sectors.

(b) Strategic plans containing long-term objectives, key strategies and funds requirements are drawn up, based on a 'comprehensive analysis of market attractiveness', competitors and so on.

(c) At corporate level, these plan are reviewed. Head office takes all the different plans, and, with a 7-10 year planning horizon, the total risk, profitability, cash flow and resource requirements are assessed. Business sectors are allocated specific targets and funds.

2   Concepts in established and emergent thinking in strategic management

Introduction

This section is quite theoretical but keep in mind certain organisations work flexibly and **evolve**. They inspire creativity and initiative. Others are more rigid and the **rational model** we studied previously suits their management style better.

We also look at **resource-based strategy** where organisations get ahead by exploiting their individual competences and resources. This approach contrasts the **positioning approach** which fits into the **rational model**, whereby an organisation seeks to position itself by aligning its strategy with the external environment.

There is an argument that modern organisations need to be flexible to adapt their strategies and a positioning approach is too difficult to sustain.

2.1 Ecology, adaptation and individualisation

Some writers have applied the ideas of **evolution and natural selection** to organisations. This **ecology model** suggests that as an organisation's environment changes, it will only survive if it **adapts** and **evolves**. Business history is littered with the corpses of once powerful companies that failed to adapt. In this theory, an organisation survives if it finds a niche that provides both demand for its outputs and resources for it to use. Change plays an important role in determining whether or not an organisation finds a viable niche.

KEY POINT

> You should compare this idea with the various approaches to making corporate strategy discussed earlier. Much strategic theory makes an implicit assumption that success depends on achieving a close correspondence between what the organisation does and what its environment needs or can accept.

The rational model is, of course, an example of a strategic method that is based on careful study of the strategic environment. However, it is also, almost inevitably, a **rather bureaucratic method** and suffers from the common weaknesses of bureaucracy, including inflexibility of method, complexity of process, poor communication, ponderousness and a tendency to play safe.

Some large commercial organisations, such as *General Electric, 3M, Unipart* and *Asea Brown Boveri*, seem to have achieved a more responsive and agile approach to strategic management. The methods employed by these companies are described by *Ghoshal and Bartlett* in their book *The Individualized Corporation*.

In a dynamic global environment in which competition is increasingly service-based and knowledge-intensive, they recognised that human creativity and individual initiative were far more important as sources of competitive advantage than homogeneity and conformity.

Ghoshal and Bartlett suggest that these companies have three distinguishing characteristics.

(a)   They are able to inspire **individual creativity** and **initiative** in their people, based on a fundamental faith in them.

(b)   They build on pockets of entrepreneurial activity and expertise by building an integrated process of **organisational learning**.

(c)   They continuously **renew** themselves.

Developing the ability to operate in this way requires a new approach to human behaviour and organisational management (at least in so far as it affects middle and senior managers: this is not a recipe

for lower-level supervisors). The organisation's **behavioural context** must be changed from one of
repression to one of **renewal**. Each type of context has four important characteristics.

2.1.1 The repressive context

Compliance with central policy ensures that the direction set by top management is followed by all.
However, it also results in inflexible procedures and intolerance of dissent, the latter leading to the
perpetuation of the former even when they become obsolete.

Control of divisionalised companies, intended to enhance accountability through sophisticated budgeting
systems, can lead to defensiveness and risk-aversion.

Contract is the basis of some adversarial relationships that grow up as a result of massive restructuring
programmes with their attendant downsizing; people distance themselves emotionally from the
organisation and see their relationship with it as legalistic and financially based.

Constraint prevents the inefficient use of resources by clearly defining the boundaries of corporate strategy
and delegated responsibility.

2.1.2 The context for renewal

Discipline becomes 'an embedded norm that makes people live by their promises and commitments'.

Support replaces control: the role of managers becomes one of coaching, helping and guiding both
subordinates and colleagues.

Trust is built by transparency, openness and fairness. It allows people to rely on each other's judgements
and make reciprocal commitments to one another.

Stretch liberates and energises by lifting individual aspirations and expectations of themselves.

2.2 Resource-based strategy

2.2.1 The positioning approach v the resource-based approach

We have seen that a rational approach to strategy involves analysis of the environment of the organisation
to identify (internal) strengths and weaknesses and (external) opportunities and threats to the competitive
position of the organisation. However, there are two approaches to dealing with this information.

(a)   The **positioning approach** suggests that the main source of competitive advantage lies in how the
       organisation fits its strategy to its external environment. Strategic objectives are set by reference to
       product/market opportunities and threats – and organisational resources are developed and
       deployed to exploit those conditions and get the organisation to where it wants to be. (This is the
       basis of strategic planning: environmental analysis, corporate appraisal and the selection of best-fit
       strategies.)

(b)   The **resource based approach** suggests that the main source of competitive advantage lies in how
       the organisation exploits its distinctive (unique, hard to imitate, competitively value-adding)
       internal competences and resources. Strategic objectives are set by reference to what the
       organisation is best able to do (or able to do better than competitors).

2.2.2 Criticisms of the positioning approach

Various writers have argued that sustainable competitive advantage can no longer be assured using a
positioning approach.

(a)   The **rate of environmental change is too great** for effective positioning strategies to be developed.
       The rate of economic and social change brought about by globalisation, rapid technological

innovation, and changing consumer taste make a measured response out of date before it can take effect.

(b) **Positioning advantages cannot be sustained in the long term**. Advantageous product-market positions are too easy to copy to last long and more rapid product lifecycles erode initial advantage.

(c) It is **more difficult to adapt the organisation than to adopt a new environment**. The positioning approach may require significant change within the firm, which is difficult to achieve. It may be easier to move to a market environment that suits existing arrangements, skills, culture and capabilities.

2.2.3 Core resources and competences

Resources may be obvious things such as favoured access to a particular **raw material** or a piece of legally protected **intellectual property**; they may also take less tangible forms, such as a well known **brand**.

Core competences can be very specialised indeed or may be transferable between markets. For example, *Enron*, in its early days, established a core competence in price risk management that was equally applicable to the oil and gas industries. It is important to realise that it is possible to acquire or develop new competences, but this takes time. The possession of a particular advantage thus constitutes a competitive advantage but its validity may decline if other firms develop equivalent capabilities. Competences must therefore be developed and kept up to date on a continuing basis.

KEY TERM

Johnson, Scholes and Whittington (2008) define CORE COMPETENCES as 'the skills and abilities by which resources are deployed through an organisation's activities and processes such as to achieve competitive advantage in ways that others cannot imitate or obtain.'

The concept of core competences is key to the modern trend to **outsourcing**: organisations focus their activity on core competences, and contract non-core activities to other organisations which do have distinctive resources and capabilities to add more value than the outsourcing organisation could do in-house.

2.2.4 Assessing resource based theory

(a) Core competences are **difficult to identify and assess**: a wrong appraisal could lead to the loss of wider competence or source of advantage by misdirected outsourcing.

(b) Attempts to apply core competences (or other resources) widely across a range of markets and operations may make the firm **vulnerable to more focused, single market operations**.

(c) The emphasis on unique resources is reminiscent of the 'product orientation' decried by marketing experts: competitors who are more in touch with **market requirements** may be more successful. On the other hand, a strategy based on a sequence of unique products, as in the pharmaceutical industry, can be successful.

(d) **Investors** may or may not be convinced by the resource based view. Where there is a clear, identifiable and credible strategy, they may well maintain their support. However, a strategy based on exploiting existing markets may be more intuitively acceptable.

(e) The competence approach seems to support ideas such as cross-functional, activity based management, team working and the use of network structures both within the organisation and in its relations with suppliers and customers. However, the need to safeguard core competence capability against erosion by staff turnover and direct sharing of know-how may lead to a **perceived need for close control of activities** and narrow limits on outsourcing.

Section summary

Organisations can attempt to adapt in an **ecological** way to their changing environment. A bottom-up, empowering philosophy is one approach.

Exam alert

The different approaches to strategy may seem heavily theoretical, but they lead themselves to examination in various ways.

3 The transaction cost approach

Introduction

This is another theoretical approach but bear with us! The **transaction cost approach** seeks to answer the question of why firms exist. Why not have individuals transacting with each other instead? *Williamson* answered the question by explaining that firms have advantages over individuals making contracts which he explained by **uncertainty and bounded rationality.**

He then explained that firms are set up to allow **asset specificity or** using specialised assets in the business.

3.1 Markets and hierarchies

Transaction cost analysis is an aspect of economics that deals with the way resources are organised for production. It is an important contribution to thinking about the nature of business and has important implications for both business strategy and business structure. In its simplest form, this analysis is concerned with the question of why firms exist and grow; and why production is not undertaken by self-employed individuals contracting with one another for the supply of goods and services. This is sometimes referred to as the '**markets or hierarchies**' question.

Example

Consider the following example covering **economic efficiency**. In a transaction such as the supply of a book by an author to a publisher, is it a better use of resources for the author to be a full-time employee or to be an independent supplier with a contract for services? There are **transaction costs** involved in both methods, over and above the direct reward from the publisher to the writer: the employee must be provided with an office, furniture, (probably) a computer for word processing, medical insurance and so on, while the independent contract approach incurs expense associated with the contract itself, including legal costs and the cost to the publisher of negotiating, administering and enforcing it.

KEY TERMS

A TRANSACTION is an economic event in which a good or service is transferred from one economic entity to another.

TRANSACTION COSTS are the costs associated with performing a transaction.

Ronald Coase addressed the question of why firms exist in his 1937 essay *The Nature of the Firm*; he suggested that, initially at least, an entrepreneur will find cost advantage in employing people and resources in a coherent business organisation. Later, as the firm grows, overhead costs also grow and mistakes in resource allocation increase. Under these conditions, the market approach may be preferable.

3.2 Problems with contracts

This basic idea was refined by *Oliver Williamson*. The market or contractual approach, he suggested, was hampered in the long term by a combination of **uncertainty** and **bounded rationality**.

(a)   **Environmental uncertainty** means we must expect economic relationships to change as time passes.

(b)   **Bounded rationality** is our acceptance of the fact that we cannot have perfect knowledge of those changes in advance.

Taken together, uncertainty and bounded rationality mean that in the longer term, satisfactory contracts are not feasible: the range of possibilities they must cover is impossibly large. The incessant search for economic advantage means that the contracting parties could not trust one another not to take advantage of a new opportunity to benefit at the other's expense.

Short-term contracts allowing for renegotiation when conditions change can overcome this problem to some extent, but they increase the associated transaction costs of negotiation and so on.

Example

A very important problem with the market approach lies in **asset specificity**. Relationship-specific assets are those that have little or no application outside a given commercial relationship. For example, imagine a catering firm that contracts to supply meals to an airline. In the interests of speed of delivery it builds a new kitchen at the airport used by the airline as its main operational base. So long as the contractual relationship continues, the kitchen is an important asset to the catering company. If, however, the contract is not renewed when it comes to an end, the asset may be worthless if it cannot be sold to a successful competitor and even then a good price with only one possible purchaser may be unobtainable.

Now, from the point of view of economic efficiency, it is often better to employ specialised assets rather than general purpose ones. The related disadvantage illustrated above can be overcome if the operations involved are undertaken by a single firm. Asset specificity has thus been suggested as a major driver of **vertical integration** in organisations.

There are six different types of asset specificity.

(a)   **Physical asset** specificity arises from unique physical properties, such as rare mineral deposits. It must be distinguished from:

(b)   **Dedicated asset** specificity: this arises in a man-made asset that has only one application, such as the 'Guppy' aircraft build to ferry Airbus wings from the UK to France.

(c)   **Site** specificity arises from location: the airport kitchen we described earlier is a good example.

(d)   **Human asset** specificity arises from skills or knowledge that are relevant to the requirements of a single organisation.

(e)   **Temporal** specificity arises from an ability that is constrained to a given time, such as a landing slot at an airport.

(f)   **Brand name** specificity is **brand equity** that is not susceptible to **brand extension**: that is, the value of the brand will deteriorate if it is spread over too many products. Any well-known motor manufacturer's brand would be an example.

3.3 Problems with hierarchies

Williamson also pointed out problems with the hierarchy approach. He noted the tendency of managers to pursue personal or systems objectives (such as control or growth) rather than the overall corporate objective; the continued existence of inefficiency traceable to monopolistic practices; and the limits to organisational size and hierarchical complexity imposed by communication and control difficulties in large bureaucracies.

3.4 Insights

Transaction cost analysis has some important insights for the way firms go about their business.

KEY POINT

(a) There is the tendency to **vertical integration** discussed above.

(b) **Resource based strategy** can be supported by transaction cost ideas: the acquisition and
exploitation of distinctive capabilities is an obvious route to lower costs and greater control when
compared with the purchase of the same thing on the open market.

(c) The whole field of **outsourcing**, **network organisations** and **virtual organisations** is also susceptible
to transaction cost analysis. In essence, it is logical to suggest that a business should examine all
of its processes to see if any can be performed at less cost by external contractors, due
consideration being given to problems of control, security and asset specificity.

(d) The **divisional form of organisation (more of which in E3)** was supported by *Williamson* as
tending to reduce both the size of the operating bureaucracy (several small ones instead of one
huge one) and the scope for managers to pursue personal or systems goals.

Section summary

Transaction cost analysis compares the relative cost advantage of organising production on either a
market or a **hierarchy** basis. It suggests that **asset specificity** may drive vertical integration and that
outsourcing every activity that is not a core competence should be considered.

4 Mission

Introduction

An organisation should have a **vision** of what it is trying to achieve overall. Such a vision, or **strategic
intent**, is a kind of overall aspiration, perhaps with emotional overtones. It sets the scene for the
development of a clear idea of what the mission is.

4.1 What is 'mission'?

KEY TERM

MISSION 'describes the organisation's basic function in society, in terms of the products and services it
produces for its clients' (*Mintzberg*).

CASE STUDY

In its *Vision for the new Millennium*, CIMA defined its mission like this:

'To be the acknowledged world leader in:

(a) The qualification and support of Chartered Management Accountants
(b) The science of Management Accountancy'

It is possible, however, to give a broader definition of mission to include **four elements**.

Elements	Comments
Purpose	Why does the organisation exist and for whom (eg shareholders)?
Strategy	Mission provides the operational logic for the organisation: • What do we do? • How do we do it?
Policies and standards of behaviour	Mission should influence what people actually do and how they behave: the mission of a hospital is to save lives, and this affects how doctors and nurses interact with patients.
Values	What the organisation believes to be important: that is, its principles.

CASE STUDY

CIMA's *Vision for the new Millennium* went on to state its **vision** and **strategy**.

The Vision

(a)   An Institute renowned and respected for the quality of its members, staff, qualification, technical products and services

(b)   An Institute which stands out by reason of its effectiveness, its ability to anticipate and its agility in delivery

(c)   An Institute which thrives on partnerships, worldwide

(d)   An Institute which is inventive and innovative, and which maximises the potential of technology

The Strategy

(a)   To make the CIMA qualification relevant and accessible in key markets

(b)   To establish a network of alliances and partnerships to enable the Institute to increase its influence and/or penetration in those key markets

(c)   To develop, maintain and exploit a range of management accountancy products which anticipate and meet the needs of members and business

(d)   To anticipate and respond speedily to customer demand and market opportunities by structuring the institute accordingly

(e)   To attract, develop and retain talented staff who are empowered to reach stretch goals, and who are directly responsible and accountable for their performance

4.2 Mission statements

This topic is covered in more detail in E3

KEY TERM

A MISSION STATEMENT is a generalised statement of the overriding purpose of the organisation. It should cover the **purpose**, **scope**, **strategy** and **principles** of the organisation.

Mission statements might be reproduced in a number of places, such as at the front of an organisation's annual report, on publicity material, in the chairman's office and in communal work areas. There is no standard format, but they should have certain qualities.

(a)   **Brevity** will make them easier to understand and remember.
(b)   **Flexibility** will enable them to accommodate change.
(c)   They should be **distinctive**, to make the firm stand out.

Scott Adams, creator of *Dilbert*, defines a mission statement as 'a long awkward sentence that demonstrates management's inability to think clearly'. This illustrates the main problem with mission statements, which is getting people to take them seriously.

CASE STUDY

The following statements were taken from annual reports of the organisations concerned. Are they 'mission statements'? If so, are they any good?

(a) **GlaxoSmithKline (GSK)**: 'Our global quest is to improve the quality of human life by enabling people to do more, feel better and live longer.

(b) **IBM (UK)**: 'We shall increase the pace of change. Market-driven quality is our aim. It means listening and responding more sensitively to our customers. It means eliminating defects and errors, speeding up all our processes, measuring everything we do against a common standard, and it means involving employees totally in our aims'.

(c) **Guinness Group**:' Guinness plc is one of the world's leading drinks companies, producing and marketing an unrivalled portfolio of international best-selling brands, such as Johnnie Walker, Bell's and Dewar's Scotch whiskies, Gordon's and Tanqueray gins, and Guinness stout itself – the world's most distinctive beer. The strategy is to focus resources on the development of the Group's alcoholic drinks businesses. The objectives are to provide superior long-term financial returns for shareholders, to create a working environment in which people can perform to their fullest potential and to be recognised as one of the world's leading consumer brand development companies.'

(d) **British Film Institute**. 'The BFI is the UK national agency with responsibility for encouraging and conserving the arts of film and television. Our aim is to ensure that the many audiences in the UK are offered access to the widest possible choice of cinema and television, so that their enjoyment is enhanced through a deeper understanding of the history and potential of these vital and popular art forms.'

4.3 The role of mission

Although the mission statement might be seen as a set of abstract principles, it plays an important role in the planning process.

(a) **Planning**. Objectives should be set that support the mission: if an objective is attained, the mission should be forwarded. At the corporate appraisal stage, mission is an essential element in the definition of just what constitutes a strength, weakness, opportunity or threat: any factor only qualifies in one of these categories if it relates as such to the furtherance of the mission.

(b) **Evaluation and screening**. Mission acts as a **yardstick** by which plans are judged. Take the example of a financial services organisation that runs a number of ethical investment funds that exclude from their portfolios shares in firms involved in alcohol, tobacco and armaments. If a new fund manager proposed to invest in shares of a diversified company, it would be examined to see if its activities included those that the investment fund considered unethical. The investment strategy would be assessed with reference to the investment fund's mission. Mission helps to ensure **consistency in decisions**.

(c) **Implementation**. Mission also affects the implementation of a planned strategy and can be embodied in the **policies and behaviour standards** of the firm.

There is a clear link here with the standard criteria for strategy evaluation: sustainability, acceptability and feasibility.

Section summary

A **vision** is an overall aspiration for the future, as is strategic intent. **Mission** includes both the organisation's value system and an answer to the question 'What business are we in?' A mission (sometimes referred to as 'official goals') is often embodied in a mission statement.

Exam alert

You may be asked to consider mission in the context of a rational approach to formulating strategy.

As a rule of thumb, if you have any difficulty, ask yourself 'What and whom is this organisation for?' and possibly 'What does this organisation do?'

5 Goals, aims and objectives

Introduction

Goals and objectives are derived from mission and should support it. They provide the detail of what must be done if mission is to be achieved. There should be a **hierarchy of objectives** (or *goal structure*), cascading downwards from the general to the specific, each level supporting the one above.

5.1 The nature of goals and objectives

Different terminology is used in this area. We will distinguish between terms, for clarity.

KEY TERM

GOALS: 'The intentions behind decision or actions' (*Henry Mintzberg*) or 'a desired end result' (*Shorter Oxford English Dictionary*)

There are two types of goal.

(a) Non-operational, **qualitative** goals (**aims**). For example, a university's may be: 'to seek truth'. (You would not see: 'increase truth by 5%')

(b) Operational, **quantitative** goals (**objectives**).

Characteristics	Example
Objectives are SMART	• Operational goal: cut costs
• Specific	• Objective: reduce budgeted expenditure on office stationery by 5% by 31 December 2009
• Measurable	
• Achievable	
• Relevant	
• Time-bounded	

Exam alert

There are numerous versions of the SMART criteria. (Specific; Measurable; Agreed; Achievable; Attainable; Relevant; Results-orientated; Time bound). Candidates should consider as wide a range of criteria as possible when answering exam questions.

Question 11.2	Aims and objectives

Learning outcome A2c

Most organisations establish closed or quantifiable objectives. Give reasons why aims (non-operational goals) might still be important.

Here is an example.

(a) **Mission**: deliver a quality service
(b) **Goal**: enhance manufacturing quality
(c) **Objectives**: over the next twelve months, reduce the number of defects to 1 part per million

Note that not all goals can be easily measured, or can ever be attained completely. **Customer satisfaction** is a goal, but satisfying customers and ensuring that they remain satisfied is a **continuous process** that does not stop when one target has been reached.

5.2 The purpose of organisational objective setting

'Objectives are needed in every area where performance and results directly and vitally affect the survival and prosperity of the business' (*Drucker*). Objectives in these key areas should support management in:

(a) **Planning**. Objectives are the targets which the plan aims to meet.

(b) **Responsibility**. Objectives are given to individuals and departments for which they have responsibility.

(c) **Integration**. If objectives are consistent then they should aid goal congruence within an organisation.

(d) **Motivation**. The setting of targets (especially when success is linked to promotion or bonuses) may increase motivation.

(e) **Evaluation**. Senior management control the business by evaluating the performance of the managers responsible for each of its divisions.

(Note the acronym **PRIME** for learning this.)

5.3 The hierarchy of objectives

There is a **hierarchy of objectives**, with one primary corporate objective (restricted by certain constraints on corporate activity) and a series of subordinate objectives/goals which should combine to ensure the achievement of the overall objective.

5.3.1 Primary objectives

People might disagree on the choice of the overall corporate objective, although for a business it must be a **financial objective,** such as profitability, return on capital employed or earnings per share.

Profit, in its broadest sense, measures the creation of value, the relationship of inputs to outputs. It thus integrates cost behaviour and revenue performance for the whole organisation. Profit also is a key indicator for shareholders, and one of several measures that can be compared across organisations. However, profit has limitations as a measure of success.

(a) It is an **accounting convention** and is subject to technical **adjustment** and managerial **manipulation**.

(b) It is a **retrospective, annual measure**: it does not necessarily reflect current strategy and is anyway short-term in its focus.

(c) It is of little use as a measure of success in the **early years** of a business venture (as are cashflow measures) because of the heavy investment normally required at this stage.

5.3.2 Secondary objectives

Secondary or subordinate goals and objectives support the primary goal. They can be listed under the following broad headings.

(a) **Market position**

Total market share of each market; growth of sales, customers or potential customers; the need to avoid relying on a single customer for a large proportion of total sales; what markets should the company be in?

(b) **Product development**

Bring in new products; develop a product range; investment in research and development; provide products of a certain quality at a certain price level.

(c) **Technology**

Improve productivity; reduce the cost per unit of output; exploit appropriate technology.

(d) **Employees and management**

Train employees in certain skills; reduce labour turnover; create an innovative, flexible culture; employ high quality leaders.

Question 11.3	Primary and secondary objectives

Learning outcome A2c

Review the list of secondary objectives above. How do you think of each of them relates to financial objectives?

5.3.3 Balanced scorecard

This topic is covered in more detail in E3.

Kaplan and Norton suggested a **balanced scorecard** approach that looks at the business in four perspectives; performance in all must be satisfactory if the business is to prosper.

(a)   The **financial perspective**, or 'how do we look to shareholders?'
(b)   The **customer perspective**, or 'how do customers see us?'
(c)   The **internal business perspective**, or 'what must we excel at?'
(d)   The **innovation and learning perspective**, or 'can we continue to improve and create value?'

It is necessary for each business to set **goals** and establish **performance measures** for each perspective. Some will be fairly simple and traditional. For instance, shareholders will want to see their company survive and grow; suitable measures here might be cash generation and profits respectively. The internal perspective will vary widely between companies but will concentrate on efficiency goals and measures. Measuring customer satisfaction can be done in a variety of ways such as counting complaints or starting a programme of interviews. The innovation and learning perspective will, perhaps, be the most difficult to handle. Kaplan and Norton give the example of an electronics company with several goals in this perspective; one is technology leadership and the chosen measure is how long it takes to develop a new generation of product.

5.4 Trade-off between objectives

When there are several key objectives, some might be achieved only at the expense of others. For example, attempts to achieve a good cash flow or good product quality, or to improve market share, might call for some sacrifice of profits.

There will be a trade-off between objectives when strategies are formulated, and a choice will have to be made. For example, there might be a choice between the following two options.

Option A   15% sales growth, 10% profit growth, a £2 million negative cash flow and reduced product quality and customer satisfaction.

Option B   8% sales growth, 5% profit growth, a £500,000 surplus cash flow, and maintenance of high product quality/customer satisfaction.

If the firm chose option B in preference to option A, it would be trading off sales growth and profit growth for better cash flow, product quality and customer satisfaction. Note that the long-term effect of reduced quality has not been considered.

5.4.1 Long-term and short-term objectives

Objectives may be long-term or short-term.

(a)   A company that is suffering from a recession in its core industries and making losses in the short term might continue to have a primary objective in the long term of achieving a steady growth in earnings or profits, but in the short term, its primary objective might switch to survival.

(b)   Secondary objectives will range from the short term to the long term. Planners will formulate secondary objectives within the guidelines set by the primary objective, after selecting strategies for achieving the primary objective.

For example, a company's primary objective might be to increase its earnings per share from 30p to 50p in the next five years. Strategies for achieving the objective might include those below.

(a)   Increasing profitability in the next twelve months by cutting expenditure
(b)   Increasing export sales over the next three years
(c)   Developing a successful new product for the domestic market within five years

Secondary objectives might then be re-assessed.

(a)   Improving manpower productivity by 10% within twelve months

(b)   Improving customer service in export markets with the objective of doubling the number of overseas sales outlets in selected countries within the next three years

(c)   Investing more in product-market research and development, with the objective of bringing at least three new products to the market within five years

5.4.2 Cyert and March's organisational coalition model

The American management writers *Cyert and March* suggest that traditional ideas on organisational objectives are too simplistic and do not recognise managerial and economic reality.

(a)   The firm is **an organisational coalition** of stakeholders: shareholders, managers, employees, suppliers and customers.

(b)   This network has **potentially competing goals and interests**. There is a need for 'political' compromise in establishing the goals of the firm. Each group must settle for less than it would ideally want to have. Shareholders must settle for less than maximum profits, managers for less than maximum utility, and so on.

(c)   Organisations have **responsibilities** to (and constraints imposed by) various stakeholder groups. These may be *internal* considerations, based on stakeholder influence and the organisation's values. They may also be *external* considerations, such as legislation. (We will look at this further.)

Cyert and March conclude that 'organisations cannot have objectives, only people have objectives'.

5.4.3 How trade-offs are made

There are conflicts between different types of goals (eg long-term vs short-term). *Daft* indicates four ways of dealing with **goal conflict**.

(a)   **Bargaining**. Managers with different goals will compete with each other, and will form alliances with other managers to achieve them.

(b) **Satisficing**. Organisations do not aim to maximise performance in one area if this leads to poor performance elsewhere. Rather they will accept satisfactory, if not excellent, performance in a number of areas.

(c) **Sequential attention**. Goals are dealt with one by one, as it were, in a sequence.

(d) **Priority setting**. Certain goals get priority over others. This is determined by senior managers, but there are quite complicated systems to rank goals and strategies according to certain criteria.

| Question 11.4 | Trade-offs |

Learning outcome A2c

What type of trade-off mechanisms are being used in the following cases?

(a) 'Next year, we'll flood the market with the stuff. But we've got to get the quality right first.'

(b) 'Don't bother about the third coat of varnish, as long as we get the job done by Saturday.'

5.5 Goal structure

If an organisation is to achieve its corporate objectives, the individuals and groups within it need goals which are relevant to their own roles, but which are co-ordinated with each other and which contribute towards overall objectives. There is said to be a 'cascade' of objectives from the organisational level to the individual level.

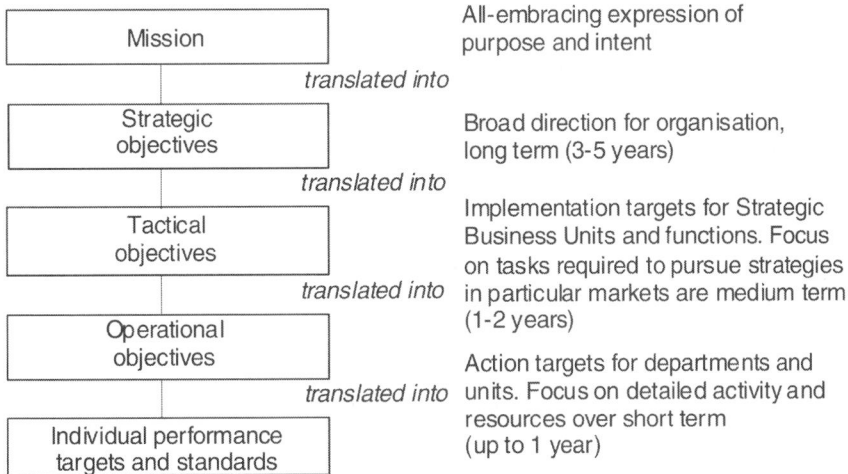

Mission	All-embracing expression of purpose and intent
translated into	
Strategic objectives	Broad direction for organisation, long term (3-5 years)
translated into	
Tactical objectives	Implementation targets for Strategic Business Units and functions. Focus on tasks required to pursue strategies
translated into	in particular markets are medium term (1-2 years)
Operational objectives	
translated into	Action targets for departments and units. Focus on detailed activity and resources over short term (up to 1 year)
Individual performance targets and standards	

This flow-down of objectives and plans is designed to ensure:

(a) **Vertical alignment**: lower level objectives are designed to further corporate objectives and mission, so that there is unity of direction.

(b) **Horizontal alignment**: the objectives of different groups and functions dovetail with each other, so that there is co-ordinated effort, and so that the organisation presents a coherent and consistent face at its points of contact with the outside world.

5.5.1 Goal structure in action: Management by Objectives (MbO)

The diagram of the hierarchy of objectives above shows a cascade of objectives from the organisation to the individual. Integrating all these objectives is not always easy to achieve. However, a method of doing so was suggested by proponents of **Management by Objectives** (originally, *Peter Drucker*).

Exam alert

Note that management by objectives is another 'integrating' topic: think how it also applies to our discussion in early chapters of this Text about managerial control and performance management.

Management by Objectives (MbO) is a process whereby individual goals are integrated with the corporate plan, as part of an on-going programme of goal-setting and performance review involving all levels of management. The stages in developing such a programme are as follows.

STEP 1 Clarifying **organisational goals and objectives**: MbO will only be effective within the framework of a coherent strategic plan.

STEP 2 Collaboratively defining each individual's major **areas of responsibility** and their purpose within the corporate plan.

STEP 3 Jointly defining and agreeing the **key tasks** which are directly related to the achievement of objectives, and in which any performance shortfall would negatively impact on the organisation's effectiveness.

STEP 4 Jointly defining and agreeing **key results** (which must be achieved in order for the key tasks to be successfully performed and objectives met) and methods of monitoring and measuring performance in these areas.

STEP 5 Agreeing individual **performance improvement plans** for a defined planning period: selecting specific improvement objectives for each key task and formulating an action plan to achieve those objectives. This will include measures to be taken by the job-holder, resources to be provided by superiors (eg guidance, training) and dates for review.

STEP 6 **Monitoring, self-evaluation and review** of performance at agreed intervals, with revision of objectives, targets and action plans as required.

STEP 7 **Periodic review of performance** against individual improvement objectives and key results (reflected at the organisation level in a review of performance against the corporate plan).

A fresh cycle of planning and control would then continue the process.

5.5.2 Evaluating MbO

There are a number of **advantages** to an MbO programme.

(a) Clarifying organisational and sub-unit **goals**. This is crucial in establishing direction and co-ordination. It helps to focus organisation structures according to defined responsibilities. The goal clarification exercise may also encourage the flow of multi-directional communication and identify needs for innovation, change and development.

(b) Focusing organisational attention on **key tasks**, results and problem areas, for more efficient targeting of effort.

(c) Systematically converting strategic plans into **co-ordinated** managerial action plans and budgets. Each individual manager knows clearly what is expected of him or her, while retaining a big-picture perspective and unity of purpose.

(d) Securing the **commitment** of individuals to defined targets and areas of accountability, as well as potentially improving morale and motivation through greater involvement and discretion in performing tasks (within defined targets).

(e) **Systematic information** for managerial planning and control, individual performance appraisal, reward and development planning.

There are **disadvantages** too.

(a) Potential **rigidity**: individual objectives must be set and, once set, are not changed because the overall plan is difficult to revise. There must be **flexibility**, especially:

    (i) In flexible working environments where individual 'jobs' are no longer rigidly defined

    (ii) Where individual results are less relevant (or measurable) because of teamworking

    (iii) Where a less hierarchical management authority structure is preferred (eg self-managed teamworking)

    (iv) Where jobs are less amenable to measurement and the setting of specific quantitative targets (eg interpersonal roles such as counselling)

(b) Potential requirement for a significant **change** in attitudes, the style of leadership and organisation structure. This may involve time and labour costs of change management – and may ultimately be unsuccessful if not supported (and sustained) by senior management.

(c) Potential for **conflict** and de-motivation: staff may perceive increasing accountability for defined results as a command-and-control pressure tactic, thinly disguised as involvement/empowerment.

5.6 Critical success factors (CSF)

This topic is covered in more detail in E3.

KEY TERM

CRITICAL SUCCESS FACTORS (CSFs) are a small number of areas in which (a) satisfactory results will enable successful competitive performance and (b) an organisation *must* excel in order to outperform competition. Control and improvement can be achieved by setting **KPIs** in these areas and monitoring progress against targets.

As an alternative to a systematic goal-structure approach, an organisation may focus on critical success factors. Having determined its competitive strategy, the organisation identifies those factors which are essential and effective in delivering competitive advantage (CSFs). It can then identify the business processes and activities which yield each CSF: this focuses on the organisation's core competences. For each of these processes and activities, key performance indicators (KPIs) can be defined in order to evaluate and measure performance in delivering the CSFs.

CASE STUDY

As long ago as 1955 *Lewis* made a study of *GEC*'s management reporting system and found that it produced reports on the following factors.

(a) Profitability
(b) Market share
(c) Productivity
(d) Product leadership

(e) Personnel development
(f) Employee attitudes
(g) Public responsibility
(h) Balance between short-range and long-range goals

5.6.1 CSF analysis

Johnson and Scholes describe six stages in the process of managing strategy using CSFs.

STEP 1 Identify the **CSFs**. This will require both experience of the organisation and its activities and sound judgement. The emphasis is not on what activities must be undertaken, but on what must be achieved in broad terms. Johnson and Scholes recommend that the number of CSFs identified should be restricted to six or fewer.

STEP 2 Identify the **competences** that must be displayed if the CSFs are to be achieved. Note that the emphasis has now changed from what must be achieved (CSFs) to the special skills and processes that will enable the required achievement (core competences).

STEP 3 The core competences identified must then be considered to determine whether they are adequate to provide genuine **competitive advantage**, or whether they must be improved or supplemented.

STEP 4 A **key performance indicator (KPI)** must be identified for each competence so that strategic control may be exercised.

STEP 5 When we discussed **resource based strategy** earlier, we noted that core competences were defined as 'the skills and abilities by which resources are deployed through an organisation's activities and processes such as to achieve competitive advantage in ways that others cannot imitate or obtain.' The fifth step is to ensure that this is, in fact, the case. If it is not, competitive advantage will not be achieved.

STEP 6 **Competitors' responses** must be monitored and their effects on the CSF structure forecast.

Section summary

Goals give flesh to the mission. They can be quantified (**objectives**) or not quantified (**aims**). Most organisations use a combination of both. Quantified or specific objectives have **SMART** characteristics.

There is a **hierarchy of objectives**. A primary objective of a business might be profit; secondary objectives relate to ways to achieve it.

Objectives are sometimes in **conflict**. In such a case, managers can adopt four ways of reconciling them.

- Internal bargaining
- Satisficing
- Sequential attention
- Priority setting

The term **goal structure** is given to the hierarchy of objectives whereby mission flows down to strategic objectives, which in turn are translated into tactical, operational and individual objectives.

Techniques have been suggested to break down organisational goals into targets for departments and individuals. **Management by Objectives** is one such technique.

The identification of **Critical Success Factors (CSFs)** provides a flexible basis for identifying strategic goals, as an alternative to a comprehensive hierarchy of objectives.

6 Implementation

Introduction

The formulation of strategic plans is one thing: implementing them is quite another. **It is impossible to plan for every eventuality.** Some decisions of strategic importance may not be anticipated in the strategic plan. Implementation often involves adjusting the plan in the light of changed conditions.

The relative abstraction of the strategy is made real by the work of many individuals, sometimes in isolation, sometimes in small teams, sometimes in large organisational formations.

KEY POINT

Implementation of strategy is a ground level issue. An organisation has to decide how its resources are deployed.

(a)   At **corporate level** (between different businesses)
(b)   At **unit level** (between functions, departments and so forth)

6.1 Resource planning

Resource planning involves allocating the resources (and identifying potential resources) of the undertaking in order that the defined and agreed corporate objectives may be achieved. At operational level, there are four stages in resource planning.

(a)   Establishing currently available and currently obtainable resources (by category) and details of any which are not available or readily obtainable – making a resource audit.

(b)   Estimating what resources would be needed to pursue a particular strategy and deciding whether there would be enough resources to pursue it successfully.

(c)   Assigning responsibilities to managers for the acquisition, use and control of resources.

(d)   Identifying all constraints and factors exerting an influence on the availability and use of resources (internal and external environments).

Resource plans can be prepared in detail providing organisations know what they need to achieve.

(a)   **Critical success factors (CSFs)** 'are those factors on which the strategy is fundamentally dependent for its success'.

(b)   **Key tasks** are what must be done to ensure each critical success factor is achieved.

(c)   **Priorities** indicate the order in which tasks are achieved.

6.2 Operations planning

Linneman says operations planning has two aspects.

(a)   Deciding what is to be accomplished, by whom and when, and at what cost.
(b)   Setting up control points and methods of measuring and monitoring performance.

This planning process spans plans at the corporate level, for product-market areas (subsidiaries or divisions), for functional areas and for lower echelons of management.

Operations plans are relatively short. Major items would need to be quantified – such as sales, cost of sales, operating profit, other income, non-current asset details, inventory levels, working capital investment and production targets (if appropriate). Budgets add flesh and muscle to the bones of these skeleton operations plans.

Plans for functional departments must also be prepared, below the overall corporate level. In a manufacturing company, major functional plans will be for **marketing** and **production**.

6.3 Review and control

Successful implementation of the corporate plan demands the continued interest of senior management.

(a)   Strategic plans must be converted into action plans (ie operations plans and budgets).

(b)   Responsibilities must be allocated and authority given to individual managers to use resources (eg spend money sufficient to allow them to achieve their individual targets).

(c)   Checkpoints must be established to monitor activities.

(d)   Pressure must be exerted for control action where necessary, to ensure that things get done according to the aims of the corporate plan.

Control checkpoints or milestones should monitor factors such as those below.

(a)   Have deadlines been met and are future deadlines going to be met?

(b)   Are any targets in danger of being missed?

(c)   Will the required resources be available to make the products/services?

(d)   Will the products be available in sufficient numbers to achieve the aims of the product– market plan?

A control system requires organisation.

(a)   The responsibilities of divisions, departments and individual managers must be documented.

(b)   Responsibility charts for managers at divisional, departmental and subordinate levels must be prepared.

(c)   Activity schedules for managers at divisional, departmental and subordinate levels must be prepared.

Section summary

Implementation requires detailed planning and hands on management of resources and operations. Progress and performance must be properly measured and reported.

Chapter Roundup

✓   Organisations can attempt to adapt in an **ecological** way to their changing environment. A bottom-up, empowering philosophy is one approach.

✓   Transaction cost analysis compares the relative cost advantage of organising production on either a **market** or a **hierarchy** basis. It suggests that **asset specificity** may drive vertical integration and that outsourcing every activity that is not a core competence should be considered.

✓   A **vision** is an overall aspiration for the future, as is strategic intent. **Mission** includes both the organisation's value system and an answer to the question 'What business are we in?' A mission (sometimes referred to as 'official goals') is often embodied in a mission statement.

✓   **Goals** give flesh to the mission. They can be quantified (**objectives**) or not quantified (**aims**). Most organisations use a combination of both. Quantified or specific objectives have **SMART** characteristics.

There is a **hierarchy of objectives**. A primary objective of a business might be profit; secondary objectives relate to ways to achieve it.

Objectives are sometimes in **conflict**. In such a case, managers can adopt four ways of reconciling them.

- Internal bargaining
- Satisficing
- Sequential attention
- Priority setting

The term **goal structure** is given to the hierarchy of objectives whereby mission flows down to strategic objectives, which in turn are translated into tactical, operational and individual objectives.

Techniques have been suggested to break down organisational goals into targets for departments and individuals. **Management by Objectives** is one such technique.

The identification of **Critical Success Factors (CSFs)** provides a flexible basis for identifying strategic goals, as an alternative to a comprehensive hierarchy of objectives.

✓   **Implementation** requires detailed planning and hands on management of resources and operations. Progress and performance must be properly measured and reported.

Quick Quiz

1   Complete the statement below by using one of the list of phrases given in brackets.

'A strategy of vertical integration is likely to be supported by ....'

(core competences; bounded rationality; transaction cost analysis; system goals)

2   An approach to strategy which works 'from the inside out, seeking to identify strategic activities for which the organisation is best equipped, is called:

A   A positioning approach
B   A resource based approach

3   What do you understand by the acronym SMART?

4   How must objectives be interlocked?

Answers to Quick Quiz

1   Transaction cost analysis.

2   B   Make sure you understand the distinction.

3   Specific, measurable, achievable, relevant, time-bounded

4   Vertically; horizontally (across departments); over time

Answers to Questions

11.1   Levels of strategy

The corporate objective is profit growth. The corporate strategy is the decision that this will be achieved by entering new markets, rather than producing new products. The business strategy suggests that those markets include Latin America. the operational or functional strategy involves the decision to invest in new plant (the production function) which is to be financed by shares rather than loans (the finance function).

11.2   Aims and objectives

Aims can be just as helpful: customer satisfaction, for example, is not something which is achieved just once. Some goals are hard to measure and quantify, for example 'to retain technological leadership'. Quantified objectives are hard to change when circumstances change, as changing them looks like an admission of defeat: aims may support greater flexibility.

11.3   Primary and secondary objectives

(a)   Markets are customers. Customers are source of revenue. Markets are where organisations compete with each other. Gaining market share now helps future profitability – but may be expensive in the short term.

(b)   Product development is another way of competing, to make profits to satisfy the corporate objectives.

(c)   and (d) are to do with organising the production process, making operations efficient and effective.

11.4   Trade-offs

(a)   Sequential attention
(b)   Satisficing

Now try the question below from the Exam Question Bank

Number	Level	Marks	Time
Q11	Examination	10	18 mins

GENERAL ENVIRONMENT

In the last two chapters we considered models of strategy and managing strategy. Now we move on to look at the **external environment** in which the organisation is managed.

Organisations interact with their environment and you should expect the environment to have a significant effect on the organisation. The rational model of strategy-making includes an analysis of the environment and is highly dependent on this information to make decisions. Other strategy models are less formal in their use of this knowledge but will use it as they emerge/muddle through or make incremental decisions.

PEST is the best-known of the external environmental analyses. It scans the environment using political, economic and social and technological factors. Variants on PEST include **PESTEL** which adds environmental and legal factors.

Stakeholder **mapping** considers the stakeholders who are the constituency of the organisation. They have an influence and an interest in what the organisation does.

In Section 7, on **the competitive advantage of nations**, we learn how the domestic origins of an industry can affect its competitive success.

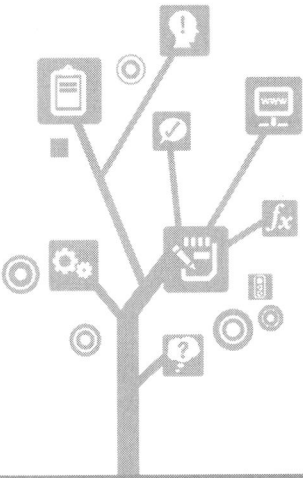

12

topic list	learning outcomes	syllabus references	ability required
1 Relating the organisation to its environment	A1a	A1(i)	analysis
2 The political and legal environment	A1a	A1(i)	analysis
3 The economic environment	A1a	A1(i)	analysis
4 The social and cultural environment	A1a	A1(i)	analysis
5 The technological environment	A1a	A1(i)	analysis
6 Stakeholder goals and objectives	A1a	A1(ii)	analysis
7 The competitive advantage of a nation's industries: Porter's diamond	A1b	A1(vii)	comprehension

1 Relating the organisation to its environment

Introduction

It is usual to consider the organisation as having boundaries that separate it from its environment. You must remember that it can be useful to regard organisation and environment as inextricably linked to one another in a wide range of ways. This is consistent with the modern emphasis on stakeholders, organisational networks and the strategic importance of human resource management.

Exam alert

The topics in this chapter have not been examined at this level recently. They were previously in Paper P6 which was a strategic-level paper in the previous syllabus and the exams tested their application at a high level. You will need to be able to discuss the use of PEST and stakeholder analysis. In a longer scenario question, expect to apply these models as at this level more than knowledge is expected of you.

1.1 Environmental factors

Organisations exist within an environment which strongly influences what they do and whether they survive and develop. Strategic planners must take account of potential environmental impacts in order to produce plans that are realistic and achievable. Where international or even global operations are undertaken, it is important to understand that there may be important differences between the environments present in the various regions and countries involved.

The environment of an organisation is everything outside its boundaries. It may be segmented according to the diagram below.

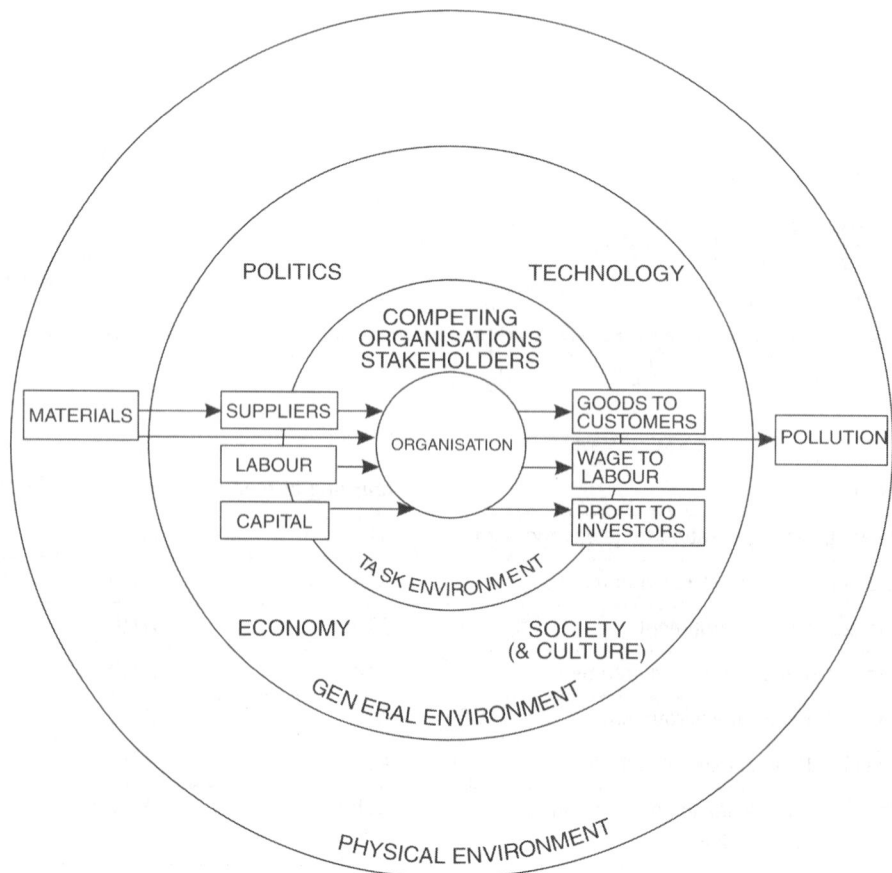

KEY TERMS

The GENERAL ENVIRONMENT covers all the political/legal, economic, social/cultural and technological (**PEST**) influences in the countries an organisation operates in.

The TASK ENVIRONMENT relates to factors of particular relevance to a firm, such as its competitors, customers and suppliers of resources.

The mnemonic PEST is often used in environmental analysis. **PEST** stands for political, economic, social and technical; legal matters are considered under the political heading and cultural matters under the social heading. Increasing public concern for the natural environment and corporate sensitivity about protest groups has led in recent years to the inclusion of a second 'E' in the mnemonic, to stand for environment. This has given rise to new arrangements such as **STEEPLE** and **PESTEL**.

An even more exotic analysis is DEEPLIST: demographic, environment, economics, politics, law, information, society, technology.

Exam alert

The PEST model is a useful checklist for general environmental factors – remember that in the real world they are **interlinked** and any given environmental development is likely to qualify under two or more of the PEST or PESTEL headings.

1.2 Environmental fit

One approach to strategy is to seek **environmental fit**, relating a company to its environment.

Any strategy is made in conditions of **partial ignorance**. The environment is a major cause of such 'ignorance'.

(a)   It contains **opportunities and threats** which may influence the organisation's activities and may even threaten its existence.

(b)   The environment is sometimes so **varied** that many organisations will find it difficult to discern its effects on them.

(c)   Firms can conduct **audits** to identify which of the many different sorts of environmental factors have had a significant influence.

(d)   Environmental conditions **change**.

1.3 Complexity and dynamism

Johnson and Scholes contrast the concepts of **environmental complexity** (how many influences and the inter-relationships between them) and **environmental dynamism** (the rate of change).

Together, complexity and dynamism create **uncertainty**.

1.3.1 The strategic impact of uncertainty

A high degree of uncertainty can have an important impact on the strategic management of a business.

(a)   There is likely to be a wish for **more and better information** in order to enhance the likelihood of making useful forecasts. The difficulty of achieving this is likely to lead to a **close planning time horizon**.

(b)   Decisive moves to new strategies are unlikely: strategy is likely to be **conservative** and new ideas may only appear as **emergent strategies**.

1.4 Time horizon

You should bear in mind which environmental issues are of:

- **Long-term impact**, which can be dealt with in advance
- **Short-term impact**, which require crisis management

CASE STUDY

Text messages

In many countries, text messaging is growing rapidly as a significant use of mobile phones. In the UK and Germany, for example, almost 40 text messages are sent by each mobile subscriber per month. The big operators make $50bn in annual revenues.

However, in France and the USA, sending text messages is far less popular. Both are wealthy, technologically advanced, IT-literate societies. What environmental factors might cause the difference?

The USA

In the USA, there are several incompatible technologies still in place. Voice calls on mobile phones are cheaper than in other countries so there is less incentive to save money by texting. Also, texting is an extra paid-for service. To summarise, the business model is different.

France

In France, only 65% of the population have a mobile phone compared to 90% in the UK, Spain or Italy. Some people explain this as a result of lack of competition, as Orange, the main mobile phone operator, is part of France Telecom which benefits from Orange's revenues and cash flows. French operators were slow to introduce texting, but even so, texting is still not so attractive. *The Economist* (7/10/2004) suggested that 'it is difficult to avoid the conclusion that cultural factors also play a role: perhaps mobile phones simply do not fit in with the relaxed French lifestyle'.

1.5 Environmental interactions

We have mentioned the various mnemonics used to help in making a comprehensive analysis and assessment of the general environment and, indeed, we will use the PEST approach to give structure to much of the rest of this chapter. It is very important that you understand that **this framework is merely one of convenience**. Environmental influences on business do not appear in neatly packaged groups: they interact and take effect in complex ways. A good example is the way in which **government policy affects economic factors**. Policy is by definition a political matter, but it is inevitable that economic conditions and developments will be heavily influenced by policy developments. Similarly, policy itself is likely to evolve in the face of demographic change or the development of opinion in society. Advanced nations are currently very concerned about the aging of their populations, for example, while the growth of concern over green issues has led to subsidy for power generation that does not produce carbon dioxide.

Section summary

The environment exists outside an organisation's boundaries, and organisations survive and prosper in this context. To secure **environmental fit**, an analysis of the environment therefore is required. PEST is a useful mnemonic to discuss these issues. Uncertainty in the environment arises from complexity and dynamism.

2 The political and legal environment

Introduction

The **political environment** affects the firm in a number of ways.

- A basic legal framework generally exists

- The government can take a particular stance on an issue of direct relevance to a business or industry

- The government's overall conduct of its economic policy is relevant to business

Exam alert

PEST analysis is a useful tool to employ in the long questions as an initial survey of conditions and options. But remember the real world doesn't have neatly defined categories like a model does; for example, political and economic factors often overlap. Use the model to generate ideas, but do not be too concerned with attributing factors to a specific category: identifying relevant factors is more important.

2.1 The political and legal environment

Laws come from common law, parliamentary legislation and government regulations derived from it, and obligations under treaties such as those establishing the European Union.

Some legal factors affect all companies, for example tax law (corporation tax, sales tax, income tax); employment law; health and safety law; and company law which governs directors and their duties, reporting requirements, takeover proceedings and shareholders' rights.

Other legal and regulatory factors affect **particular industries**, where the public interest is served by doing so. For example, electricity, gas, telecommunications, water and rail transport are subject to **regulators** (Ofgem, Oftel, Ofwat, Ofrail) who have influence over market access, competition and pricing policy (can restrict price increase)

This is because either:

- The industries are, effectively, monopolies
- Large sums of public money are involved (eg in subsidies to rail companies)

CASE STUDY

The National Lottery in the UK is one of the most highly regulated lotteries in the world. Under the terms of its licence, Camelot (the operator) is required to operate the lottery in an efficient and socially responsible way, protecting players and the integrity of the lottery, and to ensure that it generates the maximum amount of money for the 'Good Causes' which are designated by Parliament:

- The Community Fund
- The Millennium Commission
- The Sports Council
- The Heritage Lottery Fund
- The Arts Council
- New Opportunities Fund

The National Lottery Commission regulates the operation of the lottery. It has the right to award and revoke the operating licence, determine the number of games that can be offered and to carry out compliance audits (such as making sure there are no sales to under 16s).

Camelot's strategic objectives are clear:

(i)   Deliver target returns to Good Causes in a socially responsible way
(ii)   Increase the number of players and total sales
(iii)   Maximise player and retailer satisfaction
(iv)   Retain the trust and support of the general public
(v)   Deliver healthy returns for shareholders

However, it sees the regulatory regime in which it operates (there are over 2,000 regulations) as a barrier to a rapid response to an increasingly competitive market. Unequal tax regimes are a prime concern. The tax on bingo has been abolished, and it seems likely that regulation over competitors to the Lottery will be further reduced. Camelot believes that the only way to achieve a more effective balance between its own commercial requirements and the needs of customers is to allow it greater self regulation. It believes that its experience of running the Lottery since inception is testament to its integrity and ability.

2.2 The impact of government

Porter notes several ways whereby the **government** can directly affect the **economic structure** of an industry. They are explained below.

Capacity expansion	Government policy can encourage firms to increase or cut their capacity. (a) The UK tax system offers 'capital allowances' to encourage investment in equipment (b) A variety of incentives, funded by the EU and national governments, exist for locating capacity in a particular area (c) **Incentives** are used to encourage investment by overseas firms. Different countries in the EU have 'competed' for investment from Japan, for example
Demand	(a) The government is a major customer (b) Government can also influence demand by legislation, tax reliefs or subsidies
Divestment and rationalisation	In some European countries, the state takes many decisions regarding the selling off or closure of businesses, especially in sensitive areas such as defence.
Emerging industries	Can be promoted by the government or damaged by it.
Entry barriers	Government policy can discourage firms from entering an industry, by restricting investment or competition or by making it harder, by use of quotas and tariffs, for overseas firms to compete in the domestic market.
Competition	(a) The government's **purchasing decisions** will have a strong influence on the strength of one firm relative to another in the market (eg armaments). (b) **Regulations and controls** in an industry will affect the growth and profits of the industry – eg minimum product quality standards. (c) As a supplier of **infrastructure** (eg roads), the government is also in a position to influence competition in an industry. (d) Governments and supra-national institutions such as the EU might impose policies which keep an industry **fragmented**, and prevent the concentration of too much market share in the hands of one or two producers.

In some industries, governments regulate the adoption of **new products**. This is well illustrated by the **pharmaceuticals industry**, where new drugs or medicines must in many countries undergo stringent testing and obtain government approval before they can be marketed.

National and EU institutions also affect the operating activities of some organisations, for example:

- Anti-discrimination legislation
- Health and safety legislation
- **Product safety and standardisation** (especially EU standards)
- Workers' rights (eg unfair dismissal, maternity leave)
- Training and education policies can determine the 'standard' of recruits

| Question 12.1 | Government impact |

Learning outcome A1a

How do you think government policy affects the pharmaceutical industry in your country?

2.3 Influencing government

Businesses are able to influence government policies in a number of ways.

(a)   They can employ **lobbyists** to put their case to individual ministers or civil servants.

(b)   They can give MPs **non-executive directorships**, in the hope that the MP will take an interest in all legislation that affects them.

(c)   They can try to **influence public opinion**, and hence the legislative agenda, by advertising.

Of particular importance is the need to influence the decision making processes of the European Commission. EU regulations, for practical purposes, take priority over national law. They are arrived at after a great deal of negotiation, and for this reason alone, are difficult to change. It is therefore much better to influence the **drafting process** of new regulations than to try and get them changed once they have been implemented.

The EU will have an increasing role in the conduct of **European businesses** in:

(a)   Product standards
(b)   Environmental protection
(c)   Monetary policy (a **European Central Bank** might set interest rates)
(d)   Research and development
(e)   Regional policy
(f)   Labour costs (wages, pensions)

2.4 Political risk and political change

Changes in UK law are often predictable. A government will publish a **green paper** discussing a proposed change in the law, before issuing a **white paper** and passing a bill through Parliament. Plans should be formulated about what to do if the change takes place.

The political environment is not simply limited to legal factors. Government policy affects the whole **economy**, and governments are responsible for enforcing and creating a **stable framework** in which business can be done. A report by the World Bank indicated that the quality of **government policy is important in providing the right**:

(a)   Physical infrastructure (eg transport)
(b)   Social infrastructure (education, a welfare safety net, law enforcement)
(c)   Market infrastructure (enforceable contracts, policing corruption)

However, it is **political change** which complicates the planning activities of many firms. Many economic forecasts ignore the implications of a change in government policy.

(a) At **national level**, political influence is significant and includes legislation on trading, pricing, dividends, tax, employment as well as health and safety (to list but a few).

(b) Politics at **international level** also has a direct bearing on organisations. EU directives affect all countries in the EU.

The **political risk** in a decision is the risk that political factors will invalidate the strategy and perhaps severely damage the firm. Examples are wars, political chaos and regime change, social unrest, corruption and nationalism.

Political risk checklist

A political risk checklist was outlined by Jeannet and Hennessey. Companies should ask the following six questions.

1	How stable is the host country's political system?
2	How strong is the host government's commitment to specific rules of the game, such as ownership or contractual rights, given its ideology and power position?
3	How long is the government likely to remain in power?
4	If the present government is succeeded, how would the specific rules of the game change?
5	What would be the effects of any expected changes in the specific rules of the game?
6	In light of those effects, what decisions and actions should be taken now?

It is also important to remember that there are many countries that do not conform to the Western model of the **rule of law**. Political power may well be extra legal, with the legal system being manipulated or even ignored by government or by other powerful groups such as political parties.

Question 12.2   Political risk

Learning outcome A1a

For a business of your choice, identify the most significant areas of political risk.

2.5 International trade

The political environment is of particular importance in **international trade**. Such trade is governed by an extra layer of legislation contained in treaties and agreements and is potentially subject to a **higher level of political risk**. This may be manifested in a variety of ways, such as taxation law, labour regulation and economic policy on such matters as ownership. At worst, there is a threat of expropriation or nationalisation. Failure to repress lawlessness and corruption are further complicating factors, as is open or covert refusal to consider international bidders for government contracts.

2.6 Global business regulation

The wider political and legal environment interacts with the immediate task environment in the sphere of business regulation. Here, industry-specific rules are laid down and enforced.

Braithwaite and Drahos, in their book *Global Business Regulation*, discuss the way that the development of globally effective regulation has taken place. They argue that, while laws are passed by national legislatures, the rules they embody are actually created by discussion, negotiation and agreement among a **variety of expert bodies** including states, corporations and international bodies.

The emergence of global regulation does not necessarily march in step with the globalisation of either markets or business organisations. Gambling, for example, *via* the Internet, is a global market, but it is regulated in different ways by different states. By contrast, regulations relating to prescription drugs are now largely global in effect, but national markets are kept isolated from one another by differences in government policy on medicine as a welfare benefit. Pharmaceutical firms, however, are among the best established of global businesses.

Common features in global regulation

The processes that result in developments in global regulation are complex and vary from industry to industry. But some common features emerge.

(a)   **Power of individual countries**. The **USA** has huge influence over the globalisation of regulation; the **EU** is beginning to have similar influence. Among individual countries, the **UK** is second to the US in influence.

(b)   **International organisations** such as the World Trade Organisation, IMF and International Chamber of Commerce also have extensive power to influence the development of regulations.

(c)   **US corporations** are very effective at enrolling the power of their own government and international bodies to promote their interests. For example, at one time, the technical committees of the International Telecommunications Union nearly all had chairmen and vice-chairmen that had been nominated by US companies. As a result, US patented systems become global standards.

(d)   Change in global regulatory regimes often results from two contrasting sequences: the proactive and the reactive.

   (i)   The **proactive** sequence involves the promotion of regulatory innovation to one or more early mover organisations: these organisations will initially suffer a cost disadvantage but if the new standard is globalised, they will enjoy early mover benefits.

   (ii)   The **reactive** sequence starts with a disaster, followed by media hypes and public unrest: subsequent adoption of regulation placates the public.

However, despite any changes in the level at which regulation is made, it is still in the interests of businesses to **remain alert to the general thrust of regulation** as it affects their industries, and to participate in the processes of lobbying and representation in order to preserve their self-interest.

Section summary

Government policy influences the economic environment, the framework of laws, industry structure and certain operational issues. Political instability is a cause of risk. Different approaches to the political environment apply in different countries. International trade is subject to a further layer of international law and regulation.

---

3   The economic environment

3.1 The importance of the economic environment

Introduction

The economic environment is an important influence at local and national level. Here are some factors that firms must attend to.

Factor	Impact
Overall growth or fall in Gross Domestic Product	Increased/decreased demand for goods (eg dishwashers) and services (holidays).
Local economic trends	Type of industry in the area. Office/factory rents. Labour rates. House prices.
National economic trends:	
Inflation	Low in most countries; distorts business decisions; wage inflation compensates for price inflation
Interest rates	How much it costs to borrow money affects **cash flow**. Some businesses carry a high level of debt. How much customers can afford to spend is also affected as rises in interest rates affect people's mortgage payments.
Tax levels	Corporation tax affects how much firms can invest or return to shareholders. Income tax and Sales tax affect how much consumers have to spend, hence demand.
Government spending	Suppliers to the government (eg construction firms) are affected by spending.
The business cycle	Economic activity is always punctuated by periods of growth followed by decline, simply because of the nature of trade. The UK economy has been characterised by periods of 'boom' and 'bust'. Government policy can cause, exacerbate or mitigate such trends, but cannot abolish the business cycle. (Industries which prosper when others are declining are called counter-cyclical industries.)
Productivity	An economy cannot grow faster than the underlying growth in productivity, without risking inflation. UK manufacturing productivity is still lower than that of its main competitors, but in services, the UK is relatively efficient.

The **forecast state of the economy** will influence the planning process for organisations which operate within it. In times of boom and increased demand and consumption, the overall planning problem will be to **identify** the demand. Conversely, in times of recession, the emphasis will be on cost-effectiveness, continuing profitability, survival and competition.

3.1.1 Growth of the service sector

There is a trend in many developed economies, such as the UK, the US and so on, for **services** to account for a growing proportion of national economic activity and employment. The **service sector** accounts for most output. Services include activities such as restaurants, tourism, nursing, education, management consultancy, computer consulting, banking and finance. Manufacturing is still important, especially in exports, but it employs fewer and fewer people.

KEY TERM

SERVICES are value-creating activities which in themselves do not involve the supply of physical product. Service provision may be subdivided into:

(a) *Pure services*, where there is no physical product, such as consultancy
(b) *Service with a product attached,* such as the design and installation of a computer network
(c) *Products with services attached,* such as the purchase of a computer with a maintenance contract

3.1.2 Impact of international factors on a country's economy

Factor	Impact
Exchange rates	Cost of imports, selling prices and value of exports; cost of hedging against fluctuations
Characteristics of overseas markets. Different rates of economic growth and prosperity, tax etc	Desirable overseas markets (demand) or sources of supply
Capital flows and trade	Investment opportunities, free trade, cost of exporting
Globalisation	Increased competition, increasing prosperity

3.2 Government economic policy

Governments generally accept that they have a role to play in the management of the macroeconomy. Their objectives are generally to achieve satisfactory and stable **growth**, while controlling **inflation** and avoiding significant changes in the value of their **currencies**. Growth is required since it enhances general economic **well-being** and provides for high levels of **employment**.

A government can use various policy tools as follows.

Fiscal policy	• Taxation and other sources of income • Government spending • Borrowing whenever spending exceeds income • Repaying debt when income exceeds expenditure
Monetary policy	• Interest rates • Exchange rates or exchange controls • Control of the money supply • Controls over bank lending and credit (rarely used nowadays)

Businesses are affected by a government's tax policy (eg corporation tax rates), and monetary policy (high interest rates increase the cost of investment, or depress consumer demand).

In practice, governments are making use of these tools in different ways.

In the UK, the USA and the Euro-zone, control of **monetary policy** (interest rates) is set by independent bodies (the Bank of England, the Federal Reserve, the European Central Bank), over which governments have little direct influence. In other countries, this is not the case.

Some countries use exchange rate policy and exchange controls to affect economic activity. Not all currencies are fully convertible into others. The government of Malaysia used this approach, by restricting the import and export of Malaysian *ringgit*, in the financial crises of Asia in the late 1990s.

Finally, there is pressure in some jurisdictions for co-ordination of fiscal policies.

3.2.1 Government spending

Governments nationally and locally spend money on the following.

- Payments of wages and salaries to employees, and of pensions to old age pensioners
- Payments for materials, supplies and services
- Purchases of capital equipment
- Payments of interest on borrowings and repayments of capital

Tax and spending decisions have the effect of increasing or decreasing the amount that consumers have to spend generally and **re-allocating resources** in the economy to the public sector activities.

3.2.2 Involvement of the private sector

In many countries, various areas of the public sector have been delivered to the private sector in a process of **privatisation**. Where these were utilities, these organisations are regulated by bodies such as Ofcom. This process has had a number of sometimes conflicting objectives.

(a) **Reductions in public sector borrowing** and expenditure to finance tax cuts and/or spending.

(b) **Greater investment** which the government is unwilling or unable to fund from its own resources. Privatised utilities are then **free to borrow**.

(c) **New management practices** are introduced.

(d) Privatisation can encourage **competition**, but some utilities have been sold off as **monopolies**, subject to a regulator.

Privatisation is now relatively uncontroversial in the UK, but still causes political hostility in the developing world.

The blurring of boundaries between public and private sector continues.

(a) **Contracting out**. Some work which was previously done by government employees has been contracted out to firms in the private sector.

(b) **Welfare spending**. Government policy has been to shift some welfare spending to individuals, for example in personal pensions.

(c) **Private finance initiative**. In the UK, the private sector is involved in financing public projects, such as roads and hospitals.

In some countries, therefore, government policy has been to purchase welfare services from private sector suppliers rather than manage them directly.

3.2.3 Inflation and interest rates

Inflation can be a deterrent to real economic growth, creating expectations of further inflation and undermining business confidence. The consequences include the following.

(a) A demand for **higher money wages** to be paid to employees to compensate for the fall in value of their wages.

(b) A demand for **high interest rates**, so that investors can be compensated for inflation and borrowers are deterred.

3.2.4 The housing market

An important feature of the UK and other countries is the **housing market**. Events from 2007 onwards affected the ability to borrow to buy a house. This meant many young buyers with limited funds, were unable to borrow enough to buy a house. It may be some years before the housing market returns to stability.

(a) The **housing market** is a key factor for people in the UK and many other countries. Most houses are owner-occupied, and most people's wealth is tied up in their homes. UK borrowers generally borrow at variable rates of interest, so are vulnerable to changes in interest rates.

(b) **Rising prices** encourage people to take out extra loans to spend on other things. This was held to lead to inflation.

(c) Most of the debt owed by UK borrowers is at **variable rate**. Changes in interest rates have an immediate effect on people's pockets. This is not necessarily the case elsewhere.

3.3 International trade and exchange rates

International trade and finance consists of:

- Trade in goods and services, forming the **balance of trade**
- Long-term and short-term **investments** from other countries and into other countries
- Movements in a government's **official reserves** of foreign currency, gold etc

Faced with a **trade deficit**, a government might once have considered **protectionist measures** and, in the case of developing countries, **exchange controls**.

However, a government's long-term strategy for a balance of trade deficit should be to improve conditions in the domestic economy.

(a)   The improvements required could include bringing inflation under control, encouraging investment in domestic industries and depressing consumer demand.

(b)   The **quality** of the deficit is an important consideration. If capital goods are imported, this might mean only a short-term deficit, as the machinery enhances the productivity and export capacity of domestic firms in the long term. If consumer goods are imported, this might not be as sustainable in the long run.

Question 12.3
Single currency

Learning outcome A1a

What might be the implications of the single European currency, for the following UK businesses?

(a)   A package holiday firm, mainly selling holidays to France and Germany.
(b)   An exporter of power station generating equipment to developing countries in Asia.
(c)   An importer of wine from Australia.

Do this exercise twice, firstly on the assumption that the UK adopts the Euro, swapping sterling for the Euro, and secondly on the assumption that it keeps sterling as its currency.

3.4 Economic factors and the management accountant

The management accountant may be asked to estimate the effect of particular economic factors on the firm's operations.

(a)   **Interest rates**

  (i)   A rise might increase the cost of any borrowing the company has undertaken, thereby reducing its profitability. It also has the possible effect of raising a firm's cost of capital. An investment project therefore has a higher hurdle to overcome to be accepted. If, on the other hand, a firm has surplus cash, this can be invested for a higher return.

  (ii)   Interest rates also have a general effect on consumer confidence and liquidity, and hence demand, especially in relation to the housing markets.

(b)   **Inflation.** For an economy has a whole, inflation works as a 'tax on savers' given that it reduces the value of financial assets and the income of those on fixed incomes.

  (i)   It requires high **nominal interest rates** to offer investors a real return.

  (ii)   Inflation makes it hard for businesses to plan, owing to the uncertainty of future financial returns. Inflation and expectations of it help explain '**short-termism**'.

  (iii)   Inflation has a number of effects on how firms report their performance and how they plan.

Exchange rate volatility affects the cost of imports from overseas, and the prices that can be charged to overseas customers. A high value to the pound means that customers must be charged more in their local currencies – and imports are cheaper.

Exchange rates do not only affect imports and exports. Many firms invest large sums of money in factories in overseas markets.

(a) The **purchasing power parity** theory of exchange rate suggests that, in the long term, differences in exchange rates caused by inflation or higher interest rates will even out. It looks at what people can buy in their own country and uses this to compare economic performance. The Chinese economy is, measured in US $, much smaller than the US economy: the difference in size is not so marked when purchasing power parity is used for comparisons.

(b) Firms are very vulnerable to changes in exchange rates over the short to medium term, especially as a subsidiary's reported profit can affect the reported profit of the holding company and hence, by implication, its share price. Firms can guard against the risk of exchange rates by a number of financial instruments such as **hedges**.

Section summary

Economic factors include the overall level of growth, the business cycle, official monetary and fiscal policy, exchange rates and inflation.

---

4 The social and cultural environment

Introduction

Social change involves changes in the nature, attitudes and habits of society. Social changes are continually happening, and trends can be identified, which may or may not be relevant to a business. Culture is often spoken of as 'the way we do things round here' certainly in organisations. In society however culture is broader than this and encompasses customs, attitudes, characteristic ways of viewing the world and behaviour. Most countries contain several subcultures.

4.1 Social change and social trends

CASE STUDY

In January 2006, *Canterbury Foods*, a manufacturer of food products such as pastries, sausages and hamburgers, collapsed into insolvency with debts of £15m. The Chief Executive, Paul Ainsworth, had said in September 2005 that the TV campaign by celebrity chef Jamie Oliver to drive up the quality of school meals had helped to undermine the company's position, though commentators noted that it had been heavily indebted and trading at a loss for some time. Britain's largest catering firm, *Compass*, said that sales of several food companies had been hit by the school meals campaign: 'there has been a move away from Turkey Twizzlers'.

4.2 Demography

KEY TERM

DEMOGRAPHY is the study of populations and communities. It provides analysis of statistics on birth and death rates, age structures of populations, ethnic groups within communities and so on.

Demography is important for these reasons.

- Labour is a factor of production
- People create demand for goods, services and resources
- It has a long-term impact on government policies
- There is a relationship between population growth and living standards

Here are some statistics, which might help to explain the importance many businesses are placing on overseas markets. The figures are taken from *Social Trends*.

	1994 Population	*2025 Population*	*% increase*
	(millions)	*(millions) estimated*	*1994-2025*
World population	5,665.5	8,472.4	49%
Europe (including Baltic states)	512.0	541.9	5%
Former USSR (excluding Baltic states)	284.5	344.5	21%
Canada and USA	282.7	360.5	27%
Africa	681.7	1,582.5	132%
Asia	3,233.0	4,900.3	52%
Latin America	457.7	701.6	53%
Oceania (including Australia)	27.5	41.3	50%

The following demographic factors are important to organisational planners.

Factor	Comment
Growth	The rate of growth or decline in a national population and in regional populations.
Age	Changes in the age distribution of the population. In the UK, there will be an increasing proportion of the national population over retirement age. In developing countries there are very large numbers of young people.
Geography	The concentration of population into certain geographical areas.
Ethnicity	A population might contain groups with different ethnic origins from the majority. In the UK, about 5% come from ethnic minorities, although most of these live in London and the South East.
Household and family structure	A household is the basic social unit and its size might be determined by the number of children, whether elderly parents live at home etc. In the UK, there has been an increase in single-person households and lone parent families.
Social structure	The population of a society can be broken down into a number of subgroups, with different attitudes and access to economic resources. Social class, however, is hard to measure (as people's subjective perceptions vary).
Employment	In part, this is related to changes in the workplace. Many people believe that there is a move to a casual flexible workforce; factories will have a group of **core employees**, supplemented by a group of insecure **peripheral employees**, on part time or temporary contracts, working as and when required. Some research indicates a 'two-tier' society split between 'work-rich' (with two wage-earners) and 'work-poor'. However, despite some claims, most employees are in permanent, full-time employment.
Wealth	Rising standards of living lead to increased demand for certain types of consumer good. This is why developing countries are attractive as markets.

4.2.1 Implications of demographic change

(a) **Changes in patterns of demand**: an ageing population suggests increased demand for health care services: a 'young' growing population has a growing demand for schools, housing and work.

CASE STUDY

The UK disposable nappy market turnover fell by 18% to £344m between 1999 and 2003, according to *Mintel*, a market research company. This fall echoes a 15% fall in live births between 1998 and 2004.

(b) **Location of demand**: people are moving to the suburbs and small towns.

(c) **Recruitment policies**: there are relatively fewer young people so firms will have to recruit from less familiar sources of labour.

(d) **Wealth and tax**.

We looked at culture in Part A, in some detail and in the context of the organisation. Here we look at the external cultural influences in an organisation and its strategy.

4.3 Culture

KEY TERM

CULTURE is used by sociologists and anthropologists to encompass 'the sum total of the beliefs, knowledge, attitudes of mind and customs to which people are exposed in their social conditioning.'

Through contact with a particular culture, individuals learn a language, acquire values and learn habits of behaviour and thought. Culture has the following characteristics.

(a) **Beliefs and values**. Beliefs are what we feel to be the case on the basis of objective and subjective information (eg people can believe the world is round or flat). Values are beliefs which are relatively enduring, relatively general and fairly widely accepted as a guide to culturally appropriate behaviour.

(b) **Customs:** modes of behaviour which represent culturally accepted ways of behaving in response to given situations.

(c) **Artefacts:** all the physical tools designed by human beings for their physical and psychological well-being: works of art, technology, products.

(d) **Rituals.** A ritual is a type of activity which takes on symbolic meaning, consisting of a fixed sequence of behaviour repeated over time.

The learning and sharing of culture is made possible by language (both written and spoken, verbal and non-verbal).

CASE STUDY

Islamic banking

Islamic banking is a powerful example of the importance of culture in an economy. The Koran forbids the charging of interest, which is usury. However whilst interest is banned, profits are allowed. A problem is that there is no standard interpretation of the sharia law regarding this. Products promoted by Islamic banks include:

(a) Leasing (the Islamic Bank TII arranged leases for seven Kuwait Airways aircraft)
(b) Trade finance
(c) Commodities trading

The earlier Islamic banks offered current accounts only, but depositors now ask for shares in the bank profits. To tap this market, Citibank, the US bank, opened an Islamic banking subsidiary in Bahrain.

4.3.1 Importance of culture for business

Knowledge of the culture of a society is clearly of value to businesses in a number of ways.

(a) **Marketers** can adapt their products accordingly, and be fairly sure of a sizeable market. This is particularly important in export markets.

(b) **Human resource managers** may need to tackle cultural differences in recruitment. For example, some ethnic minorities have a different body language from the majority, which may be hard for some interviewers to interpret.

Culture in a society can be divided into **subcultures** reflecting social differences. Most people participate in several of them.

Subculture	Comment
Class	People from different social classes might have different values reflecting their position in society.
Ethnic background	Some ethnic groups can still be considered a distinct cultural group.
Religion	Religion and ethnicity are related.
Geography or region	Distinct regional differences might be brought about by the past effects of physical geography (socio-economic differences etc). Speech accents noticeably differ most.
Age	Age subcultures vary according to the period in which individuals were socialised to an extent, because of the great shifts in social values and customs in this century. ('Youth culture'; the 'generation gap' etc.)
Sex	Some products are targeted directly to women or to men.
Work	Different organisations have different corporate cultures, in that the shared values of one workplace may be different from another.

Cultural change might have to be planned for. There has been a revolution in attitudes to female employment, despite the well-publicised problems of discrimination that still remain.

Question 12.4   Social trends

Learning outcome A1a

Club Fun is a UK company which sells packaged holidays. It offers a standard 'cheap and cheerful' package to resorts in Spain and the Greek islands. It was particularly successful at providing holidays for the 18-30 age group.

What do you think the implications are for Club Fun of the following developments?

- A fall in the number of school leavers
- The fact that young people are more likely now than in the 1960s to go into higher education
- Holiday programmes on TV which feature a much greater variety of locations
- Greater disposable income among the 18-30 age group
- Increasing levels of Internet access

Section summary

Social and cultural factors relate to two main issues. **Demography** is the study of the population as a whole: its overall size, whether it is growing, stable, or falling; the proportion of people of different age groups – in industrial countries the proportion of elderly people is increasing; where people live and work; ethnic origin. **Culture** includes customs, attitudes, characteristic ways of viewing the world and behaviour: most countries contain several subcultures.

5 The technological environment

Introduction

In the most general sense, technology contributes to overall **economic growth**. Consider the **production possibility curve** which describes the total production in an economy. Technology can shift this curve, increasing total output, by enabling:

- Gains in productivity (more output per units of input)
- Reduced costs (eg transportation technology, preservatives)
- New types of product

Technological change is rapid, and organisations must adapt themselves to it. Technological change can affect the activities of organisations as follows.

(a) **The type of products or services that are made and sold.** For example, consumer markets have seen the emergence of personal computers, DVDs, digital cameras and digital TV; industrial markets have seen the emergence of custom-built microchips, robots and local area networks for office information systems.

CASE STUDY

The development of the transistor made valve radios obsolete. Japanese firms were thus able easily to enter the consumer electronics market, where they are now key competitors. Japanese firms had no previous investment in valve radio production.

(b) **The way in which products are made.**

  (i) Modern production equipment reduces the need for labour.
  (ii) Technology can also develop new raw materials.

(c) The way in which services are provided, for example travel agencies over the internet.

(d) The way in which markets are identified. Database systems make it much easier to analyse the market place.

(e) The way in which firms are managed. IT has helped in the 'delayering' of organisational hierarchies (in other words, the reduction of management layers between the senior managers and the workforce), but requires greater workforce skills. Using technology often requires changes in working methods. Information technology, in particular, requires skills at manipulating and interpreting abstract data.

(f) The means and extent of communications with external clients.

Impact of technological change

The impact of technological change also has potentially important social consequences.

(a) Whereas people were once collected together to work in factories, **home working** will become more important.

(b) Certain sorts of skill, related to **interpretation** of data and information processes, are likely to become more valued than manual or physical skills.

(c) Technology increases manufacturing productivity, so that more people will be involved in **service** jobs.

It is extremely difficult to **forecast** developments beyond more than a few years. For example, many of the current developments in information technology would have seemed almost impossible not much more than a decade ago.

(a) **Futurology** is the science and study of sociological and technological developments, values and trends with a view to planning for the future.

(b)   The **Delphi model** involves a panel of experts providing views on various events to be forecast such as inventions and breakthroughs, or even regulations or changes over a time period in to the future.

(c)   In some cases, instead of technical developments being used to predict future technologies, future social developments can be predicted, in order to predict future **customer needs**.

It is also possible that one particular invention or technique will have wide ranging applications. Such a technology might be called a **meta-technology**.

CASE STUDY

An example of a meta-technology might be the technology behind lasers. Lasers are used for a huge variety of jobs.

- Eye surgery (eg on the cornea, as it is more precise than a scalpel, and the heat effectively seals the wound)

- Industrial cutting

- Illuminating public monuments at night

- Reading data from compact disks or DVDs (for recorded music, interactive video games, interactive encyclopaedias, publishing)

- Discotheques

CASE STUDY

Ethanol in Brazil

The need to consider the general environment as an integrated whole and not as a group of separate influences is illustrated by the history of the ethanol fuel industry in Brazil.

Ethanol as an alternative or supplement to petroleum products for motor vehicle fuel came back into prominence in 2005 because of major demand-driven rises in the global price of oil. In January 2006, *The Financial Times* reported that the Brazilian ethanol industry had been established in response to the oil crises of the 1970s. Subsidies for cane mills and price controls had helped to create a major industry. Here we see a problem that combines politics and economics being solved with a combination of politics, economics and technology.

During the 1980s, nearly all cars in Brazil were running on ethanol, so there was clearly a significant social effect in terms of acceptance. Unfortunately, in 1989, world sugar prices spiked and ethanol producers shifted their raw material (sugar cane) to the production of sugar. The price of ethanol was still controlled, so the inevitable result was a major shortage of the fuel, which prejudiced consumers against it for a decade. Once again, politics, economics and social factors interact. A prejudice was created against ethanol fuelled cars, focussing on their inferior performance. This has only recently been overcome by the introduction of higher technology 'flex fuel' cars that adjust a mix of ethanol and petrol to boost performance.

Section summary

Technological factors have implications for economic growth overall, and offer opportunities and threats to many businesses. Meta-technologies are technologies that are applicable to many applications.

6 Stakeholder goals and objectives

STAKEHOLDERS are 'those persons and organisations that have an interest in the strategy of an organisation. Stakeholders normally include shareholders, customers, staff and the local community.'

(CIMA Official Terminology)

Introduction

There are three broad types of stakeholder in an organisation, as follows.

- **Internal** stakeholders (employees, management)
- **Connected** stakeholders (shareholders, customers, suppliers, financiers)
- **External** stakeholders (the community, government, pressure groups)

6.1 Internal stakeholders: employees and management

Because **employees and management** are so intimately connected with the company, their objectives are likely to have a strong influence on how it is run. They are interested in the following issues.

(a) The **organisation's continuation and growth**. Management and employees have a special interest in the organisation's continued existence.

(b) Managers and employees have **individual interests** and goals which can be harnessed to the goals of the organisation.

Internal stakeholder	Interests to defend	Response risk
Managers and employees	• Jobs/careers • Money • Promotion • Benefits • Satisfaction	• Pursuit of 'systems goals' rather than shareholder interests • Industrial action • Negative power to impede implementation • Refusal to relocate • Resignation

6.2 Connected stakeholders

Writing in *Management Accounting* (November 1997) Malcolm Smith stated that increasing shareholder value should assume a core role in the strategic management of a business. If management performance is measured and rewarded by reference to changes in **shareholder value** then shareholders will be happy, because managers are likely to encourage long-term share price growth.

Connected stakeholder	Interests to defend	Response risk
Shareholders (corporate strategy)	• Increase in shareholder wealth, measured by profitability, P/E ratios, market capitalisation, dividends and yield • Risk	• Sell shares (eg to predator) or boot out management
Bankers (cash flows)	• Security of loan • Adherence to loan agreements	• Denial of credit • Higher interest charges • Receivership

Suppliers (purchase strategy)	• Profitable sales • Payment for goods • Long-term relationship	• Refusal of credit • Court action • Wind down relationships
Customers (product market strategy)	• Goods as promised • Future benefits	• Buy elsewhere • Sue

CASE STUDY

A survey of FTSE 100 companies conducted by the *Financial Times* asked what part leading shareholders play in the running of companies and what top directors think of their investors.

Almost half of those surveyed felt that their main shareholders 'rarely or never' offered any useful comments about their business. 69% of respondents however felt that their major investors understood their business well or very well. 89% did not feel hampered by shareholders in taking the correct long term strategy.

Almost all directors felt their biggest shareholders were in it for the long term. This latter point probably reflects the fact that the top ten fund managers own 36 per cent of the FTSE 100 – few fund managers can afford to move out of a FTSE 100 company altogether and therefore remain long term shareholders whether the investment is liked or not.

There is a perceived trend towards greater involvement and communication. To quote one director: 'Investors are much more sensitive to their responsibilities than in the past because they are looked on as the guardians of the corporate conscience.'

6.3 External stakeholders

External stakeholder groups – the government, local authorities, pressure groups, the community at large, professional bodies – are likely to have quite diverse objectives.

External stakeholder	Interests to defend	Response risk
Government	• Jobs, training, tax	• Tax increases • Regulation • Legal action
Interest/pressure groups	• Pollution • Rights • Other	• Publicity • Direct action • Sabotage • Pressure on government

6.4 The nature of stakes

Stakes may be analysed in several ways.

(a)   Local, national or international

(b)   Single or multiple issues

(c)   Economic or social (ie financial– or concern-based: the latter would include interests such as equal opportunities)

(d)   Concrete or symbolic: symbolic stakes are hard to define but important to the persons concerned and include general concern, anxiety and the need for respect

6.5 Primary and secondary stakeholders

Stakeholders may also be analysed by reference to whether they have a **contractual relationship** with the organisation. Stakeholders who have such a relationship are called **primary stakeholders**, while those who do not are known as **secondary stakeholders**. The primary stakeholder category thus includes **internal** and **connected** stakeholders, while the secondary stakeholders category equates to **external** stakeholder status.

6.6 Stakeholder conflicts

The analysis above demonstrates that conflict is likely between stakeholder groups simply because of the divergence of their interests. The picture is complicated when individuals are members of more than one stakeholder group and when members of the same stakeholder group do not share the same principal interest. Both cases are illustrated by considering a workforce, some of whose members are also shareholders and some of whom are not.

6.7 Dependency

A firm might depend on a stakeholder group at any particular time.

(a)   A firm with persistent cash flow problems might depend on its bankers to provide it with money to stay in business at all.

(b)   In the long term, any firm depends on its customers.

The degree of dependence or reliance can be analysed according to these criteria.

(a)   **Disruption.** Can the stakeholder disrupt the organisation's plans (eg a bank withdrawing overdraft facilities)?

(b)   **Replacement.** Can the firm replace the relationship?

(c)   **Uncertainty.** Does the stakeholder cause uncertainty in the firm's plans? A firm with healthy positive cash flows and large cash balances need not worry about its bank's attitude to a proposed investment.

The way in which the relationship between company and stakeholders is conducted is a function of the parties' **relative bargaining strength** and the philosophy underlying **each party's objectives**. This can be shown by means of a spectrum.

	Weak		Stakeholders' bargaining strength			Strong
Company's conduct of relation-ship	Command/ dictated by company	Consultation and consideration of stakeholders' views	Negotiation	Participation and acceptance of stakeholders' views	Democratic voting by stakeholders	Command/ dictated by stakeholders

6.8 Stakeholder mapping: power and interest

In an earlier chapter, we looked at stakeholder power and how this was managed in respect of projects. This was explained by Mendelow's model of stakeholder mapping. The model can be applied to stakeholders in general and we will run through the general principles again here.

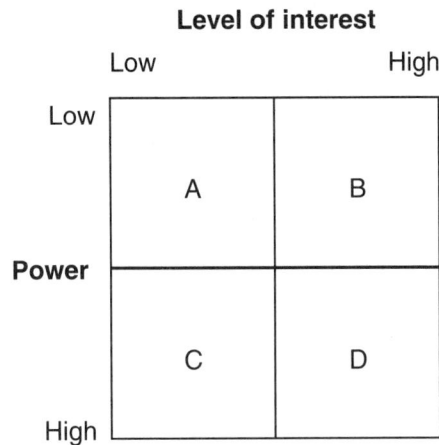

Level of interest

	Low	High
Low	A	B
High	C	D

Power

(a)   **Key players** are found in segment D: strategy must be *acceptable* to them, at least. An example would be a major customer.

(b)   Stakeholders in segment C must be treated with care. While often passive, they are capable of moving to segment D. They should, therefore be **kept satisfied.** Large institutional shareholders might fall into segment C.

(c)   Stakeholders in segment B do not have great ability to influence strategy, but their views can be important in influencing more powerful stakeholders, perhaps by lobbying. They should therefore be **kept informed.** Community representatives and charities might fall into segment B.

(d)   Minimal effort is expended on segment A.

A single stakeholder map is unlikely to be appropriate for all circumstances. In particular, stakeholders may move from quadrant to quadrant when different potential future strategies are considered.

Stakeholder mapping is used to assess the **significance** of stakeholder groups. This in turn has implications for the organisation.

(a)   The framework of **corporate governance** should recognise stakeholders' levels of interest and power.

(b)   It may be appropriate to seek to **reposition** certain stakeholders and discourage others from repositioning themselves, depending on their attitudes.

(c)   Key **blockers** and **facilitators** of change must be identified.

Stakeholder mapping can also be used to establish political priorities. A map of the current position can be compared with a map of a desired future state. This will indicate critical shifts that must be pursued.

In *Power In and Around Organisations*, *Mintzberg* identifies groups that not only have an interest in an organisation but power over it.

The external coalition	The internal coalition
• Owners (who hold legal title) • Associates (suppliers, customers, trading partners) • Employee associations (unions, professional bodies) • Public (government, media)	• The chief executive and board at the strategic apex • Line managers • Operators • The technostructure (more in **E3** on this) • Support staff

Each of these groups has three basic choices.

- **Loyalty**. They can do as they are told.

- **Exit**. For example by selling their shares, or getting a new job.

- **Voice**. They can stay and try to change the system. Those who choose **voice** are those who can, to varying degrees, influence the organisation. Influence implies a degree of power and willingness to exercise it.

Existing structures and systems can channel stakeholder influence.

(a) They are the **location of power**, giving groups of people varying degrees of influence over strategic choices.

(b) They are **conduits of information**, which shape strategic decisions.

(c) They **limit choices** or give some options priority over others. These may be physical or ethical constraints over what is possible.

(d) They **embody culture**.

(e) They **determine the successful implementation** of strategy.

(f) The **firm has different degrees of dependency** on various stakeholder groups. A company with a cash flow crisis will be more beholden to its bankers than one with regular cash surpluses.

Question 12.5   Stakeholder influences

Learning outcome A1a

Ticket and Budget International is a large multinational firm of accountants. The firm provides audit services, tax services, and consultancy services for its many clients. The firm has a strong Technical Department which designs standardised audit procedures. The firm has just employed a marketing manager. The marketing manager regards an audit as a 'product', part of the entire marketing mix including price (audit fees), place (usually on the client's premises) and promotion (advertising in professional journals) The marketing manager is held in high regard by the firm's senior partner. The marketing director and the senior partner have unveiled a new strategic plan, drawn up in conditions of secrecy, which involves a tie-up with an advertising agency. The firm will be a 'one-stop shop' for business services and advice to management on any subject. Each client, or 'customer' will have a dedicated team of auditors, consultants and advertising executives. Obviously, a member of staff will be a member of a number of different teams.

The firm has recently settled a number of expensive law suits for negligence (which it has, of course, 'contested vigorously') out of court, without admitting liability. The Technical Department is conducting a thorough review of the firm's audit procedures.

In the light of what we have covered in this section, what do you think will be the organisational and stakeholder influences on the proposed strategy?

So, different stakeholders will have their own views as to strategy. As some stakeholders have **negative power**, in other words power to impede or disrupt the decision, their likely response might be considered.

Exam alert

In an exam question, you will usually have to:

- Identify the stakeholders in the situation
- Identify what their particular interests are

You may also have to:

- Explain the importance of developing and maintaining relationships with them
- Explain how their varying interests may be reconciled

6.9 The strategic value of stakeholders

The firm can make strategic gains from managing stakeholder relationships. Studies have revealed the following correlations.

(a)   A correlation between **employee** and **customer loyalty** (eg reduced staff turnover in service firms generally results in more repeat business).

(b)   **Continuity** and **stability** in relationships with employees, customers and suppliers is important in enabling organisations to respond to certain types of change, necessary for business as a sustained activity.

Responsibilities towards customers are mainly those of providing a product or service of a quality that customers expect, and of dealing honestly and fairly with customers.

Responsibilities towards suppliers are expressed mainly in terms of trading relationships.

(a)   The organisation's size could give it considerable power as a buyer. One ethical guideline might be that the organisation should not use its power unscrupulously.

(b)   Suppliers might rely on getting prompt payment in accordance with the terms of trade negotiated with its customers.

(c)   All information obtained from suppliers and potential suppliers should be kept confidential.

6.10 Measuring stakeholder satisfaction

If it is accepted that stakeholders other than shareholders have a legitimate interest in what the firm does, it is appropriate to consider measuring the degree of success it achieves in satisfying those interests.

We have already considered ways in which stakeholders may be classified and given some instances of their probable interests. Measuring the satisfaction of stakeholder interests is likely to be difficult, since many of their expectations relate to **qualitative** rather than **quantitative** matters. It is, for example, difficult to measure good corporate citizenship. On the other hand, some of the more important stakeholder groups do have fairly specific interests, the satisfaction of which should be fairly amenable to measurement. Here are some examples of possible measures.

Stakeholder group	Measure
Employees	Staff turnover; pay and benefits relative to market rate; job vacancies
Government	Pollution measures; promptness of filing annual returns; accident rate; energy efficiency
Distributors	Share of joint promotions paid for; rate of stock-outs

Paper E3 requires you to be able to recommend how to manage relationships with stakeholders.

Section summary

Stakeholders are those individuals or groups that, potentially, have an interest in what the organisation does. Different stakeholder groups have different degrees of power and interest, and management must respond to each in a different way.

7 The competitive advantage of a nation's industries: Porter's diamond

Introduction

Michael Porter's *The Competitive Advantage of Nations,* suggests that some nations' industries succeed more than others in terms of international competition. UK leadership in some industries (eg ship-building) has been overtaken (by Japan and Korea).

Porter does not believe that countries or nations as such are competitive, but he asks:

(a)   'Why does a **nation become the home base** for successful international competitors in an industry?'

(b)   'Why are firms based in a particular nation able to create and **sustain competitive advantage** against the world's best competitors in a particular field?'

(c)   'Why is **one nation** often the home for **so many of an industry's world leaders**?'

The original explanation for **national** success was the theory of **comparative advantage**. This held that relative **factor opportunity costs** in countries determined the appropriateness of particular economic activities in relation to other countries. (In other words, countries should concentrate on what they are best at in relation to other countries.)

Porter argues that **industries that require high technology and highly skilled employees are less affected** than low technology industries by the relative costs of their inputs of raw materials and basic labour as determined by the national endowment of factors.

Comparative advantage is too **general a concept** to explain the success of **individual companies and industries**. If high technology and global markets allow firms to circumvent (or ignore) the constraints (or advantages) of their home country's endowment of raw materials, cheap labour, access to capital and so forth, how can they be successful internationally?

Porter identifies determinants of national competitive advantage which are outlined in the diagram below. *Porter* refers to this as the **diamond.**

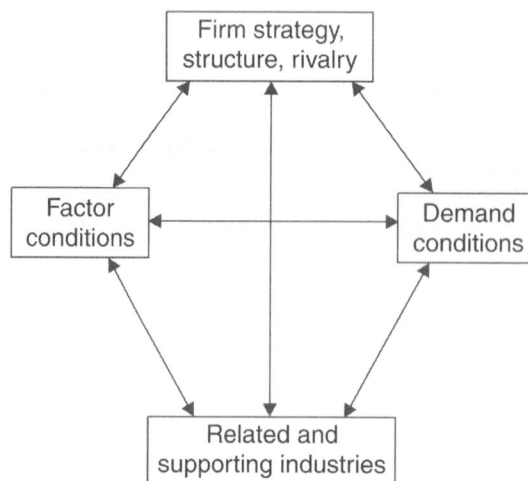

Each element of the diamond is capable of enhancing national competitive advantage. Conversely, a nation that enjoys competitive advantage will find it diminishes if the elements cease to work positively.

7.1 Analysing the diamond

7.1.1 Factor conditions

Factor conditions are a country's endowment of inputs to production.

(a)   **Human resources** (skills, motivation, industrial relations)
(b)   **Physical resources** (land, minerals, climate, location relative to other nations)
(c)   **Knowledge** (scientific and technical know-how, educational institutions)
(d)   **Capital** (amounts available for investment, how it is deployed)
(e)   **Infrastructure** (transport, communications, housing)

Porter distinguishes between:

(a)   **Basic factors:** natural resources, climate, semiskilled and unskilled labour. Basic factors are inherited, or at best their creation involves little investment.

(b)   **Advanced factors** include modern digital communications, highly educated personnel research laboratories and so forth. They are necessary to achieve high order competitive advantages such as differentiated products and proprietary production technology.

Inappropriate decisions and economic policy, in particular, can lead to erosion of advantageous factor conditions. This is particularly true of advanced factor conditions, which require significant investment, but even the advantage provided by basic physical factors can be eroded if markets change significantly. For example, there is plenty of coal left under England but it is difficult to work underground and open-cast extraction is politically unacceptable because of its environmental effects.

KEY POINT

An abundance of factors is not enough. It is the efficiency with which they are deployed that matters. The former USSR had an abundance of natural resources and a fairly well educated workforce, but was an economic catastrophe.

7.1.2 Demand conditions: the home market

The **home market determines how firms perceive, interpret and respond to buyer needs.** This information puts pressure on firms to innovate and provides a launch pad for global ambitions.

(a)   There are **no cultural impediments** to communication.

(b)   The **segmentation** of the home market shapes a firm's priorities: companies will be successful globally in segments which are similar to the home market.

(c)   **Sophisticated and demanding buyers** set standards. ('The British are known for gardening, and British firms are world class in garden tools.')

(d)   **Anticipatory buyer needs:** if consumer needs are expressed in the home market earlier than in the world market, the firm benefits from experience.

(e)   The **rate of growth**. Slow growing home markets do not encourage the adoption of state of the art technology.

(f)   **Early saturation** of the home market will encourage a firm to export.

(g)   Serving a substantial home market allows the attainment of **economies of scale**.

Advantage here can be eroded if a gap emerges between local and foreign demand.

7.1.3 Related and supporting industries

Competitive success in one industry is linked to success in related industries. Domestic suppliers are preferable to foreign suppliers, as 'proximity of managerial and technical personnel, along with cultural similarity, tends to facilitate free and open information flow' at an early stage. However, it is easy for this aspect of the diamond to lose its advantage if individual companies do not remain competitive or mutually supportive. See below for a case study on the situation in Italy.

7.1.4 Firm strategy, structure and rivalry

Structure. National cultural factors create certain tendencies to orientate business people to certain industries. German firms, according to Porter, have a strong showing in 'industries with a high technical content'.

Strategy. Industries in different countries have different **time horizons**, funding needs and so forth.

(a)   **National capital markets** set different goals for performance. In some countries, banks are the main source of capital, not equity shareholders.

(b)   When an industry faces difficult times, it **can either innovate within the industry**, to sustain competitive position or **shift resources from one industry to another** (eg diversification).

Domestic rivalry is important because:

(a)   With little domestic rivalry, firms are happy to rely on the home market
(b)   Tough domestic rivals teach a firm about competitive success
(c)   Each rival can try a different strategic approach

If rivalry collapses, perhaps because of consolidation, standards are likely to slip, reducing competitiveness.

7.1.5 Losing competitive advantage

It is important to remember that the factors which create competitive advantage are dynamic, and so over time they may deteriorate eroding a nation's competitive advantage.

(a)   Factor conditions may deteriorate due to a lack of investment in technology or education.

(b)   Demand conditions may deteriorate due to a recession or deflationary government policies.

(c)   Supporting clusters may collapse as firms diversify and therefore stop concentrating on their own business.

7.2 Influencing the diamond

7.2.1 Interactions between the determinants

The factors in the diamond are interrelated. Competitive advantage rarely rests on only one element of the diamond.

(a)   **Related industries** affect **demand conditions** for an industry. An example from the context of international marketing is piggy-back exporting in which an exporting company also exports some of the products of related industries.

(b)   **Domestic rivalry** can encourage the **creation of more specialised supplier industries.**

Porter says that a nation's competitive industries are **clustered**. Porter believes clustering to be a key to national competitive advantage. A cluster is a linking of industries through relationships which are either vertical (buyer-supplier) or horizontal (common customers, technology, skills). For example, the UK financial services industry is clustered in London.

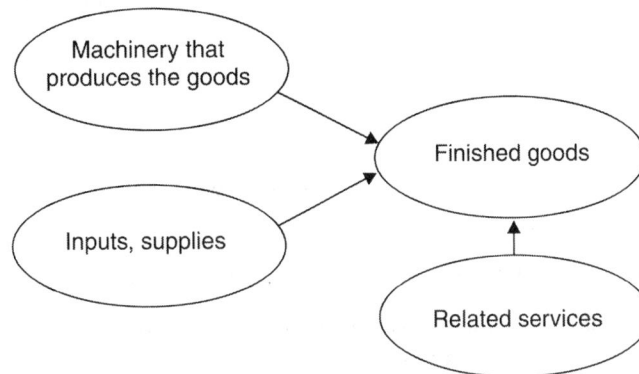

The **individual** firm will be more likely to succeed internationally if there is a **supporting cluster.** Such a cluster can lead to lower costs or the achievement of differentiation; the presence of advanced factors such as skilled labour and digital infrastructure; the transfer of expertise; and a degree of vertical integration through the development of network relationships among the organisations concerned.

7.2.2 Government policy

Porter also points out the importance of **government policy** in nurturing all four of the diamond factors by means of education, subsidy and the provision of services. He also reminds us that **chance** plays an important part.

CASE STUDY

Lack-lustre clusters

Time was when the only thing more fashionable than an Italian suit was the cluster that made it.

The small companies that both competed and co-operated with each other in industrial districts all over Italy – some making shoes, some clothing and others machine tools – were regarded as an example to the rest of the world. Their flexibility contrasted with slow-moving manufacturers that depended on mass production and suffered heavily in the recession of the early 1990s.

The pendulum always swings back and it has done so viciously in the case of Italy's clusters. The country faces an industrial crisis caused by the high euro and competition from low-wage countries. Companies making footwear, textiles and leather goods – specialisms of some northern regions – struggle to compete against China.

The problem goes deeper than labour costs and an expensive currency. The clusters are showing their age as a way to organise businesses in a mature economy. Some have become conservative and inward-looking, more focused on finding outlets for goods they have traditionally made locally than designing and marketing innovative products.

While the Lira could be devalued and competition with China was restrained by trade barriers, any structural weaknesses among the 500,000 companies in Italy employing fewer than 20 people remained hidden.

Italy is trying to adjust. Many industrial companies outsource some production to eastern European countries such as Romania and Slovakia and to China. Some industrial districts have taken similar steps. The Montebelluna cluster of companies producing sports shoes set up an industrial park in Romania. But clusters that do everything from weaving cloth to making clothes can find it harder to discard local jobs and craft skills in favour of production abroad than bigger manufacturers which have less at stake.

Small companies that mainly interact with others in their district may also lack the expertise to manage a global supply network, a comparative advantage of big companies.

Above all, clusters face the problem of being rooted in craft industries rather than value-added services such as design and marketing. In the days when consumers were less demanding, if was sufficient to buy in such services from agencies in Milan and Rome. But they must now compete with rivals that focus all their efforts on services instead of manufacturing.

(John Gapper, *Financial Times*, 26 May 2005)

7.2.3 Overcoming lack of advantage

If a UK firm wishes to compete in an industry in which there is no national competitive advantage, it can take a number of steps to succeed.

(a)   **Compete in the most challenging market,** to emulate domestic rivalry and to obtain information.

(b)   **Spread research and development** activities to countries where there is an established research base or industry cluster already.

(c)   Be prepared to **invest heavily in innovation**.

(d)   **Invest in human resources**, both in the firm and the industry as a whole.

(e)   **Look out for new technologies** which will change the rules of the industry.

(f)   **Collaborate with foreign companies.** American motor companies successfully learned Japanese production techniques.

(g)   **Supply overseas companies**. Japanese car plants in the UK have encouraged greater quality in UK components suppliers.

(h)   **Source components from overseas**. In the UK **crystal glass industry**, many firms buy crystal glass from the Czech Republic, and do the cutting and design work themselves.

(i)   **Exert pressure on politicians** and opinion formers to create better conditions for the diamond to develop (eg in education).

| Question 12.6 | National advantage |

Learning outcome A1b

The Republic of Albion, an island in the North East Atlantic inhabited by about 40m people, has a climate which is plagued by fog, damp and rain. Life is a battle to keep dry. In this battle, the Republic has set up 20 research institutes into 'Water and Aridity Studies'. A variety of companies compete in devising new ways of keeping houses (and their owners!) dry, involving advanced technology. A recent innovation is the ionising umbrella, with an electric field that drives away water particles. The country imports most of its raw materials. The water problem is so bad that the country has a network of canals taking surplus water to the sea, through a network of hydroelectric turbines.

What do you think are the possible competitive advantages of the industries of the Republic of Albion?

7.3 The diamond and competitive strategy

Porter's description of the diamond is more a piece of positive economic theory than a useful strategic tool. Individual companies cannot rely on favourable diamond conditions to provide them with competitive advantage. Countries with extremely favourable national conditions still have their share of poor companies.

•   In international trade it is essential to study and analyse environmental conditions within the **target nation**, as discussed earlier.

- The theory of the diamond is largely based on exporting manufacturing industry: it is less relevant to service industries and any industry that expands internationally by setting up local production or provision of services.

Section summary

Four factors support **competitive success** in a nation's industries: factor conditions, demand conditions, related and supporting industries, and firm strategy, structure and rivalry.

Chapter Roundup

✓ The environment exists outside an organisation's boundaries, and organisations survive and prosper in this context. To secure **environmental fit**, an analysis of the environment therefore is required. PEST is a useful mnemonic to discuss these issues. Uncertainty in the environment arises from complexity and dynamism.

✓ Government policy influences the economic environment, the framework of laws, industry structure and certain operational issues. Political instability is a cause of risk. Different approaches to the political environment apply in different countries. International trade is subject to a further layer of international law and regulation.

✓ Economic factors include the overall level of growth, the business cycle, official monetary and fiscal policy, exchange rates and inflation.

✓ Social and cultural factors relate to two main issues. **Demography** is the study of the population as a whole: its overall size, whether it is growing, stable, or falling; the proportion of people of different age groups – in industrial countries the proportion of elderly people is increasing; where people live and work; ethnic origin. **Culture** includes customs, attitudes, characteristic ways of viewing the world and behaviour: most countries contain several subcultures.

✓ Technological factors have implications for economic growth overall, and offer opportunities and threats to many businesses. Meta-technologies are technologies that are applicable to many applications.

✓ **Stakeholders** are those individuals or groups that, potentially, have an interest in what the organisation does. Different stakeholder groups have different degrees of power and interest, and management must respond to each in a different way.

✓ Four factors support **competitive success** in a nation's industries: factor conditions, demand conditions, related and supporting industries, and firm strategy, structure and rivalry.

Quick Quiz

1   What does PEST stand for?

2   Distinguish between the general environment and the task environment.

3   What is political risk?

4   Are the following related to government **fiscal** or **monetary** policy?

    (a)   Taxation
    (b)   Borrowing
    (c)   Interest rates
    (d)   Control of the money supply
    (e)   Exchange rates
    (f)   Government spending

5   How can technological change affect the activities of organisations? (List 4 ways).

6   What are the two axes of Mendelow's matrix?

7   There are three broad types of stakeholder

     (1)   ....

     (2)   ....

     (3)   ....

8   Fill in the diagram of Porter's diamond

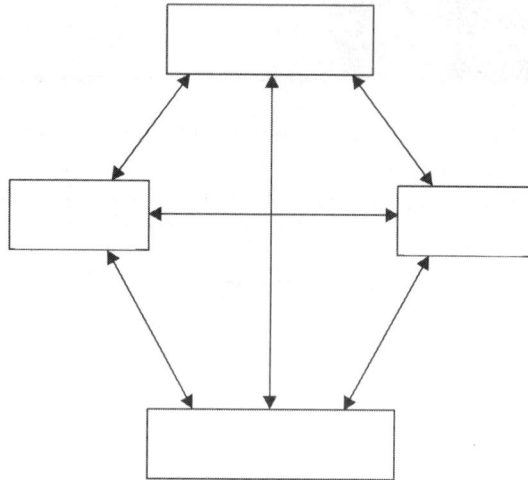

Answers to Quick Quiz

1   Political, economic, social, technological – factors which shape an organisations environment.

2   The general environment covers all the political/legal, economic, social/cultural and technological (PEST) influences in the countries an organisation operates in.

     The task environment relates to factors of particular relevance to a firm, such as its competitors, customers and suppliers of resources.

3   The political risk in a decision is the risk that political factors will invalidate the strategy and perhaps severely damage the firm. Examples are wars, political chaos, corruption and nationalisation.

4   (a)   Fiscal
         (b)   Fiscal
         (c)   Monetary
         (d)   Monetary
         (e)   Monetary
         (f)   Fiscal

5   Any 4 from:

     –   It can affect the type of products or services that are made and sold
     –   It can affect the way in which products are made
     –   It can affect the way in which services are provided (especially with the growth of the internet)
     –   It can affect the way in which markets are identified
     –   It can affect organisational structure and the way firms are managed
     –   It can affect the way organisations communicate with their customers or suppliers

6   Level of interest; power

7   (1)   Internal
     (2)   Connected
     (3)   External

8

```
              ┌──────────────────┐
              │ Firm strategy,   │
              │ structure, rivalry│
              └──────────────────┘

┌────────────┐              ┌────────────┐
│ Factor     │ ←──────────→ │ Demand     │
│ conditions │              │ conditions │
└────────────┘              └────────────┘

              ┌──────────────────┐
              │ Related and      │
              │ supporting industries│
              └──────────────────┘
```

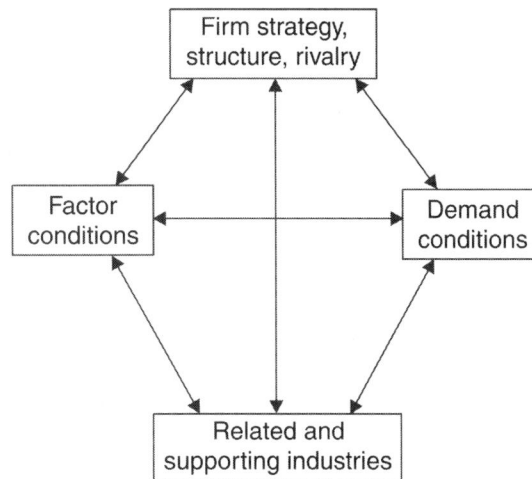

Answers to Questions

12.1 Government impact

Using the example of the UK:

(a)   The government must authorise most new drugs (eg for safety before they can be sold).

(b)   The UK government is a major purchaser of pharmaceuticals, for the national health service, and so has significant buying power.

(c)   Health education policies affect consumer demand.

(d)   Funding of universities affects the science base for recruitment.

(e)   Employment practices, such as working hours, are influenced by EU employment directives.

12.3 Single currency

We can offer no definitive solution, but here are some points to consider.

(a)   For companies trading primarily within the EU, such as the package holiday firm, adopting the Euro will mean a reduction in exchange rate volatility – businesses will be able to compete on the essentials of cost and productivity. An analogy is the USA – although there are many 'states' there is only one currency. Most British trade is with EU countries.

(b) and (c)

Companies trading outside the Euro-zone would remain subject to exchange rate risk, based on the Euro rather than sterling. It all depends on how the European Central Bank manages the currency - if the Euro becomes a 'hard' currency, with a high value, then exports will cost more to overseas customers, but imports from overseas suppliers might be cheaper. Many internationally traded goods, such as oil or aircraft, are priced in US dollars anyhow, so the impact will be indirect.

Of course, if the UK stays out of the Economic and Monetary Union (EMU) and does not adopt the Euro it will not be in a position to influence the monetary policies of countries which use the Euro, although these policies will undoubtedly affect the UK economy and British businesses.

12.4 Social trends

The firm's market is shrinking. There is an absolute fall in the number of school leavers. Moreover, it is possible that the increasing proportion of school leavers going to higher education will mean there will be fewer who can afford Club Fun's packages. That said, a higher disposable income in the population at large might compensate for this trend. People might be encouraged to try destinations other than Club Fun's traditional resorts if these other destinations are publicised on television. Growing access to the Internet makes it easier for other suppliers to compete.

12.5 Stakeholder influence

Accountants have divided loyalties – to their firm, and to their profession.

The Technical Department will almost certainly resist such a change, as the proposals devalue audit to being one of many business services to management. An audit is undertaken for the benefit of shareholders, not the company management. The Technical Department (the firm's **technostructure**) is also powerful as enforcement of the standards it will suggest should reduce professional negligence costs. The technostructure will thus exert a powerful influence over the strategy and business practices. External influences include *professional associations* which have a technostructural influence on the profession as a whole. The marketing manager may also be misled as to the degree to which *customers* want a 'one-stop shop' for accounting and advertising services. Perhaps he is overestimating the power of this factor in the external coalition.

12.6 National advantage

The only **basic factor** endowment appears to be rain. **Advanced factors** include the research institutes. The country also has very sophisticated demand conditions for umbrellas and water-proof items. There seems to be domestic competition in the industry. In addition to umbrellas, you would expect related industries (such as high-technology waterproof raincoats) to appear. The country's firms could compete successfully in global markets for waterproof materials.

It is possible that the country's inhabitants would also have certain expertise in building technologies (eg damp proofing) which could be exported to the construction industry. Finally hydro-electric turbines *might* be a source of advantage: but the amount of water-for-energy is so plentiful that only the simplest technology need be used to harness it.

Question 12.2 requires a personalised answer.

Number	Level	Marks	Time
Q12	Examination	25	45 mins

COMPETITIVE ENVIRONMENT

Chapter 12 dealt with general environmental factors in the external environment (**macro-environment**). There we looked at trends that affect most organisations to some extent.

We now narrow our focus to consider the **micro-environment** or the immediate small-scale environment of the organisation.

We start though by considering how an organisation might go about analysing its competition and what data it would need to do so.

Then we move on to consider the sources of data and the quality of data.

Most businesses compete with other firms but have a limited number of direct competitors. Competitors are a vital influence on decision-making and we discuss the five competitive forces underlying a particular industry.

We end this chapter by considering generic competitive strategies. These are strategies that organisations adopt for competitive advantage. These follow on naturally from our discussion of the competitive environment and so they appear here rather than in the discussion of strategies.

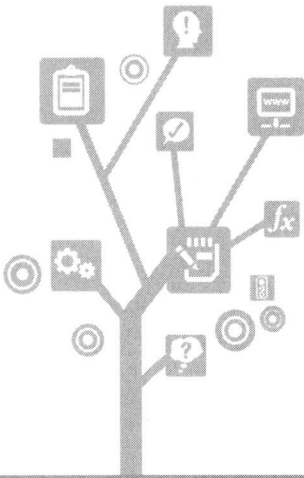

13

topic list	learning outcomes	syllabus references	ability required
1 Competitor analysis	A1a	A1(iii),(iv)	analysis
2 Accounting for competitors	A1a	A1(iii),(iv)	analysis
3 Sources, availability and quality of data for environmental analysis	A1b	A1(v)	comprehension
4 Information for planning and control	A1b	A1(v)	comprehension
5 Environmental information and analysis	A1b	A1(v)	comprehension
6 The competitive environment: the five forces	A1b	A1(vi)	comprehension
7 Competitive strategies	A2a	A2(ii)	analysis
8 Corporate appraisal (SWOT)	A1a	A1(iii)	analysis

1 Competitor analysis

Introduction

In any market where there are significant competitors, the strategic decisions and marketing decisions made by a firm will often be partly a response to what a competitor has done. This is because competitors' autonomous policies and reactions to market developments have great influence on each firm's freedom of action and ultimately on its profitability. In its simplest form, competitor analysis will be concerned with the extent to which competition exists. This is clearly bound up with the relevance of product and industry life cycles.

1.1 Who are competitors?

KEY TERM

COMPETITIVE POSITION is the market share, costs, prices, quality and accumulated experience of an entity or a product relative to competition.

Firms must be on the lookout for **potential competitors**, and the potential impact of competitor actions on their profits. For example, a competitor may introduce price cuts or aggressive advertising campaigns to increase market share, or launch a new product. Firms must be alert to these threats so that they can respond to them.

CASE STUDY

(a) The convergence of the technologies underlying imaging and communication is leading to a battle between computer manufacturers, games manufacturers and TV manufacturers to supply the environment of digital entertainment. Is the TV or the PC going to be the hub of the home entertainment system?

(b) In the UK, petrol companies have been wrong-footed by supermarkets, who now sell petrol.

A firm must **define who its current competitors actually are**. This group may be larger than is immediately apparent. *Coca-Cola*, for example, competes against the following.

- *Pepsi* in the Cola market, retailers' own brands.

- All other soft drinks.

- Tea and coffee.

- Coca-Cola's chief executive has declared that 'the main competitor is tap water: any other definition is too narrow'.

1.1.1 Types of competitor

Kotler lists four kinds of competition.

(a) **Brand competitors** are similar firms offering similar products: for example, *McDonald's* and *Burger King*.

(b) **Industry competitors** have similar products but are different in other ways, such as geographical market or range of products: for example, *Amazon* and *HMV*, or *British Airways* and *American Airways*.

(c) **Generic competitors** compete for the same disposable income with different products: for example, home improvements versus foreign vacations.

(d) **Form competitors** offer products which are technically significantly different, but satisfy the same needs: for example, manufacturers of matches and cigarette lighters.

1.2 Analysing competitors: the main issues

COMPETITOR ANALYSIS is the 'identification and quantification of the relative strengths and weaknesses (compared with competitors or potential competitors), which could be of significance in the development of a successful competitive strategy'.

(CIMA *Official Terminology*)

An important initial variable is **industry structure**. A fragmented industry with many small players is unlikely to be highly competitive overall, since most firms will seek to pursue a **niche strategy**. The situation is the opposite in a **consolidated industry**, where a small number of firms are striving for a dominating market share and **cost leadership**.

Some industries cannot easily be consolidated and the niche structure may continue indefinitely.

An organisation should look at four key factors when undertaking competitor analysis:

Factor	Comment
Competitor's goals (the firm as a whole and the business unit)	• What are the business's **stated financial goals**? What trade-offs are made between long-term and short-term objectives? • What is the competitor's attitude to **risk**? • Do **managerial beliefs** (eg that the firm should be a market leader) affect its goals? • **Organisation structure**: what is the relative status of functional areas? • What **incentive systems** are in place? • What are the **managers** like? Do they favour one particular type of strategy? • To what extent does the business **cross-subsidise** others in the group if the business is part of a group? What is the purpose of the business: to raise money for the group?
The competitor's assumptions about the industry	• What does a competitor believe to be its **relative position** in the industry (in terms of cost, product quality)? • Are there any **cultural or regional differences** that indicate the way managers are likely to respond? • What does the competitor believe about the **future** for the industry? • Does the competitor accept the industry's **'conventional wisdom'**?
The competitor's current and potential situation and strategy	• Distribution • Organisation • Operations • Research and engineering • Overall costs • Managerial ability • Marketing and selling • Products • Financial strengths
Competitor's capability	• The **competitor's core competences**. In other words, what does the competitor do distinctively well? • Does the competitor have the **ability to expand** in a particular market? • What **competitive advantages and disadvantages** does the competitor possess?

1.2.1 Competitor response profiles

All these are combined in a **competitor response profile**. This indicates the competitor's vulnerability and the right 'battleground' on which to fight.

KEY POINT

Kotler lists four response profiles.

- The **laid back** competitor does not respond
- The **tiger** responds aggressively to all opposing moves
- The **selective** competitor reacts to some threats in some markets but not to all
- The **stochastic** competitor is unpredictable

The reasons for these observed profiles may be complex. An effort should be made to understand them and how they fit into the competitor's overall strategy.

Information for strategic uses can be gathered from the following sources.

- Financial statements
- Information from common customers and suppliers
- Inspection of a competitor's products
- Information from former employees
- Job advertisements

1.2.2 Competitive significance

Competition is likely to be intense when firms have strategic similarities in such matters as those below.

- Technology used
- Management skills
- Distribution channels
- Products offered
- Geographic coverage

Even when current products are dissimilar, similarities in other areas may well see new competition emerging, as for instance when *Marks & Spencer*, an own brand clothes retailer, started selling own brand food.

1.2.3 Exit barriers

Exit barriers are those which **prevent a firm from leaving an industry**, or increase the cost of so doing. Cost-related exit barriers include the following.

(a) **Vertically integrated companies** producing products for many markets. Exiting one market would not significantly alter its cost structure. In global commodity markets, inability to buy cheaply on spot markets can be a severe hindrance to competitive pricing, as is seen for example in the UK petrol market, where supermarkets have greater flexibility than the major integrated companies who are committed to selling their own oil through their own filling stations.

(b) **Common administrative costs** might be shared over a number of different businesses. This might result in a high overhead charge, but whilst the apportionment might turn one of the businesses into a loss, closing the business down might save little of the overhead expenditure.

Question 13.1

Competitor analysis

Learning outcome A1a

Jot down a list of items of information that might be obtained from an environmental analysis of competitors. The list can be a long one!

Section summary

Firms should **analyse their competitors** and build models of how they might react based on their future goals, assumptions, capability and current situation.

2 Accounting for competitors

Introduction

Competitive strategies can be analysed in financial terms, as we know, using simple techniques such as NPV. However, simple models really require a consideration of likely competitive response if they are to be useful in forecasting the likely return on a strategic investment.

2.1 Competitor response

In practice, anticipated **competitor actions** are dealt with indirectly in the planning process. The management accounting system may not be able to identify those deficiencies in performance arising from competitors' activities **after** the plan has been implemented.

A few detergent companies own many of the brands offered to the market. This deters competitors. How do you evaluate, financially, a strategy such as this?

(a) The expenditure to **maintain market share** and sustain brands is a known cost. However the benefit is not known exactly.

(b) There might be a variety of **assumptions** about market size, market shares and the profit assumptions of a number of the scenarios identified.

(c) There are problems with forecasting the future cash flows of market share estimates.

A useful approach to take is to **analyse the anticipated loss** caused by **not** undertaking a particular course of action: the present value of this loss becomes, effectively, the maximum size of the investment. For example, A Ltd is worried that a competitor will shift the market dynamics from I to II.

	Market state	
	I	II
A Ltd's market share	20%	15%
Present value of future cash flows	£1m	£800,000

(a) There is a present value loss of £200,000. If a marketing manager suggested that spending £100,000 would see off the competitor, this action would be worth taking.

(b) There is still the problem of estimating the difference between market states I and II: after all, the marketing campaign might deter **other** competitors, or create an increase in demand. It is also impossible to be certain that the competitor will in fact be deterred by an advertising campaign.

2.2 Competitor modelling

2.2.1 Sources of information

Data sources include: published accounts and annual reports, market research reviews and reports (eg *Economist Intelligence Unit);* investment analysts' notes; industry experts and consultants; suppliers, shared customers, the competitor's marketing strategy; public communications (magazines, journals and newsletters) and the internet.

A great deal can be gleaned from using one's own company as a model, and adjusting it for significant differences in competitors' businesses. For example, a firm might make some sub-components in-house, whereas a competitor might buy them on the open market.

2.2.2 Cost structures

Important differences between firms include the following.

- Absolute cost levels
- The proportion of fixed to variable costs
- The strategic impact of outsourcing decisions on competitive flexibility
- The sales price in relation to costs, and unit costs. (This will affect a firm's ability to respond to a competitor's price cut.)
- Not all businesses require the same rate of return
- Exit costs. (If a firm has high exit costs, it is likely to stay in an industry and compete aggressively, rather than leaving the industry.)

2.2.3 Barriers to entry

Competitor analysis should also consider the costs that any potential new entrant to the industry will incur to overcome barriers to entry. (We discuss the nature of barriers to entry later in this chapter when we consider Porter's five forces model.)

Comparing entry costs with the present value of the returns the entrant could achieve will indicate the likelihood of new entrants. If revenues exceed costs the market is financially attractive to new entrants; if costs exceed revenues the threat of new entrants is reduced.

Exam alert

It is important to remember competitor analysis does not simply involve finding out information about competitors. An organisation should also consider how it can use the information it has gained to shape its own strategies.

KEY POINT

If the market appears attractive to new entrants, an organisation should compare the cost of raising new barriers (for example, by spending on a brand) to the potential loss of revenue if a new competitor does enter the market. If the potential loss of revenue from a new competitor entering the market exceeds the cost of raising new barriers, the organisation should look at raising new barriers to entry.

Section summary

The **management accountant's techniques** are useful in competitor analysis (eg by analysing how a competitor's cost structure influences the options available to it) and by modelling the impact of different strategies.

3 Sources, availability and quality of data for environmental analysis

Introduction

Data and information come from sources both inside and outside an organisation. An organisation's information systems should be designed so as to obtain – or **capture** – all the relevant data and information required.

3.1 Internal information

Capturing data and information from **inside** the organisation involves designing a system for collecting or measuring data and information which sets out procedures for:

(a)   What data and information is collected

(b)   How frequently

(c)   By whom

(d)   By what methods

(e)   How data and information is processed, filed and communicated

The accounting records

The accounting ledgers provide an excellent source of information regarding what has happened in the past. This information may be used as a basis for predicting future events.

3.2 External information

Formal collection of data from outside sources includes the following.

(a)   A company's **tax specialists** will be expected to gather information about changes in tax law and how this will affect the company.

(b)   Obtaining information about any new legislation on health and safety at work, or employment regulations, must be the responsibility of a particular person – for example the company's **legal expert** or **company secretary** – who must then pass on the information to other managers affected by it.

(c)   Research and development (R & D) work often relies on information about other R & D work being done by another company or by government institutions. An **R & D official** might be made responsible for finding out about R & D work in the company.

(d)   **Marketing managers** need to know about the opinions and buying attitudes of potential customers. To obtain this information, they might carry out market research exercises.

Informal gathering of information from the environment occurs naturally, consciously or unconsciously, as people learn what is going on in the world around them – perhaps from newspapers, television reports, meetings with business associates or the trade press.

Organisations hold external information such as invoices, letters, advertisements and so on **received from customers and suppliers**. But there are many occasions when an active search outside the organisation is necessary.

KEY TERM

The phrase ENVIRONMENTAL SCANNING is often used to describe the process of gathering external information, which is available from a wide range of sources.

Sources of external information include:

(a)   The government

(b)   Annual reports and press statements of competitors or other firms

(c)   Advice or information bureaux

(d)   Consultants

(e)   Newspaper and magazine publishers

(f)   Market research and other report, for example from Mintel or the Economist Intelligence Unit

(f)   **Libraries** and information services

(g)   Increasingly businesses can use each other's systems as sources of information, for instance via extranets or **electronic data interchange** (**EDI**).

(h)   **Electronic sources** of information are becoming increasingly important.

  (i)   For some time there have been 'viewdata' services such as **Prestel** offering a very large bank of information gathered from organisations such as the Office for National Statistics, newspapers and the British Library. **Topic** offers information on the stock market. Companies like **Reuters** operate primarily in the field of provision of information.

  (ii)   The **Internet** is a vast source of information. A number of journals and articles are now published on line, and many organisations now also display information about themselves on their home pages.

Question 13.2   Decisions

Learning outcome A1b

Information is often required by people **outside** the organisation for making judgements and decisions relating to an organisation. Give four examples of decisions which may be taken by outsiders.

Section summary

An information system should be designed to obtain information from **all relevant sources** – both internal and external.

Exam alert

Make sure the sources of information you recommend are practical and relevant to the context of the scenario.

---

4   Information for planning and control

Introduction

Remember the levels of the organisation we looked at earlier in the syllabus? We now consider what sorts of decisions are made at the **strategic level** and the **operational level**. These decisions are affected by risk and uncertainty in the environment.

KEY TERM

STRATEGIC PLANNING is a process of deciding on objectives of the organisation, on changes in these objectives, on the resources used to attain these objectives and on the policies that are to govern the acquisition, use and disposition of these resources.

Strategic decision making:

(a)   Is medium– to **long-term**
(b)   Involves high levels of **uncertainty** and risk (the future is unpredictable)
(c)   Involves situations that **may not recur**
(d)   Deals with **complex** issues

KEY TERM

Operational control ensures that specific tasks are carried out effectively and efficiently. It focuses on individual tasks, and is carried out within the strictly defined guidelines issued by strategic planning and tactical control decisions.

4.1 The decision-making process

The stages in making a decision are as follows.

STEP 1 Problem recognition

STEP 2 Problem definition and structuring

STEP 3 Identifying alternative courses of action

STEP 4 Making and communicating the decision

STEP 5 Implementing the decision

STEP 6 Monitoring the effects of the decision

Information and decision-making

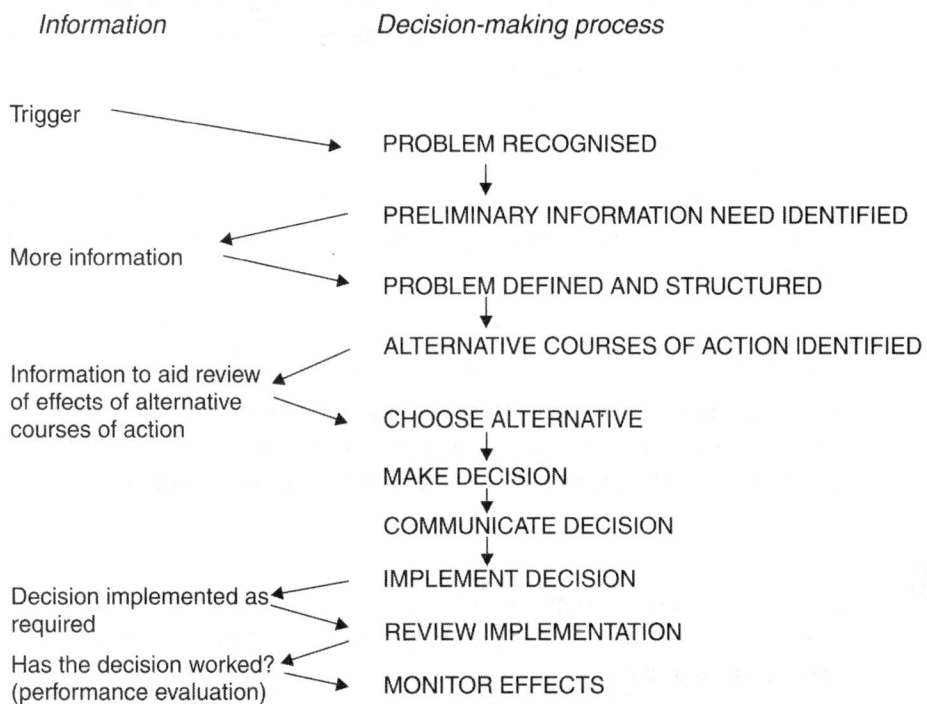

Information	*Decision-making process*
Trigger	PROBLEM RECOGNISED
	↓
	PRELIMINARY INFORMATION NEED IDENTIFIED
More information	
	PROBLEM DEFINED AND STRUCTURED
	↓
	ALTERNATIVE COURSES OF ACTION IDENTIFIED
Information to aid review of effects of alternative courses of action	CHOOSE ALTERNATIVE
	↓
	MAKE DECISION
	↓
	COMMUNICATE DECISION
	↓
Decision implemented as required	IMPLEMENT DECISION
	REVIEW IMPLEMENTATION
Has the decision worked? (performance evaluation)	MONITOR EFFECTS

4.1.1 Problem recognition

Decisions are not made without **information**. The decision-maker needs to be informed of a problem in the first place. This is sometimes referred to as the **decision trigger**.

4.1.2 Problem definition and structuring

Normally **further information** is then required. This further information is **analysed** so that the problem can be **defined** precisely.

Consider, for example, a company with falling sales. The fall in sales would be the **trigger**. **Further information** would be needed to identify where the deficiencies were occurring. The company might discover that sales of product X in area Y are falling, and the problem can be **defined** as:

'Decline of sales of product X in area Y due to new competitor: how can the decline be reversed?'

One of the purposes of **defining** the problem is to identify the **relationships** between the **various factors** in it, especially if the problem is complex.

4.1.3 Identifying alternative courses of action

Where alternative courses of action are identified, **information** is needed about the likely effect of each, so they can be assessed.

As a simple example, if our company wishes to review the price of product X in area Y, information will be needed as to the effect of particular price levels on demand for the product. Such information can include external information such as market research (demand at a particular price) and the cost of the product, which can be provided internally.

4.1.4 Making and communicating the decision

The decision is **made** after review of the information relating to alternatives. However, the decision is useless if it is not **communicated**. So, in our example, if the **marketing director** decides to lower the price of product X and institute an intensive **advertising** campaign, nothing will happen unless the advertising department is informed, and also the **manufacturing** department, who will have to prepare new packaging showing the lower price.

4.1.5 Implementation of the decision

The decision is then **implemented**. For large-scale decisions (for example to relocate a factory 100 miles away from its current site), implementation may need substantial **planning**, detailed information and very clear communication.

4.1.6 Monitoring the effects of the decision

Once a decision has been implemented, information is needed so that its effects can be **reviewed**. For example, if a manufacturing organisation has installed new equipment in anticipation of savings in costs, then information will need to be obtained as to whether these are achieved in practice.

Exam alert

You could use this six-stage process as a means of analysing an exam question scenario and as a structure for your answer. What is the problem; what are the alternatives; how will your solution be implemented, and so on.

4.2 Risk and uncertainty in decision making

Decision making involves **making decisions now about what will happen in the future**. Obviously, decisions can turn out badly, or actual results can prove to be very different from the estimates on which the original decision was made because the necessary **information is not available** when the decision is made.

KEY TERMS

RISK involves situations or events which may or may not occur, but whose probability of occurrence can be calculated statistically and the frequency of their occurrence predicted from past records.

UNCERTAINTY involves situations or events whose outcome cannot be predicted with statistical confidence.

The management accountant, who must present relevant cost and revenue data to assist a manager who is about to make a decision, should consider two things.

(a)   If the figures are **only slightly in doubt** or the amounts themselves are not material, a **best estimate** with a note that the figures are not certain may be good enough.

(b)   If the amount or the **degree of uncertainty was large**, to present just one set of forecast figures would be unwise. For example, if a forecast of sales demand is 'anywhere between 1,000 and 10,000 units', it would be naive and unhelpful to prepare a **single point estimate** of sales – just one forecast figure – of, say, 5,000 units.

If the uncertainty in a situation does warrant special attention in the figures, the next problem is **how the uncertainty** in the figures should be presented.

There are various methods of bringing uncertainty and risk analysis into the evaluation of decisions. They include the following.

(a)   **Conservative estimates:** estimating outcomes in a conservative manner in order to provide a built-in safety factor.

(b)   Looking at the **worst possible** and **best possible** outcomes, as well as the most likely outcome, and reaching a decision which takes these into account.

(c)   **Sensitivity analysis:** any technique that tests decision options for their vulnerability to changes in a 'variable' such as expected sales volume.

(d)   Assessing **probabilities** and calculating, for each decision alternative, either the **expected value** of costs or benefits with, possibly, the standard deviation of the possible outcomes, or a probability distribution of the possible outcomes. **Decision trees** might be used to illustrate in a 'pictorial' or 'graphical' form the alternatives facing the decision-maker.

4.3 Perfect information

KEY TERMS

PERFECT INFORMATION is information that predicts the future with perfect accuracy.

IMPERFECT INFORMATION is information which cannot be guaranteed to be completely accurate. Almost all information is therefore imperfect – but may still be very useful.

Obtaining more information first about what is likely to happen can sometimes reduce the uncertainty about the future outcome from taking a decision. We can categorise information depending upon **how reliable** it is likely to be for predicting what will happen in the future and hence for helping managers to make better decisions.

Section summary

Control information, to be useful, must aid the decision-making process.

5 Environmental information and analysis

5.1 Environmental analysis and uncertainty

Introduction and Key Point

Johnson and Scholes suggest that a firm should conduct an **audit of environmental influences**. This will identify the environmental factors which have had a significant influence on the organisation's development or performance in the past.

Strategic decisions are made in partial ignorance, as we have seen, because the environment is **uncertain**. As we mentioned earlier, uncertainty arises from the **complexity and dynamism** of the environment.

(a)   **Complexity** arises from:

(i)   The **variety of influences** faced by the organisation. The more open an organisation is, the greater the variety of influences. The greater the number of markets the organisation operates in, the greater the number of influences to which it is subject.

(ii)   The amount of **knowledge** necessary. All businesses need to have knowledge of the tax system, for example, but only pharmaceuticals businesses need to know about mandatory testing procedures for new drugs.

(iii)   The **interconnectedness** of environmental influences. Importing and exporting companies are sensitive to exchange rates, which themselves are sensitive to interest rates. Interest rates then influence a company's borrowing costs.

(b)   **Dynamism**. Stable environments are unchanging. Dynamic environments are in a state of change. The computer market is a dynamic market because of the rate of technological change, for example.

Question 13.3   Contrasting environment

Learning outcome A1b

Analyse the environments of the two situations below according to the criteria given above.

(a)   A new product has just been introduced to a market segment. It is proving popular. As it is based on a unique technology, barriers to entry are high. The product will not be sold outside this market segment.

(b)   A group of scientists has recently been guaranteed, by an EU research sponsoring body, funds for the next ten years to investigate new technologies in the construction industry, such as 'smart materials' (which respond automatically to weather and light conditions). This is a multi-disciplinary project with possible benefits for the construction industry. A number of building firms have also guaranteed funds.

The implication is that the type of business strategy adopted, and indeed the approach to making business strategy, will depend on the type of environment the firm inhabits.

5.2 Impact of uncertainty

If an organisation is operating in a highly uncertain environment this will affect its strategy.

•   **The planning horizon will be shortened** because the uncertainty will mean that management will not dare plan too far ahead.

- **Strategies may be more conservative** because management are unlikely to risk anything new. However, the counter argument to this is that management may want to try something new, because the uncertainty could mean that the existing strategies will no longer work.

- **Emergent strategies may be encouraged**, instead of planned strategies. Advocates of emergent strategies argue they are more appropriate to periods of uncertainty because of their adaptability to changing circumstances.

- **Increased information requirements**. Management will require more regular information to allow them to monitor and assess the changing conditions. Uncertainty will make forecasting harder, so management will need more information to gauge their strategic position.

- **Firms may follow multiple strategies**. Firms may respond to risk and uncertainty by trying to develop a number of alternative options. For example, in the current climate of uncertainty surrounding oil reserves and production, oil firms may try to develop multiple sources of oil around the world, to avoid being dependent on a particular region or a particular extraction technology.

5.3 Forecasts

A FORECAST is 'a prediction of future events and their quantification for planning purposes'.

(CIMA *Official Terminology*)

Forecasting attempts to reduce the uncertainty managers face. In **simple/static conditions the past is a relatively good guide** to the future. Techniques are:

(a) **Time series analysis.** Data for a number of months/years is obtained and analysed. The aim of time series analysis is to identify:

(i) Seasonal and other cyclical fluctuations
(ii) Long term underlying trends

An example of the use of this approach is the UK's monthly unemployment statistics which show a 'headline figure' and the 'underlying trend'.

(b) **Regression analysis** is a quantitative technique to check any underlying correlations between two variables (eg sales of ice cream and the weather). Remember that the relationship between two variables may only hold between certain values.

(c) **Econometrics** is the study of economic variables and their interrelationships.

(i) **Leading indicators** are indicators which change before market demand changes. For example, a sudden increase in the birth rate would be an indicator of future demand for children's clothes.

(ii) The ability to predict the span of time between a change in the indicator and a change in market demand. Change in an indicator is especially useful for demand forecasting when they reach their highest or lowest points (when an increase turns into a decline or vice versa).

In **dynamic/complex conditions**, the picture is different.

- **Future developments:** the past is not a reliable guide.

- Techniques such as **scenario building** are useful as they can propose a number of possible futures.

- **Complex environments** require techniques to reduce the effects of complexity on organisational structure and decision-making.

Some firms aim to deal with planning in complex environments by techniques such as scenario building.

5.4 Strategic intelligence

If a key task of strategic management is to ensure environmental fit, managers need a willingness and an ability to understand the environment and to anticipate future trends.

- A separate strategic planning department collects data on trends
- The marketing department identifies customer needs
- The R&D department identifies new technology
- The production department suggests process innovation

Arguably, as strategy is about the whole organisation, there are dangers in restricting the gathering of strategic information to functional departments. The whole firm needs to be aware of **strategic intelligence**.

KEY TERM

STRATEGIC INTELLIGENCE, according to Donald Marchand, is defined as 'what a company needs to know about its business environment to enable it to anticipate change and design appropriate strategies that will create business value for customers and be profitable in new markets and new industries in the future'.

A model of the process of creating strategic intelligence is outlined below.

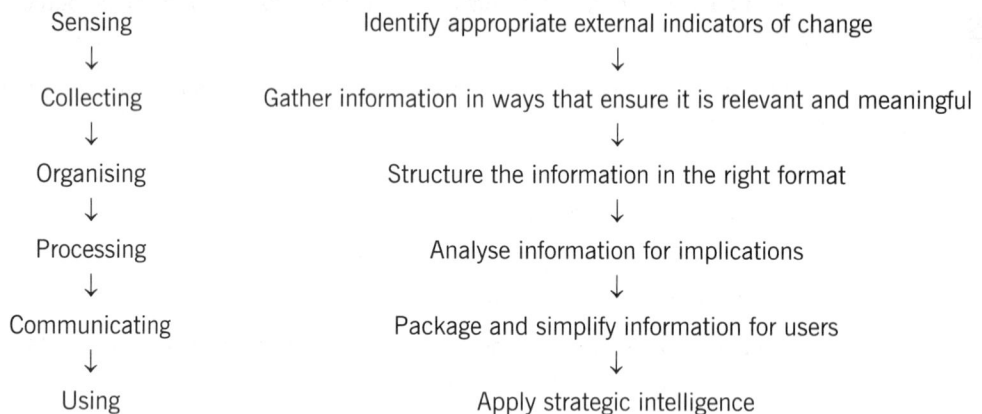

Sensing   Identify appropriate external indicators of change
↓   ↓
Collecting   Gather information in ways that ensure it is relevant and meaningful
↓   ↓
Organising   Structure the information in the right format
↓   ↓
Processing   Analyse information for implications
↓   ↓
Communicating   Package and simplify information for users
↓   ↓
Using   Apply strategic intelligence

Key dimensions of strategic intelligence

Information culture	What is the role of information in the organisation? Is it only distributed on a 'need to know basis' or do people have to give specific reasons for secrecy?
Future orientation	Is the focus on specific decisions and trade-offs, or a general attitude of enquiry?
The structure of information flows	Is communication vertical, up and down the hierarchy, or lateral?
Processing strategic intelligence	Are 'professional' strategists delegated to this task or is it everybody's concern?
Scope	Is strategic intelligence dealt with by senior management only, or is intelligence built throughout the organisation?
Time horizon	Short-termist or orientated towards the long term?
The role of IT	Some firms are developing sophisticated knowledge management systems to capture the information needed?
Organisational 'memory'	In other words, do managers keep in mind the lessons of past successes or failures?

There are many **sources** of strategic intelligence.

(a)   **Internal sources** or sources relatively close to the company.

    (i)   The **sales force** deals with customers, and so is in a position to obtain customer and competitor information.

    (ii)   Many companies conduct **market research**. Although generally this deals with specific issues, it can indicate general environmental concerns (eg consumers' worries).

    (iii)   The management information system may generate information about the environment, although its main focus is internal.

(b)   **External sources** of environmental data are various.

    (i)   **Media**. Newspapers, periodicals and television offer environmental information.

    (ii)   Sometimes, more detailed country information is needed than that supplied by the press. **Export consultants** might specialise in dealing with particular countries, and so can be a valuable source of information. The **Economist Intelligence Unit** offers reports into particular countries.

    (iii)   Academic or **trade journals** might give information about a wide variety of relevant issues to a particular industry.

    (iv)   **Trade associations** also offer industry information.

    (v)   The government can be a source of statistical data relating to money supply, the trade balance and so forth, which is often summarised in newspapers. The Department for Business Enterprise and Regulatory Reform also publishes **Overseas Trade**, concentrating on export opportunities for UK firms.

    (vi)   Sources of technological environmental information can include the **Patent Office**.

    (vii)   **Stockbrokers** produce investment reports for the clients which involve analysis into particular industries.

    (viii)   Specialist **consultancy firms** (eg CACI census data) provide information.

    (ix)   The **Internet**.

5.5 Database information

A **management information system** or **database** should provide managers with a useful flow of relevant information which is easy to use and easy to access. Information is an important corporate resource. Managed and used effectively, it can provide considerable competitive advantage and so it is a worthwhile investment. Large scale databases are created and stored on **computer systems,** using **database application packages** such as **Microsoft Access**.

It is now possible to access large volumes of generally available information through databases held by public bodies and businesses.

(a)   Some **newspapers** offer free or paid-for access on the web to both current and archived editions, with search facilities looking for information on particular companies or issues.

(b)   Public databases are also available for inspection. **Dun and Bradstreet** provide general business information. **AC Nielsen** operate on-line information regarding products and market share.

(c)   Developments in information technology allow businesses to have access to the databases of **external organisations**. Reuters, for example, provides an on-line information system about money market interest rates and foreign exchange rates to firms involved in money market and foreign exchange dealings, and to the treasury departments of a large number of companies. The growing adoption of technology at **point of sale** provides a potentially invaluable source of data to both retailer and manufacturer.

CASE STUDY

CACI is a company which provides market analysis, information systems and other data products to clients. It advertises itself as 'the winning combination of marketing and technology'.

As an illustration of the information available to the marketing manager through today's technology, here is an overview of some of their products.

Paycheck: this provides income data for all 1.6 million individual post codes across the UK. This enables companies to see how mean income distribution varies from area to area.

People UK: this is a mix of geodemographics, life stage and lifestyle data. It is person rather than household specific and is designed for those companies requiring highly targeted campaigns.

InSite: this is a geographic information system (GIS). It is designed to assist with local market planning, customers and product segmentation, direct marketing and service distribution.

Acorn: this stands for A Classification of Residential Neighbourhoods, and has been used to profile residential neighbourhoods by post code since 1976. ACORN classifies people in any trading area or on any customer database into 54 types.

Lifestyles UK: this database offers over 300 lifestyle selections on 44 million consumers in the UK. It helps with cross selling and customer retention strategies.

Monica: this can help a company to identify the age of people on its database by giving the likely age profile of their first names. It uses a combination of census data and real birth registrations.

Legislation and regulation exists to protect consumers form misuse of **personal details** held on computer, unsolicited mail and invasion of privacy.

(a) There are now stringent trading practices and regulations in the direct mail industry, administered by the **Direct Mail Services Standards Board** (DMSSB) and **Mail Order Protection Scheme** (for display advertisements in national newspapers that ask for money in advance).

(b) The **Mailing Preference Service** allows customers to state whether they would – and more often, would not – be willing to receive direct mail on a range of specific areas.

(c) The **Data Protection Acts 1984 and 1998** provide that data users (organisations or individuals who control the contents of files of personal data and the use of personal data) must register with the Data Protection Registrar. They must limit their use of personal data (defined as any information about an identifiable living individual) to the uses registered.

CASE STUDY

Retailers have been collecting data about their customers, through loyalty card schemes, for a number of years, in order to target their marketing more effectively.

5.5.1 Environmental data

Nine areas of environmental data that ought to be included in a database for strategic planners could be as follows.

(a) **Competitive data.** This would include information derived from an application of Porter's Five Forces analysis.

(b) **Economic data.** Details of past growth and predictions of future growth in GDP and disposable income, the pattern of interest rates, predictions of the rate of inflation, unemployment levels and tax rates, developments in international trade and so on.

(c) **Political data.** The influence that the government is having on the industry.

(d) **Legal data.** The likely implications of recent legislation, legislation likely to be introduced in the future and its implications.

(e) **Social data**. Changing habits, attitudes, cultures and educational standards of the population as a whole, and customers in particular.

(f) **Technological data**. Technological changes that have occurred or will occur, and the implications that these will have for the organisation.

(g) **Geographical data**. Data about individual regions or countries, each of them potentially segments of the market with their own unique characteristics.

(h) **Energy suppliers data**. Energy sources, availability and price of sources of supply generally.

(i) **Data about stakeholders in the business**. Employees, management and shareholders, the influence of each group, and what each group wants from the organisation.

In other words data which covers the key elements of the general and market environment should be included in a database for strategic and marketing planners.

As well as obtaining data from its own internal database system an organisation can obtain it from an **external database** operated by another organisation.

5.5.2 A word of caution

Most external databases are on-line databases, which are very large computer files of information, supplied by **database providers** and managed by **host** companies whose business revenue is generated through charges made to **users**.

Information sources have to be used with caution. The Internet, in particular, has made data more available: but this data is unvetted and often unmediated.

Section summary

A company's response to the environment is influenced by its complexity and its dynamism. The value of forecasts varies according to these factors.

An organisation should plan to obtain **strategic intelligence** as a basis for future strategies. Internal and external databases should be maintained and the data they contain assessed and applied.

---

6 The competitive environment: the five forces

Introduction

Porter suggests that five **competitive forces** influence the state of competition in an industry, which collectively determine the **profit** (ie long-run return on capital) potential of the industry as a whole. Read the section, learn what the forces are and then note the evaluation of the model at the end. Always apply these models with a critical eye and an appreciation of their limitations.

We must make a basic distinction between the **market** and the **industry**.

KEY TERMS

A MARKET comprises the customers or potential customers who have needs which are satisfied by a product or service.

An INDUSTRY comprises those firms which use a particular competence, technology, product or service to satisfy customer needs.

Question 13.4   Industries and markets

Learning outcome A1b

Assume that you are based in London and that you need to attend a meeting in Glasgow. Which industries can satisfy your need to attend the meeting?

KEY TERM

COMPETITIVE FORCES/FIVE FORCES. CIMA defines these as 'external influences upon the extent of actual and potential competition within any industry which in aggregate determine the ability of firms within that industry to earn a profit'. Porter argues that a firm must adopt a strategy that combats these forces better than its rivals' strategies if it is to enhance shareholder value.

KEY POINT

In discussing competition, *Porter* (*Competitive Strategy*) distinguishes between factors which characterise the nature of competition:

(a)   **In one industry compared with another** (eg in the chemicals industry compared with the clothing retail industry) and make one industry as a whole potentially more profitable than another (ie yielding a bigger return on investment).

(b)   **Within a particular industry.** These relate to the competitive strategies that individual firms might select.

Porter suggests that five **competitive forces** influence the state of competition in an industry, which collectively determine the profit (ie long-run return on capital) potential of the industry as a whole. **Learn them.**

- The threat of **new entrants** to the industry
- The threat of **substitute** products or services
- The bargaining power of **customers**
- The bargaining power of **suppliers**
- The **rivalry** amongst current competitors in the industry

Source: adapted from Porter *(Competitive Strategy)*

Exam alert

This model is fundamental to business strategy. You must know it and be able to apply it to circumstances as set out in questions. Not all five forces will necessarily be represented in a scenario and so it may not provide an exhaustive answer. However, it should provide a good framework to build on.

6.1 The threat of new entrants (and barriers to entry to keep them out)

A new entrant into an industry will bring extra capacity and more competition. The strength of this threat is likely to vary from industry to industry, depending on:

- The strength of the **barriers to entry**. Barriers to entry discourage new entrants.
- The likely **response of existing competitors** to the new entrant.

Barriers to entry	Comment
Scale economies	As scale of operations increases, unit costs tend to fall. This means that new entrants must start their operations on a large scale or suffer a vast disadvantage. A high level of fixed costs, with a consequent high breakeven point also requires entry on a large scale. If the market as a whole is not growing, the new entrant has to capture a large slice of the market from existing competitors.
Product differentiation	Existing firms in an industry may have built up a good brand image and strong customer loyalty over a long period of time. A few firms may promote a large number of brands to crowd out the competition.
Capital requirements	When capital investment requirements are high, the barrier against new entrants will be strong, particularly when the investment would possibly be high-risk.
Switching costs	Switching costs refer to the costs (time, money, convenience) that a customer would have to incur by switching from one supplier's products to another's. Although it might cost a consumer nothing to switch from one brand of frozen peas to another, the potential costs for the retailer or distributor might be high.
Access to distribution channels	Distribution channels carry a manufacturer's products to the end-buyer. New distribution channels are difficult to establish, and existing distribution channels hard to gain access to.
Cost advantages of existing producers, independent of economies of scale	Include: - Patent rights - Experience and know-how (the learning curve) - Government subsidies and regulations - Favoured access to raw materials

Japanese firms

CASE STUDY

A little while ago, it was assumed that, following the success of Japanese firms worldwide in motor vehicles (Nissan, Honda, Toyota) and consumer electronics (eg Sony, JVC, Matsushita), no Western companies were safe from Japanese competition. Kao (household goods), Suntory (drinks), Nomura (banking and securities) were seen as successors to firms such as Procter and Gamble, Heineken etc.

This has not happened: for example, Japanese pharmaceutical firms, such as Green Cross, have not achieved world domination. US and European firms are still dominant in this industry.

Perhaps cars and consumer electronics were the exception rather than the rule. The reason for this might be distribution. Normally, outsiders do not find it easy to break into established distribution patterns. However, distribution channels in cars and consumer electronics offered outsiders an easy way in.

(a) The car industry is vertically integrated, with a network of exclusive dealerships. Given time and money, the Japanese firms could simply build their own dealerships and run them as they liked, with the help of local partners. This barrier to entry was not inherently complex.

(b) **Consumer electronics**

    (i) In the early years, the consumer electronics market was driven by technology, so innovative firms such as Sony and Matsushita could overcome distribution weaknesses with innovative products, as they had plenty to invest. This lowered entry barriers.

    (ii) Falling prices changed the distribution of hi-fi goods from small specialist shops to large cut-price outlets, such as Comet. Newcomers to a market are the natural allies of such new outlets: existing suppliers prefer to shun 'discount' retailers to protect margins in their current distribution networks.

Japanese firms have *not* established dominant positions in:

(a) Healthcare, where national pharmaceuticals wholesalers are active as 'gatekeepers'.
(b) Household products, where there are strong supermarket chains.
(c) Cosmetics, where department stores and specialist shops offer a wide choice.

Entry barriers might be **lowered** by:

(a) Changes in the environment
(b) Technological changes
(c) Novel distribution channels for products or services

6.2 The threat from substitute products

A **substitute product** is a good/service produced by **another industry** which satisfies the same customer needs.

CASE STUDY

The Channel Tunnel

Passengers have several ways of getting from London to Paris, and the pricing policies of the various industries transporting them there reflects this.

(a) 'Le Shuttle' carries cars in the Channel Tunnel. Its main competitors come from the *ferry* companies, offering a substitute service. Therefore, you will find that Le Shuttle sets its prices with reference to ferry company prices, and vice versa.

(b) Eurostar is the rail service from London to Paris/Brussels. Its main competitors are not the ferry companies but the *airlines*. Initially, prices on the London-Paris air routes fell with the commencement of Eurostar services, and some airlines curtailed the number of flights they offer. Low-cost airlines have changed this equation by offering a cheaper alternative.

6.3 The bargaining power of customers

Customers include both the **ultimate consumer** and the buyers forming the **distribution channel**. Customers want better quality products and services at a lower price. Satisfying this want might force down the profitability of suppliers in the industry. Just how strong the position of customers is dependent on several factors.

(a) How much the **customer buys**
(b) How **critical** the product is to the customer's own business
(c) **Switching costs (ie the cost of switching supplier)**
(d) Whether the products are **standard items** (hence easily copied) or specialised
(e) The **customer's own profitability**

(f)   Customer's **ability to bypass** the supplier or might take over the supplier

(g)   The **skills** of the customer **purchasing staff**, or the price-awareness of consumers

(h)   The importance of **product quality** to the customer

CASE STUDY

Although the Ministry of Defence may wish to keep control over defence spending, it is likely as a customer to be as concerned that the products it purchases perform satisfactorily than with getting the lowest price possible for everything it buys.

6.4 The bargaining power of suppliers

Suppliers can exert pressure for higher prices but this is dependent on several factors.

(a)   Whether there are just **one or two dominant suppliers** to the industry, able to charge monopoly or oligopoly prices

(b)   The threat of **new entrants** or substitute products to the **supplier's industry**

(c)   Whether the suppliers have **other customers** outside the industry, and do not rely on the industry for the majority of their sales

(d)   The **importance of the supplier's product** to the customer's business

(e)   Whether the supplier has a **differentiated product** which buyers need to obtain

(f)   Whether **switching costs** for customers would be high

6.5 The rivalry amongst current competitors in the industry

The **intensity of competitive rivalry** within an industry will affect the profitability of the industry as a whole. Competitive actions might take the form of price competition, advertising battles, sales promotion campaigns, introducing new products for the market, improving after sales service or providing guarantees or warranties.

The intensity of competition will depend on the following factors.

Factor	Comment
Market growth	Rivalry is intensified when firms are competing for a greater market share in a total market where growth is slow or stagnant.
Cost structure	High fixed costs are a temptation for to compete on price, as in the short run any contribution from sales is better than none at all.
Switching	Suppliers will compete if buyers switch easily (eg Coke vs Pepsi).
Capacity	A supplier might need to achieve a substantial increase in output *capacity*, in order to obtain reductions in unit costs.
Uncertainty	When one firm is not sure what another is up to, there is a tendency to respond to the uncertainty by formulating a more competitive strategy.
Strategic importance	If success is a prime strategic objective, firms will be likely to act very competitively to meet their targets.
Exit barriers	Make it difficult for an existing supplier to leave the industry. • Fixed assets with a low break-up value (eg there may be no other use for them, or they may be old). • The cost of redundancy payments to employees. • If the firm is a division or subsidiary of a larger enterprise, the effect of withdrawal on the other operations within the group.

Read the following case study from 2005 and relate it to the factors in the table above.

CASE STUDY

Low cost airlines

Low cost airlines first appeared in Europe in 1997 after aviation liberalisation. Firms such as *Ryanair* and *EasyJet* copied American companies. They undercut the major carriers on price. The business model included:

- A single-type fleet of planes
- Fast turnaround at airports
- No frills
- Low fares, which only rose when seats were filled
- Cost advantages such as non-unionised labour

Things have changed.

In the US, the budget carriers are moving up market, offering well-defined service, not only low prices. The bigger they grow, the less easy they are to distinguish from their more upmarket rivals.

In Europe, the market for low cost flights is relatively young. There is overcapacity as new entrants spring up and disappear rapidly. EasyJet and Ryanair issued profit warnings in 2004. In Europe the low-cost airline faces several threats.

- An all out price war between airlines.

- Low barriers to entry with a glut of second hand aircraft, off the shelf software and low interest rates.

- Established competitors such as BA have adopted some of the innovations of the low-cost airlines, cut their prices and offer better service. Also they have a dominating presence in the most central and attractive airports.

New capacity is being added, as EasyJet and Ryanair buy more planes. Finally, most of the low cost trade is VFR – visiting friends and relatives. The danger is that the 'low-cost' airlines will end up attracting some higher costs in their pursuit of growth.

6.6 Complements

An important aspect of industries is the existence of **complements**. This is a concept you should recall from your basic economics studies: a complement is a product that is consumed at the same time as another one and both are, therefore, required. For example, a CD player is useless without CDs. In modern high technology industries, the existence of such complements is very important and fundamental to growth. The existence or otherwise of complements may almost be regarded as another competitive force, in that the more of them there are, the better for all concerned. Thus, the growth of IT based industries requires a kind of mutual support between telecomms companies, mobile phone manufacturers, chip manufacturers, software houses and so on. This implies that **collaboration** and **co-operation** are important aspects of strategy in these industries.

6.7 The impact of information technology on the competitive forces

The **Internet** has had a variety of impacts.

CASE STUDY

The *Financial Times* reported that German companies were losing lucrative niche markets because the Internet made it easier for customers to compare prices from other suppliers by obtaining other information over the Internet. High prices made German retailers vulnerable in an age when 'a shopper with a credit card and computer could sit at home and could order from around the world'.

The Internet is a competitive weapon. Supermarket home shopping service are supported by Internet technology.

6.7.1 Barriers to entry and IT

(a) **IT can raise entry barriers** by increasing economies of scale, raising the capital cost of entry or effectively colonising distribution channels by tying customers and suppliers into the supply chain or distribution chain.

(b) **IT can surmount entry barriers**. An example is the use of telephone banking.

6.7.2 Bargaining power of suppliers and IT

(a) **Increasing the number of** accessible **suppliers.** IT enhances supplier information available to customers.

(b) **Closer supplier relationships.** Suppliers' power can be shared. Computer Aided Design can be used to design components in tandem with suppliers. Such relationships might be developed with a few key suppliers.

(c) **Switching costs.** Suppliers can be integrated with the firm's administrative operations, by a system of electronic data interchange.

6.7.3 Bargaining power of customers

IT can 'lock customers in'.

(a) IT can raise switching costs.

(b) Customer information systems can enable a thorough analysis of marketing information so that products and services can be tailored to the needs of certain segments.

6.7.4 Substitutes

In many respects, **IT itself is 'the substitute product'**. Here are some examples.

(a) Video-conferencing systems might substitute for air transport in providing a means by which managers from all over the world can get together in a meeting.

(b) IT is the basis for leisure activities (eg games) which substitute for TV, cinema, music or other pursuits.

(c) E-mail might substitute for some postal deliveries and phone calls. Mobile text messages can substitute for email.

(d) Digital cameras, with output via computer, can substitute for traditional film and film processing labs.

6.7.5 IT and the state of competitive rivalry

(a) IT can be used in support of a firm's **competitive** strategy of cost leadership, differentiation or focus. These are discussed later in this text.

(b) IT can be used in a **collaborative** venture, perhaps to set up new communications networks. Competitors in the financial services industry share the same ATM network.

6.8 Evaluation of the five forces model

The five forces model offers a comprehensive framework into which appropriate aspects of economic theory, such as scale economies, may be fitted alongside elements of commercial practice, such as price negotiations. **Segmental analysis models** such as the five forces and PEST and its variants have much to offer the business strategist.

(a)   They point out **key strategic uses**.

(b)   They permit strategic analysis to be **divided up** among staff.

(c)   Their wide acceptance provides a **clear basis for discussion**.

(d)   They provide for **comprehensive analysis**.

Nevertheless, Porter's five forces model has **come in for criticism.**

(a)   The model relies on a **static picture of the competition** and therefore plays down the role of innovation.

(b)   It overemphasises the importance of the **wider environment** and therefore ignores the significance of possible individual company advantages with regard to resources, capabilities and competence.

(c)   Its model of government is essentially **passive** – as a referee in the competitive battle – rather than an active agent and shaper of the competitive environment.

6.9 Negotiation with customers and suppliers

To survive and prosper, a business must **create value** on a long term basis; this ultimately boils down to operating profitably. Costs and revenues have obvious impact on profitability and, therefore, purchasing and selling prices must be managed appropriately. While it is tempting to see trade with suppliers and customers as mutually beneficial and the prosperity of trading partners as a continuing desirable outcome, the strategic control of a business requires a firm control of trading relationships. This can only be achieved through **negotiation**, unless the business is in a position simply to accept the terms it is offered: this will anyway be impracticable for firms selling to the general public.

(a)   Terms of business are usually drafted to confer maximum advantage on the drafting organisation: they will often clash with those of trading partners and when this cannot be resolved by simple insistence; **mutually agreeable terms** must be arranged. This is particularly important when considering payment terms and the passing of property and risk in goods.

(b)   Trading relationships between **unequal partners** are frequently one-sided. The weaker partner must be sure that the terms and their impact are understood in detail.

(c)   Price structures can be made deliberately complex and difficult to understand: **quantity and settlement discounts** must be managed with care.

(d)   Price is an important aspect of the marketing mix and, especially in consumer markets, can send important messages about **quality**.

(e)   Weaker partners can gain advantage from membership of **purchasing and selling consortia**.

6.10 The industry life cycle

We have already defined an industry, earlier in this section. It may be possible to discern an **industry life cycle**, which will have wider implication for the nature of competition and competitive advantage. This cycle reflects changes in demand and the spread of technical knowledge among producers. Innovation creates the new industry, and this is normally **product innovation**.

Later, innovation shifts to processes in order to maintain margins. The overall progress of the industry lifecycle is illustrated below.

	Inception	Growth	Maturity/shakeout	Decline
Products	Basic, no standards established	Better, more sophisticated, differentiated	Superior, standardised	Varied quality but fairly undifferentiated
Competitors	None to few	Many entrants Little concentration in industry	Competition increases, weaker players leave	Few remain. Competition may be on price
Buyers	Early adopters, prosperous, curious must be induced	More customers attracted and aware	Mass market, brand switching common	Enthusiasts, traditionalists, sophisticates
Profits	Negative – high first mover advantage	Good, possibly starting to decline	Eroding under pressure of competition	Variable
Strategy	Dominate market, build quality	React to competitors with marketing spend	Cost reductions sought	Control costs

6.11 Survival and success factors

We have already made reference to critical success factors (CSFs). **Survival and success factors** (SSFs) are rather different. While CSFs are vital aspects of an individual organisation's activity, SSFs relate to a **complete industry**. If an organisation wishes to operate in an industry at all, it must deploy survival factors; if it wishes to succeed, it must deploy success factors. Generally, survival and success will represent two different degrees of achievement in similar fields. Thus, in a technically complex manufacturing industry, a survival factor would be technical competence with existing technology, while the equivalent success factor might be the ability to introduce technical innovations on a continuing basis.

The identification of survival and success factors should be one of the outcomes of environmental analysis.

Section summary

A market is a group of customers with needs to satisfy. An industry is the companies that use similar technologies to satisfy those needs. For any industry, **five forces** determine its profitability: 'threat of new entrants, substitute products, customers, suppliers and the intensity of competition'.

Trading relationships have strategic impact and, while mutual benefit may be desirable, they must be firmly managed.

Industries may display a **lifecycle**: this will affect and interact with the five forces.

7 Competitive strategies

Introduction

In any market where there are competitors, strategic and marketing decisions will often be in response to what a competitor has done.

Competitive advantage is anything which gives one organisation an edge over its rivals. Porter argues that a firm should adopt a competitive strategy which is intended to achieve some form of competitive advantage for the firm. A firm that possesses a **competitive advantage** will be able to make profit exceeding its cost of capital: in terms of economic theory, this is '**excess profit**' or '**economic rent**'. The existence of excess profit tends to be temporary because of the effect of the **five competitive forces**. When a company can continue to earn excess profit despite the effects of competition, it possesses a **sustainable competitive advantage**.

KEY TERM

COMPETITIVE STRATEGY means 'taking offensive or defensive actions to create a dependable position in an industry, to cope successfully with ... competitive forces and thereby yield a superior return on investment for the firm. Firms have discovered many different approaches to this end, and the best strategy for a given firm is ultimately a unique construction reflecting its particular circumstances'.

(Porter)

7.1 The choice of competitive strategy

Porter believes there are three **generic strategies** for competitive advantage. To be successful, Porter argues, a company must follow only one of the strategies. If they try to combine more than one they risk losing their competitive advantage and becoming 'stuck in the middle.'

KEY TERM

COST LEADERSHIP means being the lowest cost producer in the industry as a whole.

DIFFERENTIATION is the exploitation of a product or service which the **industry as a whole** believes to be unique.

FOCUS involves a restriction of activities to only part of the market (a segment) through:

- Providing goods and/or services at lower cost to that segment (**cost-focus**)

- Providing a differentiated product or service to that segment (**differentiation-focus**)

Cost leadership and differentiation are industry-wide strategies. Focus involves segmentation but involves pursuing, within the segment only, a strategy of cost leadership or differentiation.

7.1.1 Cost leadership

A cost leadership strategy seeks to achieve the position of lowest-cost producer in the **industry as a whole**. By producing at the lowest cost, the manufacturer can compete on price with every other producer in the industry, and earn the higher unit profits, if the manufacturer so chooses.

How to achieve overall cost leadership

- Set up production facilities to obtain **economies of scale**

- Use the **latest technology** such as Computer Aided Design and Manufacture and computerised inventory and logistics control to reduce costs and/or enhance productivity

- Exploit the **learning curve effect**

- Concentrate on **improving productivity**

- **Minimise overhead costs**

- **Get favourable access to sources of supply**

- **Relocate to cheaper areas**

- Use **IT** to record and analyse costs

Classic examples of companies deliberately pursuing cost leadership are Black and Decker and South West Airlines.

CASE STUDY

Watermark is a supplier of catering and other services to airlines. It had a good six months in the first half of 2005, with turnover increasing from £30.5m to £35.2m and profits rising from £1.6m to £2.4m. John Caulcott, the CEO, declared that the company's business was, in essence, finding savings in the airlines' supply chain: 'we can sell the savings to our clients and keep some of it for ourselves'.

7.1.2 Differentiation

A differentiation strategy assumes that competitive advantage can be gained through **particular characteristics** of a firm's products. Products may be categorised as:

(a) **Breakthrough products** offer a radical performance advantage over competition, perhaps at a drastically lower price (eg float glass, developed by Pilkington).

(b) **Improved products** are not radically different from their competition but are obviously superior in terms of better performance at a competitive price (eg microchips).

(c) **Competitive products** derive their appeal from a particular compromise of cost and performance. For example, cars are not all sold at rock-bottom prices, nor do they all provide immaculate comfort and performance. They compete with each other by trying to offer a more attractive compromise than rival models.

How to differentiate

(a) **Build up a brand image**
(b) **Give the product special features** to make it stand out
(c) **Exploit other activities of the value chain** such as marketing and sales or service
(d) Use **IT** to create new **services** or **product features**

Advantages and disadvantages of industry-wide strategies

Competitive force	Advantages		Disadvantages	
	Cost leadership	Differentiation	Cost leadership	Differentiation
New entrants	Economies of scale raise entry barriers	Brand loyalty and perceived uniqueness are entry barriers		
Substitutes	Firm is not so vulnerable as its less cost effective competitors to the threat of substitutes	Customer loyalty is a weapon against substitutes		

Competitive force	Advantages		Disadvantages	
	Cost leadership	Differentiation	Cost leadership	Differentiation
Customers	Customers cannot drive down prices further than the next most efficient competitor	Customers have no comparable alternative Brand loyalty should lower price sensitivity		Customers may no longer need the differentiation factor Sooner or later, customers become price sensitive
Suppliers	Flexibility to deal with cost increases	Higher margins can offset vulnerability to supplier price rises	Increase in input costs can reduce price advantages	
Industry rivalry	Firm remains profitable when rivals go under through excessive price competition	Unique features reduce direct competition	Technological change will require capital investment, or make production cheaper for competitors Competitors learn via imitation Cost concerns ignore product design or marketing issues	Imitation narrows differentiation

7.1.3 Focus (or niche) strategy

In a focus strategy, a firm concentrates its attention on one or more particular segments or niches of the market, and does not try to serve the entire market with a single product. **IT** can be useful in establishing the exact determining characteristics of the chosen niche, using existing customer records.

(a)   A **cost-focus strategy**: aim to be a cost leader for a particular segment. This type of strategy is often found in the printing, clothes manufacture and car repair industries.

(b)   A **differentiation-focus strategy**: pursue differentiation for a chosen segment. Luxury goods suppliers are the prime exponents of such a strategy. *Ben and Jerry's* ice cream is a good example of a product offering based on differentiation-focus.

CASE STUDY

In 2005, the *Financial Times* reported on *Tyrrells' Potato Chips*, a niche manufacturer of crisps that uses potatoes produced on its own farm. William Chase, owner of the company, set it up in part to escape from dependence on the major supermarkets and in part to add extra value to his basic product, potatoes. A major feature of his strategy is to sell mainly though small retailers at the upper end of the grocery and catering markets. The *Financial Times* summarises the Tyrells' strategy under six headings.

*   **Branding**. Tyrrells' marketing taps into the public's enthusiasm for 'authenticity' and 'provenance'. Its crisp packets tell the story of Tyrrells'. Pictures of employees growing potatoes on the Herefordshire farm and then cooking them illustrate the journey from 'seed to chip'.

*   **Quality**. Tyrrells' chips are made from traditional varieties of potato and 'hand-fried' in small batches.

*   **Distribution**. Tyrrells' sells directly to 80 per cent of its retail stockists. Students from a local agricultural college are employed to trawl through directories and identify fine-food shops to target with samples. After winning their business, Tyrrells' develops the relationship though personal contact.

*   **Diffusion strategy**. Selling to the most exclusive shops creates a showcase for Tyrrells' to target consumers who are not sensitive to price, allowing it to grow profitably.

- **New product development**. Tyrrells' is constantly bringing out new flavours and products. Experimental recipes are produced in sample runs and given free to shops to test with customers. Recent introductions include apple chips, honey glazed parsnips and Ludlow sausage with wholegrain mustard.

- **Exporting**. This has created a further sales channel through fine-food stores. Yet it has also forced greater dependency on distributors, introducing an unwelcome layer between itself and its customers.

Porter suggests that a focus strategy can achieve competitive advantage when '**broad-scope**' businesses fall into one of two errors.

(a)   **Underperformance** occurs when a product does not fully meet the needs of a segment and offers the opportunity for a **differentiation focus** player.

(b)   **Overperformance** gives a segment more than it really wants and provides an opportunity for a **cost focus** player.

Advantages of a focus strategy

- A niche is more secure and a firm can insulate itself from competition.

- The firm does not spread itself too thinly.

Drawbacks of a focus strategy

(a)   The firm sacrifices economies of scale which would be gained by serving a wider market.

(b)   Competitors can move into the segment, with increased resources (eg the Japanese moved into the US luxury car market, to compete with Mercedes and BMW).

(c)   The segment's needs may eventually become less distinct from the main market.

7.2 Which strategy?

Although there is a risk with any of the generic strategies, Porter argues that a firm must pursue one of them. A **stuck-in-the-middle** strategy is almost certain to make only low profits. 'This firm lacks the market share, capital investment and resolve to play the low-cost game, the industry-wide differentiation necessary to obviate the need for a low-cost position, or the focus to create differentiation or a low-cost position in a more limited sphere.'

Question 13.5   Hermes

Learning outcome A2a

The managing director of Hermes Telecommunications plc is interested in corporate strategy. Hermes has invested a great deal of money in establishing a network which competes with that of Telecom UK, a recently privatised utility. Initially Hermes concentrated its efforts on business customers in the South East of England, especially the City of London, where it offered a lower cost service to that supplied by Telecom UK. Recently, Hermes has approached the residential market (ie domestic telephone users) offering a lower cost service on long-distance calls. Technological developments have resulted in the possibility of a cheap mobile telecommunication network, using microwave radio links. The franchise for this service has been awarded to Gerbil phone, which is installing transmitters in town centres and stations etc.

What issues of competitive strategy have been raised in the above scenario, particularly in relation to Hermes Telecommunications plc?

In practice, it is rarely simple to draw hard and fast distinctions between the generic strategies as there are conceptual problems underlying them.

(a) **Problems with cost leadership**

   (i) **Internal focus.** Cost refers to internal measures, rather than the market demand. It can be used to gain market share: but it is the **market share that is important,** not cost leadership as such. Economies of scale are an effective way to achieve low costs, but they depend on high volumes. In turn, high volumes may depend on low prices, which, in turn, require low costs. There is a circular argument here.

   (ii) **Only one firm.** If cost leadership applies cross the whole industry, only one firm will pursue this strategy successfully.

   (iii) **Higher margins can be used for differentiation.** Having low costs does not mean you have to charge lower prices or compete on price. A cost leader can choose to 'invest higher margins in R&D or marketing'. Being a cost leader arguably gives producers more freedom to choose other competitive strategies.

(b) **Problems with differentiation.** Porter assumes that a differentiated product will always be sold at a higher price.

   (i) However, a **differentiated product** may be sold at the same price as competing products in order to **increase market share.**

   (ii) **Choice of competitor.** Differentiation from whom? Who are the competitors? Do they serve other market segments? Do they compete on the same basis?

   (iii) **Source of differentiation.** This includes **all** aspects of the firm's offer, not only the product. However, it is difficult to achieve differentiation purely by **promotion**, though some managers think it can be done this way.

Focus probably has fewer conceptual difficulties, as it ties in very neatly with ideas of market segmentation. In practice most companies pursue this strategy to some extent, by designing products/services to meet the needs of particular target markets.

'Stuck-in-the-middle' is therefore what many companies actually pursue quite successfully. Any number of strategies can be pursued, with different approaches to **price** and the **perceived added value** (ie the differentiation factor) in the eyes of the customer.

7.3 Limitations of the generic strategy approach

Porter's model depends on clear notions of what the **industry** and **firm** in question are. However, this may not be clear, since many companies are part of larger organisations and many 'industries' have boundaries that are hard to define. Also, we are faced with the difficulty of determining whether strategies should be pursued at Strategic Business Unit or corporate level, and in relation to exactly which category of products. For example, *Proctor and Gamble* have a huge range of products and brands: are they to follow the same strategy with all of them?

There have been several criticisms of Porter's approach. One is that it does not allow for **expansion into new industries**, perhaps as the result of creative innovation, as was the case with *Apple's iPod*. This is not really valid: Porter may be silent on this topic, but his model does not preclude it.

A second erroneous criticism is to see the model as dividing products into basic goods and luxury goods. This is to over simplify the model. Cost leadership might well be pursued over a wide range of product quality, though it seems likely that the emphasis will shift to differentiation where the higher quality products are concerned.

A further questionable point that may be raised is that the model does not allow for technical obsolescence and the introduction of new products. This is simply incorrect, as shown by *Black and Decker's* regular new product launches. These, generally, are marketed on the basis of high volume and low price, economies of scale being the basis of the business model.

CASE STUDY

Petrol is a commodity product, so it is difficult for suppliers to base their strategies on factors such as brand image and product characteristics. Instead, they tend to concentrate on cost reduction and operational efficiencies.

Mobil took this one step further in the late 1990s. Because some competitors had access to low cost crude, it realised that a cost leadership strategy was unlikely to be sustainable in the long run. Mobil's strategy for growth therefore aimed to attract customers who bought more petrol than average, were willing to pay higher prices for Mobil petrol, and who would also provide non-petrol revenue (eg from the forecourt's convenience store). To help in this, they identified five distinct consumer segments in the gasoline buying public and targeted the top three.

Section summary

Porter suggests there are three generic strategies: **cost leadership**, **differentiation**, and **focus.**

8 Corporate appraisal (SWOT)

KEY TERM

CORPORATE APPRAISAL: 'Critical assessment of the strengths and weaknesses, opportunities and threats (**SWOT** analysis) in relation to the internal and environmental factors affecting an entity in order to establish its condition prior to the preparation of the long-term plan.'

CIMA Official Terminology

Introduction

Corporate appraisal centres on a consideration of internal **strengths** and **weaknesses** and external **opportunities** and **threats**. This is known, unsurprisingly, as **SWOT analysis**.

8.1 Internal appraisal: strengths and weaknesses

A strengths and weaknesses analysis will identify two things.

(a) The areas of the business that have **strengths** that should be exploited by suitable strategies

(b) The areas of the business that have **weaknesses** which need strategies to improve them.

The strengths and weaknesses analysis is internal to the company and intended to shape its approach to the external world. For instance, the identification of shortcomings in skills or resources could lead to a planned acquisition programme or staff recruitment and training. The strengths and weaknesses part of the SWOT analysis involves looking at the findings of the position audit. At the end of the internal appraisal a firm should have some ideas as to its core competences.

8.2 External appraisal: opportunities and threats

An **external appraisal** is required to identify profit-making opportunities that can be exploited by the company's strengths and also to anticipate environmental threats against which the company must protect itself. The external appraisal is the **opportunities and threats** part of SWOT analysis.

BPP LEARNING MEDIA

Opportunities

(a)   What opportunities exist in the business environment?

(b)   What is their inherent profit-making potential?

(c)   Can the organisation exploit the worthwhile opportunities?

(d)   What is the comparative capability profile of competitors?

(e)   What is the company's comparative performance potential in this field of opportunity?

Threats

(a)   What threats might arise to the company or its business environment?

(b)   How will competitors be affected?

(c)   How will the company be affected?

8.3 Resource-based and positioning-based strategies

The SWOT analysis can be used in one of two ways.

(a)   The firm can develop **resource-based strategies** which depend on two things.

(i)   What the firm is good at and what are its strengths and competences are

(ii)   Where these strengths can be deployed

This is common in retailing, for example, as supermarket chains extend their own brands from food to pharmaceuticals.

(b)   The firm can develop **positioning-based strategies**. These are based on product market opportunities, in other words identifying what opportunities are available and what the firm has to do to align its resources with environmental conditions.

SWOT can usefully be combined with a **comparative analysis** of performance.

(a)   **Anticipated** and **past** performance can be compared.

(b)   A company's performance can be assessed in relation to its **competitors** and **industry norms**.

(c)   Industry **best practice** can be used as a yardstick, perhaps via the techniques given below.

(i)   **Competitor profiles**: analysis of the performance of key competitors.

(ii)   **Benchmarking**. Benchmarks are goals of performance which an organisation wishes to achieve in particular value activities. A benchmark for quality would be so many reject parts per million. This is to identify best practice and so achieve it. Benchmarks are often based on the most efficient competitors.

Section summary

The environmental assessment and the analysis of internal resources and capabilities are summarised in a **corporate appraisal**, or **SWOT** analysis. This stage explores the interplay between these factors preparatory to the generation of possible strategic courses of action.

Chapter Roundup

✓ Firms should **analyse their competitors** and build models of how they might react based on their future goals, assumptions, capability and current situation.

✓ The **management accountant's techniques** are useful in competitor analysis (eg by analysing how a competitor's cost structure influence the options available to it) and by modelling the impact of different strategies.

✓ An information system should be designed to obtain information from **all relevant sources** – both internal and external.

✓ Control information, to be useful, must aid the decision-making process.

✓ A company's response to the environment is influenced by its complexity and its dynamism. The value of forecasts varies according to these factors.

✓ An organisation should plan to obtain **strategic intelligence** as a basis for future strategies. Internal and external databases should be maintained and the data they contain assessed and applied.

✓ A market is a group of customers with needs to satisfy. An industry is the companies that use similar technologies to satisfy those needs. For any industry, **five forces** determine its profitability: 'threat of new entrants, substitute products, customers, suppliers and the intensity of competition'.

   Trading relationships have strategic impact and, while mutual benefit may be desirable, they must be firmly managed.

   Industries may display a **lifecycle**: this will affect and interact with the five forces.

✓ Porter suggests there are three generic strategies: **cost leadership**, **differentiation** and **focus**.

✓ The environmental assessment and the analysis of internal resources and capabilities are summarised in a **corporate appraisal**, or **SWOT** analysis. This stage explores the interplay between these factors preparatory to the generation of possible strategic courses of action.

Quick Quiz

1   Distinguish 'market' from 'industry'

2   **Fill in the blanks** in the statement below, using the words in the box.

     (1) .... competitive forces influence the state of competition in an (2) .... , which collectively determine the (3) .... of the industry as a whole:

     •   the threat of (4) .... to the industry

     •   the threat of (5) ....

     •   the (6) .... power of (7) ....

     •   the bargaining power of (8) ....

     •   the (9) .... amongst current (10) ....

• industry	• five	• profit	• new entrants
• bargaining	• competitors	• substitutes	• rivalry
• customers	• suppliers		

3   Define a switching cost.

4   Strategically useful information will rarely be obtained from sources internal to the organisation.

☐   True

☐   False

5   What is the difference between data and information?

Answers to Quick Quiz

1   The market comprises the customers or potential customers who have needs which are satisfied by a product or service.

     The industry comprises those firms which use a particular competence, technology, product or service to satisfy customer needs.

2   (1) five (2) industry (3) profit (4) new entrants (5) substitutes (6) bargaining (7) customers (8) suppliers (9) rivalry (10) competitors

3   Switching costs refer to the costs (time, money, convenience) that a customer would have to incur by switching from one supplier's products to another's.

4   False. Many organisations possess large amounts of strategically useful information in their internal records.

5   Information is data that is organised in some useful way.

Answers to Questions

13.1   Competitor analysis

(a)   Who are the existing competitors? How much of the market do they hold in each segment of the markets (eg in each particular region or country?)

(b)   Who are potential competitors? How soon might they enter the market?

(c)   How profitable are existing competitors? What is their EPS, dividend yield, ROCE etc?

(d)   What do the goals of each competitor appear to be, and what strategies have they adopted so far?

(e)   What products/services do they sell? How do they compare with the organisation's own products or services?

(f)   How broad is their product line? (eg Are they up-market high quality, or down-market low quality, low price and high volume producers?)

(g)   What is their distribution network?

(h)   What are their skills and weakness in direct selling, advertising, sales promotions, product design etc.

(i)   What are their design skills or R&D skills? do they innovate or follow the market leader with new product ideas?

(j)   What are their costs of sales and operational capabilities? With respect to equipment, technology, intellectual property etc?

(k)   What are their general managerial capabilities? How do these compare with those of the organisation?

(l)   Financial strengths and weaknesses. What is the debt position and financial gearing of each competitor? Do they have easy access to sources of new finance? What proportion of profits do they return in the business in order to finance growth?

(m)   How is each competitor organised? How much decentralisation of authority do they allow to operating divisions, and so how flexible or independent can each of the operating divisions be?

(n)   Does the competitor have a good spread or portfolio of activities? What is the risk profile of each competitor?

(o)   Does any competitor have a special competitive advantage – eg a unique government contract or special access to government authorities?

(p)   Does any competitor show signs of changing strategy to increase competition to the market?

13.2 Decisions

There are many possible suggestions, including those given below.

(a)   The organisation's **bankers** take decisions affecting the amount of money they are prepared to lend.

(b)   The **public** might have an interest in information relating to an organisation's products or services.

(c)   The **media** (press, television etc) use information generated by organisations in news stories, and such information can adversely or favourably affect an organisation's relationship with its environment.

(d)   The **government** (for example the Department for Business Enterprise and Regulatory Reform) regularly requires organisational information.

(e)   **HM Revenue and Customs** requires information for taxation and VAT assessments.

(f)   An organisation's **suppliers** and **customers** take decisions whether or not to trade with the organisation.

13.3 Contrasting environment

(a)   The environment is simple, as the product is only being sold in one market. The environment is dynamic, as the product is still at the introduction stage and demand might be predicted to increase dramatically.

(b)   The environment is complex, but stable. The knowledge required is uncertain, but funds are guaranteed for ten years.

13.4 Industries and markets

(a)   The airline industry: a number of airlines will compete to fly you from London to Glasgow.

(b)   The railways: it is possible that two railway companies will compete to take you there.

(c)   The car industry, if you have purchased a car.

(d)   The bus industry: several bus firms will compete to drive you to Glasgow.

(e)   The telecommunications industry. You may not need to travel at all, if the conference can be held via a video-conferencing system or even something simpler like a 'conference call'. Telecommunications firms might compete to provide this service.

13.5 Hermes

(a)   Arguably, Hermes initially pursued a cost-focus strategy, by targeting the business segment.

(b)   It seems to be moving into a cost leadership strategy over the whole market although its competitive offer, in terms of lower costs for local calls, is incomplete.

(c)   The barriers to entry to the market have been lowered by the new technology. Gerbil phone might pick up a significant amount of business.

Now try the question below from the Exam Question Bank

Number	Level	Marks	Time
Q13	Examination	25	45 mins

EXAM QUESTION AND ANSWER BANK

What the examiner means

The table below has been prepared by CIMA to help you interpret exam questions.

Learning objectives	Verbs used	Definition
1 Knowledge		
What are you expected to know	• List	• Make a list of
	• State	• Express, fully or clearly, the details of/facts of
	• Define	• Give the exact meaning of
2 Comprehension		
What you are expected to understand	• Describe	• Communicate the key features of
	• Distinguish	• Highlight the differences between
	• Explain	• Make clear or intelligible/state the meaning of
	• Identify	• Recognise, establish or select after consideration
	• Illustrate	• Use an example to describe or explain something
3 Application		
How you are expected to apply your knowledge	• Apply	• Put to practical use
	• Calculate/ compute	• Ascertain or reckon mathematically
	• Demonstrate	• Prove with certainty or to exhibit by practical means
	• Prepare	• Make or get ready for use
	• Reconcile	• Make or prove consistent/compatible
	• Solve	• Find an answer to
	• Tabulate	• Arrange in a table
4 Analysis		
How you are expected to analyse the detail of what you have learned	• Analyse	• Examine in detail the structure of
	• Categorise	• Place into a defined class or division
	• Compare and contrast	• Show the similarities and/or differences between
	• Construct	• Build up or compile
	• Discuss	• Examine in detail by argument
	• Interpret	• Translate into intelligible or familiar terms
	• Prioritise	• Place in order of priority or sequence for action
	• Produce	• Create or bring into existence
5 Evaluation		
How you are expected to use your learning to evaluate, make decisions or recommendations	• Advise	• Counsel, inform or notify
	• Evaluate	• Appraise or assess the value of
	• Recommend	• Propose a course of action

This list is very important, and guidance in our Practice and Revision Kit focuses on verbs.

1 S and C (Integrated Management (IM) 11/05)   18 mins

Learning outcome C2a

S has recently been appointed as the Finance Department Manager in Z Company. During the first month in her new role she has observed that one member of staff, C, is underperforming. C is frequently arriving late to work with no explanation and he is taking extended lunch breaks without permission. He is also making errors and refuses to do certain tasks which are part of his role. One of his colleagues has spoken to S confidentially, saying that C's poor performance in his work is having an adverse impact on the rest of the team. It is apparent that the problems have been going on for some time but the previous manager had preferred to ignore them. S has decided that she must now take action on what appears to be a disciplinary case, but is unclear on how to deal with the situation.

Required

Explain to S the stages involved in taking disciplinary action against C.   **(10 marks)**

2 Performance appraisal systems   45 mins

Learning outcome C2d

(a)   What are the features of an effective performance appraisal system?   **(13 marks)**

(b)   What are the advantages and disadvantages of performance appraisal systems?   **(12 marks)**

(Total = 25 marks)

3 The accounting function   18 mins

Learning outcome C2c

The accounting function is one of several key functions within an organisation, all of which integrate to ensure that the organisation is able to deliver its products or services as efficiently and effectively as possible.

Required

(a)   Explain the purpose of the accounting function within an organisation and identify and briefly describe how it interacts with **any two other** functional areas.   (6 marks)

(b)   Identify and describe the key factors which might affect the type of accounting system used within an organisation.   (4 marks)

(Total = 10 marks)

4 Communication (IM 5/08)   18 mins

Learning outcome C2b

P is the project manager responsible for managing the relocation of H Company's head office to new premises. He thought all was going well with the project and is very surprised when he learns that various project stakeholders are complaining about his poor communication skills.

Some of the complaints made relate to the complex messages he sends and his use of very technical language associated with the project. Whilst he feels he is keeping the project team members up to date, they feel they are overloaded with e-mails covering lots of different issues, not all of which are relevant to them.

Required

Explain to P what he could do to ensure that his communications with stakeholders about the relocation project are more effective. **(10 marks)**

5 Corporate culture

18 mins

Learning outcome C1b

Handy defines 'culture' as 'the way we do things around here'. What precisely does this mean? How does a corporate culture come into existence? What are the benefits and disadvantages of a strong corporate culture (like that commonly attributed to organisations like IBM)? **(10 marks)**

6 MFS

45 mins

Learning outcome B1a, b, c

You are employed by Metropolitan Financial Services (MFS), a company employing 1,200 staff based in your own country. As a systems accountant, one of your responsibilities is to improve the systems development process. In particular, the managing director has expressed concern at the length of time that systems development takes. The MD recently stated 'we have highly trained staff with excellent technical skills but we still seem to fall behind schedule on all of our systems development projects'.

Current systems development

Most concern at the moment relates to a project agreed upon nine months ago. The project goal is to centralise the management information systems for the three operational units by the installation of a new centralised server, and the consolidation of each unit's IT staff into a new IT team based at head office. It was planned that the transition would be completed within eighteen months. Interim plans were made to facilitate the change, for example one unit would deal with all payroll processing, one with all customer ledger activities and so on, using existing systems.

Problems encountered

At the end of nine months it has become apparent that the eighteen-month timeframe was over-optimistic.

The installation work on the new server at head office has progressed steadily, but the writing of the new software required for the centralised system is yet to start. As a result, a decision has been taken to defer the 'go live' date for the new system by six months, extending the transitional period to two years.

The redistribution of much of the back office and administrative work between units has proved difficult. The resulting operational problems have led to publication of regulatory body information being delayed. There is real concern that breaches of rules may occur.

Staff concerns

Senior management has been aware of the generally slow progress, and is now also becoming aware of the problems arising from the transitional arrangements.

In addition, users are concerned that they have had very little input to date on the development of new systems they will be dependent on. The disruption caused by the transitional arrangements has made users' jobs more difficult, for example staff often have to switch terminals depending on what type of information they need to access.

The three main areas affected by the changeover are:

(a) The Management Information System (MIS) developed in-house. This includes 'front-office' functions such as dealing/trading, and 'back-office' functions such as settlement and reporting.

(b) 'Office' type software including spreadsheet, word-processing, e-mail and database.

(c)   Access to a third party on-line information service.

The existing MIS has attracted user criticism. In particular, staff involved in dealing activities are unhappy with the way they have to navigate between screens when working in a high-pressure and fast-moving environment.

Users are satisfied with the office type software (running under Windows) and the access to, and information provided by, the third-party system.

Discussions with senior IT staff have revealed that the company uses a traditional systems development cycle that requires minimal user involvement until the implementation stage.

Required

The managing director has requested a report explaining the principles of project management and how these could be applied to systems development projects at MFS Ltd.   **(25 marks)**

7 C Hospital (IM 5/06)   45 mins

Learning outcome B1d

The main agenda item at the meeting of the Executive Board of C Hospital is to discuss the new pay and reward system. The hospital needs to make changes to the existing pay systems to respond to government requirements to reform reward systems as part of its pay modernisation agenda. The aim is to harmonise the payments systems for different categories of workers in the hospital on to one pay scale. This will mean that there is one pay scale for all employees of the hospital including nurses, physiotherapists, radiographers, technicians and support staff (ie cleaners, porters, and kitchen staff). The rationale for the new system is to achieve greater flexibility, to assist in recruitment and retention of staff and to reward people for their contribution to the achievement of hospital targets.

The hospital has twelve months in which to design and implement the new system in order to meet the government target of May 20X7. There is a huge amount of work that will need to be undertaken to deliver the new system, and a number of different stakeholders to satisfy.

At the meeting of the Board there was some discussion concerning who should be responsible for undertaking all tasks and activities associated with the development of the new system. The Human Resource (HR) director proposed that a project manager should be appointed and a project team set up. Whilst he would expect some members of his HR team to be part of the team, he is adamant that although his staff are responsible for administering the current payroll system and dealing with staff enquires about pay and rewards, designing a new pay system should not form part of the 'business as usual' work for the HR department.

Required

(a)   Describe the attributes of the proposed project in C Hospital that distinguish it from 'business as usual' work.   **(10 marks)**

(b)   Produce an outline of the different stages in the project to design and implement a new pay and reward system for C Hospital.   **(15 marks)**

(Total = 25 marks)

8 Critical path analysis

18 mins

Learning outcome B1e

You are the project manager responsible for a proposed new computer-based application for a medium sized retail chain.

You have drawn up an outline timetable for the introduction of the new system. The first draft of this is shown below.

Task	Description	Planned duration (weeks)	Preceding activities
A	Communication – inform staff at each shop of the proposal and indicate how it will affect them	1	–
B	Carry out systems audit at each shop	2	A
C	Agree detailed implementation plan with board of directors	1	B
D	Order and receive hardware requirements	4	C
E	Install hardware at all shops	4	D
F	Install software at all shops	2	D
G	Arrange training	3	D
H	Test systems at all shops	4	E and F
I	Implement changeover at all shops	10	G and H

Required

Produce a critical path analysis of the draft implementation plan. (This should identify the critical path and the total elapsed time.)
(10 marks)

9 Z Company (IM 11/05)

45 mins

Learning outcome B1, j

T has just returned to his job in the Finance Department of Z Company, having spent the last six months as a member of a project team working on the development of an Educational Visitor Centre for the company.

Reflecting on his experiences whilst working on the project, he feels that most of his time was spent in meetings that did not achieve anything, but rather wasted his time. He also feels that the final stages of the project were not dealt with effectively, with the project members going back to their functional jobs without any discussion or feedback on the project performance and outcomes.

He has now been asked to take on the role of project manager for a new project and is determined that he will improve the experience for his project team.

Required

(a) Discuss the problems that may be associated with project meetings. Make recommendations on the methods T could use to ensure the meetings he arranges as project manager, are effective.
(15 marks)

(b) Evaluate the contribution of the various activities that should be carried out as part of project closure, the post completion review and audit of the project.
(10 marks)

(Total = 25 marks)

10 Four Star Products

45 mins

Learning outcome A2b

Four Star Products plc is a major manufacturing organisation with a range of consumer products. Founded over seventy years ago and run for many years by the founder and his family, the company was rather traditional in its strategy, tending to stick to the hardware and other household goods that it understood. A formal system of strategic planning was introduced in 1962 and remains in place today, with a 47 person planning department reporting to a Planning Director.

Since a financial crisis in 1994, the dominance of the founding family has been diluted by banker power and the appointment from outside of a new CEO, a new CFO and three non-executive directors. The CEO has a reputation for turning companies around and his strategy has been to move into the IT and telecommunications sectors in force. He has made little use of the work of the planning department, preferring to commission research externally. Unfortunately, the collapse of the Internet bubble and fall in interest in IT and telecomms shares has led to Four Star suffering significant losses and a fall in its share price. One of the CEO's plans for cost reduction is to abolish the planning department.

Required

(a)   Is the CEO justified in his attitude towards the planning department?   **(15 marks)**

(b)   Explain how the formal planning process is intended to deal with events such as the collapse of the Internet business model.   **(10 marks)**

(Total = 25 marks)

11 Mission statement

18 mins

Learning outcome A2c

The managing director of TDM plc has recently returned from a conference entitled 'Strategic planning today'. Whilst at the conference, she attended a session on Corporate Mission Statements. She found the session very interesting but it was rather short. She now has some questions for the accountant.

'What does corporate mission mean? I don't see how it fits in with our strategic planning processes.'

'Where does our mission come from and what areas of corporate life should it cover?'

'Even if we were to develop one of these mission statements, what benefits would the company get from it?'

You are required to prepare a memorandum which answers the managing director's questions.

(10 marks)

12 National advantage

45 mins

Learning outcome A1b

D4D is a politically stable, developing country enjoying a temperate climate and a young, educated population, many of whom are educated to graduate level. Those who have studied at this level have tended to do so abroad since there are limited opportunities to do so in D4D.

The economy is mixed, based on agriculture and some light manufacturing but has enjoyed considerable revenue from oil exploration and production which is based offshore in its territorial waters. Some of this revenue is generated by providing services for the oil industry but the majority comes from a tax on every barrel of oil which the foreign oil companies extract.

The Government has used the revenue to keep personal and property taxes low and to support the largely uneconomic local industry. It now recognises that, although politically popular, this decision might not have been in the best long-term interests of the country.

The Finance and Trade Minister of D4D is aware that the oil revenue may only last a further ten years. He wishes to build a competitive advantage over the neighbouring countries. The Prime Minister is sceptical and has made the observation that 'companies have competitive advantages not countries'.

As a management accountant within the Ministry of Finance and Trade you have been asked to produce a number of documents, for both the Prime Minister and the Finance and Trade Minister, considering how competitive advantage could be achieved for D4D and examining the possibilities of attracting inward investment from foreign companies.

Required

(a) Using any models you consider appropriate, explain the factors which lead to competitive advantage being present in particular countries. **(7 marks)**

(b) Identify the aims that D4D should try to achieve in attracting appropriate investors into the country. You should also compare and contrast those aims with the likely aims of any company investing in D4D. **(10 marks)**

(c) Explain the steps that D4D should take to make the country more attractive to appropriate inward investment. **(8 marks)**

(Total = 25 marks)

13 X Company (IM 5/06)   45 mins

Learning outcome A1b

X Company is a manufacturer of non alcoholic soft drinks and has a well established position and brand recognition in country Z. The potential for future growth in country Z is, however, limited, with the market reaching saturation. One option for expansion is to move into new markets in other countries offering its existing product range.

The business development team is evaluating this option and is currently working on proposals to sell the company's range of drinks in country Y. One possible strategy to achieve market entry that the team is investigating is through a joint venture with a company that is already established in country Y, and is in the drinks distribution business.

The Board of X Company has given the business development team the task of undertaking a feasibility study to explore the viability of the proposed strategy. As part of the feasibility study there needs to be some assessment of industry competition and the attractiveness of the market in country Y. The feasibility study also needs to assess the cultural compatibility of the ways of doing business in country Y compared to how X Company currently operates in country Z.

Required

(a) Advise the business development team on how Porter's five forces model could be used to assess industry competition in country Y. **(15 marks)**

(b) Discuss how Hofstede's research could be used to assess the compatibility of X Company's strategy with the culture of country Y. **(10 marks)**

(Total = 25 marks)

1 S and C

> **Text references.** Chapter 1.
>
> **Top tips.** You need a good **knowledge** of the appropriate area of employment law to answer this question: there is an unspoken assumption that a proper answer will reflect modern attitudes to the relationship between employer and employee.
>
> Our answer is based on UK law and procedure, which can be taken as representative of the situation in the EU generally. You could use another legal system as a basis for an answer if you were more familiar with it.
>
> **Easy marks.** Employment law is complex and it would not be appropriate to approach this question looking for easy marks.

Disciplinary action is undertaken to improve future behaviour. It has considerable potential for creating serious disputes, so managers should always act consistently and in accordance with their organisation's established procedures. All disciplinary incidents should be **thoroughly investigated** and a written record kept by the manager concerned.

Stage – informal advice/coaching or counselling

Many minor cases of poor performance or misconduct are best dealt with by informal advice, coaching or counselling. S should certainly start by taking this course of action, using the medium of an **informal interview**. C should be informed that his behaviour has caused concern and be asked to account for it. This should focus his mind and reveal if there are any extenuating circumstances, such as illness or a family crisis. In the absence of such circumstances, C should be informed firmly that an improvement is required. A record should be made of the interview.

Stage – formal disciplinary procedures

Should there be no improvement, it may be necessary to deal with C through more formal disciplinary procedures. In the UK, such procedures are governed by the **ACAS code of practice**, which among other things, provides for full investigation, a right to be accompanied at any disciplinary proceeding and a right of appeal against sanctions. S, as a newly appointed manager should take advice from HRM professionals within Z Company.

The next stage would be the issue of a warning. This could be oral or written.

(a)   An **oral warning** should include the reason for issuing it; notice that it constitutes the first stage of the disciplinary procedure; and details of the right of appeal. A note of the warning should be kept on file but disregarded after a specified period, such as six months.

(b)   A **first written warning** is appropriate in more serious cases. It should inform the employee of the improvement required and state that a **final written warning** may be considered if there is no satisfactory improvement. A copy of a first written warning should be kept on file but disregarded after a specified period, such as twelve months.

(c)   A first written warning may also be appropriate if there has not been satisfactory improvement after an oral warning.

In the case of C, an oral warning is probably appropriate, as the disciplinary offences are fairly minor.

If the first warning is still current and there is no improvement, S may have to consider disciplinary sanction. Any sanction must be preceded by a **final written warning**.

The ultimate disciplinary sanction is dismissal. This is only appropriate for the most serious breaches of discipline. Demotion and suspension without pay are less drastic alternatives, but they must be provided for in the contract of employment.

Background material

In the UK, any imposition of disciplinary sanction must be in accordance with the statutory procedure introduced on 1 October 2004. This has three steps.

STEP ①   S writes to C stating why disciplinary action is being taken and inviting him to meeting to discuss the matter. C has the right to be accompanied by an advisor at the meeting.

STEP ②   At the meeting, S must explain the problem and allow C to respond. S must decide what is to be done and, after the meeting, explain her decision and inform C that he has the right to appeal to a different and preferably senior manager.

STEP ③   C may appeal and has the right to be accompanied by an adviser at the appeal meeting.

2 Performance appraisal systems

Top tips. Appraisal was quite a popular examination topic under the previous syllabus. This is not an exam standard question, but it will have enabled you to cover a great deal of important basic material.

(a)   **Features of an effective performance appraisal system**

Most large firms have a regular system of appraising staff. **The objectives of staff appraisal systems** are to **help in developing staff members to their full potential** and **to enable the organisation to allocate their human resources in the most efficient way possible**. To achieve these objectives an **effective appraisal system is likely to incorporate certain key characteristics**.

(i)   **Reports on employees should be made out in writing and at fixed intervals**. Staff appraisal is a sensitive operation and a written record of the assessment may remove any doubts or uncertainties which arise at a later date. The report is part of a record, the personnel record, which charts an employee's progress within the organisation. The intervals at which the appraisal should be carried out depend on the nature of the employee's work. For specialist staff who move from one long-term assignment to another, appraisal may be appropriate after each assignment is completed. For staff engaged in more routine work, an interval of six months or a year may be suitable.

(ii)   **Written reports should be objective**. An employee's superior may be inclined to assess harshly to excuse his own poor performance; alternatively, an easy-going relationship during day-to-day work may make a superior feel reluctant to be critical, especially if his subordinate's promotion prospects may be harmed. One way of improving objectivity is to make the assessment form very detailed: the more specific the assessor is required to be, the less margin there is for subjective responses.

(iii)   **Appraisal should be consistent throughout the organisation**. This can cause problems in organisations which, like banks, have many semi-autonomous branches. Again, the use of detailed assessment forms (standard throughout the organisation) will help, but the assessment form is only the beginning of the appraisal process and care must be taken to ensure consistency in the later stages too.

(iv)   **Assessments should be discussed with the person assessed**. If employees do not know what is being written about them they will not be able to improve in areas where shortcomings have been noted. This could cause particular frustration if the assessment system is used as part of a process of selecting staff for promotion.

(v)   **Persons conducting the appraisal interviews should be trained and experienced** in the necessary techniques.

(vi) **The employee should be encouraged to contribute to the appraisal process**. Ideally, he should have sight of the written assessment in time to consider his response before being called to interview. During the interview the emphasis ought not to be on problems and obstacles, but on opportunities. The interviewee should be encouraged to talk about his career plans, his knowledge and skills and how they could be put to better use, and to make suggestions for improving the way his work is carried out.

(vii) **There should be adequate follow-up after the interview has taken place**. If the system is to be effective, staff must have confidence in it. This will only happen if results are seen to follow from the assessments.

(b) **Advantages of appraisal systems**

(i) **They enable the organisation to gather information about the skills and potential** of employees and to identify training needs.

(ii) **They provide a system on which salary reviews and promotions can be based**.

(iii) **They help to develop the employee's potential** by directing his attention to particular strengths and weaknesses.

(iv) **They allow the employee and his assessor to discuss and agree on personal objectives**.

(v) **They** may **contribute to staff motivation**.

Disadvantages of appraisal systems

(i) **The subjective element in such systems cannot be entirely eliminated**.

(ii) **They depend for their success on a mutual confidence** between the assessor and the employee assessed. In practice, it is difficult to achieve that confidence.

(iii) **It is difficult to go beyond appraisal of past performance**, which may be an inadequate guide to future performance in a different job. If an appraisal scheme is used as a guide to promotion potential this is a serious disadvantage.

(iv) **They often do not lead to improvements in performance**. Criticism of areas where performance has been weak can lead to a defensive response and future performance may actually deteriorate.

(v) **There are many posts, particularly in technical roles, where further promotion is impossible**, performance is standardised at a high level and experience is infinitely valuable. To the incumbents of such posts a formal appraisal system may seem like a waste of time.

3 The accounting function

> **Helping hand**. We have given more than two examples of functional areas in part (a). This is to give you some alternatives for when you revise.

(a) **The work of the accounting function** can be seen as encompassing two areas of responsibility:

(i) **Handling the financial operations** of an organisation. This involves activities such as handling **receipts and payments**, receiving and checking **invoices from suppliers**, chasing payment from **customers**, accounting to the government for **tax**, borrowing money and repaying loans and preventing errors or fraudulent practices.

(ii) **Providing information and advice** to the managers of other departments to help them to do their work better. The accounts department has to liaise with other departments all the time. Information may be required for planning, control and one-off decision making purposes. In each case, information from other departments is necessary to carry out the accounting activity, and the procedures for interdepartmental communication may be formally set out.

Accounting management provides a good example of the need for close co-ordination.

Department	Accounts section	Relationship
Purchases dept (PD)	Purchase ledger (PL)	PD advises PL of purchase orders
		PD indicates valid invoices
	Cashier (C)	C informs PD and PL of payment
Personnel dept	Payroll	Personnel gives details of wage rates, starters and leavers, to payroll
Sales dept (SD) Credit control (CC)	Sales ledger (SL)	SD advises SL of sales order
		SL might give CC information about overdue debts
		SL might give details about debtors ageing and other reports
Operations, stock controllers	Cost accounting staff	Operations might give details of movements of stock, so that the accounts staff can value stock and provide costing reports
Senior management	Financial accounting and cost accounting staff	The accounts department as a whole produces management information for decision making and control

(b)   **Key factors affecting the type of accounting system used in an organisation**

The accounting function is part of the broader business system, and does not operate in isolation. Accounts are produced to aid management in planning, control and decision making and to comply with statutory regulations. The accounting system must be adequate to fulfil these functions. An organisation's accounting systems are affected by the nature of its business transactions and the sort of business it is.

The key factors which might affect the type of accounting system used within an organisation are as follows.

(i)   **Size**. A **small business** like a greengrocer will have a simple, accounting system, where the main accounting record will probably be the till roll. A **large retail business**, such as a chain of supermarkets, will have elaborate accounting systems covering a large number of product ranges and sites.

(ii)   **Type of organisation.** A **service business** might need to record the time employees take on particular jobs. Accounting on a **job or client basis** might also be a feature of service businesses. A **public sector organisation**, such as a government department, may be more concerned with the **monitoring of expenditure** against performance targets than recording revenue. A **manufacturing company** will account both for unit sales and revenue, but needs to keep **track of costs** for decision-making purposes and so forth.

(iii)   **Organisation structure**. In a business managed by **area**, accounts will be prepared on an area basis. In a functional organisation, the accounts staff are in a separate department.

4 Communication

Text references. Chapter 4 has a good section on communication.

Top tips. This question was set in a previous syllabus and the examiner's comments are quite helpful still so we have included them here. Do not be fooled into thinking this is a question about project management! You need to use your knowledge of communication to explain to P how he could make communication more effective. We have included a little preamble explaining how communication is used in project teams which sets the context for the answer. Start by thinking about the possible barriers to effective communication that may impede P's success. Refer to information in the brief scenario to back up your argument. The examiner uses a visual model of communication in her suggested answer which we suggest you consult on the CIMA website as this is a good summary of the process of communication. The examiner awarded a mark for each aspect of this model giving a maximum of ten marks. For instance, there would be a mark for use of appropriate language, medium selected as appropriate to the message and explanation of noise.

Easy marks. There are clues in the scenario such as 'complex', 'technical' and 'overloaded' which tell you where P's communication is ineffective.

In an organisational context communication has a variety of purposes. Among these is providing information to support managerial decision-making and to co-ordinate the plans and activities of different units and functions. Project teams usually communicate laterally and the project manager needs to use communication to co-ordinate the work of several stakeholders who are individuals and possibly departments with a stake in the project.

There are certain general problems in communication that can arise. Based on the information in the scenario, relevant problems would include **distortion** whereby the meaning of a message is lost between sender and receiver. **Misunderstanding** is also arising due to lack of clarity or technical jargon. It also appears that **overload** is an issue whereby the recipients of the information are being given too much information to digest in the time available. Certainly senior management would not be able to read detailed information and it would have to be edited for them. Timing may also be an issue here if information is being sent which has no immediate use. It is safe to say that there are also **poor communication skills** between P as sender and his audience although it is unclear whether this is two-sided as the team have made the complaints but are unlikely to admit any fault in their part.

Given the problems identified there are several suggestions to make communication more effective:

Give P training and guidance in communication skills including how to consider the information needs of the recipients of his messages, listening to them and acting on their feedback. **P needs to encourage feedback** as this is an important part of the communication process. **P also needs clear objectives about what he wants to achieve as a project manager** and this should frame his approach to communication. This would help P overcome problems with using inappropriate language unsuited to his audience, in his case, technical jargon.

It may be that P is uncomfortable with face to face communication. In this case, P could be given training on how to run meetings and make presentations. This would include looking at his non-verbal skills and giving him advice on how to make these cues consistent with the message he communicates verbally. In this way, he would also enhance personal interaction between the project team members, spread important information to all members at the same time and build relationships in a way that is not possible with remote ways of communicating.

Establish suitable communication channels and mechanisms that are suitable to all recipients. So the project group could agree to meet to update themselves if this was more suitable or agree the timing and form of regular email updates to avoid the danger of becoming overloaded with information (or 'noise'). The most appropriate medium for updating the team depends on factors such as complexity (face to face is often better here), urgency (email is best here), permanency (any written form) and cost effectiveness.

P needs to anticipate the reaction of those receiving the message so that any bad news is probably better communicated face to face.

5 Corporate culture

Top tips. This is another introductory question covering basic material. Our answer is not exhaustive and you may have chosen to cover a variety of other relevant topics such as the Harrison; Miles and Snow; and Denison models.

Defining culture

Handy's definition neatly sums up the meaning of culture, which is the complex body of shared values and beliefs of an organisation.

Schein has defined culture in a more detailed way as 'the pattern of basic assumptions that a given group has invented, discovered or developed, in learning to cope with its problems of external adaptation and internal integration, and that have worked well enough to be considered valid and therefore, to be taught to new members as the correct way to perceive, think and feel in relation to these problems.'

IBM has been cited in the question as a company with a strong culture. Other examples of 'the way we do things around here' can be found at Procter and Gamble and at Hewlett Packard. At Procter and Gamble all parts of the organisation's activities focus on product quality. At Hewlett Packard all employees are encouraged to be innovative and the culture is one which encourages individuals to experiment.

How a corporate culture comes into existence

Corporate culture develops along with the organisation as it grows. The development of a particular culture may be deliberate, perhaps through the issuing of policy documents and by selecting and retaining only certain types of employee. Alternatively, the culture may develop more naturally as a result of the leadership style of the organisation's senior managers.

It has been suggested that an **organisation's culture develops from three main sources**: the **organisation's origins**, its **technology** and the **dramatic events in its history**.

To demonstrate the effect of an organisation's **origins** on the development of culture we can cite the two founders of Philips, who had distinct personal work preferences. One founder preferred technical work, the other concentrated on sales and commercial work.

An organisation's **technology** can give clues to the development of the underlying culture. For example an engineering culture will be very different from mass production culture.

Dramatic events include events such as a recession, a major new product development or a significant lay-off of staff, which could change or mould an organisation's set of shared values or beliefs.

The benefits of a strong corporate culture

A strong corporate culture exists where there is a very clear set of values and beliefs in the organisation. There are a number of benefits in this and *Peters and Waterman*, in their book *In search of excellence* found that '**dominance and coherence of culture**' was an essential feature of '**excellent**' companies. The benefits can be listed as follows.

(a) **Motivation and satisfaction of employees** may be improved by encouraging commitment to the organisation's values and objectives, fostering satisfying team relationships and using 'guiding values' instead of rules and controls.

(b) **The organisation will present a positive image in its environment**. The cultural attributes of an organisation will affect its appeal to potential customers and suppliers, employees, potential shareholders and so on.

(c) **An organisation's culture may encourage adaptability**, by supporting innovation, risk-taking, willingness to embrace new methods and so on.

(d)   **A background of unchanging values** (or values which change more slowly, over a longer time-scale, as a result of mere superficial changes) can act as a platform for change, and for the acceptance of change by individuals who may desire some familiarity and security to be retained.

The disadvantage of a strong corporate culture

(a)   **Culture may be an obstacle to change because by its nature it is a force for continuity and cohesion.** If culture itself is continually adapting, there will be none of the sense of security and order and coherent self-image that Peters and Waterman observe in successful business cultures.

(b)   **Culture establishes patterns of thought and behaviour as a basis for future action.** In other words, it establishes *attitudes*. Attitudes are notoriously hard to change – harder than behaviour.

(c)   **Culture tends to be a force for cohesion and may cause a tendency for 'groupthink' or a cosy complacency**, a consensus which is resistant to outsider input and information which contradicts or threatens the group. This sense of infallibility and blindness to dangers in the present course can obviously be detrimental to an organisation's prospects of survival in a changing environment.

6 MFS

> **Top tips.** As with many questions, there are a wide range of possible answers that could have scored well. The suggested approach to project management in the answer below shows how theories may be adapted to suit the circumstances described in the question.

REPORT

To: Managing Director MFS Ltd
From: Systems Accountant
Date: May 200X
Subject: Project management at MFS

The introduction of a new computer system has the potential to cause considerable disruption to an organisation.

Some problems are presently being experienced at MFS, particularly in connection with the transitional arrangements during the development of the new system. For example the 'going live' extension from 18 months to 2 years suggests that personnel costs will be at least one third over budget.

Project management techniques can help monitor and control projects. The principles are outlined below.

A **project** involves the management of a number of **disparate, yet interdependent tasks**, within a **timetable** and a **budget** set in advance. A particular project is unique, in that by its nature once done it is never repeated.

Efficient management of the resources and process of the project is vital if the project is to be completed successfully – that is on time, within budget and to the required quality.

The consistent lateness of IT related projects at MFS Ltd implies the organisation would benefit from the application of appropriate project management techniques. Workable policies need to be developed as soon as possible to prevent further damage being done to the company, for example through regulatory breaches and a further reduction in employee morale.

A suggested approach to project management

STEP 1 **Form the Project Board or steering committee**. A steering committee comprising senior user department personnel, a member of the finance department and various systems professionals should be appointed to oversee the project.

STEP 2 **Appoint a project manager**. This person will manage and oversee the execution of the project, and is responsible for its successful completion. The project manager presents the timetable and budget to the steering committee for their approval and authorisation.

STEP 3 **Plan the project**. The **goals** of the project are identified, and the **tasks needed to achieve them** are outlined. These are then matched to the manpower resources available, so that a **Project Plan** can be outlined and agreed. Tools such as work-breakdown structure, Critical Path Analysis and Gantt charts are useful aids. The schedule will indicate **when** each task has to be completed, and in **which order**. **Each stage** of the project is then planned in its own right. The stages of the project may be determined by the systems development methodology adopted.

STEP 4 **Control the project**. Actual outcomes are compared to the plan, and any discrepancies investigated and addressed as soon as they become apparent.

The monitoring process should take into account four criteria.

- **Time**, by reference to critical path analysis or Gantt charts.
- **Resources**, by measuring available resources and percentage utilisation.
- **Costs**, by reference to the MIS and budgets.
- **Quality**, as appropriate.

Regular progress meetings should be held by the project manager with members of the project team to monitor performance.

Specified **documentation** is produced at the end of each stage for review and approval, in accordance with quality control criteria established.

At the end of each stage, progress will be reported to the steering committee. **Users** should be consulted, as their approval is necessary to demonstrate that the project is meeting its objectives.

STEP 5 **Complete the project**. The resulting system must meet the technical criteria (Quality) specified (eg response times). All relevant documentation must be completed to an adequate standard, project files must be complete and there should be a clear relationship evidenced between the work done in the various successive stages of the project.

STEP 6 **Post-implementation audit**. The project should be reviewed in terms of both the **technical quality** of the output, and the **efficiency** with which project tasks and management were carried out.

Stakeholders' feedback should be gained to ensure all viewpoints are covered.

Lessons that can be learned from the project should be documented to prevent the same mistakes being made on similar projects in the future.

7 C Hospital

(a) **Attributes of project working**

In general the work which organisations undertake may be classified as either '**business as usual**' or **projects**. Whether an activity is classified as a project is important, as projects require management using specialised project management techniques.

A project has a number of attributes that distinguish it from 'business as usual'.

(i) **Projects have a defined beginning and end** – unlike operations which tend to be on-going. So, for example, the C Hospital project has a defined duration of 12 months to meet its deadline of May 20X7. This often allows them to be perceived in terms of a 'life cycle' of defined stages, from project definition and planning through implementation and control to closure and review.

(ii) **Projects have resources allocated specifically to them**, although often on a shared basis. This is reflected in the HR director's insistence on separating responsibility for the development of the new system, and staff involvement in it, from 'business as usual' working in the form of administering the system and dealing with staff enquiries. At the close of the development project, staff will return to their departments.

(iii) **Projects are often unique or 'one-off'**: intended to be done only once, in contrast to operations which involve recurring tasks. Thus the development of the new system is distinguished from its on-going operation.

(iv) **Projects follow a specific plan towards a clear intended end-result** (in this case, implementation of the new system), in contrast to operations for which goals and deadlines may be more general. There will be a specific schedule and resource plan for the system development project.

(v) **Projects often cut across organisational and functional lines**, while operations usually follow the organisation or functional structure. So, for example, the HR director argues that HR staff will only be one part of the project team, since a number of other stakeholders will need to be involved (including, say, payroll and accounts, IT, worker representatives and hospital management).

(b) **Outline stages for the systems design project**

The life cycle of the project to design and implement a new pay and reward system for C Hospital will include the following four main phases:

Identification of a need

Projects start when someone becomes aware of the **need** for one. This can occur at any level and in any context, though more formal business projects of management significance will normally be originated within the area of responsibility of the sponsoring manager.

At C Hospital the need has arisen as a result of the need to respond to government requirements to reform reward systems. A key first step is to **identify the goals and objectives** of the project – why we are doing it and what are we seeking to achieve. At this early stage one of the most important things to get under control is the **scope** of the project; that is, just what is included and what is not. A firm grasp of the agreed scope of the project must be maintained throughout its life. Government requirements in relation to reward systems will play a major role in shaping the scope of the project.

The **project team** will also be assembled at this stage and should include representatives from HR, Finance and those who can speak on behalf of each of the employee groups affected. The **project manager** will take ultimate **responsibility** for ensuring the desired result is achieved on time and within budget. A person should only take on the role of project manager if they have the time available to do the job effectively. Since that person is to be held responsible for the project, they must be given the **resources** and **authority** to complete project tasks.

Development of a solution

Planning is a key duty of the project manager and the initial outline planning will include:

(i)   Developing project targets such as overall costs or timescales.

(ii)   Dividing the project into activities and placing these activities into the right sequence.

(iii)   Developing a framework for procedures and structures needed to manage the project – this could include weekly team meetings, performance reviews and so on.

Detailed planning may include use of techniques such as work breakdown structure and network analysis in order to produce a schedule of activities to be undertaken.

Implementation

This is the **operational** phase of the project. Planning will continue as required to in order to control agreed changes and to deal with unforeseen circumstances, but the main emphasis is on **getting the work done**.

There are several important aspects to this phase. **Management** and **leadership** assume a greater importance as the size of the project work force increases. **Time**, **cost** and **quality** must be kept under control, as must the tendency for **changes** to proliferate.

Problems are bound to arise and must be solved sensibly and expeditiously. At C Hospital the objective of the project, pay harmonisation, is potentially extremely contentious and it will be very important to resolve employee concerns quickly without imposing an ongoing insupportable financial burden upon the hospital.

Completion

The final phase of the project is **completion and review**. This phase involves a number of important but often neglected activities.

Completion itself is often neglected. All activities must be properly and promptly finished and **documentation** must be completed. This is particularly important on a payroll project where accuracy and timeliness of payment are of crucial importance.

At some point the HR department must formally **accept** that the project is **complete** and **take responsibility** for any future action that is required in relation to the new pay system, such as the maintenance of the system. The HR department will want to ensure that the project being handed over **conforms** to the latest **requirements definition** and **project specification**.

Completion will involve the **disbandment** of the project team. It is important for future projects that before the team members return to their previous roles there is a **formal process** that gathers the **lessons learned** so that they are available to future project teams and help those projects to avoid any mistakes or difficulties encountered whilst developing the payment system.

8 Critical path analysis

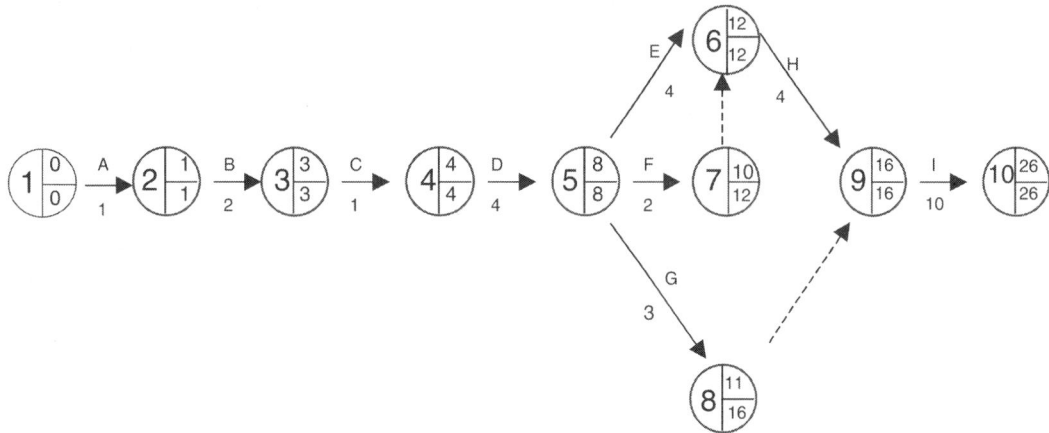

Critical path analysis [One of the following]

Activity on line presentation

The critical path is A, B, C, D, E, H, I. The total elapsed time is 26 weeks.

Activity on node presentation

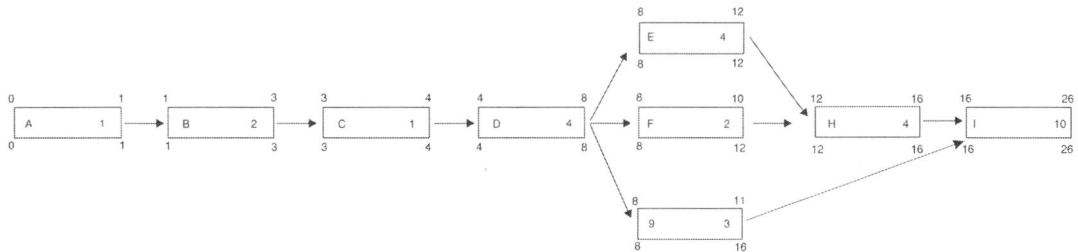

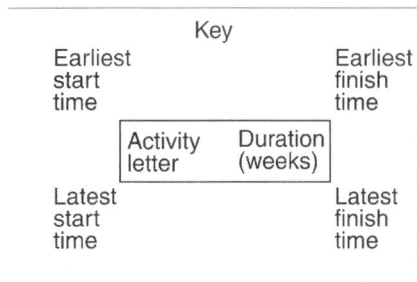

		Key		
Earliest start time			Earliest finish time	
	Activity letter	Duration (weeks)		
Latest start time			Latest finish time	

9 Z Company

Text references. Chapter 9.

Top tips. Part (a) is more about meetings than it is about project management, because, while project meetings may deal with matters peculiar to a given project, organising, chairing and participating in them is not different from doing the same things in some other kind of meeting.

Easy marks. You either have an idea of how to run meetings, or you don't. If you do, this is easy stuff.

(a) **Problems associated with project meetings and recommendations to resolve them**

Unnecessary meetings

The effectiveness of every hour the individual spends in a meeting has to be considered in terms of opportunity cost. **T needs to ensure that he gets value for money**. The first question about any proposed meeting should be whether or not it should be held at all. If the meeting will purely be a forum for disseminating information, a memo may be a more efficient means of communication.

Unsuitable participation in the meeting

Participants who have nothing to contribute, or to whom the meeting is irrelevant, are wasting time. Only those people with a genuine need to be at a meeting, and a genuine contribution to make, should be invited. This is an important consideration for project meetings, because of the need for stakeholder representation and communication.

Unclear objectives and remit

Unclear objectives will lead to irrelevancies being discussed. T should decide the objectives or desired outcomes of the meeting, and design the agenda (and conduct the discussion) accordingly. Project problem-solving meetings should have clear guidance on their decision-making authority.

Lack of planning and co-ordination

When involving a number of people, particularly when they do not work at the same location, **lack of planning can sabotage the meeting** (by preventing key stakeholders from attending), its tone (by creating frustration) and its effectiveness (eg by failing to include vital items on the agenda). T must give plenty of notice of the meeting, and send a formal notification of the meeting with either an agenda or a request for any further items for the agenda. (This is important to ensure that all stakeholder concerns and inputs have an opportunity to be aired.)

Poorly constructed agenda

Lack of a detailed pre-planned agenda causes problems by not allowing participants to prepare themselves for discussion and (even more crucially) not providing a framework for the meeting. It will be much harder for T to keep the meeting 'on track' if there is no 'track'! In order to minimise this problem, T should ensure that the agenda:

(i) **Follows a logical order**, with the most important and time-consuming matters in the middle (to focus quality attention)

(ii) **Gives sufficient detail about the purpose of each item** to guide preparation and discussion

(iii) **Shows the start and finish times of the meeting**, and also roughly how much time will be allocated to each item, in order to facilitate time-keeping

Poor chairing/leadership of the meeting

Whoever is leading the project meeting must be aware of the role of chair (leader or facilitator) and should have appropriate skills. Poor leadership can cause problems such as: the meeting getting off-agenda; uncontrolled conflict and 'power plays' by different participants; lack of equitable contribution (so that some stakeholders fail to get heard or give their input); lack of protocols for conduct and processes such as debate and decision-making; and failure to get to 'closure' (all discussion, no decision). These problems may have contributed to T's dissatisfaction with the earlier project meetings he attended.

A skilled and experienced chair or discussion facilitator should be appointed for the task. This may be T as project manager, or it may be a role that revolves among the project team over the period of the project. The leader should be supported by a secretary (or minutes taker) to record the discussion and decisions.

Lack of minutes and follow-up action

Lack of record of decision can create uncertainty and conflict about what was agreed and whose responsibility it was to take action. Lack of defined responsibilities for action can lead to inaction! All meetings should be minuted. After the meeting the person responsible for taking minutes needs to check with the chair that minutes and action points are a fair reflection of events. Action points should specify the action to be taken, by whom the action should be taken, and by when. There should be follow up and progress check on those with responsibilities before the next meeting.

(b) **Project closure and review**

> **Text references.** Maylor's model is covered in Chapter 7.
>
> **Top tips**. The question which comes from the predecessor syllabus, uses the word 'contribution'. It is clear that this doesn't mean revenue minus variable costs. We must assume it means something like the contribution proper project closure makes to the organisation generally, rather than to the process of project management itself, which would be a rather smaller target.
>
> **Easy marks**. The final D as in 'develop the process' of *Maylor's* 4D model answers this question succinctly and accurately.

T is quite right to be concerned about failure to finish off a project properly. Because project management is episodic in nature, it is **difficult to improve**. The lack of continuous operation means that the skills and experience developed during a project are likely to fragment and atrophy after it is complete. The completion and review phase involves a number of important but often neglected activities that T should ensure are carried out at the conclusion of his new project.

(i) **Completion** itself is often neglected. All project deliverables must be, in fact, delivered and all activities properly and promptly finished; care must be taken that contractors do not either leave small things undone or, if paid by time, spin things out for as long as possible.

(ii) **Documentation** must be completed. This is important on any project but it is vital if there are quality certification issues or it is necessary to provide the user with operating documentation. Indeed, these two types of documentation should be specified as deliverables at the outset. Contracts, letters, accounting records and so on must be filed properly.

(iii) **Project systems** must be closed down, but in a proper fashion. In particular, the project accounts and any special accounting systems must remain in operation and under control until all costs have been posted but must then be closed down to avoid improper posting.

(iv) **Handover** must take place where the project has been managed for a client under contract. At some point the client must formally accept that the contract is complete and take responsibility for any future action that may be required, such as the operation and maintenance of a system.

(v) **Immediate review** is required to provide staff with immediate feedback on performance and to identify short-term needs such as staff training or remedial action for procedure failures.

The review process

A thorough review is the organisation's opportunity to make significant **improvements in how it manages its projects**. T should ensure that his review clear **terms of reference** and covers all aspects of the project, possibly organised on a functional basis. This cannot be done on the cheap: appropriate quantities of management time and attention must be allocated to the review process and to the assimilation of its results and recommendations.

Post Completion Audit

The post completion audit is the final stage of the review process. **It is a formal review of the project that examines the lessons that may be learned and used for the benefit of future projects.**

Did the end result of the project meet the client's expectations: was it delivered on time and on budget? Was the management of the project as successful as it might have been, or were there bottlenecks or problems?

The audit helps to identify problems that might occur on future projects with similar characteristics, as well as to provide feedback for improvement of the performance of the project team. In other words any project is an opportunity to learn how to manage future projects more effectively. It should be clear that the audit has the potential to reduce the costs associated with future projects.

Longer-term review

Longer-term review is useful for the consideration of **lifetime costs**; which should be the eventual criterion for project success. It also allows individuals time to reflect on their experiences and to learn more thoroughly from them.

10 Four Star Products

Part (a)

Top tips. This is a relatively simple question to start this subject with. It will give you good practice at marshalling your knowledge and presenting it in a way that is related to the scenario, both of which are essential skills for this subject.

Do not worry if you reach a different conclusion from the one in the suggested solution, or even no conclusion at all. It is very important to understand that there are few absolutely correct answers to questions in strategic management. Success does not just depend on learning. You must be familiar with the material, certainly, but you must also be able to apply it to an infinite variety of problems.

What is important in questions of this type is that you offer reasoning that is both theoretically sound and relevant to the setting.

Answer plan

NB Q not so much about the planning department as about what it does. Therefore answer requires critique of formal planning approach.

Against

Difficulty of forecasting discontinuities
Linear approach – annual cycle
Isolation of planners from operations
Politics
Implementation
Learning

For

Systematic approach
Sets targets
Co-ordination of objectives, departments, activities
Organised attention to environment

Criticisms of the rational model concern both the theory behind it and how it has worked in practice. Empirical studies have not proved that formal planning processes contribute to success.

Planning theory assumes that the development of the business environment can be forecast, and to some extent controlled. In conditions of stability, forecasting and extrapolation make sense. But forecasting cannot cope with sudden **discontinuities** and **shocks**, such as the change from mainframe computing to PCs, which nearly destroyed IBM.

Part of the problem is the **linear approach** sometimes adopted, using an annual cycle. Unfortunately, strategically significant events outside the organisation are rarely synchronised with the annual planning cycle. Four Star's financial crisis in the early 1990s is, perhaps, an example.

Another problem is that formal planning can **discourage strategic thinking** among operational managers. Once a plan is locked in place, people are unwilling to question it. The internal significance of the chosen performance indicators leads managers to focus on fulfilling the plan rather than concentrating on developments in the environment. Strategy becomes something for specialists.

A complementary problem arises when the planners are separated from the operational managers; the implication is that the planners do not really need day-to-day knowledge of the product or market. However, small-scale developments can have important strategic influence and should not be ignored.

The rational model by definition assumes that an **objective approach** prevails. Unfortunately, no account is taken of the essentially political processes that determine many plans. There are also problems of implementation. Managers are not all-knowing, and there are limits to the extent to which they can control the actual behaviour of the organisation. This places limits upon what can be achieved. Discovering strengths and weaknesses is a learning process. Implementing a strategy is necessary for learning – to see if it works.

On the other hand, we can discern an important role for **formal planning activities**. Apart from anything else, a desire to do things in a systematic way naturally leads to rational planning; deciding what to do, and when and how it should be done. Such an approach can make management control more effective by developing detailed and explicit targets. This shows managers at all levels where they fit in and forces them to confront the company's expectations of them.

The development of a plan for a large organisation such as Four Star includes an important element of **co-ordination**. Long-term, medium-term and short-term objectives, plans and controls must be made consistent with one another. Similarly, the activities of the different business functions must be directed towards a common goal.

Also, companies cannot remain static: they have to cope with and exploit changes in the **environment**. It is clear from the CEO's use of external agencies and his new strategy for Four Star that he understands this. We may speculate that he is not so much an enemy of strategic planning as much as he is unimpressed with the performance of the Four Star planning department.

Part (b)

> **Top tips**. This part of the question is fairly unusual in that there is pretty much a single correct approach to a good answer; that is, this question is about the environmental analysis aspect of the rational planning model and not very much else will do. However, notice that a good answer will point out the weakness of the forecasting process: the future is essentially unknowable and the danger of detailed research is that we forget this and come to believe that we do indeed know just what is going to happen.

Answer plan

Nature of environmental analysis
The environment – divisions
Desk research
Market research
Informal research
Technical nature of Internet boom
Importance of judgement
Relationship of formal planning to strategic decision-making support

Environmental analysis is a fundamental part of strategic business management. The aim of the analysis is to identify opportunities and threats and to assess their significance. The environment itself may be divided both according to its proximity to the organisation and according to its inherent features. Thus, the task environment, dealing with suppliers, customers, competitors and so on, may be differentiated from the wider, general environment and, indeed, from the global physical environment. The general, or macro, environment is often analysed under such headings as political, economic, social and technological.

The work of analysis can be carried on to a great extent by **desk research**. This may be quite adequate for keeping abreast of the more general aspects of the macro environment, and even for some parts of the task environment, such as changing labour costs and the fortunes of competitors. However, more complex and expensive methods, such as market research surveys may be required for some aspects of the task environment, and more intuitive ones, such as personal contact between senior managers for others.

In the case of the Internet business model, which was given enormous publicity, it should have been easy to obtain a full understanding of both principle and technique by the methods outlined above. The problem with the collapse of confidence in the model was that foretelling was very much a matter of **judgement**. Extremely large sums of money were invested on quite rational grounds and very few commentators took a pessimistic view.

This is not a failure of the formal planning process as such, but rather a failure of strategic judgement at the highest levels of the organisations concerned. Planning techniques cannot foretell exactly what the future holds, let alone control it. Their purpose is to support those who must take strategic decisions, not to replace them.

11 Mission statement

> **Top tips**. The question asks for a memorandum. Do not throw away the mark that may be available for creating a memo-like heading such as the one we use. We have provided a fairly extensive discussion in our suggested solution, so if your solution was less detailed do not be alarmed.

To: Managing Director
From: Anne Accountant
Date: 29 February 200X
Subject: Mission Statements
Contents: Introduction
            Mission statements and strategic planning
            Originating a mission statement
            The scope of mission statements
            The benefits of mission statements

Introduction

A *mission* can be defined as a business's basic function in society. It is often visionary, open-ended and has no time limit for achievement. It is possible, however, to reach a more expanded definition of mission to include four elements.

(a)   **Purpose**. Why does the company exist, or why do its managers and employees feel it exists?

    (i)   To create wealth for shareholders, who take priority over all other stakeholders.
    (ii)   To satisfy the needs of all stakeholders (including employees, society at large, for example).
    (iii)   To reach some higher goal and objective ('the advancement of society' and so forth).

(b)   **Strategy**. This provides the commercial logic for the company, and so defines two things.

    (i)   The business the company is in
    (ii)   The competence and competitive advantages by which it hopes to prosper

(c) **Policies and standards of behaviour**. Policies and strategy need to be converted into everyday performance. For example, a service industry that wished to be the best in its market must aim for standards of service, in all its operations, which are at least as good as those found in its competitors. In service businesses, this includes simple matters such as politeness to customers, speed at which phone calls are answered, and so forth.

(d) **Values**. These relate to the organisation's culture, and are the basic, perhaps unstated beliefs of the people who work in the organisation. For example, a firm's moral principle might mean not taking on an assignment if it believes the client will not benefit, even though this means lost revenue. An example of this can be found in the standards of professional ethics required of accountants.

A **mission statement** is a document embodying some of the matters noted above. A mission statement might be a short sentence, or a whole page. It is intentionally unquantified and vague, and is sometimes seen as a statement of the guiding priorities that govern a firm's behaviour. Mission statements are rarely changed, as otherwise they have less force, and become mere slogans.

(a) **Purpose**

   (i) The firm's purpose might be described in terms of more than just self interest. A pharmaceutical company might define its corporate mission as 'the well-being of humanity'.

   (ii) The firm's responsibility to its stakeholders.

(b) **Strategy**

   (i) The statement should identify the type of business the firm is engaged in.

   (ii) The statement should perhaps identify the strategy for competitive advantage the firm intends to pursue.

(c) **Values**

   (i) The statement should identify values that link with the firm's purpose.
   (ii) The values should reinforce the corporate strategy.

(d) **Behaviour standards**

   (i) Defined standards of behaviour can serve as benchmarks of performance.
   (ii) Individual employees should be able to apply these standards to their own behaviour.

(e) **Character**

   (i) The statement should reflect the organisation's actual behaviour and culture, or at least its aspirations for improved behaviour and culture.

   (ii) The statement should be easy to read.

Objectives, on the other hand, are the embodiment of a mission statement in a commercial context. They specify the meaning of a mission in a particular period, market, or situation.

Mission statements and strategic planning

The relationship between mission statements and strategic planning is an ambiguous one. In some cases, the mission statement is prepared after the strategic plan is drawn up as a sort of summary of it. However this would only be done if there was a major change in the company's direction.

Whilst the mission inspires corporate objectives, the strategy is a means for fleshing them out. The strategy also provides directions for specific context. The mission statement cannot institute particular strategies but it can indicate priorities. Say an investment company prided itself on investing funds in companies which it regarded as behaving ethically, and its mission statement contains a clause which says that the company is 'to invest clients' funds in companies whose products promote health'. It would be unlikely to invest in tobacco firms, but no indication is given as to which shares to buy, on which stock exchanges, when to sell, what returns to expect, and so forth.

Originating a mission statement

A mission statement originates at the highest levels of the organisation. It is possible that, given a mission statement is meant to inspire as well as direct, a process of consultation with employees should take place to determine what the mission statement should be, or to assess what would be laughed out of courts. A company which declared its commitment to customer service in a mission statement, but whose practices for years had been quite the opposite, would have problems in persuading employees to take it seriously. The fact that the employees were consulted about the current ethos in a formal procedure would make the mission statement more effective. The mission statement would be introduced as part of an attempt to change the culture of the organisation.

The scope of mission statements

All areas of corporate life can be covered by a mission statement. This is because it is broadly based, and as a statement of an organisation's values and objectives, it should affect everyone in the organisation. That means its scope is wide-ranging. If it did not affect everybody in each department, from managing director to clerk, then its power would be lessened, and its purpose poorly satisfied.

For example, if a company's mission highlights the provision of *good quality* products and services, then this does not only include the way in which products are made and services delivered, but the way in which commercial relationships are conducted. Given that a successful business requires, in the long term, good commercial relationships, 'quality' applies to these as well.

The benefits of mission statements

The benefits of mission statements are that they:

(a) Describe what the company is about

(b) Provide a guiding philosophy where there are doubts about the direction a company should take, or a decision an individual manager or employee should make

(c) Display the area in which the company is operating

(d) Enable the communication of a common culture throughout the whole organisation

(e) Stimulate debate as to how the mission can be implemented.

12 National advantage

Part (a)

> **Text reference**. Porter's diamond is dealt with in Chapter 12 of your BPP Study Text.
>
> **Top tips**. Although you are invited to use 'any models you consider appropriate': there is only one model that is really appropriate here, and that is Porter's diamond. Unusually, in this question there is no explicit requirement to apply theory to the scenario, but we have demonstrated how you might do so (briefly) by way of introducing the model you have chosen to use. However, remember this part of the question is only worth 7 marks, so you mustn't spend too long trying to link the model to the scenario.
>
> **Easy marks**. This is a relatively easy question, in which a sensible explanation of Porter's theory of national advantage should produce a pass mark. Note that there would be no marks for drawing the diagram: it adds nothing to an explanation of the theory.
>
> This is, in fact, a general rule at this level of examination: do not draw diagrams unless there is no other way of providing the information efficiently in the time available – and unless the question asks you to 'outline' or 'describe'. (A diagram by itself is unlikely to 'explain', 'evaluate' or 'discuss' a model...)

Porter notes that some nations' industries succeed more than other in terms of international competition. He does not suggest (as the D4D Prime Minister rightly notes) that countries as such are competitive, but that various factors support or inhibit the ability of the industries and firms *within* them to compete successfully on the international stage. Porter's 'diamond' model suggests that the degree of competitive advantage enjoyed by different nations results from the interaction of four basic factors.

Factor conditions

Factor conditions are a country's endowment of inputs to production. This includes **human resources, physical resources, knowledge, capital and infrastructure** (transport, communications etc). D4D appears to benefit from positive basic factor conditions (oil reserves and related revenues, temperate climate, a young tertiary-educated population, political stability) – but there are limitations (eg lack of local education institutions) and risks (eg dwindling oil reserves). D4D does not currently have advanced factors which are necessary to achieve high-order competitive advantages such as their own production technologies.

Demand conditions

The home market determines how firms perceive, interpret and respond to buyer needs. Strong and sophisticated demand encourages **growth, high quality, innovation and economies of scale**: all these build competences for competing more effectively abroad. Given the recent revenue D4D has earned from oil, it is possible that it has not been focusing on demand conditions very closely. If that is the case, then the short tern benefits from oil could potentially be weakening its competitive advantage in the longer term.

Firm strategy, structure and rivalry

Capital markets, ownership structures, attitude to time horizons, degree of **innovation and entrepreneurship** vary from country to country. National cultures have been shown to orient business towards certain industries: in D4D's case, agriculture and light manufacturing.

Meanwhile, **domestic rivalry makes exporting attractive** and keeps firm on their toes, while the opposite is also true: as in D4D's case, lack of domestic rivalry stunts competitive development and encourages firms to rely on the home market.

The government could be more pro-active in fostering innovation and entrepreneurship among firms to encourage them to become more successful, but it appears to be happy to support the uneconomic local industry.

Related and supporting industries

Competitive success in one industry is linked to success in related industries, by creating a pool of managerial and technical talent, the exchange of information for organisational/industry learning and benchmarking, and a robust supply market for parts and components.

Clustering

A 'cluster' is a linking of industries through network relationships which are either vertical (within the supply chain) or horizontal (common customers, technology or skills). Porter believes clustering to be a key to national competitive advantage: firms will be more likely to succeed internationally if there is a supporting cluster which supports lower costs, infrastructure development, transfer of expertise and so on.

Part (b)

> **Top tips**. What is required here is a statement of the things D4D is trying to get out the foreign direct investment it seeks, compared with what the investors want to get out of it. The requirement asks you to 'compare and contrast' – so this should have given you an indication that D4D's aim are likely to be different to the investors.
>
> **Easy marks**. The marking scheme suggested when this was set as an exam question that it would be just possible to achieve a pass mark by identifying the aims of the parties concerned: half a mark per point up to a maximum of three marks for each party. However, a safer way to arrive at a pass mark would be to score some of the four marks available for *comparing* and *contrasting*.

Aims of the D4D government in attracting inward investment

D4D should be seeking to achieve:

(i)   **Economic growth**, through additional economic activity and related investment in infrastructure. The latter may be particularly important to D4D in terms of information and communications technology (ICT) development, say, and the development of domestic higher education institutions.

(ii)   **Technology and knowledge transfer**, through the importing of international managerial and technical expertise and proprietary technologies, and the technical training of domestic employees

(iii)   The creation of **well-paid and responsible employment** in a range of industries that have potential for further growth

(iv)   Related benefits through the production of **goods for export** and **increased domestic production** of goods that are currently imported. The government should also aim to maximise the overall increase in national income resulting from the **multiplier effect**.

(v)   **Minimisation of negative externalities** associated with economic growth: investment by firms with a good record of corporate governance, legal compliance, environmental protection, ethical employment practices and other indicators of corporate social responsibility

(vi)   **Positive public relations** with its own citizens and corporate sector, through proactive stakeholder consultation, marketing and issues management (eg in regard to the erosion of past protections for domestic industry, or the risk of cultural erosion).

Aims of companies considering investment in D4D

Companies considering investment in D4D will primarily be interested in:

(i)   **Political and economic stability**, in order to minimise political and business risk to their investments

(ii)   The **availability of human resources** (skills, educational levels, industrial relations climate) at competitive cost, since one of the principal attractions of off-shoring is economies through **low-cost labour**

(iii)   **Supportive physical infrastructure** (transport, communications, education etc), political climatic (a government oriented towards facilitating business), legal and regulatory regime (without onerous constraints or duties) and tax regime

(iv)   **Financial incentives and assistance** (eg tax breaks or regional development grants)

(v)   **Developed business and trading networks** (particularly within neighbouring markets, supporting use of D4D as an export base or 'hub') (vi)　Safe, attractive, economically viable **lifestyle and amenities** for foreign residents, to facilitate the posting of managerial and technical staff to D4D where necessary.

Comparison and contrast

These aims are not all mutually incompatible. Indeed, in order for them to be achieved, there will have to be some dovetailing of aims towards a mutually satisfying 'win-win' outcome. D4D and potential foreign investors will have a 'symbiotic' relationship, in which the success of one depends on the success of the other. So for example:

(i)　D4D's aim of increased economic activity and infrastructure is likely to be met *through* firms fulfilling their aims of successful trading and growth, while the firms' need for suitable infrastructure and human resources is likely to be met *through* fulfilling D4D's aims of attracting investment and knowledge sharing in those areas.

(ii)　Political and economic stability are desired conditions for both parties.

The overall aim will thus be **mutual value gains** – but the aims of the two 'sides' also reflect a degree of competition for **share** of those value gains, and to this extent, the **sets of aims are somewhat different**. So, for example:

(i)　D4D will want its people to be **paid as well as possible** (given the need for competitive HR costs), while firms will seek the **lowest possible wages cost** (given the need for ethical compliance).

(ii)　D4D may be **relying on foreign investment to provide technical infrastructure**, while firms will be seeking an **existing supportive infrastructure** – unless competitive advantage can be gained by investment in its development (eg exclusive use or specificity/customisation creating barriers to entry to other firms, or concessions in other areas).

Negotiation will be required to attain a mutually satisfying set of outcomes.

Part (c)

Top tips. Note the requirement to '*explain*'. A generic list of points will not suffice; you must explain why the steps you advocate will make the country more attractive for foreign investment.

Easy marks. Some of the points already made can be recycled in this part of the question. For example, we have said in part (b) that firms will seek a good infrastructure. We can now advise the government to invest in road building and communications systems.

Examiner's comments. Most answers were adequate, but the usual common error of not relating the points made to D4D was widespread.

Steps to make D4D more attractive to appropriate inward investment

Government can influence national competitive advantage both indirectly by promoting the development of advanced factors and directly by supporting individual industries and companies with financial and other means such as business-friendly regulation. There are a number of factor related things the government could do.

(i)　**Developing a robust capital market within the country**

Promoting the development of liquid and flexible capital markets will benefit both domestic and arriving companies and will encourage the local population to save and invest.

(ii)　**Investment in infrastructure**

Direct investment in **transport infrastructure** will have wide benefits for agriculture and manufacturing industries, reducing costs associated with the supply chain and facilitating international trade.

Direct investment in the **digital communications infrastructure** would bring many related benefits such as cost reduction and improved innovation, as well as facilitating the growth of both domestic and international service and knowledge-based industries.

Incoming companies will require a significant local infrastructure of **supply and service industry**: this could be encouraged with government contracts and the provision of training within local firms. This would also help to strengthen the productivity and competitiveness of local firms, supporting business investment and skilling – and creating the 'clusters' regarded as key to national competitive advantage.

(iii) **Investment in education and training**

A particular need has been identified to **invest in domestic universities**, because most of D4D's graduates are currently being educated abroad, with the risk of a 'brain drain' if they choose to remain abroad. However, emphasis may also be required on vocational and professional education at all levels to **provide the skills required by potential investors**.

There may be potential for foreign companies to develop sponsorship or apprenticeship schemes, or R & D/ learning partnerships with local universities. This should be supported by a robust **intellectual property protection** regime to reduce the business risk of knowledge/technology sharing.

(iv) **Investment-friendly tax regime**

The corporation and personal **tax regime** will be very important, as will the prospect of government incentives to business. Foreign investors will want to benefit from high public spending (on infrastructure etc) and low taxes.

However, while this may be a way of attracting foreign investment in the short term, in the longer term the government will need to balance these incentives with its own economic constraints to achieve a balance between **business incentive** and **state activity**.

(v) **Legal/regulatory regime**

Since the aim is to promote 'appropriate' inward investment, D4D should protect its interests by ensuring that, while not unduly restrictive or onerous (which would deter investors), the law and regulations affecting business are ethical and adequate. This applies to areas such as planning, competition, the environment, health and safety, employment rights and so on. In addition to benefiting D4D, this should also contribute to the foreign firms' management of ethical, compliance and reputational risk.

13 X Company

(a) **Using the five forces model to assets industry competition in country Y**

> **Text references.** Chapter 13 covers Porter's five forces and Chapter 4 covers *Hofstede's model*.
>
> **Top tips.** *Michael Porter's* five competitive forces should be well known to students. It is very important to understand their purpose, to be able to apply them to a situation and to know how the results of any analysis should be interpreted.
>
> **Easy marks.** Easy marks could be gained by identifying the five forces. To gain the bulk of the marks however it was necessary to set out how, in general terms, they could be used to assess industry competition and then to set out in relation to each force the market circumstances which would tend to increase or reduce the strength of that force, with intelligent application to the drinks industry.

The level of competition which X Company and its joint venture partner will face in country Y will depend on the strength of the competitive forces at work in that country.

Michael Porter identified **five market factors**, or forces, that will drive the competitive position of a given supplier in a given market.

These five forces, taken together, will provide an overall assessment of X Company's competitive position in country Y. Entry into country Y would be suggested if, overall, the five forces were found to be weak and the prospective returns high.

Taking each force in turn:

Barriers to entry

X is considering **entry to the market** via a joint venture with a partner established in the drinks distribution business in country Y. This approach may facilitate its entry and enable it to overcome barriers to entry and commence operations relatively quickly.

Substitutes

Substitutes are products that differ from the product in question but provide similar satisfactions. In the case of soft drinks, substitutes might include some alcoholic drinks, such as beer; beverages such as tea and coffee; and small luxury or 'treat' items such as sweets and ice cream. X Company could use the experience of its partner to assess the importance of such substitutes.

Customers' bargaining power

Customers will be looking to achieve lower prices or to obtain a higher quality soft drink. If they have the power to get what they want they will force down the profitability of the firms in the drinks industry.

The strength of the threat from the **bargaining power of customers** will depend on a number of factors.

(i)   **The level of differentiation amongst soft drink manufacturers** (including 'intangible' aspects such as brand strength).

(ii) **The cost to the customer of switching from one supplier to another** – X company's customers are likely to be retailers in which case they will exercise considerable power via their ability to switch easily between suppliers.

(iii) **Whether a customer's purchases from the industry represent a large or small proportion of the customer's total purchases**. In this case retailers could represent a material threat if – as in the UK – a small number of very large retailers account for a substantial proportion of soft drink sales and are in a position to drive a very hard bargain in relation to the prices paid to the manufacturers. X company could seek to counter such a threat by investment in their brands.

Suppliers' bargaining power

Suppliers can influence the profitability of a firm by exerting pressure for higher prices or by reducing the quality of the goods and services which they supply.

The **bargaining power of the supplier** depends on a number of factors.

(i)   The number of suppliers in the industry
(ii) The importance of the supplier's product to the firm
(iii) The cost to the firm of switching from one supplier to another.

Given the widely available nature of the ingredients needed for soft drink manufacture it is unlikely that suppliers to X Company will be limited and hence the power of suppliers is likely to be modest.

Competitive rivalry

The intensity of **competitive rivalry** within the soft drinks industry will be driven by the number of companies operating in this sector, the anticipated industry growth rates and the profitability of the industry as a whole. If the market is dominated by multinationals with strong brands and there is modest growth and profitability levels this market will not be attractive to Company X. If at the other extreme a large number of small local suppliers dominate the market place, the margins being achieved are substantial and there are no well established brands the market opportunities for X Company could be significant.

(b)   **Using the Hofstede model**

> **Top tips.** *Hofstede's* work on national cultural differences is found in the chapter on culture and students should not have found this question difficult. Students would have done well to adopt an approach that began with a **summary** of Hofstede's findings and their **significance** in terms of their impact on the behaviour of individuals at work and the way things are done in organisations. Of the ten marks available here, aim for two marks for each dimension and the remainder on an introduction explaining the model. This was a question in the previous syllabus May 2006 exam and the examiner said that many candidates seemed unprepared for it.
>
> **Easy marks.** Easy marks could be gained by setting out the four dimensions of the Hofstede model in which national culture varies and explaining what each seeks to measure. More marks were available to those students able to explain how a country's position on the scale was likely to be reflected in that country's managerial style.

National cultures and **value systems** can be as distinctive as corporate cultures and value systems. It is potentially very important therefore for Company X to assess the compatibility of its strategy with the culture of country Y.

Hofstede sought to explain national differences by identifying key dimensions in the value systems of all countries. Each country is represented on a scale for each dimension so as to explain and understand values, attitudes and behaviour.

In particular, *Hofstede* pointed out that countries differ on the following dimensions.

(i)   **Power distance**. This dimension measures how far superiors are expected to exercise power. In a high power-distance culture, the boss decides and people do not question. X Company needs to find out what organisations in Country Y fit into this continuum especially in relation to its current business model and possibly modify its local operation accordingly.

(ii)   **Uncertainty avoidance**. Some cultures prefer clarity and order, whereas others are prepared to accept novelty. This affects the willingness of people to *change* rules, rather than simply obey them. X Company may need to tailor its current operations to suit the way the local workforce makes decisions.

(iii)   **Individualism-collectivism**. In some countries individual achievement is what matters. In a collectivist culture people are supported and controlled by their in-group and put the interests of the group first. For X, this means the local organisation would need to think about how important individual achievement, relationships in the organisation and achievement of the task is.

(iv)   **'Masculinity'**. In 'masculine' cultures assertiveness and acquisitiveness are valued. 'Masculine' cultures place greater emphasis on possessions, status, and display as opposed to quality of life and caring for others. X needs to understand how local norms would alter its management of the local business and educate its managers to expect possible differences.

Hofstede grouped countries into **eight clusters** using these dimensions. Countries in the 'Anglo group' (the UK, the USA) for example were found to be comfortable with less direction and order than their counterparts in the 'more developed Asian group' (ie Japan). This suggests that typical UK management styles may not work well in Japan and vice-versa.

Hofstede's work will be of particular relevance to X Company's intentions to joint venture with a company in country Y. Ideally, there should be minimal differences between the two cultures. Where differences are found to exist, plans should be made to overcome any problems that might result.

INDEX

Note: **Key Terms** and their references are given in **bold**.

Review Form & Free Prize Draw – Paper E2 Enterprise Management **(5/09)**

All original review forms from the entire BPP range, completed with genuine comments, will be entered into one of two draws on 31 January 2010 and 31 July 2010. The names on the first four forms picked out on each occasion will be sent a cheque for £50.

Name: _____   **Address:** _____
_____
_____

How have you used this Interactive Text?
(Tick one box only)

☐ Home study (book only)

☐ On a course: college _____

☐ With 'correspondence' package

☐ Other _____

Why did you decide to purchase this Interactive Text? *(Tick one box only)*

☐ Have used BPP Texts in the past

☐ Recommendation by friend/colleague

☐ Recommendation by a lecturer at college

☐ Saw information on BPP website

☐ Saw advertising

☐ Other _____

During the past six months do you recall seeing/receiving any of the following?
(Tick as many boxes as are relevant)

☐ Our advertisement in *Financial Management*

☐ Our advertisement in *Pass*

☐ Our advertisement in *PQ*

☐ Our brochure with a letter through the post

☐ Our website www.bpp.com

Which (if any) aspects of our advertising do you find useful?
(Tick as many boxes as are relevant)

☐ Prices and publication dates of new editions

☐ Information on Text content

☐ Facility to order books off-the-page

☐ None of the above

Which BPP products have you used?

Text	☑	*Success CD*	☐
Kit	☐	*i-Pass*	☐
Passcard	☐	*Interactive Passcard*	☐

Your ratings, comments and suggestions would be appreciated on the following areas.

	Very useful	Useful	Not useful
Introductory section	☐	☐	☐
Chapter introductions	☐	☐	☐
Key terms	☐	☐	☐
Quality of explanations	☐	☐	☐
Case studies and other examples	☐	☐	☐
Exam skills and alerts	☐	☐	☐
Questions and answers in each chapter	☐	☐	☐
Section summaries and chapter roundups	☐	☐	☐
Quick quizzes	☐	☐	☐
Question Bank	☐	☐	☐
Answer Bank	☐	☐	☐
Index	☐	☐	☐

Overall opinion of this Study Text	Excellent ☐	Good ☐	Adeqate ☐	Poor ☐

Do you intend to continue using BPP products?   Yes ☐   No ☐

On the reverse of this page are noted particular areas of the text about which we would welcome your feedback. The BPP Learning Media author of this edition can be e-mailed at: helendarch@bpp.com

Please return this form to: Nick Weller, CIMA Publishing Manager, BPP Learning Media Ltd, FREEPOST, London, W12 8BR

Review Form & Free Prize Draw (continued)

TELL US WHAT YOU THINK

Please note any further comments and suggestions/errors below

Free Prize Draw Rules

1   Closing date for 31 January 2010 draw is 31 December 2009. Closing date for 31 July 2010 draw is 30 June 2010.

2   Restricted to entries with UK and Eire addresses only. BPP Learning Media Ltd employees, their families and business associates are excluded.

3   No purchase necessary. Entry forms are available upon request from BPP Learning Media Ltd. No more than one entry per title, per person. Draw restricted to persons aged 16 and over.

4   Winners will be notified by post and receive their cheques not later than 6 weeks after the relevant draw date.

5   The decision of the promoter in all matters is final and binding. No correspondence will be entered into.